Sacred Species and Sites

Advances in Biocultural Conservation

It is being increasingly recognised that cultural and biological diversity are deeply linked and that conservation programmes should take into account the ethical, cultural and spiritual values of nature.

With contributions from a range of scholars, practitioners and spiritual leaders from around the world, this book provides new insights into biocultural diversity conservation. It explores sacred landscapes, sites, plants and animals from around the world to demonstrate the links between nature conservation and spiritual beliefs and traditions. Key conceptual topics are connected to case studies, as well as modern and ancient spiritual insights, guiding the reader through the various issues from fundamental theory and beliefs to practical applications.

It looks forward to the biocultural agenda, providing guidelines for future research and practice, and offering suggestions for improved integration of these values into policy, planning and management.

GLORIA PUNGETTI is Research Director of the Cambridge Centre for Landscape and People (CCLP) and Chair of the Darwin College Society at the University of Cambridge. Aiming to integrate the spiritual and cultural values of land and communities into landscape planning, nature conservation and sustainable development, she has published widely on these topics and chairs the IUCN-CCLP 3S Initiative on Sacred Species and Sites.

GONZALO OVIEDO is the Senior Adviser for Social Policy at IUCN. In this position he facilitates IUCN's global work on topics such as livelihood security, poverty reduction, indigenous peoples and rural communities, and assists the IUCN programmes worldwide on matters of social equity and human well-being in their conservation work.

DELLA HOOKE is an Honorary Fellow in the Institute for Advanced Research in Arts and Social Sciences at the University of Birmingham. She is an historical geographer and has published extensively upon the historical development of the British landscape. Her research inter... d-scape, and combining ecological and cul... nd and parks.

Sacred Species and Sites

Advances in Biocultural Conservation

Edited by

GLORIA PUNGETTI
University of Cambridge, UK

GONZALO OVIEDO
International Union for Conservation of Nature (IUCN), Switzerland

DELLA HOOKE
University of Birmingham, UK

CAMBRIDGE
UNIVERSITY PRESS

CAMBRIDGE UNIVERSITY PRESS
Cambridge, New York, Melbourne, Madrid, Cape Town,
Singapore, São Paulo, Delhi, Mexico City

Cambridge University Press
The Edinburgh Building, Cambridge CB2 8RU, UK

Published in the United States of America by Cambridge University Press, New York

www.cambridge.org
Information on this title: www.cambridge.org/9780521110853

© Cambridge University Press 2012

First published 2012

Printed in the United Kingdom at the University Press, Cambridge

A catalogue record for this publication is available from the British Library

Library of Congress Cataloguing in Publication data
Sacred species and sites : advances in biocultural conservation / edited by
Gloria Pungetti, Gonzalo Oviedo, Della Hooke.
    p. cm.
Includes index.
ISBN 978-0-521-11085-3 (hardback)
1. Sacred space. 2. Human ecology – Religious aspects. 3. Conservation of natural
resources – Religious aspects. 4. Plants – Religious aspects. 5. Animals – Religious
aspects. I. Pungetti, Gloria. II. Oviedo, Gonzalo. III. Hooke, Della.
BL580.S233 2012
203′.5 – dc23   2011042604

ISBN 978-0-521-11085-3 Hardback
ISBN 978-0-521-12575-8 Paperback

Contents

v

The colour plates will be found between pages 228 and 229.

Contributors

Editors:

Gloria Pungetti

Research Director, Cambridge Centre for Landscape and People (CCLP); Darwin College, University of Cambridge, Cambridge, UK.

Gonzalo Oviedo

Senior advisor on social policy, International Union for Conservation of Nature (IUCN), Gland, Switzerland.

Della Hooke

Honorary Fellow, Institute for Advanced Research in Arts and Social Sciences, University of Birmingham, Birmingham, UK.

Other authors:

Ethel Allué

Institute of Human Palaeoecology and Social Evolution (IPHES), Rovira i Virgili University, Tarragona, Spain.

Mijasoa M. Andriamarovololona

PhD Candidate, Social and Cultural Anthropology, VU University, Amsterdam.

Jeneda Benally

Save the Peaks Coalition, Dine' (Navajo), Arizona, USA.

Edwin Bernbaum

Senior Fellow, The Mountain Institute (TMI), Berkeley, California, USA.

Shonil A. Bhagwat

Senior Research Fellow, School of Geography and the Environment, University of Oxford, Oxford, UK.

Malin Blomqvist
Swedish Digital National Monuments Record, Swedish National Heritage Board, Stockholm, Sweden.

Radhika Borde
PhD Researcher, Wageningen University, the Netherlands.

Stephen Browne
Asia-Pacific Senior Programme Manager, Fauna & Flora International, Cambridge, UK.

Sebastian Catanoiu
Park Manager, Vanatori Neamt Nature Park, Neamt, Romania.

Natalie Ceperley
Yale School of Forestry and Environmental Studies, New Haven, CT, USA.

Federico Cinquepalmi
Sapienza University of Rome, Villa Giulia, Rome, Italy.

The Revd Nigel Cooper
University Chaplain (Diocese of Ely), Anglia Ruskin University, Cambridge, UK.

Alexander N. Davydov
Ass. Prof. Head of Laboratory of Protected Areas and Ecology of Culture, Institute of Ecological Problems of the North, Ural Branch of the Russian Academy of Sciences, Archangel, Russia.

Ahmed Djoghlaf
Former Executive Secretary, Convention on Biological Diversity, Montreal, Canada.

William J. Douros
Regional Director, West Coast Region, Office of National Marine Sanctuaries, National Oceanic and Atmospheric Administration (NOAA), Monterey, California, USA.

Nigel Dudley
Industry Fellow, School of Geography, Planning and Environmental Management, University of Queensland, Australia.

Grazia Francescato
National Committee of Sinistra Ecologia Liberta' (Left Ecology Freedom), Rome, Italy.

Katsue Fukamachi
Associate Professor, Laboratory of Landscape Ecology and Planning, Graduate School of Global Environmental Studies, Kyoto University, Kyoto, Japan.

Lucy Garrett
PhD Researcher, School of International Development and School of Environmental Science, University of East Anglia, UK.

Leif Gren
Swedish National Heritage Board, Stockholm, Sweden.

Liza Higgins-Zogib
Director, DiversEarth – for nature, culture and spirit, Gland, Switzerland.

Father Peter Hughes OSB CAM
Benedictine Monastery of the Camaldoli Order, Rome, Italy.

Julia P. G. Jones
Senior Lecturer in Conservation, School of Environment, Natural Resources and Geography, Bangor University, Wales, UK.

Prashant Kakoday
Activities Coordinator, Brahma Kumaris, Inner Space, Cambridge, UK.

Ven Lama Karma Samten Gyatso
Karma Choeling Tibetan Buddhist Monastery, Albany, Auckland, New Zealand.

Jyotish Kumar Kerketta
Birsa Agricultural University, Ranchi, Jharkhand, India.

Richard J. Ladle
Institute of Biological and Health Sciences, Federal University of Alagos, Maceió, AL, Brazil.

Jala Makhzoumi
Professor of Landscape Architecture, IBSAR Centre for Nature Conservation and Sustainable Futures, American University of Beirut, Beirut, Lebanon.

Josep-Maria Mallarach
President Silene Association, Olot, Catalonia, Spain.

Kate Mannle
Program Development Manager, Rare, Arlington, VA, USA.

Philip J. K. McGowan
Director, World Pheasant Association, Newcastle upon Tyne, UK.

Anna McIvor
Visiting Academic, Department of Geography, University of Cambridge,
Cambridge, UK.

Jacob Mhando Nyangila
Programme Specialist, African World Heritage Fund, Midrand, South Africa.

Alison Ormsby
Associate Professor of Environmental Studies, Eckerd College, St Petersburg,
Florida, USA.

Thymio Papayannis
Director Mediterranean Institute for Nature and Anthropos (Med-INA),
Athens, Greece.

Llorenç Picornell-Gelabert
Seminary of Studies and Research into Prehistory (SERP), Department of
Prehistory, Ancient History and Archaeology, University of Barcelona,
Barcelona, Spain.

Oliver Rackham
OBE, Honorary Professor, and Honorary Director, Cambridge Centre for
Landscape and People (CCLP); Corpus Christi College, University of
Cambridge, UK.

Elizabeth Reichel
Research Fellow, Department of Archaeology and Anthropology, University
of Wales Trinity Saint David at Lampeter, UK.

Santiago Riera
Seminary of Studies and Research into Prehistory (SERP), Department of
Prehistory, Ancient History and Archaeology, University of Barcelona,
Barcelona, Spain.

Mere Roberts
Faculty of Maori Development, Auckland University of Technology,
Auckland, New Zealand.

Guillermo E. Rodriguez-Navarro
Fundraising Consultant Fundacion Pro-Sierra Nevada de Santa Marta, Jardin
Etnobotanico Villa Ludovica, Colombia.

Gabriel Servera-Vives
Seminary of Studies and Research into Prehistory (SERP), Department of
Prehistory, Ancient History and Archaeology, University of Barcelona,
Barcelona, Spain.

Paul Sharman
Ranger Naturalist for the National Trust for Scotland on the dual World
Heritage Site of St Kilda, UK.

Robert E. F. Smith
Late Honorary Fellow of the Institute for Advanced Research in Arts and
Social Sciences, University of Birmingham, Birmingham, UK.

Kalliopi Stara
Department of History and Archaeology, University of Ioannina, Ioannina,
Greece.

Stan Stevens
Senior Lecturer in Geography and Conservation, Department of Geosciences,
University of Massachusetts, Amherst, MA, USA.

Daniela Talamo
International Organisation and European Affairs, Federparchi, Rome, Italy.

Joseph S. Te Rito
Ngati Hinemanu; Chair, Puketapu/Fernhill ReserveTrust; Chair, Omahu
Maori Committee; Nga Pae o te Maramatanga, New Zealand's Indigenous
Centre of Research Excellence, University of Auckland, Auckland, New
Zealand.

Rigas Tsiakiris
Department of Ecology, School of Biology, Aristotle University, Thessaloniki,
Greece.

Bas Verschuuren
Co-Chair of the IUCN WCPA Specialist Group on Cultural and Spiritual
Values of Protected Areas, Biocultural Researcher with EarthCollective,
Coordinator for the Sacred Natural Sites Initiative.

Wang Nan
College of Nature Conservation, Beijing Forestry University, Beijing, China.

Jenny Wong
Wild Resources Limited, Bangor, Gwynedd, Wales, UK.

Foreword

AHMED DJOGHLAF

There is clear and growing evidence of strong links existing between cultural diversity and biodiversity, between sacred sites and a concentration of often unique species. There is in effect an intrinsic relationship between culture, religion, spirituality and the environment.

Sacred sites often provide sanctuaries for rare and endangered species, and contain important reservoirs of genetic and species diversity. They play an important role as a potential gene pool that can be used to restore degraded environments and can help protect ecosystems against other environmental threats.

In many societies, traditional sacred sites fulfil similar functions to protected areas. Due to the spiritual values attributed to these sites, restrictions on access and use often apply, and many such sites remain in a natural or near-natural condition. In sacred sites, human disturbance has usually been reduced or prevented, often for long periods of time, resulting in high levels of biodiversity. We can then say that sacred sites represent the oldest protected areas of the planet.

Because of their cultural and interdisciplinary character, sacred sites are also means for environmental education, cross-cultural learning and the intergenerational transmission of spiritual and biocultural knowledge. For example, at the Tibetan Phags Mo Gling Lamasary in China's western Sichuan Province, lamas regularly survey the land by walking on paths lined with prayer flags and other offerings. They conduct trail maintenance and monitor bird diversity, floral health and soil composition, among other activities. The lamas have also developed a bird guide and regularly lead tourists on bird-watching treks on the sacred mountain.

In many ways and in many places, sacred sites, beliefs, faith groups and protected areas meet. For example, the Boabeng-Fiema Monkey Sanctuary, in Ghana, is considered as a sacred grove because it supports populations of black and white colobus monkey (*Colobus vellerosus*) and mona monkey (*Cercopithecus mona*), both of which are revered and strictly protected as sons of the gods of the people of Boabeng and Fiema villages. Another example is Argentina's Lanin National Park, famous for its monkey puzzle tree (*Araucaria araucana*), which is sacred to the Mapuche Indians, or the 'Earth people'.

Many natural sacred sites are associated with indigenous cultures. Historical, cultural and spiritual aspects of indigenous peoples' lives are grounded in the biodiversity, ecosystems and land that surround them. Traditional knowledge and practices often make indigenous peoples highly skilled and respectful stewards of biodiversity. Thus, indigenous peoples are most important to consider in exploring the relationships between sacred species and sites, biodiversity and conservation.

Biological diversity is intricately linked to cultural diversity. The traditional songs, prayers, names and languages associated with sacred sites reflect the deep knowledge and spirituality of indigenous cultures. For example, of the 6000 human languages counted by UNESCO, more than 2500 are threatened with extinction, and thousands of others are suffering a gradual loss of functionality because their environmental dimension is becoming impoverished. More than 80% of countries that have great biological diversity are also places with the greatest number of endemic languages. In fact, biological, cultural and linguistic diversity are co-evolved, interdependent and mutually reinforcing. Each culture possesses its own set of representations, knowledge and cultural practices which depend upon specific elements of biodiversity for their continued existence and expression. Many of the world's endangered species today are known only to certain peoples whose languages are dying out. As they die, they take with them all the traditional knowledge associated with these species.

Cultural groups develop and maintain significant ensembles of biological diversity, with knowledge and practice as the media for their management. Together, cultural diversity and biological diversity hold the key to ensuring resilience in both social systems and ecosystems. The Convention on Biological Diversity has recognised this important link, amongst other things, through its work developing the *Akwe Kon* guidelines for the conduct of cultural, environmental and social impact assessments regarding developments proposed to take place on, or which are likely to impact on, sacred sites and on lands and waters traditionally occupied or used by indigenous and local communities.

Sadly, sacred species and sites are under major threat. They are subject to a wide range of pressures, such as illegal extraction of timber and wildlife, impacts from extractive industries' operations, encroachment by outsiders, disrespectful tourism, poverty and population dynamics, and degradation of neighbouring environments. Moreover, the close interconnections of many sacred areas with cultural and biological diversity mean that, if any one of these three is threatened or endangered, then the others may be as well. There is an urgent need to help indigenous people and local communities safeguard their heritage, which in turn can do much to conserve the biological diversity upon which we all depend. Biocultural conservation is a successful and cost-effective approach to protecting biodiversity, strengthening traditional systems, and helping to preserve culture in a holistic and synergistic way.

In order to truly protect biodiversity, we need to think outside of the economic model of asking how much a species is worth, or of what use it is to humans. The value of certain sites and species is often not quantifiable in monetary terms. Yet, does that give us the right to abuse these natural resources? Understanding and conserving biodiversity has to come from values and respect. Thus, at a time when the current rate of species extinctions is higher than at any time since the disappearance of the dinosaurs 65 million years ago, the recognition and protection of sacred species and sacred sites are needed more than ever before for the survival of biodiversity, and accordingly that of humans. Hence, the publication of the book *Sacred Species and Sites: Advances in Biocultural Conservation* is extremely timely and truly encouraging. I would like to congratulate and thank all those who contributed to this important book.

Dr Ahmed Djoghlaf is the former Executive Secretary of the Convention on Biological Diversity (CBD). Dr Djoghlaf has lectured frequently on topics related to biodiversity and is the author of a number of articles on topics ranging from the spiritual and ethical dimensions of the environment to the environmental dimension of peace and security.

Preface

> For us Indians there is just the pipe, the Earth we sit on and the open sky. The spirit is everywhere. Sometimes it shows itself through an animal, a bird or some trees and hills. Sometimes it speaks from the Badlands, a Stone or even from the water. That smoke from the peace pipe, it goes straight up to the spirit World.
>
> Lame Deer

At a time when many animal and plant species, as well as long-established cultural traditions, are threatened by the homogenising effects of modern society and its globalising economies and value systems, this book provides an in-depth investigation of the interaction between traditional spiritual beliefs and practices and nature conservation. Spiritual and cultural values have developed as part of people's relationship with their natural environment. Nature, culture and spirituality are in turn interdependent dimensions shaping our understanding of the existence on this planet. Therefore, the consideration of traditional practices can offer valuable guidance for the future preservation of biological and cultural diversity.

The need to consider ethical, cultural and spiritual values of nature has been increasingly recognised by conservation programmes around the world. International institutions and initiatives are starting to develop legal and policy frameworks based on the integration of such values, together with guidelines for implementation. The recognition of the role of sacred natural sites is one aspect of the holistic conservation approach, as awareness of the cultural and spiritual values of the species and sites of our planet can certainly help to sustain biological and landscape diversity. Despite these recent developments, the specific consideration of the role that sacred species might play in conservation efforts has not yet been comprehensively explored. There is certainly a dearth of studies on species – in terms of plants and animals – which are considered sacred, and on the interrelation between sacred species and sacred sites.

Cultural and biological diversity are indeed deeply linked, and the rich diversity of human cultures, with their knowledge, beliefs and practices related to the natural environment, is fundamental to global sustainability, their interactions contributing to the resilience and health of our planet. However, effective integration of biological and cultural diversity in conservation and development is still a challenge, and much remains to be done.

The research illustrated in this volume demonstrates that human perception of nature, ecosystems and species embrace both material and non-material perspectives, within tangible and intangible realms, including the ethical, cultural and spiritual values mentioned above. It also shows some of the efforts currently being made to increase awareness of the importance of integrated approaches to nature conservation.

The chapters bring together efforts and learning from IUCN, the International Union for Conservation of Nature, and CCLP, the Cambridge Centre for Landscape and People, a research group of the University of Cambridge. IUCN encompasses projects and working groups dealing with social, economic and cultural aspects of nature conservation; CCLP supports research on biocultural and spiritual values of landscape and nature conservation, among which is the 3S Initiative on Sacred Species and Sites under CSVPA, the IUCN's Specialist Group on Cultural and Spiritual Values of Protected Areas of WCPA, the IUCN World Commission on Protected Areas.

This volume is the combined result of the work of CSVPA members and of other scholars, practitioners and spiritual leaders from different affiliations and disciplines working in related subjects around the world. Several participated at the 3S Conference on Sacred Species and Sites organised by CCLP in Cambridge in 2007. Two of the editors, Gloria Pungetti and Gonzalo Oviedo, are part of the Steering Committee of CSVPA.

The goal of this publication, and of the continuing liaison between those involved, is to facilitate cross-organisational and interdisciplinary dialogue on the spiritual values of species and sites, discussing recent research findings and improving their recognition and understanding globally. It provides a comprehensive look at their sacred dimension, with regard to their natural and cultural values and the people who interact with them. The cases presented demonstrate their importance to nature conservation across the globe.

Following varied illustrations of the connections between biological and cultural diversity at different levels, suggestions are offered for improving policy frameworks and action programmes. It is therefore hoped that this publication will contribute to strengthening the bonds between biological and cultural diversity in nature and landscape conservation, further developing the biocultural agenda and, finally, promoting the integration of biocultural values into policy, planning and management.

The chapters include conceptual topics as well as case studies, with a structured sequence of seven parts of four chapters each, aimed at guiding the reader through the various issues, from fundamental theory to practical applications. An account of each chapter is provided in the Introduction. Chapters have been clustered in the seven parts according to their main area of focus as follows:

1. discussion on the topic of sacred species and sites, and on relevant concepts and know-how;
2. sacred landscapes;
3. the bond between sacred sites and people;
4. sacred species in general, further specified in Parts V and VI;
5. sacred animals;
6. sacred groves and plants; and
7. the implementation of the principles and conclusions, followed by words of wisdom from spiritual leaders about humans and nature, and the need to care for the planet.

As editors and authors, our thoughts come from different perspectives, but all share a common mission: the preservation of the earth's well-being through a holistic approach that is cross-organisational, multicultural and interdisciplinary. We advocate that the consideration of cultural and spiritual values, and the consequent conservation of biocultural diversity, is a new paradigm in nature and landscape conservation. With this book, we trust to facilitate the establishment of new procedures for further investigation in this regard.

GLORIA PUNGETTI, GONZALO OVIEDO AND DELLA HOOKE

Acknowledgements

The editors thank all the authors of this volume for their effort, Professor Oliver Rackham for his collaboration, Daniel M. P. Shaw, from the IUCN Forest Conservation Programme, for his inputs and editorial assistance in some chapters, and the publishing team for valuable cooperation.

The principal editor is grateful to the other editors for precious work in the preparation of this book: to Gonzalo Oviedo for its initial inspiration and to Della Hooke for exceptional editing. Gloria Pungetti is also indebted to those who provided beautiful pictures and verses to enlighten this volume, and in particular to Venerable Lama Karma Samten Gyatso, Ahmhed Djoghlaf, Stephen Browne, Federico Cinquepalmi, Aldo Cosentino, and the Italian Ministry for the Environment, Land and Sea (MATTM). She is grateful to MATTM, Fauna & Flora International (FFI) and the Cambridge University Library for giving permission to reproduce their material.

Gloria Pungetti is also thankful, to IUCN, WWF and Yuman for their support given to the 3S Conference on Sacred Species and Sites held under the Cambridge Centre for Landscape and People (CCLP) in Cambridge in 2007. She is grateful to the big 3S Community, including the conference participants and the book authors, for their exceptional contribution. CCLP is honoured by the endorsement of IUCN-CSVPA Specialist Group and the Council of Europe European Landscape Convention for being a Focal Point for research on sacred landscape, heritage and human rights.

Nigel Cooper is very grateful to Della Hooke and David Andrews for their comments.

Joseph Te Rito thanks Janneen Love for her photographs; Nga Pae o te Maramatanga, University of Auckland, for its support, and the Omahu Maori Committee and WAi 127 Hinemanu Claimants for access to their archival records.

Mijasoa Andriamarovololona and Julia Jones thank all those who have cooperated with them and the Parcs Nationaux Madagascar and the Direction des Eaux et Forêts for permission to carry out their research. They also thank H. Andrianetrazafy, N. Hockley and G. Rajoelison for helpful discussion and the Leverhulme Trust and FFI for funding.

The research carried out by Wang Nan and his team is a collaborative project of the Beijing Forestry University and the World Pheasant Association and was supported by the latter with the Critical Ecosystem Partnership Fund, Rufford Small Grant and the Oriental Bird Club. Constructive advice was provided by E. J. Milner-Gulland (Professor in Conservation Science, Imperial College London) and Stephen Browne (Asia-Pacific Regional Coordinator, FFI). The team thanks Alexander Pack-Blumenau and Karl-Heinz Grabowski for their assistance during the first period of fieldwork in Daocheng County and their advice. They are especially grateful to Maotianxue for introducing them to the local people, and thank the Sichuan Province Forestry Bureau, the Daocheng County Forestry Bureau, and the Daocheng County Religion Bureau for support in various ways throughout the project.

Bob Smith thanks Chushaka Shibata for sending a copy of Nakamoto, *Upaskama*.

The work of Kate Mannle would not have been possible without the financial support of the Royal Geographical Society, the Tropical Agriculture Award Fund, Rio Tinto, Green College, Oxford, and Nomad Medical Supplies. Kate thanks also James MacKinnon, Alex Totomarovario, Hugh Felton, Rachel Lenane, Stuart Higgs, Romeo Jaomaharavo and the residents of the Bay of Antsiranana.

Shonil Bhagwat acknowledges the 3S Conference participants for comments and useful discussion. His work at the School of Geography and the Environment at the University of Oxford has been funded by the Leverhulme Trust.

Alison Ormsby appreciates the hospitality of the residents of Tafi Atome, Boabeng and Fiema and their participation in interviews. Special thanks to Prosper Gayibor, Delali Dovie, Robert Kwaku Egbeako, Duodu Kwame Michael, Reuben Otto, Bright Obeng Kankam and John Effah for assistance with preparations and in the field. She is grateful to Lizzie McGurk and Sharon Oegerle for help with data analysis, and to Moani Hibbard for map-making. Funding was provided by the Ford Foundation and the Kellogg Foundation.

Research for the articles of Alexander Davydov has been carried out within the Program of Fundamental Research of the Presidium of Russian Academy of Sciences 'Adaptation of peoples and cultures to changes of nature environment and to social and technogenous transformations'.

The study of Kalliopi Stara is co-funded by the European Union, the Ministry of Development, General Secretariat of Research and Technology of Greece, and private sources through the 3rd Community Support Program 'PENED' (Action 8.3 Operational Program 'Competitiveness').

The study by Llorenç Picornell Gelabert, Gabriel Servera Vives, Santiago Riera and Ethel Allué was carried out in the context of an interdisciplinary project 'Producing, Consuming, Exchanging. Exploitation of Resources and External Interaction of the Balearic Communities during Late Prehistory', HAR2008–00708 (Ministry of Science and Innovation, Spanish Government).

Introduction

GLORIA PUNGETTI, GONZALO OVIEDO and DELLA HOOKE

Conservation of biocultural diversity

The year 2010 was declared by the United Nations (UN) as the International Year of Biodiversity, indicating its now widely accepted vital importance. The conservation of biodiversity – the variability and diversity of living organisms on the planet – is fundamental to the health, resilience and sustainability of life on Earth. At a time when many species have been driven to extinction as a direct result of the actions of humankind, with many more similarly threatened, conservation of biodiversity is one of the challenges of our century.

Yet, while the importance of biodiversity and its conservation increasingly gathers momentum, attention is now being drawn to the importance of preserving 'biocultural' diversity, as confirmed for example by the 'Biocultural Diversity Journey' at the IUCN World Conservation Congress in Barcelona in 2008 (McIvor et al., 2009) and the publication in 2010 of *Biocultural Diversity Conservation: A Global Sourcebook* (Maffi and Woodley, 2010). The Convention on Biological Diversity also convened in 2010 the 'International Conference on Biological and Cultural Diversity: Diversity for Development – Development for Diversity', with the aim of advancing development of a programme of work on the subject (Convention on Biological Diversity, 2010).

The UNESCO Universal Declaration on Cultural Diversity (UNESCO, 2002) reaffirms that 'culture should be regarded as the set of distinctive spiritual, material, intellectual and emotional features of society or a social group, and that encompasses, in addition to art and literature, lifestyles, ways of living together, value systems, traditions and beliefs' (p. 12). Cultural diversity, the Declaration states, 'is embodied in the uniqueness and plurality of the identities of the groups and societies making up humankind' (Art. 1, p. 13).

Not only does the concept of biocultural diversity combine cultural diversity, or the variety and richness of cultures in human societies with biological diversity, as shown in Chapter 1, but it recognises that the two should not be considered apart, since cultural diversity is profoundly interrelated with the diversity of the natural environment (Maffi and Woodley, 2010). Loh and Harmon (2005) define global biocultural diversity as the total sum of the world's differences, no matter what their origin. It comprises biological diversity at all its levels, cultural diversity in all its manifestations (including linguistic diversity), ranging from individual ideas to entire cultures; and, importantly, the interactions among all these'. It is, in sum, the diversity of life in all of its manifestations – biological, cultural and linguistic – which are interrelated (and likely co-evolved) within a complex socio-ecological adaptive system (Maffi and Woodley, 2010).

Accepting the biocultural view, thus, means that conservation efforts should not ignore the local human cultural context and should, moreover, only expect to achieve optimum results when undertaking an approach that involves and fully integrates cultural perspectives in nature conservation.

Old values for a new future

From the point of view of the largely positivist tradition of 'Western' thought and science, this new direction is in a sense a return to values that were gradually suppressed. As discussed in Chapter 1, the concept of 'nature' developed from the wider connotation of the Latin *natura*, and the anthropocentric interlinked cultural and natural view during the Renaissance, to a more material meaning during the scientific revolution.

Building on this inheritance, thinkers such as Claude Levi-Strauss began to explore the cultures of other societies, particularly indigenous peoples, no longer viewing them as 'savages' or 'brutes' as had been the case prior to Darwin. Meanwhile, the Western philosophical tradition began to re-engage with questions concerning the natural world and its values: the subdisciplines of environmental philosophy and environmental ethics were born, inspiring and encouraging nature conservation. More recently, the world's major faiths have also rediscovered ecological resonances in their traditional teachings.

While Western societies, religions and politics rediscovered the values of nature, ethnologists revealed that many indigenous peoples had retained an identity and culture which was inseparable from their natural environment. The spirituality and religions of such groups were found to almost invariably hold nature, or certain of its elements – such as a particular species, sites or landscape – to be sacred or divine. Furthermore, indigenous and traditional peoples, living by spiritual value systems founded upon their precious natural environments, were found to have been living 'sustainably' for centuries, even millennia, before the term 'sustainable development' was even coined.

Political leaders of the indigenous peoples' movement put the dimension of cultural rights on the global agenda, and suddenly, worldviews and cosmologies hitherto considered 'primitive' were seen to be in alignment with the most innovative environmental thinkers of 'global' society, and were recognised as an integral part of the search for new approaches to development, conservation and politics.

Some contemporary philosophies of nature closely connect with traditional value systems and worldviews. For example, there are indigenous traditions that believe natural elements to be manifestations of worldly spirits, including human spirits. Such beliefs, along with the consequent human identification with nature, lead smoothly to a form of 'biocentric egalitarianism' (Næss, 1973, 1989) similar to that promulgated by the contemporary American philosopher Paul Taylor. Taylor surpasses sentience-based environmental ethics to argue that each living thing is of equal inherent worth – and therefore of intrinsic value – by possessing a 'teleological centre of life', i.e. pursuing its own good in its own distinct manner (Taylor, 1986). His 'biocentric outlook' has four main parts which are very reminiscent of certain indigenous worldviews.

1. Humans are members of the community of life on the same terms which apply to non-humans.
2. The Earth's natural ecosystems are a complex web of interconnecting elements, each part interdependent on the others.
3. Each individual centre of life in its own way pursues its own good.
4. It is incorrect and prejudiced to claim human superiority in terms of inherent worth.

Taylor concludes that if we assume the biocentric outlook, we are already behaving as moral agents and are thus adopting a certain ultimate environmental moral attitude toward the natural world. He calls this attitude 'respect for nature'. In adopting an attitude of respect for nature, one is morally bound to promote and protect the good of all living things as individuals. Obligations to groups, species and ecosystems are derived from the interests of their individual constituents (Taylor, 1986).

However, many indigenous value systems go further than biocentric egalitarianism in that they believe the spirit world, and therefore values, permeates all parts of the natural world, not just those that are living. They often go beyond the life-centred to include non-living things – such as water, rocks, celestial bodies;

and natural phenomena – from mountains, rivers and the land itself, to thunder, seasons and winds.

The American twentieth-century conservationist Aldo Leopold, one of the influential figures in the early years of the United Nations Environment Programme (UNEP), similarly went beyond biocentrism in valuing nature. Searching for a 'Land Ethic', Leopold (1987) urged people to realise their symbiotic relationship with the earth and to push back the ethical 'frontier' in order to value the biotic community, or 'the land', in itself (see Chapter 1). For Leopold, we are equal members of this community, which comprises both the living and non-living elements of nature. However, Leopold valued the community, the ecosystem, first: individuals, be they a particular plant, species, site or landscape, are valuable only as they are parts of the community.

Therefore, the world's traditional and indigenous spiritualities and cultures have as much to teach us, and each other, about the values of nature, our place within it and the art of sustainable living as some of the most progressive environmental thinkers and conservationists at the global level. Moreover, the survival and diversity of these traditions are inseparably linked to the well-being of their environments, and their experience and knowledge in living sustainably, while caring successfully for nature, in most cases goes back to times immemorial. The conservation of biocultural diversity aims to protect and maintain this survival and richness.

Learning and gathering knowledge on those things held most sacred by traditional cultures – their venerated species and sites – and researching the effects, linkages and implications for nature conservation, is an important part of working on biocultural diversity. However, there is currently a gap in literature on sacred species and sites with regard to conservation efforts. It is hoped that this book will not only serve as a significant 'brick' in filling that gap, but that it will also serve to inspire a broad research agenda exploring sacred species and sites, and their potential for improved environmental and biocultural conservation. An account of the Parts and chapters of the book is given below.

Part I: From concepts to knowledge

Part I starts with *Sacred species and sites: dichotomies, concepts and new directions in biocultural diversity conservation*, a theoretical preamble to the topic of sacred species and sites, including key issues in biocultural diversity, by Gloria Pungetti. Dichotomies, from the ancient meaning of nature to the modern scientific thinking, are discussed, and definitions of keywords and concepts related to the themes of this book are provided. The state of the art in biocultural diversity is illustrated with an indication of the new research directions on sacred species and sites.

Following that, *Spiritual values and conservation*, a personal account by Gonzalo Oviedo, builds on the discussion between natural, cultural and ethical values in conservation, drawing on examples from both local experiences with indigenous peoples of South America and global conservation efforts. After elaborating on the sometimes tragic tensions between colonial and native traditions regarding sacred nature, we learn of optimistic recent developments, also illustrated in the rest of this book. The author finally calls for the conservation community to consider new approaches to integrate biocultural diversity and spiritual values in development efforts.

In *Protected areas and sacred nature: a convergence of beliefs*, Nigel Dudley and Liza Higgins-Zogib present us with the findings of their research, looking into links between protected areas and sacred lands and waters. As the authors explain, the two principal reasons for designating a protected area are either to preserve its biodiversity or because it is considered sacred. The two different reasons have much more in common than might be apparent initially.

In Chapter 4, *Ancient knowledge, the sacred and biocultural diversity*, Federico Cinquepalmi and Gloria Pungetti delve into the heritage of Italy, and the links between the sacred, the natural sites and their landscape. They contemplate the spiritual role of waters in various ancient traditions and the interactions and connections between Christian and Pagan sites. The authors stress the crucial importance of the traditional sacred sites of Europe for its modern societies in order to fully understand the relationship between communities, their cultures and spiritualities, and the features of their natural environment.

Part II: Sacred landscapes

Ecological and spiritual values of landscape: a reciprocal heritage and custody is the first of four chapters looking at spirituality and natural landscapes. Gloria Pungetti, Father Peter Hughes and Oliver Rackham examine the case of the Casentino forested landscape in Italy, tracing the harmonious development of its natural, cultural and spiritual heritages. We learn how a monastic order has quietly taken the lead as custodian of the local site and species, with the local communities following suit. This shared sense of responsibility, the authors argue, allows a holistic view of the landscape to be promoted, advancing an integrated, biocultural approach to sustainable development in the area.

Edwin Bernbaum, in *Sacred mountains and national parks: spiritual and cultural values as a foundation for environmental conservation*, focuses on mountainous landscapes. He echoes the call for conservation programmes to include the spiritual values of sacred sites and species in furthering their work. Without this integration, he warns, conservation efforts may lose the support of local communities and stakeholders. His examples from around the world demonstrate, furthermore, that this applies equally to indigenous, as well as contemporary, secular societies.

Within the context of such a modern society, in the next chapter, *The history of English churchyard landscapes illustrated by Rivenhall, Essex*, Nigel Cooper traces the historical origins and developments of English churchyards. He contemplates their original selection, their expansion and recent approaches to churchyard care. Importantly, he highlights the recent recognition of the exceptional biodiversity value of the churchyard landscape, relating to their spiritual value and their ongoing relevance to contemporary society.

Another case from Great Britain is presented in Chapter 8, *Exmoor dreaming*. Paul Sharman draws on Norberg-Schultz's theory of Genius Loci to argue for sacred site and species status at Dunkery Beacon, the highest point on Exmoor – an upland region of south-west England. Sharman calls it 'an ordinary place ritually made extraordinary' and describes how even in a secular context a landscape, or site, and its species can be considered sacred.

Part III: The bond between sacred sites and people

From the 'old' world of Exmoor and England, we then travel with Elizabeth Reichel to the 'new', in a case study of two indigenous Amazonian populations, *The landscape in the cosmoscape, and sacred sites and species among the Tanimuka and Yukuna Amerindian tribes (north-west Amazon)*. With an interest in the 'anthropology of landscape', the author investigates how these indigenous peoples maintain rainforest landscapes and biodiversity through the implementation of shamanic cosmologies in sacred sites and species. She looks at the importance of gender, shamanism, patrilinearity and cosmology in this context, compares this landscape's conservation with that of an adjacent park and concludes by suggesting changes in official conservation management and participatory practices with indigenous peoples.

In Chapter 10, *Sacred natural sites in zones of armed conflicts: the Sierra Nevada de Santa Marta in Colombia*, Guillermo Rodriguez-Navarro describes how indigenous peoples of that region believe in equilibrium between humans and nature, which is vulnerable to human irresponsibility. However, as he points out, this balance refers not only to natural resource management, but also to the spiritual and moral balance of the human individual and, by extension, that of the group to which people belong.

We then move to *Struggles to protect Puketapu, a sacred hill in Aotearoa*, which chronicles the efforts of the Maori group of Ngati Hinemanu in New Zealand to protect the sacred hill of Puketapu. The author, Joseph Selwyn Te Rito, is a member of that group and so, as readers, we are treated to an insider's explanation of the spiritual and cultural values traditionally held by the Ngati Hinemanu.

Part III finishes with a return to Italian ancient beliefs and traditions, with Grazia Francescato and Daniela Talamo's chapter, *The Roman goddess Care: a therapy for the planet*. Taking the goddess *Dea Cura* as a starting point, the authors look at the history and status of links between conservation, spirituality and indigenous traditions. Sharing personal experiences and insights, the authors conclude by calling for spiritual values to be included in the mission, vision and policy statements of global conservation organisations and institutions.

Part IV: Sacred species

Although sacred species hold conservation significance, many are endangered. In this context, Anna McIvor and Gloria Pungetti present a pilot study on the conservation status of sacred species, in *The conservation status of sacred species: a preliminary study*, exploring whether being considered sacred is a protector from threats. Their review of the literature reveals interesting examples from around the world and highlights the need for further research in this area. In concluding that sacredness alone is not enough to protect a sacred species, the authors show that in the contemporary world an integrated, holistic approach is required, as no one set of values will be enough on its own to achieve ideal conservation outcomes.

Chapter 14, *The role of taboos and traditional beliefs in aquatic conservation in Madagascar*, examines the role of ancestor worship and the complex system of taboos in Madagascar, called *fady*, in relation to natural species and their conservation. The two authors, Mijasoa Andriamarovololona and Julia Jones, share their wealth of knowledge and insight into this subject and call for an improved cultural understanding in the quest for solutions to the numerous challenges faced by efforts to conserve Madagascar's aquatic species and their natural environments.

Water is still addressed by Willam Douros in Chapter 15, *Sacred species of national marine sanctuaries of the United States' West Coast*. Here, we encounter both modern and traditional spiritual values of North America regarding a host of different species, and their interaction and correlation with legally protected marine and freshwater sanctuaries.

Chapter 16, *Integrating biocultural values in nature conservation: perceptions of culturally significant sites and species in adaptive management*, by Bas Verschuuren, investigates the role of sacred species and their sites in newly emerging biocultural approaches to conservation and ecosystem management, something that has until recently been largely ignored. Speaking practically and concretely, Verschuuren explains how investigating the sacred dimensions of species and sites for various peoples could help to develop new approaches to adaptive management, indicators and participatory monitoring.

Part V: Sacred animals

Mere Roberts takes us back to New Zealand in Chapter 17, *Genealogy of the sacred: Maori beliefs concerning lizards*. For Mere Roberts, indigenous knowledge, 'developed over long periods of time and involving close intimacy between peoples and place', should not be ignored if we want to develop conservation programmes that include local people. We should be inspired by the proverbial Maori description of themselves as a people who 'walk backwards, so that the past is in front of them and constantly guides future actions and decision'.

The first Asian perspective is presented by Wang Nan, Lucy Garrett and Philip McGowan, who describe *Pheasant conservation, sacred groves and local culture in Sichuan, China* in Chapter 18. Their work confirms once again the inseparability of people and nature as we learn of the specific case of natural, cultural and spiritual coincidence in western Sichuan. The authors quite rightly point out that, since China's forests can be considered a result of natural and cultural actions, their safe management and conservation for the future should similarly include cultural values and practices.

Moving further north, Robert Smith then recounts *The bear cult among the different ethnic groups of Russia*. Remarkably, despite numerous political and religious shifts, the ancient veneration, respect and fear of the bear is still intact across Russia and even beyond its borders. The relationship that people and societies in this part of the world have with this enigmatic land mammal is complex, with a whole host of taboos and a rich mythological tradition.

Links between taboos and nature are further explored in Chapter 20, as we return to Madagascar. Kate Mannle and Richard Ladle take us deeper into the world of *fady* with *Specific-species taboos and biodiversity conservation in Northern Madagascar*. We are also introduced to the complex concept of *tsiny*, a spirit type distinct to animals with particularly interesting consequences for nature conservation.

Part VI: Sacred groves and plants

After the animal kingdom, we turn to that of the plants and its own sacred species and sites. Della Hooke examines England's ancient beliefs in sacred trees, in *The sacred tree in the belief and mythology of England*. Despite the anti-pagan efforts of Christianity at various points in history to suppress what it perceived as tree worship, the iconic role of trees is still alive and visible in various cultural and natural examples across the country today. The worship of trees and forests was certainly not unique to Britain and we witness this today in two other contrasting examples from India and Kenya (Chapters 22 and 23, respectively).

In *Sacred groves and biodiversity conservation: a case study from the Western Ghats, India*, Shonil Bhagwat recommends that the profile of sacred sites be raised in international fora, in order to attract the funding that will be required for their conservation. As he explains, such sites cover a highly substantial surface of the Earth, and are therefore of enormous potential for maintaining biodiversity.

Alison Ormsby seconds this statement in *Cultural and conservation values of sacred forests in Ghana*, with a research carried out in two case studies of Monkey sanctuaries in Africa. Although these are officially protected sites, the majority are culturally protected lands vulnerable to the changing values and practices of the people living around them. The results of her investigation outline the need for additional research in evaluating the role that sacred groves play.

A final case also comes from Africa: *Sacred species of Kenyan sacred sites*, by Jacob Mhando Nyangila. In Kenya, as elsewhere, sacred sites are becoming more vulnerable to destruction as their cultural significance gradually wanes due to societal and demographic changes. Partnership is a must in their preservation, as demonstrated by the example of collaboration between communities and the National Musems of Kenya in conservation of the Kayas. Stakeholders working together are surely crucial anywhere on the planet where biocultural conservation is concerned.

Part VII: Implementation, case studies and conclusions

The concluding chapters provide examples for the implementation of the theory illustrated before, integrating the spiritual value of species to their sites. Gloria Pungetti and Shonil Bhagwat edit a series of case studies, summarised in eight boxes, on holy animals and holy plants. *Sacred species and biocultural diversity: applying the principles* presents study areas from Pan-Europe, Africa, the Middle East and Asia, with worldwide cases from Fauna & Flora International.

Sacred sites, sacred landscapes and biocultural diversity: applying the principles, edited by Gloria Pungetti and Federico Cinquepalmi, proposes case studies on holy landscapes and their peoples, including holy ancient mountains, divided in six boxes. Study areas from Europe, Asia and North America are completed by additional worldwide examples on sacred natural sites and landscapes in technologically developed countries.

The editors of the book, Gloria Pungetti, Gonzalo Oviedo and Della Hooke, wrap up the discussion in *Conclusions: the journey to biocultural conservation*. Natural and spiritual life, traditional ecological knowledge, and lessons from the field are discussed. Several approaches to biocultural conservation for sacred species and sites are proposed: (a) know-how, empowerment and participation; (b) evolution; (c) ethics; (d) sustainability; (e) biocultural conservation; and (f) advancement – the consideration of future directions.

After contemplating the agenda that lies ahead, the volume closes with spiritual accounts on nature and culture from a number of ancient traditions in Chapter 28: *Epilogue: a spiritual circle*.

The above chapters show an undeniable paradigm shift in nature conservation, with a new agenda put forward by the organisations promoting such a paradigm. Their recent advances are delineated in this publication, which aims to provide a background for future studies.

References

Convention on Biological Diversity. (2010). *In-Depth Review of the Implementation of the Programme of Work on Protected Areas*. UNEP/CBD/SBSTTA/14/L.5. Nairobi: CBD.

Leopold, A. (1987). *A Sand County Almanac: and Sketches Here and There* (1st edn. Oxford, 1949). Oxford: Oxford University Press.

Loh, J. and Harmon, D. (2005). A global index of biocultural diversity. *Ecological Indicators*, **5**, 231–41.

Maffi, L. and Woodley, E. (2010). *Biocultural Diversity Conservation: A Global Sourcebook*. London: Earthscan.

McIvor, A., Fincke, A. and Oviedo, G. (2009). *Bio-Cultural Diversity and Indigenous Peoples Journey*. Report from the 4th IUN World Conservation Congress Forum, 6–9 October 2008, Barcelona, Spain. Gland, Switzerland: IUCN.

Næss, A. (1973). The shallow and the deep, long-range ecology movement. *Inquiry*, **16**, reprinted in *Sessions* 1995, pp. 151–5.

Næss, A. (1989). *Ecology, Community, Lifestyle*, trans. and ed. D. Rothenberg. Cambridge: Cambridge University Press.

Taylor, P. (1986). *Respect for Nature*. Princeton, NJ: Princeton University Press.

UNESCO. (2002). *Universal Declaration on Cultural Diversity*. Paris: UNESCO.

PART I   CONCEPTS AND KNOWLEDGE

1

Sacred species and sites: dichotomies, concepts and new directions in biocultural diversity conservation

GLORIA PUNGETTI

Introduction

This chapter aims to introduce the topics of this volume and to provide the reader with keywords and works of reference for the understanding of the complex subject addressed.

First, it explains dichotomies such as: biological and cultural diversity; nature and culture; sciences and humanities; mind and soul; tangible and intangible values; divine and animistic views.

Second, it illustrates key concepts for the sacred dimension of biocultural diversity, offering a broad comprehension of meanings and definitions on the precise topics and those related to them.

Third, it outlines the state of the art and new directions in the conservation of biocultural diversity, taking into account sacred species and sites.

Dichotomies

Conservation of biodiversity is one of the challenges of our century and in situ conservation is a strategy to achieve it (Harmon and Putney, 2003, p. 3). Biocultural diversity relates largely to intangible values, which tend to be referred to as the enrichment of intellectual, psychological, emotional, spiritual, cultural and artistic aspects of well-being. Although these values contrast with the Western tendency to base knowledge on scientific and technical evidence, and economic and tangible criteria, intangible values are increasingly being recognised (UNESCO,

Sacred Species and Sites: Advances in Biocultural Conservation, ed. Gloria Pungetti, Gonzalo Oviedo and Della Hooke. Published by Cambridge University Press. © Cambridge University Press 2012.

1998, 2002; Makhzoumi and Pungetti, 1999; Posey, 1999; Oviedo *et al.*, 2000; Maffi, 2001; Lee and Schaaf, 2003; Schaaf and Lee, 2006; Persic and Martin, 2008).

The modern concept of 'nature' developed after the scientific revolution in Europe, moving from the Latin word *natura* with a wider meaning, to a restrictive sense of a material dimension. *De Rerum Natura*, the poem by Lucretius (died about 55 BC: Rouse, 1937), based on an Epicurean approach, bridges physics and philosophy to explain the nature of the mind and the soul, thoughts and sensations, terrestrial and celestial phenomena. The poem is not strictly about the physical world, as Epicureanism also offers guidelines for human conduct and relationships, leaving hope for happiness in a world imperfectly suited to our existence. Conversely, it already becomes detached from the spiritual perspective, proclaiming that the universe is ruled by chance and not by gods, thus underlining a sense of personal responsibility.

'Nature the creature' and 'nature the divine creator', in contrast, have been addressed by several authors including Botkin (1990), describing first the Earth as a created living being, i.e. the creature, and second seeing it as a celestial form of stable and perfect order, i.e. the creator.

In the Renaissance view, cultural and natural worlds were interlocked in every way. Nature was perceived in relation to humans and as for their benefit. Plants and animals not only provided food, medicine, clothing and shelter, but also reflected and symbolised moral and religious values (Thomas, 1983). In this period, nature is helped by art to become more fertile and man serves this purpose. Renaissance gardens, therefore, are not characterised in terms of man dominating nature, but rather as a mutual exchange between culture and nature. Leonardo da Vinci, for example, speaks of the artist as an interpreter between 'nature and art' (Tyler, 1964).

The scientific tradition was then influenced by Descartes with *Meditations on First Philosophy*, published in Latin in 1641 (died 1650: Cottingham, 1986). With the development of Cartesian mechanisms in the eighteenth century, the concept of 'nature the machine' emerged, continuing to pervade twentieth-century ecological thinking (Makhzoumi and Pungetti, 1999, p. 8) as well as the dominant Western scientific mindset even in this century. The Cartesian distinction drawn between the material and spiritual worlds swiftly permeated all fields of thought and was spread around the world along with colonialism, Christian evangelism and what we now call globalisation. Nevertheless, these are not the only modern philosophical schools of thought that can be compared to, or have even been influenced by, the mindsets of other cultures. The Cartesian distinction in reality does not hold true in many traditional cultures where nature, encompassing universal values, connects earth with sky. A combination of the divine and animistic vision of nature, and of global ecology and human ecology, led to concepts such as the Gaia hypothesis (Lovelock, 1979), 'deep ecology' and 'biocentric egalitarianism'

(Næss, 1973, 1989), and the view of 'nature as a biosphere' (Naveh, 1995; Naveh and Lieberman, 1984).

One hundred and fifty years after its publication, *The Origin of Species* (Darwin, 1859), with its open and inclusive approach to phenomena and its inexhaustible range of applications and concerns, provides a model of the ecological knowledge still in use today (Wallace, 1998). Darwin's theory of biological evolution has challenged the view of man as standing at the centre of creation. The relativist door was accordingly open for a re-questioning of both natural and cultural values. The attitude of man, proclaimed engineer of nature with the task of creating his paradise on Earth, has outlined a position of superiority which continues to the present day, especially in architecture, planning and construction.

Environmental ethics, nonetheless, has been addressed by Leopold (1987) in his work on the development of modern environmental ethics and wilderness preservation, stating that the right approach is to preserve the integrity, stability and beauty of the biotic community. He has argued that 'conservation is a state of harmony between men and land' and has introduced 'ecological conscience' into conservation biology with a non-fiction book in which he develops the concept of 'land ethic', a perspective in environmental ethics dealing with man's relation to land and to the animals and plants which live and grow on it (Leopold, 1987, p. 204).

Parallel to this, the deep ecology movement, starting from Scandinavian discussions between Næss, Kvaløy and Faarlund, supports a 'biospheric egalitarianism', i.e. the view that all living things have equal value in their own right (Næss, 1973, 1989). This implies respect for such intrinsic value, taking great care of the Earth and its living organisms (Taylor, 1981, 1986).

Nature, finally, today embraces both tangible and intangible values. Among the latter, ethical, cultural and spiritual values are at the core of new research centres, e.g. CCLP, the Cambridge Centre for Landscape and People (Pungetti, 2008). An example of such a duality is the natural and the cultural landscape. The former refers to a product of nature, i.e. to the physical effects and interactions of its abiotic (land forms, soil, water and air) and biotic (species) elements; the latter to a product of man, i.e. to the shaping of the land by human impact, often over a long period of time (Pungetti, 1996, p. 20; Makhzoumi and Pungetti, 1999, p. 7).

For a broad comprehension of biocultural meanings and the topics related to them, key concepts and definitions are illustrated in the next section.

Concepts and definitions

Biodiversity

'Biodiversity', short for 'biological diversity', means, for the Convention on Biological Diversity (Art. 2), variability among living organisms from all sources including, inter alia, terrestrial, marine and other aquatic ecosystems and the eco-logical complexes of which they are a part; this comprises diversity within species, between species and of ecosystems (Secretariat of the Convention on Biological Diversity, 2003, p. 4). Hence it refers to the number and kind of organisms on the planet, including genetic diversity, ecosystem diversity and taxonomic (species and infraspecies) diversity.

Cultural diversity

'Cultural diversity' is the variety and richness of cultures in human soci-eties (Skutnabb-Kangas *et al.*, 2003, p. 53). It encompasses the mosaic of individuals and groups with varying traditions, backgrounds, experiences, styles and percep-tions. It thus describes the differences in race, ethnicity, language, nationality, beliefs, values and religion, as well as the variety of human cultures within a community, organisation, region or nation. It refers accordingly to the practice of enhancing the acceptance, tolerance and understanding of cultural differences within the above communities and organisations.

The first instrument that poses cultural diversity at the level of a common heritage for humanity is the UNESCO Declaration on Cultural Diversity (UNESCO, 2002), which states that cultural diversity is embodied in the uniqueness and plurality of identities of the groups and societies making up humankind (see the Introduction). As a source of exchange, innovation and creativity, cultural diversity is as necessary for humankind as biodiversity is for nature. In this sense, it is the common heritage of humanity and should be recognised and affirmed for the benefit of present and future generations (Art. 1). Cultural diversity, moreover, widens the range of options open to everyone; it is one of the roots of development, understood not simply in terms of economic growth, but also as a means to achieve a more satisfactory intellectual, emotional, moral and spiritual existence (Art. 3). Preservation of cultural diversity, perceived as a living, dynamic and changing resource, is a process that can guarantee the survival of humanity. Therefore, the ethical imperative is bonded with individual dignity, linking further with the UN Universal Declaration of Human Rights (see below).

Traditional culture and knowledge

'Traditional culture' refers to the practice of preserving and promoting cultural practices, traditions and folklore, including traditional dance, handi-crafts, art, storytelling, myths, oral history, customs, ceremonies, beliefs, rites and ethnobiology.

Besides, 'traditional knowledge' (TK) or 'indigenous peoples' knowledge' is knowledge acquired and preserved through generations in an original or local society, consisting of experience in working to secure subsistence from nature (see Grim, 2001; Harmon, 2002; Posey, 1999; Schaaf and Lee, 2006).

According to Berkes (1999, p. 8), 'traditional ecological knowledge' (TEK) is a 'cumulative body of knowledge, practice and belief, evolving by adaptive processes and handed down through generations by cultural transmission, about the relationships of living beings (including humans) with one another and with their environment'. Moreover, TEK has been considered by Ramakrishnan (2003) as the basis for nature conservation by traditional societies. It is clearly a challenge to the positivist-reductionist paradigm in Western science, and is seen by some authors (e.g. Berkes) as a possible injection of ethics into the science of ecology and resource management.

Biocultural diversity

'Biocultural diversity' is the diversity of life on Earth in both nature and culture (Skutnabb-Kangas *et al.*, 2003, p. 53). It includes biological diversity, cultural diversity and their interactions (Loh and Harmon, 2005, p. 231). Specifically, it comprises the diversity of life manifested in biology, cultures and languages, interrelated within a 'complex socio-ecological adaptive system' (Maffi, 2001; Maffi and Woodley, 2010).

Indeed, the diversity of life is made up not only of the diversity of plants and animal species, habitats and ecosystems found on the planet, but also of the diversity of human cultures and languages. These diversities do not exist in separate and parallel realms but, rather, they interact with one another in different ways. The links among these diversities have developed over time through a mutual adaptation between man and nature.

Nature, culture and landscape

The *Oxford English Dictionary* defines 'nature' as the 'phenomena of the physical world collectively, including plants, animals, the landscape, and other features and products of the earth, as opposed to humans or human creations'. Paradoxically, nature is also described, as per Lucretius, as the inherent qualities or characteristics of a person or thing and hereditary characteristics as an influence on or determinant of personality, thus moving from a scientific to a humanistic perception.

'Culture' is, instead, defined as 'the arts and other manifestations of human intellectual achievement regarded collectively, as well as the customs, institutions and achievements of a particular nation, people or group' (*Oxford English Dictionary*). Culture is undeniably a set of distinctive spiritual, material, intellectual and emotional features of society and social groups, encompassing arts, lifestyles, traditions and beliefs. The majority of spiritual believers moreover share respect and appreciation for nature (Nasr, 1996), creating reciprocal positive efforts towards the conservation of science and culture.

'Landscape', considered as 'a dynamic process developing on the visible earth surface, resulting from the interaction between abiotic, biotic and human factors which vary according to site and time' (Pungetti, 1996, p. 20; Makhzoumi and Pungetti, 1999, p. 7) is surely an umbrella concept embracing nature and culture. Humans are undeniably as much a part of the landscape as are other species and the earth. They are all linked to one another in the same web of life by complex patterns of ecological relationships (Forman and Godron, 1986), making human presence and activities an intrinsic aspect of the development of any vision for biodiversity conservation (Oviedo *et al.*, 2000, p. 7).

This vision has been reinforced by the European Landscape Convention (Art. 1) indicating landscape as 'an area, as perceived by people, whose character is the result of the action and interaction of natural and/or human factors' (Council of Europe, 2000, p. 5).

Cultural landscape

A similar perspective has been taken by the World Heritage Convention for 'cultural landscape', identified as the 'combined works of nature and man' (UNESCO, 2008, p. 14). Specifically, cultural landscapes are represented as cultural properties 'illustrative of the evolution of human society and settlement over time, under the influence of the physical constraints and/or opportunities presented by their natural environment and of successive social, economic and cultural forces, both external and internal' (Art. 47: UNESCO, 2008).

Bearing witness to the social, cultural, artistic and spiritual energy of humanity, cultural landscapes, such as cultivated terraces, gardens and sacred places, form a consistent part of our collective identity. The concept of World Heritage Sites by UNESCO considers natural and cultural landscapes as an integrated heritage. Furthermore, their reference to landscape used sustainably by traditional societies opens up new perspectives that indicate a rediscovery of traditional knowledge (Ramakrishnan, 2003).

Indeed, cultural landscapes often reflect specific techniques of sustainable traditional land use, as well as specific spiritual relations to nature. Since protection of cultural landscapes can contribute to sustainable land use in maintaining or enhancing natural and cultural values, the protection of traditional cultural landscapes is crucial in maintaining biocultural diversity.

Sacredness and the sacred

The word 'sacred' derives from *sacer*, formed by the Indo-European root *sak-* meaning to sanctify and the suffix *-ro*, forming together the word *sakro*, becoming in Latin *sacer* with the meaning of holy, sacred, dedicated. Further connections in English are 'holiness' and 'sanctity', meaning the state of being holy, sacred, and generally referring to being set apart for the worship and service of gods, or for pursuing a sacred state. The later English word *consecrate* derives from the Latin verb *sacrare*, and other English derivates are the adverb 'sacredly' and the noun 'sacredness' (*Oxford English Dictionary*).

Sacred is commonly related to 'spiritual', representing a transcendent aspect of existence. Although the term 'sacred' could in some cultures be connected to religions, sites and species are more commonly associated with it rather than with the word 'spiritual', while reference is given to the latter in association with values. Moreover, sacredness is linked with wording such as holy, religious, veneration, sacrificial, healing, magic, ritual, totemic, traditional medicine, animist, ancestral spirits and other similar expressions. The *Oxford English Dictionary* refers clearly to sacred as 'holy' and 'connected with a deity and so deserving veneration', holding more a religious rather than a secular meaning.

Considering that in the world there are over 6000 known spoken languages, and perhaps as many sign languages (Skutnabb-Kangas *et al.*, 2003, p. 22), each with different cultural settings, their own background and consequent meanings, one can argue that the word 'sacred' could have many different connotations and implications. For example, some Western languages do not have words that link man with the universe or the Earth, while many traditional cultures have, as indicated in several passages of this volume.

Sacred species

The link with nature and culture and with ecology and society has been addressed in literary works. Ramakrishnan (2003), in particular, has shown how socially selected species are often ecologically significant keystone species, indicating that the conservation of the sacred is an important dimension in conservation biology. Moreover, it could also be a major means for community participation, as well as rehabilitation of degraded ecosystems by intervention of the local religious or secular society.

'Sacred species' are species (animals, plants, mushrooms, etc.) which are believed to embody spiritual values, e.g. religious, devotional, sacrificial, healing or ethical. They can have a positive or negative impact on the environment, and it is therefore important to assess in which way their sacredness will further conservation.

Sacred species are often connected with conservation significance, as demonstrated in the several cases recounted in this volume. However, many of these are endangered. The reason for this and the link between their sacredness and biocultural conservation have been discussed in several of the following chapters.

Sacred sites

A 'sacred site' is an area of special spiritual significance to peoples and community (Wild and McLeod, 2008, p. xi). 'Sacred natural sites' are sacred sites blending natural and spiritual values. This volume tackles both sacred sites (e.g. Paestum and Velia in Chapter 4) and sacred natural sites (e.g. Mount Kenya Biosphere Reserve in Chapter 24), although more cases fall into the second category.

Despite the fact that many sacred natural sites lie within protected areas, thousands around the world are threatened for different reasons. Great effort is needed to protect the holy lands of the planet. Interest in, and recognition of, sacred sites as elements critical for both biological and cultural preservation are certainly increasing noticeably around the world, especially in the light of globalisation and consequent biocultural diversity loss.

There is a strict link between sacred species and sacred sites, the latter usually being containers of the former. As per sacred species above, sacred sites carry a spiritual dimension embedded in associated history, mythology, beliefs, worship and consecrated uses. They might also be natural landscapes such as stones, cliffs, mountains, trees, forests, sources, lakes or rivers with religious or spiritual significance (Lee and Shaaf, 2003).

Guardians of biocultural diversity

Embracing an indigenous perspective, sacred species and sites may well be regarded as 'guardians of biocultural diversity'. A Maori worldview, for example, perceives mountains, rivers and trees as living beings equal in status to humans (see Chapter 17). Many of these, including the so-called 'inanimate objects' such as the rocks, as well as spiritual beings such as the *taniwha* (water demons), can surely act as guardians, called in Maori *kaitiaki*. In the Australian Aboriginal mind, moreover, the land is seen as guardian of the knowledge that lies embedded within it (Lee and Shaaf, 2003) and which humans can release or access by calling on it, or by singing it into being.

Furthermore, for American native peoples, sacred places guard the knowledge and wisdom belonging to that place (Basso, 1996). Events that took place many years ago in a specific area, for example, reiterate the morals and beliefs the Apache people hold dear to them. For them, place names are special words assigned to specific localities where a significant event happened. Through this belief, sacred places, enriched with cultural and spiritual meanings, became teaching tools for Apache people, who in turn have respected and protected these sites over the centuries. Yet the correlation to the Western concept of *genius loci* is close (see Norberg-Schultz, 1979).

Custodians of sacred species and sites

'Custodians of sacred species and sites' are individuals or groups of people who have the responsibility of looking after and often managing them. They generally reside in or close to the sacred sites (Wild and McLeod, 2008, p. 7) and they are linked with the history, culture and spiritual practices related to those species and sites.

'As of 2008, there are more than 120,000 nationally designated protected areas worldwide, covering 21 million square kilometres of land and sea', reported the Convention on Biological Diversity when reviewing progress in implementing its Programme of Work on Protected Areas (Convention on Biological Diversity, 2010). This is undoubtedly a great conservation achievement. On top of these, there are thousands of other areas protected voluntarily by communities. Many of these are considered sacred by their custodians, who play a key role in maintaining the uniqueness of these places, including their cultural and biological diversity. This is extraordinary, given that their custodians have to fight against many pressures and threats with little support and recognition from the international community or national governments.

Indigenous peoples, besides, are sometimes removed from their traditional territories and separated from their original sacred species and sites that they have cared for over many generations. Custodians of sacred species and sites, on the other hand, are stewards of their places and, accordingly, a must for landscape integrity. For this reason they deserve involvement in the conservation of ecocultural systems with one eye to the past and the other to the future. Undeniably we are living in a dynamic world where cultural and natural heritage coexist, and biocultural diversity is the way forward to sustain them.

New directions: a state of the art

International organisations are increasingly drawing attention to intangible values and traditional knowledge in their programmes related to nature conservation. UNESCO, in particular, has outlined the importance of safeguarding intangible cultural heritage in our age of globalisation, defined by Director-General Koïchiro Matsuura in the opening of the Intergovernmental Committee for the Safeguarding of the Intangible Heritage in Tokyo on 7 September 2007 as 'a living heritage whose fragility is a cause of concern, but whose wealth makes us proud' (UNESCO, 2007). Among the ongoing activities of UNESCO are the 1970 Man and Biosphere Programme (MAB) and its World Network of Biosphere Reserves, the already cited 1972 World Heritage Convention and its recognition and protection of cultural landscapes, the 2001 Universal Declaration on Cultural Diversity, and the 2003 Convention for the Safeguarding of the Intangible Cultural Heritage.

Besides, Earth Charter International has promoted the Earth Charter, a declaration of fundamental values and principles to build a just, sustainable and peaceful global society in the twenty-first century (Earth Council, 2000). Created by a large global consultation process, and endorsed by numerous organisations, the Earth Charter's ethical vision proposes that development, environmental protection, human rights and peace are interdependent and indivisible, and it aims to provide a new framework for addressing these issues. The Earth Charter's preamble is reported in Chapter 28.

The spiritual dimension of the environment has been taken into account by numerous religious organisations, among which is the WCRL (World Council of Religious Leaders, 2002) with the aim of preventing, resolving and healing conflicts, and addressing social and environmental problems. 'By promoting the practice of the spiritual values shared by all religious traditions, and by uniting the human community for times of world prayer and meditation, the World Council seeks to aid in developing the inner qualities and external conditions needed for the creation of a more peaceful, just and sustainable world society' (Charter WCRL: chapter 2). A Global Commission for the Preservation of Sacred Sites has been founded by the WCRL in conjunction with UNESCO and the World Monument Fund. Its function is to engage religious communities in securing sacred sites endangered by conflict and intolerance, and restoring those damaged by war. Internal issues regarding sacred species and sites and indigenous peoples, however, have still to be resolved in many countries.

The protection of sacred natural sites has also been encouraged in the 1991 Ramsar Convention on Wetlands and in the 2007 UN Declaration on the Rights of Indigenous Peoples, whilst the International Council on Monuments and Sites (ICOMOS) is working for the conservation and protection of cultural heritage places, including sacred places, monuments, buildings and landscapes. Likewise, there are the activities of the Mountain Institute illustrated in Chapter 6, and those of ARC, the Alliance for Religions and Conservation (Palmer and Finlay, 2003), described in Chapter 12. The cooperation of ARC with WWF International produced the publication *Beyond Belief* on the role that both mainstream faiths and primal or indigenous spiritual traditions have played in nature conservation all over the world (Dudley *et al.*, 2005).

To add to this list, scientific organisations and universities have contributed to the advance of knowledge in the topic via publications and symposia (Grim, 2001; McIvor and Pungetti, 2008). Among these is The Forum on Religion and Ecology, which is exploring religious worldviews and ethics in order to broaden understanding of the complex nature of current environmental concerns. The Forum recognises that religions need to be in dialogue with other disciplines – e.g. science, ethics, economics, education, gender and public policy – in seeking comprehensive solutions to both global and local environmental problems (Tucker and Grim, 2000). The 'Religions of the World and Ecology' conference series, hosted by the Center for the Study of World Religions, was the result of research conducted there by some members of the above Forum from 1996 to 1998, in collaboration with nearly 600 scholars, religious leaders and environmental specialists from around the world (see Grim, 2001). Additionally, this publication and the 3S Conference are the first outcomes of the 3S Initiative on Sacred Species and Sites coordinated by the author at the CCLP.

The Convention on Biological Diversity, further, has recognised the link between cultural diversity and biological diversity, developing, among other programmes, the Akwe Kon guidelines for the conduct of cultural, environmental and social impact assessments (Secretariat of the Convention on Biological Diversity, 2004). Developments proposed to take place on, or which are likely to impact on, sacred sites and on lands and waters traditionally occupied or used by indigenous and local communities are taken into account.

Finally, IUCN, the International Union for Conservation of Nature, counts many different groups and projects dealing with cultural and spiritual values of sacred sites especially under the Commission on Environmental Law (Bagader *et al.*, 1994) and the World Commission on Protected Areas (WCPA). The Cultural and Spiritual Values of Protected Areas (CSVPA) Specialist Group belongs to the latter.

The CSVPA Specialist Group is carrying out several initiatives including the Gran Ruta Inca, Delos, 3S and the Integration of Cultural and Spiritual Values into Protected Area Planning. The outcomes are numerous publications, workshops and projects carried out, as well as resolutions and recommendations put forward. Among these is the WPC Recommendation V. 13 'Cultural and spiritual values of protected areas', issued in 2003 at the IUCN World Park Congress in Durban, which urges that all systems of protected areas should recognise and incorporate spiritual values and culture-based approaches into their conservation efforts (IUCN, 2005). It was followed by the Resolution 3.049 'Community conserved areas' adopted by the 3rd IUCN World Conservation Congress in Bangkok in 2004. More recent is Resolution 4.038 endorsed in 2008 by the IUCN World Conservation Congress in Barcelona, 'Recognition and conservation of sacred natural sites in protected areas'.

Barcelona also hosted the launch of the IUCN and UNESCO 'SNS Guidelines for Protected Area Managers' (Wild and MacLeod, 2008), another outcome of the IUCN–CSVPA Specialist Group which summarises the experience in recognising, planning and managing sacred natural sites in a variety of protected areas. While focusing primarily on the sacred places of indigenous communities, the guidelines are also relevant for the sacred sites of mainstream faiths. They will be used to share experience with protected area managers and their colleagues around the world who are concerned about, and interested in, protecting sacred natural sites.

'IUCN has become a key player in the effort to protect sacred sites and holy lands of the planet', said Gonzalo Oviedo in Barcelona; 'we run projects in the field with custodians of sacred places, we support them at the policy level, we advocate for their recognition and support and we promote better understanding of their values' (IUCN, 2008). Nevertheless, there is still a vacuum on studies on species, in terms of plants and animals, which are considered sacred. The mentioned 3S Initiative on Sacred Species and Sites, coordinated by CCLP under the IUCN–CSVPA Specialist Group aims to cover at least in part such a big gap with this publication.

Conclusions: a paradigm shift, a new agenda

It is evident that rapid progress in the consideration of practices in sacred sites around the world has begun in academic circles and conservation programmes. Maintaining the integrity of life through cultural landscapes, traditional land use, balanced lifestyles and sustainable development is essential for the conservation of biodiversity. However, we need to respect and preserve cultural diversity, including languages and knowledge, in order to maintain biodiversity. Biocultural diversity is the way forward.

Sacred species and sites are important tools for advancing studies in biocultural diversity. Yet, it is necessary to understand their essence, context and relation to humans, for their appropriate development, conservation and management.

Past research in biocultural diversity has focused on the relationships between man and other species, and also between all species and the landscape they inhabit (Loh and Harmon, 2005). First studies on biocultural diversity have aimed to establish correlations between biological and cultural diversity, often focusing on languages and geographical areas (Manne, 2003; Sutherland, 2003), or on environmental management in indigenous communities (Maffi, 2001; Harmon, 2002).

Well before this, the United Nations Development Programme (UNDP) had pointed out the importance of looking at the future with a holistic approach. 'The Earth is one but the world is not. We all depend on one biosphere for sustaining our lives' (World Commission on Environment and Development, 1987, p. 27). Over 30 years later, as stated by Her Royal Highness Princess Basma Bint Talal (2005, p. 182) 'we are witnessing the realisation that a paradigm shift in the way we theorise development is the only way forward'.

New directions are now being taken to explore the link between sites, species and peoples in the wider landscape, bridging the divide between the evolutionary view of natural sciences and the creative perception of human sciences. Among the authors of this book, the ecological, cultural and spiritual dimensions have been investigated, per se and in relation to biocultural diversity, with the aim of advancing synergies and knowledge on biocultural conservation and of providing an integrated perspective of the total life on earth.

References

Bagader, A. A., El-Chirazi El-Sabbagh, A. T., As-Sayyid Al-Glayand, M. *et al.* (1994). *Environmental Protection in Islam*. Gland and Cambridge: IUCN.

Basso, K. H. (1996). *Wisdom Sites in Places: Landscape and Language among the Western Apache*. Albuquerque, NM: University of New Mexico Press.

Berkes, F. (1999). *Sacred Ecology: Traditional Ecological Knowledge and Resource Management*. London: Taylor & Francis.

Botkin, D. (1990). *Discordant Harmonies: A New Ecology for the Twenty-first Century*. New York and Oxford: Oxford University Press.

Convention on Biological Diversity. (2010). *In-Depth Review of the Implementation of the Programme of Work on Protected Areas*. UNEP/CBD/SBSTTA/14/L.5. Nairobi: CBD.

Council of Europe. (2000). *European Landscape Convention*. Strasbourg: Council of Europe.

Darwin, C. (1859). *The Origin of Species by Means of Natural Selection*. London: John Murray.

Descartes, R. *Meditations on First Philosophy: with Selections from the Objections and Replies*, trans. J. Cottingham (1986). Cambridge: Cambridge University Press.

Dudley, N., Higgins-Zogib, L. and Mansourian, S. (2005). *Beyond Belief: Linking Faiths and Protected Areas to Support Biodiversity Conservation*. Gland: WWF, Equilibrium and ARC.

Earth Council. (2000). *Earth Charter*. San Jose, CA: Earth Council.

Forman, R. T. T. and Godron, M. (1986). *Landscape Ecology*. New York, NY: John Wiley & Sons.

Grim, J. A., ed. (2001). *Indigenous Traditions and Ecology: The Interbeing of Cosmology and Community*. Cambridge, MA: Harvard University Press.

Harmon, D. (2002). *In Light of our Differences: How Diversity in Nature and Culture makes us Human*. Washington, DC: The Smithsonian Institution Press.

Harmon, D. and Putney, A. D., eds. (2003). *The Full Value of Parks: From Economics to the Intangible*. Lanham, MD: Rowman & Littlefield.

HRH Princess Basma Bint Talal. (2005). The only way forward. In *Toward a Sustainable World: The Earth Charter in Action*, ed. P. Blaze Corcoran, M. Vilela and A. Roerink. Amsterdam: KIT Publishers BV, pp. 182–3.

IUCN. (2005). *Benefits Beyond Boundaries*. Proceedings of the Vth IUCN World Park Congress. Gland and Cambridge: IUCN.

IUCN. (2008). *IUCN and UNESCO publish guidelines on sacred natural sites in protected areas*. WCC, 07 October 2008. Barcelona: IUCN Press Release.

Lee, C. and Schaaf, T., eds. (2003). *The Importance of Sacred Natural Sites for Biodiversity Conservation*. Proceedings of the international workshop held in Kunming and

Xishuangbanna Biosphere Reserve, People's Republic of China, 17–20 February 2003. Paris: UNESCO-MAB.

Leopold, A. (1987). *A Sand County Almanac: and Sketches Here and There* (1st edn. Oxford, 1949). Oxford: Oxford University Press.

Loh, J. and Harmon, D. (2005). A global index of biocultural diversity. *Ecological Indicators*, **5**, 231–41.

Lovelock, J. (1979). *Gaia: A New Look at Life*. Oxford: Oxford University Press.

Lucretius. *De Rerum Natura, Book 3*, trans. W. H. D. Rouse (1937). The Loeb Classical Library. London: William Heinemann.

Maffi, L. (2001). *On Biocultural Diversity: Linking Language, Knowledge and the Environment*. Washington, DC: Smithsonian Institution Press.

Maffi, L. and Woodley, E. (2010). *Biocultural Diversity Conservation: A Global Sourcebook*. London: Earthscan.

Makhzoumi, J. and Pungetti, G. (1999). *Ecological Landscape Design and Planning: The Mediterranean Context*. London: Spon-Routledge.

Manne, L. L. (2003). Nothing has yet lasted forever: current and threatened levels of biological diversity. *Evolutionary Ecological Research*, **5**, 517–27.

McIvor, A. and Pungetti, G. (2008). Can sacredness help protect species? *World Conservation*, **38**(1), 18.

Næss, A. (1973). The shallow and the deep, long-range ecology movement. *Inquiry*, **16**, reprinted in *Sessions* 1995, pp. 151–5.

Næss, S. H. (1989). *Ecology, Community, Lifestyle*, trans. and ed. D. Rothenberg. Cambridge: Cambridge University Press.

Nasr, S. H. (1996) *Religion and the Order of Nature*. Oxford: Oxford University Press.

Naveh, Z. (1995). From biodiversity to ecodiversity: new tools for holistic landscape conservation. *International Journal of Ecology and Environmental Sciences*, **21**, 1–56.

Naveh, Z. and Lieberman, A. (1984). *Landscape Ecology*. New York, NY: Springer-Verlag.

Norberg-Schultz, C. (1979). *Genius Loci: Towards a Phenomenology of Architecture*. New York, NY: Rizzoli.

Oviedo, G., Maffi, L. and Larsen, P. B. (2000). *Indigenous and Traditional Peoples of the World and Ecoregional Conservation: An Integrated Approach to Conserving the World's Biological and Cultural Diversity*. Gland: WWF International.

Palmer, M. and Finlay, V. (2003). *Faith in Conservation: New Approaches to Religions and the Environment*. Washington, DC: The World Bank.

Persic, A. and Martin, G., eds. (2008). *Links between Biological and Cultural Diversity. Report of an International Workshop*. Paris: UNESCO.

Posey, D. A., ed. (1999). *Cultural and Spiritual Values of Biodiversity*. London: UNEP/Intermediate Technology Publications.

Pungetti, G. (1996). *Landscape Research for Ecologically Sound Planning of Mediterranean Rural Areas: Applications in Sardinia*. University of Cambridge, Darwin College and Department of Geography PhD thesis. University of Cambridge.

Pungetti, G. (2008). Cultural and spiritual values in landscape conservation and management. In *Riconquistare il paesaggio: La convenzione europea del paesaggio e la conservazione della biodiversita' in Italia*, ed. C. Teofili and R. Clarino. Rome: WWF, pp. 360–6.

Ramakrishnan, P. S. (2003). Conserving the sacred: the protective impulse and the origins of modern protected areas. In *The Full Value of Parks*, ed. D. Harmon and A. D. Putney. Lanham, MD: Rowman & Littlefield, pp. 27–42.

Schaaf, T. and Lee, C., eds. (2006). *Conserving Cultural and Biological Diversity: The Role of Sacred Natural Sites and Cultural Landscapes*. Proceedings of the Tokyo Symposium, UNU, 30 May–2 June 2005. Paris: UNESCO-MAB.

Secretariat of the Convention on Biological Diversity. (2003). *Convention on Biological Diversity: Text and Annexes*. Icao: UNEP/CBD.

Secretariat of the Convention on Biological Diversity. (2004). *Akwé: Kon. Voluntary guidelines for the conduct of cultural, environmental and social impact assessment regarding developments proposed to take place on, or which are likely to impact on, sacred sites and on lands and waters traditionally occupied or used by indigenous and local communities*. Montreal: CBD Guidelines Series.

Skutnabb-Kangas, T., Maffi, L. and Harmon, D. (2003). *Sharing a World of Difference: The Earth's Linguistic, Cultural, and Biological Diversity*. Paris: UNESCO.

Sutherland, W. J. (2003). Parallel extinction risk and global distribution of languages and species. *Nature*, **423**, 276–9.

Taylor, P. (1981). The ethics of respect for Nature. *Environmental Ethics*, **3**, 197–218.

Taylor, P. (1986). *Respect for Nature*. Princeton, NJ: Princeton University Press.

Thomas, K. (1983). *Man and the Natural World: A History of Modern Sensibility*. New York, NY: Pantheon.

Tucker, M. E. and Grim, J. (2000). *Series Foreword. Religions of the World and Ecology Series*. Cambridge, MA: Center for the Study of World Religions, Harvard Divinity School, University of Harvard.

Tyler, W. (1964). *Nature and Art in the Renaissance Literature*. New York, NY: Columbia University Press.

UNESCO. (1998). *'Natural' Sacred Sites, Cultural Diversity and Biological Diversity*. Proceedings of the international symposium 'Natural' Sacred Sites. Cultural Diversity and Biological Diversity, Paris, 22–25 September 1998. Paris: UNESCO, CNRS, MNHN.

UNESCO. (2002). *UNESCO Universal Declaration on Cultural Diversity*. Paris: UNESCO.

UNESCO. (2007). *First Inscriptions on UNESCO's intangible cultural heritage lists to take place in September 2009*. Paris: UNESCO Services.

UNESCO. (2008). *Operational Guidelines for the Implementation of the World Heritage Convention* (WHC. 08/01). Paris: UNESCO World Heritage Centre.

Wallace, J. (1998). *Introduction to Charles Darwin, 'The Origin of Species'*. Ware: Wordsworth Edition.

Wild, R., and McLeod, C., eds. (2008). *Sacred Natural Sites: Guidelines for Protected Area Managers*. Gland: IUCN.

World Commission on Environment and Development. (1987). *Our Common Future*. Oxford: Oxford University Press.

World Council of Religious Leaders. (2002). *Charter World Council of Religious Leaders: An Outcome of the Millennium World Peace Summit*. Bangkok: UNESCAP.

2

Spiritual values and conservation

GONZALO OVIEDO

Introduction

The history of nature conservation is largely a history of clashes of values. It is not new, and not surprising, that the universal conservation paradigm of today represents an alternative set of values, and a response, to the value systems linked to the Industrial Revolution and the expansion of capitalism.

This modern conservation paradigm, in its many forms and developments, has often tried to explore links with ethical and cultural values, in one way or another. It has not always succeeded, however, and in fact in many instances its own sets of values have entered into conflict with beliefs and values that should have been at the core of its approach.

This is the case of spiritual values. For most of the conservation experts of the nineteenth and twentieth centuries, conservation had to be based on secular approaches rooted in natural sciences, and as such it was conceived as a universal paradigm where the only appreciated non-material values were those of aesthetics, personal contemplation and enjoyment, knowledge and planetary ethics. Not that all such values were bad – on the contrary, they were a great re-creation of ideals needed to moderate the desire for progress. However, spiritual values were largely absent.

The plight of indigenous values

When I was young I shared a large part of my life with indigenous communities of the Andes, and with them I learned about the many ways in which

Sacred Species and Sites: Advances in Biocultural Conservation, ed. Gloria Pungetti, Gonzalo Oviedo and Della Hooke. Published by Cambridge University Press. © Cambridge University Press 2012.

species and places had acquired special significance in their cultures. The land for them was full of spiritual creatures embodied in plants, animals, watercourses and hills, and many of the practices of those communities were modelled by such beliefs. Conservation, as we call it formally today, was often a result of common living, not of professional practice.

This is not news, of course, as much has been written about the conceptions, cosmologies, approaches, knowledge and values of traditional cultures and their conservation values. However, until recently, conservation institutions have not really appreciated or integrated the elements and creations of traditional cultures in their policies and practices.

I would like, nonetheless, to start the discussion with a note about the clash of spiritual values and practices regarding nature, as this is very close to my own experiences. In 1970, a Colombian botanist, Víctor Manuel Patiño, published a monumental work called *Cultivated Plants and Domesticated Animals of Equatorial America* (Patiño, 1970). I started reading that book shortly after, as I entered college, and was shocked by some of the findings, in particular by those related to what the author called 'the arboricide tradition of Catholicism'. Indeed, the Catholic Church, in colonial times, obsessed by what it called 'extirpation of idolatries', embarked in a large practice throughout the continent to eliminate many species of trees that were sacred to the Amerindians. Chroniclers of the times describe, for example, how the Muisca people of the Bogota valley had large areas of palm forests which they maintained, cared for and respected because the palm species were sacred to them; Bishop Cristobal de Torres ordered the forests to be cut down and burnt to 'extirpate that idolatry'. In my country, Ecuador, the same was the fate of the tree species called quishuar (*Buddleia incana*), a sacred species that was aggressively clear cut by the Church for the same reason, which included using the wood for Catholic statuettes, as the priests thought that in this way the indigenous people were adoring the images of Catholic saints and deities made of that wood instead of the tree. The quishuar was almost driven to extinction by the Church, and in my times with the Andean communities I would only find isolated trees of this species in inaccessible *huaycus* (ravines) in the upper hills – many of them still sacred places for the indigenous communities.

This example of the arboricide tradition of the Catholic Church of colonial times of Latin America illustrates one of the reasons why the positivist conservation paradigm of the nineteenth and twentieth centuries preferred to stay away from religious and spiritual values. The thinking was that science was the sole solid foundation for conserving nature, because some spiritual values (or other motives disguised as spirituality) had in many cases been destructive forces for nature.

Rediscovering values for a sustainable future

However, the example I have given is not necessarily a fair portrait of religions and religious values per se; it is, rather, an illustration of practices that result from the degeneration of the original values of Christianity – both in terms of nature and in terms of tolerance.

The conventional clashes of values around conservation paradigms are changing rapidly and radically. In recent years, there has been a rise in the awareness and recognition of the links between cultural and biological diversity, and in the recognition that cultural and spiritual values need to be much more integrated in the search for visions and solutions for a sustainable future.

A critical point of departure in the reflection on the links between cultural and biological diversity is the recognition that the drivers of the trends of loss, impoverishment and homogenisation of cultures and their spiritual and cultural values are the same drivers as, or are very similar to, those behind the loss of biodiversity and the degradation of ecosystems (Mallarach, 2008). Further, and in spite of the conventional discourse on development and economic growth, in many cases they are also the drivers of poverty and degradation of livelihoods.

The diversity of human cultures, with its wealth of knowledge, practices, beliefs, worldviews, values and forms of social organisation – including those of indigenous peoples – are a fundamental component of sustainability.

A reflection of this new way of thinking about conservation and sustainability was the attention that cultural and spiritual values and cultural diversity received at the IUCN 4th World Conservation Congress in Barcelona, October 2008, which addressed the overall theme of 'a diverse and sustainable world'. One of the thematic Journeys (cross-cutting streams) of the Congress specifically explored the issue of 'Bio-Cultural Diversity and Indigenous Peoples', and another related Journey discussed the connected topic of the rights of peoples and cultures in conservation and sustainable development. In its more than 60 events, the Journey on Bio-Cultural Diversity and Indigenous Peoples invited Congress participants to discuss how conservation of biodiversity in the long term could better include socio-cultural practices and values, including concrete examples from the field and global policy issues, and to help in guiding and supporting further action of the conservation community and of all people engaged in the search for sustainable living (McIvor et al., 2009).

Notable in this Journey was the participation of representatives from a variety of faith communities, indigenous peoples, custodians of sacred natural sites, protected area managers, aboriginal rangers, non-governmental organisations (NGOs) and governmental policy officers and others, from all around the world.

The conservation community has been addressing the challenges for the conservation of sacred natural sites for more than a decade (Oviedo and Jeanrenaud, 2006), but still its achievements are meagre due to the complexity and the dimension of the issue, as well as to the lack of understanding and support from public policies. The IUCN Congress reviewed the problems and discussed new strategies and opportunities, and launched publications that can guide action by the conservation community (Fincke, 2009). It conveyed a strong message about the role and value of sacred natural sites and their custodians for nature conservation and for the survival of traditional cultures.

Shared values: lingering doubts and reasons for hope

The values and management practices of indigenous and traditional peoples are increasingly considered an important part of the global efforts for the conservation of ecosystems and species. They are also critical elements for the vitality of cultures. While the values and interests of such peoples and communities are not always and not necessarily the same as those of the conservation community, the points of commonality are many, and they are the basis for strategic alliances. As indicated, beyond conservation values, a key element of the commonality of interest is the fact that both traditional cultures and conservation actors face the same powerful drivers of the destruction of nature and cultures.

New legal and policy regimes are fundamental for the maintenance of cultural and spiritual values related to nature and natural processes. Communities and cultures need recognition of their rights and responsibilities in caring for the planet and for human beings – in a climate of insecurity, violation of rights, extreme inequities, conflict and weak or nonexistent governance, no cultures can flourish and there is no room for better lives. Maintenance of cultural and spiritual values needs rights-based policies and actions, and commitment from all actors to reducing inequalities.

The role of faith-based groups and religious institutions in shaping a new ethics of development and living is increasingly recognised as important. In the last few decades, all major faiths of the world have declared their conviction that conserving nature is part of their own ethical and spiritual commitments and mandates. Some of the leaders of major religions, such as Patriarch Bartholomew of the Orthodox Church, have turned into leading thinkers and promoters of nature conservation.

All different religions share some important philosophical views. Cornerstones of their doctrines are, for example, a sense of reverence for the mystery of life and respect for species that share the planet; social ethics and the principle of redistribution of resources; a sense of responsibility for future generations. All religions call upon us to have restraints and to act as part of the whole (McIvor *et al.*, 2009). Most religions call on us to live more simply, with a view to intra- and intergenerational justice. They call on us to consider that we are not owners but caretakers of the Earth and have to act with consequential responsibility. Religions call for peace and for principles that bring justice and equity to both the poor and the natural environment (IUCN, 2008).

However, many still doubt the real commitment of religious institutions, as some of them have been traditionally linked with earthly interests and powers in ways that appear incompatible with the spiritual values of their doctrines. It is not only the sad episodes of colonial times, as in the examples I gave; it is also that even today we keep hearing disturbing messages and news about the behaviour of some religious institutions and leaders.

There is good reason to doubt, then, but there is also good reason for hope. This was the feeling that prevailed after an inspiring event of the IUCN Congress, the 'Sustainability Dialogue on Spirituality and Conservation'. Speakers representing some of the world's major religions and faith traditions, including Christianity, Islam, Jainism and Judaism, agreed that the environmental crisis should be considered a moral and spiritual issue, as values and attitudes that shape peoples' concepts of nature and influence their behaviour are greatly influenced by religions, spiritual traditions and ethical practices. They highlighted the need for more dialogue between religions, science, education, policy and economy in order to collaboratively address environmental challenges.

Globally, there seems to be a growing hunger for spirituality. As the world faces the turmoil of an economic crisis that is largely the product of deep corruption and loss of ethical values, as well as of the effects of climate change (also driven by unsustainable practices and a profoundly inequitable development model), many people are turning to ethical codes, spiritual values, new approaches to the ways of living, and learning from the wisdom of simpler societies. The emerging awareness of the potentially powerful links between spirituality and conservation, and growing recognition of the importance of partnerships, inspire hope for channelling mindsets and actions into a sustainable direction.

Challenges of indigenous and traditional peoples' spirituality today

I come back to the problem still faced today by many indigenous and traditional peoples, whose spirituality continues to be considered 'paganism' by some religious groups and churches and is therefore condemned and persecuted. I would not want to be insistent on this problem, but it serves me to make the point about the need for new ethical principles.

Indeed, the oppression of the spirituality of indigenous and traditional peoples is not a problem of the past – it is still a problem of today. A few years ago, I was in the historical Maya lands of Mexico discussing conservation of sacred natural sites with scholars, indigenous leaders and practitioners. I heard from a Mayan spiritual leader that he and other fellows of their communities were still harassed by local Catholic priests who condemned their spiritual values and practices, including the protection of sacred sites, and threatened them with excommunication. He explained that such threats meant great suffering for the people as they are deeply religious. In fact, the Amerindian communities often practice various forms of religious syncretism, where Catholicism is combined with traditional spirituality.

In February 2001, several members of an indigenous group of the Mashco-Piro people of the Peruvian Amazon were killed by colonists. The Mashco-Piro people live in voluntary isolation, avoiding contact with other groups due to their long history of being persecuted. When asked about the reason for the killing, the principal town councillor explained: 'it is [also] because of religious organisations in the area (...), "gringos" and others, that work daily in trying to reach the Mashcos, with the purpose, as they say, of "civilising" them. But we know that the Mashco-Piros oppose those intents. The attitude of these religious people confuses our brothers the Mashcos in that they believe that we [all the other people] are also in that job [of religious conversion], and it is for that reason that these bad events happen'. So deadly confrontations are also the result of the Mashco-Piro people trying to avoid harassment by religious sects, mainly originating in the USA.

Removing suppression: 'We are all in the same boat'

Lack of respect for indigenous spirituality, and failure of the state to protect the rights of indigenous peoples to their religious practices and beliefs, is still ongoing. The arrogance of Western 'civilised' people, including religious institutions, has had a profound impact on the vitality of traditional spirituality and wisdom.

In recent years, attempts to reverse this situation and initiate dialogue have taken place, including some very important initiatives. One was the invitation of Patriarch Bartholomew of the Orthodox Church to an indigenous spiritual leader of the Amazon to bless the waters of the river at the Ecological Symposium that the Patriarch organised in 2006, followed by an encounter with an indigenous community. At the closing of the event, the Patriarch reported: 'In our unique encounter with the indigenous peoples of this region, we witnessed and felt their profound sense of the sacredness of creation and of the bonds which exist between all living things and people. Thanks to them, we understand more deeply that, as creatures of God, we are all in the same boat'.

Conclusions: moving forward

As I have proposed elsewhere, we need to promote an ethical approach that fosters respect for the spiritual values of all human communities – including the values of secular, non-religious spirituality. This is a fundamental requirement for creating solid bonds among different cultures for caring for the planet. The conservation community should be supportive and engaged in promoting an approach that:

- recognises the diversity of the world's cultures and spiritualities as part of the vitality of humankind and that of the planet;
- values all forms of spirituality as they connect to nature;
- recognises that spirituality is different from religion, but that it is equally valuable;
- considers all religions as having the same value;
- considers traditional spiritualities as being equal to religions in value;
- considers also that non-religious, secular spirituality is equally as valuable as religious spirituality;
- promotes ecumenism;
- promotes dialogue among all faiths, religions and forms of spirituality, as well as with the secular world, around common values and approaches towards improving human living in a sustainable planet;
- recognises that there are multiple dynamics and changes in all forms of spirituality, as they are not static (as broadly cultures are not), and that in a world of global knowledge and cultural interactions traditional or ancient values are likely to encounter and adopt new spiritual values;
- uses a rights-based approach, which implies respecting the rights of all peoples and individuals to their own beliefs and spiritual values and practices, as long as they do not harm others, as well as the universal rights of citizens to a healthy environment and to sustainable development;
- promotes equity in conservation approaches and supports especially the vulnerable or disadvantaged groups, whose cultures and spiritual values tend to be ignored or discriminated;
- promotes the integration of scientific knowledge and technical tools with traditional management systems based on local values; and

- takes an enabling approach to communities and people, with a view to strengthening local actions, institutions and processes, including communities linked through spiritual traditions.

More dialogue and further development of these approaches is needed to achieve effective integration of biological and cultural diversity and spiritual values in conservation and development. To judge from processes and thinking such as those from which this publication is a product, there is room for hope, as an increasing number of communities and individuals are engaging in a new planetary ethics.

References

Fincke, A. (2009). *Indigenous and Traditional Peoples at the IUCN World Conservation Congress*. Report from the 4th IUCN World Conservation Congress Forum, 6–9 October 2008, Barcelona, Spain. Gland, Switzerland: IUCN.

IUCN. (2008). *Video of the Sustainability Dialogue on Spirituality and Conservation at the 4th IUCN World Conservation Congress*. URL: http://www.iucn.org/congress_08/live/streaming_sessions.cfm?1874/Spirituality-and-Conservation.

Mallarach, J.-M. (ed). (2008). *Protected Landscapes and Cultural and Spiritual Values*. Volume 2 in the series *Values of Protected Landscapes and Seascapes*, IUCN, GTZ and Obra Social de Caixa Catalunya. Heidelberg: Kasparek Verlag.

McIvor, A., Fincke, A. and Oviedo, G. (2009). *Bio-Cultural Diversity and Indigenous Peoples Journey*. Report from the 4th IUN World Conservation Congress Forum, 6–9 October 2008, Barcelona, Spain. Gland, Switzerland: IUCN.

Oviedo, G. and Jeanrenaud, S. (2006). Protecting sacred natural sites of indigenous and traditional peoples. In *Conserving Cultural and Biological Diversity, The Role of Sacred Natural Sites and Cultural Landscapes*, ed. T. Schaaf and C. Lee. Paris: UNESCO, pp. 260–6.

Patiño, V. M. (1970). *Plantas cultivadas y animales domésticos en América Equinoccial*. [*Cultivated Plants and Domesticated Animals of Equatorial Africa*.] Cali, Colombia: Imprenta Departamental.

3

Protected areas and sacred nature: a convergence of beliefs

NIGEL DUDLEY and LIZA HIGGINS-ZOGIB

Introduction: protection for biodiversity, protection for the spirit

There is now almost universal recognition that for many practical, cultural and ethical reasons parts of the world's land and water surface should be set aside from the mainstream of human activity and maintained in a natural or near-natural state. Although there are many factors influencing decisions to select and protect particular places, two currently predominate: the desire to preserve the full range of naturally occurring biodiversity and the wish to safeguard places regarded as sacred. While these motives may seem a long way apart, there is in reality a considerable overlap, which manifests practically in terms of management strategies in particular places and philosophically in the worldviews and opinions of the people involved. This chapter summarises research (Dudley *et al.*, 2005) that looks at links between protected areas and sacred lands and waters.

Sacred sites and protected areas

The contemporary growth in protected areas – such as national parks and wilderness areas – represents what is almost certainly the largest and fastest conscious deliberate change of land use in history. At the dawn of the twentieth century, a handful of national parks had been established, in the US, Australia, Africa and India. By the time of the Fifth World Parks Congress in 2003, over 10% of the world's land surface was under some form of protection, along with a relatively small but rapidly growing area of coastline and ocean (Chape *et al.*, 2003).

Sacred Species and Sites: Advances in Biocultural Conservation, ed. Gloria Pungetti, Gonzalo Oviedo and Della Hooke. Published by Cambridge University Press. © Cambridge University Press 2012.

The speed with which the world's protected area network has grown demonstrates an extraordinary response to recognition that the world is losing biological diversity, but it has not come without cost. In many countries, people, often including the poorest and politically weakest communities, have been dispossessed of their traditional land to make way for protected areas. This, along with a persistent negligence in including socio-cultural–spiritual concerns into conservation strategies, has created social tensions associated with conservation (Colchester, 2003). Additionally, not all the areas that are designated as 'protected' are in reality managed as such and many, perhaps most, protected areas face threats that in the long term mean that they continue to lose some of their values (Carey *et al.*, 2000). Modern protected area strategies need to address these issues more effectively, and links with faiths and with some of their traditional conservation methods is one way of achieving this aim.

A large proportion of the world's protected areas have links to one or more faith group; these links include all the major faiths and a host of minor faiths and belief systems of local communities and indigenous peoples. Although modern protected areas are predicated on the need to protect biodiversity, their focus on natural or near-natural habitats often brings them into close alignment with sacred sites. In many places, the main reason why areas of land or water have been left in a natural state is because they are sacred. The fact that many protected areas contain sacred sites is not a coincidence, but a meeting of aims.

To tease out this relationship, it is important to understand the variety of management and governance types in protected areas and the variety of sacredness in nature.

Protected areas are not all managed uniformly; the term embraces literally hundreds of official and unofficial ways of protecting nature. IUCN (the International Union for Conservation of Nature) provides a comprehensive typology, which divides protected areas into six categories determined by management objective (Dudley, 2008):

> Category Ia: managed mainly for science or wilderness protection;
> Category Ib: managed mainly for wilderness protection;
> Category II: managed mainly for ecosystem protection and recreation;
> Category III: managed mainly for conservation of specific natural features;
> Category IV: managed mainly for conservation of species and habitat;
> Category V: managed mainly for landscape/seascape conservation or recreation;
> Category VI: managed mainly for the sustainable use of natural resources.

A number of other important international designations exist, including natural World Heritage sites, UNESCO Man and the Biosphere reserves, and Ramsar sites in freshwater areas: these can all contain protected areas in any of the IUCN categories. Sacred elements can occur in all six management categories as shown in Table 3.1 (examples from Dudley *et al.*, 2005).

Neither are indigenous and community conserved areas all governed in the same way. While the majority of land and water set aside on a global scale is owned and controlled by governments, a substantial proportion is in private hands, or managed by communities, or management is shared between several stakeholder groups (Borrini-Feyerabend *et al.*, 2004). The significance of other governance types is increasing, including, in particular, areas set aside by communities and indigenous and traditional peoples. As with management objectives, sacredness can occur within any governance type, although is perhaps particularly suited to community conserved areas or co-management approaches where there is already a social commitment to conservation because of the sacred values of the site. Table 3.2 illustrates examples from a range of governance types.

Although protected areas are regarded as a modern phenomenon, they often have ancient antecedents. Land and water have been set aside for millennia: as hunting preserves, as in many parts of Europe (Schama, 1995); to protect grazing rights such as the traditional *hima* of the Middle East (Bagader *et al.*, 1994); to address problems of forest loss and consequent environmental problems, as in Japan and Switzerland; and, perhaps most important of all, because communities regard particular places, species or natural features as having some sacred quality. The extent of this overlap is only now being widely recognised.

So far we have referred to faith groups as if they were one homogenous category. Specifically, we use the term 'faith' as a catch-all definition and recognise its limitations in encompassing the complexity of the world's religious/belief systems and practices. We recognise, for example, that some spiritual belief systems do not rely on 'faith' at all. Moreover, we must recognise the enormous variety of belief systems between and within faiths and religions: monotheism, polytheism, belief in eternal life or reincarnation, and a vast array of different creation stories, worldviews and sacred writings. There is also an important general distinction to be made between faiths that explicitly recognise and worship god or gods through nature and those, particularly the monotheistic Jewish, Christian and Islamic traditions, which have traditionally been wary of sacred nature as a manifestation of idolatry. In practice, the links between faiths and sacred places are not only influenced by current doctrinal beliefs, but often by far older philosophies. There are many instances of places remaining sacred even after the dominant faith has changed; for example, the emergence of Islam and Christianity in Africa has not stopped the protection of many sacred natural sites that originated within older

Table 3.1 *Examples of sacred sites in protected areas with different management strategies.*

Category	Country	Protected area	Notes
Ia	Sri Lanka	Yala National Park	Significant to Buddhists and Hindus and requiring high levels of protection for faith reasons
Ib	Mongolia	Bogd Khan Mountain	Significant to Buddhism and previously to shamanism. Officially designated as a sacred mountain by the state, although evidence exists of a 'wilderness area' declaration dating from 1294
II	Australia	Kata Tjuta National Park	The park, and in particular the Uluru monolith (also known as 'Ayer's Rock'), is of religious significance to the Aborigines. Visitors are asked not to climb on the rock, but some continue to do so
III	Cambodia	Phnom Prich Wildlife Sanctuary	A small area of forest within the wildlife sanctuary is considered a Spirit Forest; beliefs passed down through generations dictate that the area should be completely untouched
IV	Czech Republic	Čertova stěna (Devil's wall)	Small reserve that also contains a rock pulpit that has been sacred to both the old animist traditions and to Christians
V	China	Xishuangbanna National Park	Landscape with several sacred sites (groves and mountains) for Daoists, which have long been managed by the community and are part of an important and biologically rich cultural landscape
VI	Tanzania	Misali Island Marine Conservation Area	Important to Islam, where religious leaders are working with fishing communities to ensure sustainable catches and maintenance of marine life
World Heritage site	Japan	Itsukushima island shrine	Important for Shinto, Buddhism and Hinduism. The island is in the Seto inland sea and has been a holy place of Shinto for centuries. It also contains large areas of protected forests
UNESCO MAB	Israel	Mount Carmel	Also IUCN Category V. Significant to Judaism. The Ha'arbaim Grove contains over 80 kermes oaks which are considered holy by local residents, who grant them special treatment and protection
Ramsar site	Peru	Lake Titicaca	Important to traditional faiths of the area. In Inca mythology, the children of the Sun emerged from the depths of Lake Titicaca to found their empire. It is also said to be the origin of all life

Table 3.2 *Examples of sacred sites in protected areas with different governance strategies.*

Governance type	Country	Protected area	Notes
State	Malawi	Nyika National Park	The upland plateau contains a sacred lake, sacred mountain and sacred waterfall, all of which are important for rain ceremonies. Once cut off from local communities, access has once again been granted by the park authorities (personal communication from Roy Bima and site visit, 2004)
Private	Lebanon	Harissa Forest	A cathedral and shrine to Our Lady lie at the heart of the forest. The Maronite Church owns a large proportion of the forest and in 2003 established a management group to oversee its ecological protection in association with the local municipality (personal communication from Martin Palmer, 2006)
Co-managed	Papua New Guinea	Madang Lagoon	Wildlife management area under customary co-management, including sacred areas where the sea spirits are thought to reside; surveys show these are richer in biodiversity than other places (personal communication from WWF Papua New Guinea office, 2005)
Community conserved area	Mexico	Wirikuta Sacred Space	Important sacred space for the Huichol people in the Chihuahua Desert, now recognised as a Sacred Natural Site by the government (Borrini-Feyerabend *et al.*, 2004)

belief systems. Even faiths that in theory disapprove of sacred natural sites often have active examples in practice.

Here data are less exact; there is no database on sacred sites equivalent to the World Database on Protected Areas. However, it is becoming increasingly clear that such sites are far more numerous and widespread than has previously been supposed. As with areas protected for nature conservation, a simple typology can be outlined describing how faiths interact with land and water:

- *Sacred natural sites.* Many, perhaps most, faiths explicitly recognise certain places as being important: because they are the home of the gods, or are a place to worship, or because they are associated with spiritually significant historical events or people. Sacred natural sites are often, but not always, distinguished by an unusual landform, species or aspect: for example, groves, ancient trees, rivers, ponds and lakes, springs, mountains, volcanoes, rock formations, islands, beaches and sometimes whole landscapes (Dudley *et al.*, 2005). Yosemite National Park in California exists on lands regarded as sacred by Native American communities, for example. Many sacred natural sites may be better protected in practice than official protected areas.

- *Sacred places on natural sites.* Even when the land itself is not regarded as sacred, the presence of sacred buildings such as temples, can in effect lead to the protection of natural or semi-natural habitats. Examples might include the forests around Angkor Wat in Cambodia, about the only surviving natural forests in a densely populated part of that country (De Lopez *et al.*, 2003), and lowland trees found in churchyards in highly modified environments in Ethiopia (Burgess *et al.*, 2004, p. 262).

- *Sacred species.* A slightly different form of protection can result if a whole species is regarded as sacred. Most sacred species are either large and charismatic animals and plants, totem species, or those species that are particularly useful to humans; for instance, the olive (*Olea europaea*) has been regarded as sacred by many faith groups (Perlin, 1989, p. 67). Recognition of the sacredness of an animal can result in the protection both of the species itself and of its supporting habitat: this happens with several crane species for example, crocodiles in parts of West Africa (Borrini-Feyerabend *et al.*, 2004), and some whale species (Lantis, 1938). Sacredness does not always mean protection and many sacred animals are hunted, but it does imply that the species will be managed sustainably.

- *Land and water owned by a faith group.* The world's larger faiths are amongst the richest and most influential institutions on Earth, with much of their wealth tied up in land and property. Some of this may be protected for practical reasons, such as the forests in Japan that have been managed sustainably to supply timber for renewing temples (Bernard, 1998). Other land may be owned for investment or to provide resources, but as faiths become attuned to environmental issues a proportion may be deliberately managed for conservation: as in the forests owned by the Lutheran Church in Sweden, which are now all certified as being sustainably managed by the Forest Stewardship Council.

- *Land or water influenced by a faith group.* More broadly, many – indeed most – politicians, business people and farmers have a religious or spiritual belief. The extent to which this influences their day-to-day activities varies, but at least some will respond to what a faith teaches about responsibility and ethics, including the ethics of good land management and environmental protection.

The interaction between protected areas and sacred areas

Protection for biodiversity and for the spirit comes together in two main ways. Many – in some countries, virtually all – protected areas also contain places or elements that are important to one or more faiths; in some cases, whole protected areas coincide with sacred places, resulting in a range of additional values often misunderstood or ignored by protected area managers and authorities. Conversely, those responsible for some of the remaining sacred natural sites wish to get them designated as protected areas in order to strengthen the safeguards that such sites need to survive. Both factors have important implications for the ways in which protected areas are selected and managed and the manner in which faiths relate to the natural world.

These interactions do not come without cost. Protected area managers are faced with addressing issues of high importance and sensitivity to members of a particular faith, but which managers are probably neither trained to address nor necessarily in tune with (they may well be of a different faith group, for instance). An important sacred site or pilgrimage route can attract huge numbers of visitors each year, which can sometimes clash with conservation aims. On the other hand, the fact that interested and often powerful faith groups are committed to protection of the site significantly increases the potential for successful conservation.

Now a convergent process is occurring, where some faith groups are actively seeking to bring their sacred sites into national protected area systems in order to ensure their survival: altering social norms and rapid change are putting many sacred sites under threat and communities are looking imaginatively at ways in which they can survive. There are many examples around the world, for example in Australia, the Kaya forests of Kenya, sacred islands offshore of Madagascar, traditional lands in the Amazon, and sacred groves in India, where communities and conservation authorities have found common cause in creating protected areas (Dudley et al., 2005).

From a conservation perspective, this only makes sense if such areas are also valuable for biodiversity. An ongoing analysis of over a hundred papers published on the biodiversity values of sacred sites (Dudley et al., 2010) suggests that many such sites do have measurable values in terms of providing habitat for rare or endangered species and in some cases may be virtually the only such sites remaining; for example, sacred forests may be the only forest areas where true old-growth characteristics exist (see, for instance, Virtanen, 2002; Wadley and Colfer, 2004; Bhagwat *et al.*, 2005). Although we still need to learn far more about the integration of sacred lands into national or regional conservation strategies, there seem to be no fundamental reasons why such integration should not be successful or mutually beneficial to faiths and nature.

However, such integration will require some practical and philosophical work within both conservation and faith groups. Conservation professionals need to become much more adept at addressing the needs and aspirations of faith groups that have links to land and water within protected areas. Faith groups need to recognise conservation priorities and in some cases to rethink or clarify their relationship with and responsibilities towards the natural world – this process appears to be ongoing in most major faith groups (Palmer and Finlay, 2003).

Some preliminary conclusions

Many sacred natural sites can and should contribute to biodiversity conservation strategies, although whether this contribution should be inside an official protected area or as part of wider landscape/seascape conservation strategies needs to be determined for each case in turn. Decisions about sites should be taken by all the stakeholders: by faith groups depending on how different strategies may affect the sacred nature of the site and by conservation specialists about whether the site will be a useful addition to protected area systems.

Conservation strategies are increasingly focusing on planning protected area networks integrated with other forms of land use. Sacred sites are in places where faiths wish them to be rather than being selected through conservation planning, but can nonetheless make important contributions to biodiversity conservation. The commonest way in which faiths and biodiversity conservation overlap is through sacred natural sites being contained within protected areas; as described above, this creates both opportunities and challenges for protected area managers. There is also increasing interest in the concept of converting an entire sacred site into a protected area, and managing it for its dual spiritual and biodiversity values. However, conferring protected area status onto sacred sites may not always be the most suitable strategy; it can, for example, be inappropriate for the faith or paradoxically encourage greater visitation and damage. Certain faiths may choose to keep their sacred sites outside the official protected area network, but still encourage them to play a role in landscape-scale conservation as buffer zones, corridors or unofficially protected sites.

Sacred buildings are often surrounded by land that can be managed for its biodiversity values. In the UK, the sacred lands project is working with over a thousand churchyards to increase their value to biodiversity. Some faith groups also own both large and small amounts of land, and even quite small changes in policy towards its management can have major implications for its conservation value.

In many cases, the protection of sacred sites can be an effective way of protecting a people, culture or ethnic group, while also recognising the role that such sites play in protecting nature. Where a sacred site exists within a protected area, the care of the site should always be an important element in management plans and practice.

There is still much to be learnt about the links between sacred sites, biodiversity and protected areas, and further research is required, particularly with respect to the location and status of sacred natural sites, their role in biodiversity conservation, their practical role in people's belief systems, the influence of mainstream faiths on land and water, and options for positive interactions.

As countries struggle to meet ambitious global targets on biodiversity protection it will be interesting to see how thinking evolves in terms of incorporating traditionally protected sites into national systems. It will then be the role of faith groups, supported by NGOs (non-governmental organisations) and others, to ensure that this is done in a respectful and collaborative manner.

References

Bagader, A. A., Al-Chirazi El-Sabbagh, A. T., As-Sayyid Al-Glayand, M., et al. (1994). *Environmental Protection in Islam*. IUCN Environmental Policy and Law paper No. 20. Rev, 1994. Gland, Switzerland: IUCN.

Bernard, R. (1998). *Shinto and Ecology: Practice and Orientations to Nature*. Harvard University: Earth Ethics 10, No. 1, Center for Respect of Life and Environment. (Website: http://environment.harvard.edu/religion/research/Shinto/home.html)

Bhagwat, S. A., Kushalappa, C. G., Williams, P. H., et al. (2005). A landscape approach to biodiversity conservation of sacred groves in the Western Ghats of India. *Conservation Biology*, **19**, 1853–62.

Borrini-Feyerabend, G., Kothari, A. and Oviedo, G. (2004). *Indigenous and Local Communities and Protected Areas*. Cardiff and Cambridge: Cardiff University and IUCN.

Burgess, N., D'Amico Hales, J., Underwood, E., et al. (2004). *Terrestrial Ecoregions of Africa and Madagascar: A Continental Assessment*. Washington, DC: Island Press.

Carey, C., Dudley, N. and Stolton, S. (2000). *Squandering Paradise?* Gland, Switzerland: WWF International.

Chape, S., Blyth, S., Fish, L., et al. (2003). *2003 United Nations List of Protected Areas*. Gland and Cambridge: IUCN and UNEP World Conservation Monitoring Centre.

Colchester, M. (2003, rev. edn). *Salvaging Nature: Indigenous Peoples, Protected Areas and Biodiversity Conservation*. World Rainforest Movement and Forest Peoples' Programme, Montevideo, Uruguay and Moreton-in-the-Marsh.

De Lopez, T., Phok Samrech, T., Sisovanna, S., *et al.* (2003). *Scoping of Nature Tourism in the Angkor-Tonle Sap Region*. Phnom Penh: Cambodian Research Centre for Development.

Dudley, N. (2008). *Guidelines for Applying Protected Area Management Categories*. Gland: IUCN

Dudley, N., Higgins-Zogib, L. and Mansourian, S. (2005). *Beyond Belief*. Gland, Switzerland and Bath, UK: WWF International and Alliance for Religion and Conservation.

Dudley, N., Bhagwat, S., Higgins-Zogib, L., *et al.* (2010). Conservation of biodiversity in sacred natural sites in Asia and Africa: a review of the scientific literature. In *Sacred Natural Sites. Conserving nature and culture*, ed. B. Verschuuren, R. Wild, J. A. McNeely and G. Oviedo. London: Earthscan, pp. 19–32.

Lantis, M. (1938). The Alaskan whale hunt and its affinities. *American Anthropologist*, **40**, 438–64.

Palmer, M. with Finlay, V. (2003). *Faith in Conservation: New Approaches to Religions and the Environment*. Washington, DC: The World Bank.

Perlin, J. (1989). *A Forest Journey: The Role of Wood in the Development of Civilisation*. Cambridge, MA: Harvard University Press.

Schama, S. (1995). *Landscape and Memory*. London: Fontana Press.

Virtanen, P. (2002). The role of customary institutions in the conservation of biodiversity: sacred forests in Mozambique. *Environmental Values*, **11**, 227–41.

Wadley, R. L. and Colfer, C. J. P. (2004). Sacred forest, hunting and conservation in West Kalimantan, Indonesia. *Human Ecology*, **32**, 313–38.

4

Ancient knowledge, the sacred and biocultural diversity

FEDERICO CINQUEPALMI and GLORIA PUNGETTI

And the Spirit of God moved upon the face of the waters.

Genesis 1 : 2

Introduction

Man's earliest attempts to seek out a supernatural dimension have often involved nature by interpreting extreme natural phenomena as a manifestation of the divine, or by associating the sacred element with places of special beauty or uniqueness.

Thunder and lightning, which bring fire down to earth, were widely considered gifts from the gods. The myth of Prometheus, who stole fire from Zeus and gave it to mortals for their use, is most probably related to this natural phenomenon (Bonnefoy, 1981):

> The child of Iapetus cheated [Zeus] by stealing the far-seen gleam of untiring fire in a hollow *narthex* [the stem of giant fennel, *Ferula communis*], Hesiod *Theogony* 565–7 [mainland Greece, *c.* 700 BC].

Various cultures, including the Rigveda and Native American tribes, also feature tales of fire being stolen from the gods and given to humans.

Italian heritage and the sacred

In Italy there is a long-standing relationship between people and their sacred landscape (Figure 4.1). In the Iron Age, rural and mountain Italic sanctuaries

Sacred Species and Sites: Advances in Biocultural Conservation, ed. Gloria Pungetti, Gonzalo Oviedo and Della Hooke. Published by Cambridge University Press. © Cambridge University Press 2012.

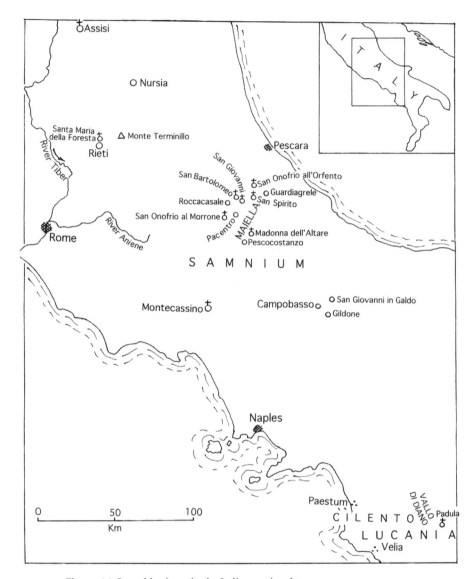

Figure 4.1 Sacred heritage in the Italian peninsula.

were important public meeting places for local communities. In archaeological research, 'sacred landscape' refers to a network of consecrated areas and temples with different functions and appeal. The construction or destruction of ancient sacred landscapes was often a result, then as now, of conflict or instability: for example, when the Romans damaged or robbed the sanctuaries of their Italic enemies (Stek, 2005).

Figure 4.2 The archaeological site of Paestum was a landscape of historical and spiritual importance during Classical times (© Italian Ministry for the Environment, Land and Sea). See colour plate section.

Sites of historical and spiritual importance are found in Molise, especially two Iron Age sanctuaries in the heartland of the Samnites, one of the tribes that were the rivals of Rome: that of San Giovanni in Galdo and that of Gildone (Pelgrom and Stek, 2006). Later, dating from Classical times, are the archaeological sites of Paestum (Figure 4.2) and Velia, and of Padula, the predecessor of the Certosa di Padula in Cilento. Cilento is an outstanding cultural and spiritual landscape with groups of sanctuaries and settlements along its mountain ridges. This region was a major route for trade, cultural and political interaction during prehistoric, Classical and medieval times: the meeting point between the Greek colonies of Magna Graecia, the Etruscans and the indigenous Lucanian peoples (Indelli, 1999).

In Abruzzo, the Maiella and other mountains contain over 40 churches, abbeys and hermitages related to St Pietro Angeleri, who after a long life in the mountains as monk, hermit, and founder of monasteries became Pope Celestine V in 1294. Among these are S. Spirito a Maiella (Figure 4.3), S. Onofrio al Morrone, S. Bartolomeo in Legio, S. Giovanni, S. Onofrio all'Orfento and Madonna dell'Altare

Figure 4.3 The Hermitage of S. Spirito a Maiella, one of many religious sites related to the monk, hermit and Pope Celestine V, in the Abruzzo mountains of the Maiella National Park (© Italian Ministry for the Environment, Land and Sea).

in the woods of Porrara. Also on the slopes of Maiella are the medieval hill-towns of Pescocostanzo, Pacentro, Guardiagrele and Roccacasale. The mountains of Abruzzo have for centuries been an ideal place for meditation and retreat, with nearly 100 hermitages (Micati, 2000). They are a particularly precious landscape, retaining a rich wildlife, fascinating views and populations (Ardito, 2000).

From a later period are the nine Sacred Mountains (*Sacri Monti*) in north-west Italy, founded from 1486 to 1712 as sites of devotion and dedicated to different aspects of the Christian faith (Melis, 2005). In addition to their symbolic and spiritual meaning, these groups of chapels are attractive and well integrated into the surrounding landscapes of hills, forests and lakes. Organised mainly by Franciscans, they house very significant wall paintings and statues of great artistic interest (Fontana *et al.*, 2004).

Present state of protection

The Cilento sites, Certosa di Padula, and the archaeological sites of Paestum and Velia were listed by the World Heritage Committee in 1998 (ICOMOS, 1998). In 2003 the Committee listed the Sacri Monti, as well as the city and Franciscan basilicas of Assisi, as representing 'the successful integration of architecture and fine art into a landscape of great beauty for spiritual reasons' (ICOMOS, 2000a, 2000b). The Cilento sites are within the National Park of Cilento and Valle di Diano, established in 1991; the Sacri Monti are part of the regional park system of Piedmont; the sacred landscape of Abruzzo is partly within the National Park of Maiella, Gran Sasso and Monti della Laga, protected since 1923.

The Holy Valley of Rieti

The best-known rural Christian sacred sites in Italy are those of St Francis and his followers. Although the saint came from Assisi in Umbria, he preferred La Verna in Tuscany (see Chapter 5) and was fond of the Valley of Rieti in Latium, Italy, where he performed many miracles.

The Holy Valley of Rieti is a very fertile plain of circular shape, enclosed by Mount Terminillo and other mountains and hills (Figure 4.1). Four Franciscan sanctuaries are situated cross-wise within this natural amphitheatre (Pampaloni, 1995). One is the Sanctuary of Santa Maria della Foresta, a secluded place ideal for those in search of tranquillity and peace, immersed in lush green woods beside natural springs. It is probably here that in 1223 the saint wrote the Canticle of the Creatures, presented in Chapter 28, and the Rule of the Franciscan Order (Cadderi, 1999).

Here nature is rich and the landscape, showing its full beauty, has apparently undergone only minor changes since the time of St Francis (Wyke, 2005). The valley is famous for its clear water and holy springs, such as the Santa Susanna, and for lakes of reeds and white waterlilies with egrets, herons, ducks and other creatures. The hills are covered by ancient woods with deciduous oaks, chestnuts, holm oaks and hornbeams at lower altitudes, and by firs, larches and holly bushes at higher altitudes.

The sites of the Valley of Rieti interlink sacred, biological and cultural diversity. They form a unique landscape mosaic made up of cultural and spiritual features interacting with ecological and natural organisms among which sacred species, like St Francis's wolf (Figure 4.4), co-exist with the local religious and secular communities.

Present state of protection

The Rieti Tourist Board, jointly with the National Forest Rangers Corps and provincial institutions, founded the 'St Francis Way', 80 km on foot, cycle, horseback, or by car. There are eight stops connected with episodes of the life of St Francis. The Way follows paths and roads travelled by the Saint, offering a simple yet impressive combination of natural and spiritual experiences.

Figure 4.4 The wolf (*Canis lupus italicus*) is a sacred species in the St Francis 'Canticle of the Creatures' (© Italian Ministry for the Environment, Land and Sea).

Ancient knowledge and sacred water

Many of the world's ancient cultures and religions illustrate the connection between water and life. The belief in the holiness of waters, especially underground waters, may have emerged as early as Palaeolithic times. Water descending from the sky as a divine gift, and springing out from the earth or flowing from caves, has become one of the four basic elements, along with Fire, Air and Earth, testifying to the power of gods. The sacredness of springs, lakes and rivers, related to the concept of water as a precious divine gift, appears in almost all religions, including the three Abrahamic religions, despite their tendency to separate the natural from the incomparable, unfathomable divine. For Babylonians the cult

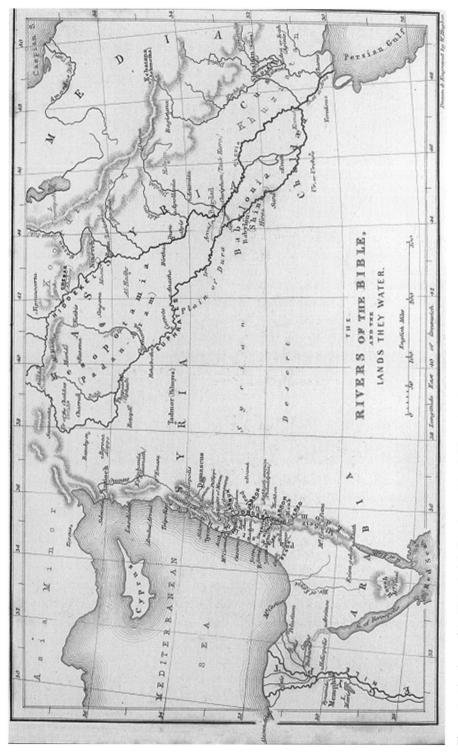

Figure 4.5 The rivers of the Bible, their holy waters and lands (Gosse, 1877).

of water was connected to a specific god, named Enki in Sumerian and Ea in Babylonian, god of the underground waters and the most protective toward humankind in the Babylonian pantheon (Golan, 2003). In Western culture the best-known text is the Hebrew Bible, with its countless examples of the perception of water in ancient times, beginning with the Exodus stories, from the Iron Age, of oases and springs (e.g. Exodus 17 : 1–7).

The Middle East and the holy geography of the Bible

The first of the two accounts of Creation in Genesis depicts God alone in the primordial vacuum, although even in a vacuum the spirit of Divinity is described as moving 'upon the face of the waters' (Genesis 1 : 2). Water was so fundamental to Middle Eastern people that it was thought of as the instrument for creating life (Eliade, 1987). It has always been strongly associated with sacredness in dry parts of the Middle East and Africa.

The ancient Hebrews shared some of their sacred or sacredly connected rivers and springs with neighbouring peoples such as Assyrians, Babylonians and Egyptians (Figure 4.5). The second account of creation sets the Garden of Eden alongside the Tigris, Euphrates, Nile and a fourth, unidentified river (Genesis 2 : 8–14). The Tigris–Euphrates delta, in some traditions the place where humankind was created (Gosse, 1877), was close to Ur, the home of the patriarch Abraham (Genesis 11 : 28). The Mesopotamian marshlands, once the largest wetland ecosystem in Western Eurasia and the home of the Marsh Arab culture since the third millennium BC, are still a unique component of our global heritage.

Present state of protection

Abu Zirig Marsh is a cultural and religious hotspot. After many years of destruction – by drainage schemes, oilfield developments, the overexploitation of rivers, Iraqi wars and the wrath of Saddam Hussein – since 2007 the marshes have been under the protection of Ramsar and listed among Wetlands of International Importance (Ramsar Convention, 2005). Restoration is being carried out by the Italian Ministry for the Environment, Land and Sea and the Free Iraq Foundation (2004) in order to reverse the draining of the delta marshlands and the destruction of the indigenous Ma'dan Arab culture.

The Roman concept of water

The Romans attributed the foundations of their religion to the semi-mythological figure of Numa Pompilius, the second king of Rome after Romulus,

FONTE DELLA NINFA EGERIA

Figure 4.6 Nymphæum dedicated to the Egeria Nymph in Caffarella Park, Rome, where its sparkling spring water is still bottled under the name of 'Acqua Santa'. Original etching on copper plate, end of the nineteenth century, Rome (Anonymous).

who married the spring goddess Egeria and received the religious rules of Roman civilisation directly from her (Ennius, *Annals*, *c*. 150, B, surviving lines 113–19: Skutch, 1985). When he died in 673 BC she was so grieved that she deliquesced into a spring, as Ovid sang long after:

> The dropping tears her eyes incessant shed, till pitying Phoebe eas'd her pious woe, thaw'd to a spring, whose streams for ever flow (*Metamorphoses* XV : 480–496, 547–551 [*c*. 1 AD]: Dryden *et al.*, 1717).

Her precepts strongly influenced all European culture (Del Ponte, 1992). Egeria was considered the Mother of Roman religion; the River Tiber was Father of the Romans (*Pater Tiber*) and protector of the state.

Mother Egeria's tears flow to this day in the Nymphæum (Figure 4.6) in Caffarella Park south of Rome city centre; her spring water, naturally sparkling, is bottled and sold, labelled *Acqua Santa*, Holy Water. Father Tiber was considered curative for a long time; even during the Renaissance, aristocrats and the Pope himself would never leave the city without a bottle of his precious waters (Petronio, 1552).

Present state of protection

The hydrological system of the Roman municipality includes the River Tiber and the Sacred Island, the valley of the tributary River Aniene, the Egeria Spring, and many other ponds and streams. They are safeguarded by RomaNatura, the Protected Areas Agency of the Municipality of Rome, which manages one of the most significant worldwide urban heritages of biodiversity and water, linking the natural and historical legacy.

'The rural areas of Rome are almost unequalled in any of the other large metropolitan cities in the world. The environment of two-thirds of the municipal land is strictly protected' (Cignini and Cinquepalmi, 2008, p. 5). A complex of natural protected zones and green urban areas, riverside areas and agricultural land, covers 860 km², 67% of the land in the city limits of Rome. The entire Historic Centre of Rome, the Properties of the Holy See Enjoying Extraterritorial Rights, and San Paolo Fuori Le Mura have also been listed as World Heritage Sites since 1980, extended in 1990 (ICOMOS, 1980, 1990).

Christian and pagan tradition

Water rituals occur in most religions, from the sacred wells and springs of the Nuragic civilisation of Iron Age Sardinia (Pungetti, 1996) to the pre-Hispanic sacred wells of the Maya and the reservoirs of the cities of Chichén-Itzá and Palenque in Mexico. In the Mediterranean, too, water formed part of the pantheistic celebration of natural phenomena in Greek and Roman cults.

In Christian tradition water plays a central role, especially associated with baptism. St John the Baptist, continuing the strong tradition of baptism among Jews in the last century BC, made the River Jordan and its waters sacred through the baptism of Jesus Christ. The ritual of baptism of the newly converted with consecrated water was considered so powerful as to become the necessary condition for soul-saving, eliminating any previous sin. Even the Emperor Constantine the Great, having granted to Christians freedom of worship all over the Roman Empire, resisted the pressure of his mother, St Helena, to become a Christian until the end of his life, keeping baptism as his last chance to cancel all his sins as emperor and to save his soul. He told the bishops he had wanted to be baptised, like Christ, in the sacred waters of the River Jordan, but left it too late to travel (Eusebius, *Life of Constantine* IV. 61, 62; Cameron and Hall, 1999).

Jordan water was considered sacred for baptism: into modern times European royal families have used these waters for christening newborn princes. Princess Ileana of Romania recalls in her memoirs that a special plane was sent

Figure 4.7 Celtic and Christian crosses in ancient sacred sites (© Gloria Pungetti).

to Palestine in the early twentieth century to collect the sacred waters to chris-ten her nephew, the crown prince and future King Michael (Ileana of Romania, 1952).

In Western Europe the Christian veneration of water partly relates to pre-Roman Celtic traditions of sacred wells, springs, and other spots as places for performing sacred rituals (Figure 4.7). Veneration of water was introduced even into lands like Wales where it was ubiquitous and not precious. The *nemeton* 'temples' of some Celts may have been sacred groves, but rivers, streams, pools, and springs could also be a focus of worship (Bord and Bord, 1985). Some of these sites maintained their sacred values after conversion. The wells of Chartres and Glastonbury may have been sacred since the Iron Age. Under Christianity, the sacredness of wells and springs became associated with specific saints and with cults such as that of St Patrick's Purgatory Well on an island in Lough Derg, Ireland, or in modern times the sacred spring of Lourdes. However, many sacred springs and wells appear to have originated long afterwards, in connection with the cult of St Ann, grand-mother of Jesus, whose church, beside a huge ancient reservoir, impressed the First Crusaders when they reached Jerusalem in 1099 (Morris, 1989).

Present state of protection

Many sacred wells and springs enjoy some form of natural or cultural protection beside their continuing sacred significance. They are often included in larger World Heritage Sites such as Chartres cathedral (1979), Chichén Itzá (1988) and Palenque (1987, also a National Park), Su Nuraxi of Barumini (1997), and the large property of Glastonbury and the Island of Avalon under the National Trust for England (Palmer and Finlay, 2003).

The River Jordan has been drunk almost dry by Israeli and Jordanian irrigation works. What is left of the sacred river, especially in the lower course, consists chiefly of sewage, but a few brave souls still manage to get baptised in it.

Sacred continuity of sites

How often has the same site been considered sacred over the centuries in the transference from one religion to another? Many sanctuaries inherited the sacredness of the place, transforming the object of the cult. Examples are sanctuaries dedicated to the Virgin Mary which had previously been dedicated to Roman or Etruscan goddesses (Ruggero, 1997, 2003).

St Benedict of Nursia, founder of western monasticism, is related to the sacred nature of the sites which were later chosen by his successors for setting up monasteries. The spread of the Benedictine Order across Europe played a vital role in preserving moral unity through the centuries between the collapse of the Western Roman Empire and the establishment of the Holy Roman Empire; it also supported the conservation of biological and cultural diversity.

St Benedict drafted his Rule in the early sixth century AD around the principles of *ora et labora* (pray and work), on which were based all the monastic systems of Western Europe (Butler, 1924). His own life, as reported from later chronicles, has connections with nature that are not purely casual. The festival of the saint's death is commemorated on 21 March, which now coincides exactly, and then coincided roughly, with the spring equinox, that in some cultures marks the end of winter and the start of the farming calendar. He founded Montecassino Abbey in the sixth century; according to St Gregory, his biographer some 60 years later, the saint seized the site and destroyed sacred groves and a still-active temple of Apollo (Gregory, *Dialogues* II. viii.10: Zimmerman, 2002).

The Rule of St Benedict was adopted in many later monasteries, particularly in northern Europe. Pope St Gregory I especially ensured the role of the Benedictine Order in the diffusion of Christianity in Europe. The Christianisation of Anglia illustrates this cause: the Pope sent as his personal emissary St Augustine, the

'Apostle of England', with 40 monks to be the first Archbishop of Canterbury in 596. The *Ecclesiastical History* of the Venerable Bede, written in the early seventh century AD, preserves Augustine's correspondence with his Pope for advice on how to deal with the problem of pre-existing cults, beliefs and traditions associated with Celtic paganism (Bede, *Ecclesiastical History*, I. 30: Colgrave and Mynors, 1969, p. 113).

The Pope recommended that Augustine should not destroy heathen shrines but convert them to Christian use, and should convert pagan festivals to Christian festivities. In other words, Christian places of worship should be erected on pagan sacred sites to 'smooth' the passage from paganism to Christianity for the local inhabitants. With this in mind, it might be logical to suppose that many of the sacred buildings of the new religion, from the island of Thanet to that of Lindisfarne and many other sacred sites in the British Isles, were erected on grounds already sacred in Germanic or Roman or even surviving Iron Age religions. This has not received much support from archaeology. The Pope probably had in mind the Pantheon or the temple of Minerva in Syracuse, which like the Parthenon were to have a longer and more illustrious after-life as cathedrals than they had had as temples. There is nothing like them in Britain, where most shrines were not substantial buildings and most excavations of churches have failed to find evidence of pre-Christian use (Morris, 1989). However, some isolated Christian shrines may be derived from the pre-existing veneration of forests, springs, mountains and especially islands (Laing, 2006).

One of the best examples of Christian sites chosen for their inherited sacred value is the island sanctuary of Mont Saint-Michel, off the French coast of Brittany, thought to have been a traditional place of worship for Druids. Mont Saint-Michel, *Mons vel tumba Beleni*, may have been the mount or tomb of Belenus, the Gaulish sun deity (Deric, 1847). Like the similar St Michael's Mount in Cornwall, it became a Benedictine abbey under the protection of St Michael the Archangel, the Christian counterpart of the god Mercury, the equivalent of Belenus in the Gaulish world (Gout, 1910) or of Apollo in the Mediterranean.

Monastic sites were established for various reasons. Solitary hermits could choose where to live: in a remote cave, under a yew tree, or where the Devil was particularly troublesome, or beside a site that was already sacred; such are the many local saints of Wales (where some of the yew trees may still exist), of Cornwall, or Greece. Anyone founding a bigger establishment had less choice and had to go where a patron could find a large enough piece of land. St Fursey (early seventh century) was an Irish monk who founded monasteries in England and France, each time getting a local potentate to give him a site such as an abandoned Roman fort (Rackham, 2007). Under the Carolingian Empire, abbeys were to be founded in order to extend control over a geographical area and to symbolise the alliance between Church and Empire. The newly consolidated link between Church and

State founded by Charlemagne rejected respect for local nature-related traditions in order to boost territorial influence (Harrison, 2004).

Not until the end of the twelfth century did St Francis, the innovator of religious practices in Europe which were often regarded with suspicion by the Church hierarchy, achieve a partial reconciliation of Christianity with nature. The Poor Man of Assisi, recalling the origin of the Church, celebrated the divine within a legitimised form of Christian pantheism of the four natural elements of earth, air, fire and water in one of the most touching elegies dedicated to the holiness of nature, the 'Canticle of the Creatures' (Doyle, 1980). However, outside Italy, most Franciscan establishments were in cities, devoted to serving urban populations.

Present state of protection

Mont Saint-Michel abbey, island and bay are managed by the French Centre des Monuments Nationaux and have been protected both for the human settlements and for natural and geological reasons as World Heritage since 1979 (ICOMOS, 1979). St Michael's Mount belongs to the English National Trust. In Assisi, the Basilica of San Francesco and the other Franciscan sites have been on the UNESCO World Heritage List since 2000: 'Assisi represents a unique example of continuity of a city-sanctuary within its environmental setting from its Umbrian-Roman and medieval origins to the present, represented in the cultural landscape, the religious ensembles, systems of communication, and traditional land-use' (ICOMOS, 2000a).

Conclusions

Urbanisation and industrialisation have created great pressure on land and natural resources in Italy as elsewhere (Leontidou et al., 1997; Pungetti and Romano, 2004). Inadequate government and cultural breakdown endanger traditional land management and also many sacred landscapes. Both cultural and biological diversity are diminishing, and the knowledge regarding the existence and location of sacred sites vanishes with them. This knowledge is part of our cultural heritage and should be preserved.

Changes in ancient local communities have been closely associated with the development of sacred places since pre-Roman times (Stek, 2005). Although, in early societies, natural phenomena may have been the criteria by which a place was deemed sacred, in more complex civilisations the sacred element was derived chiefly from particular landscape features. Springs, ponds, special trees or particular rocks have often been considered features through which the divine might manifest itself to the world of man, and are therefore venerated as 'sacred sites'. These sites are essential for an understanding of the relationship between human communities and their social, cultural and spiritual evolution across the centuries, inextricably linked to the natural features of their territory. Even if their sacredness has lapsed from recognition over time, the outstanding beauty and peculiarity of these unique sites may still be acknowledged. Many sites may have lost the intangible character connected with their worship, but still preserve their distinctive landscape and their biological and cultural diversity.

References

Ardito, S. (2000). *Guida alle Meraviglie sconosciute d'Abruzzo*. Pescara: Carsa Edizioni.

Bede. *Bede's Ecclesiastical History of England.*, ed. B. Colgrave and R. A. B. Mynors (1969). Oxford: Clarendon Press.

Bonnefoy, Y. (ed.) (1981). *Dictionnaire des Mithologies*. Paris: Flammarion.

Bord, C. and Bord, J. (1985). *Sacred Waters: Holy Wells and Water Lore in Britain and Ireland*. London: Granada.

Butler, C. (1924). *Benedictine Monachism: Studies in Benedictine Life and Rule*. London: Longmans.

Cadderi, A. (ed.) (1999). *Anonimo Reatino: Actus Beati Francisci in Valle Reatina*. Assisi: Edizioni Porziuncola.

Cignini, B. and Cinquepalmi, F. (2008). *Rome Capital of Biodiversity, Protected Areas, Flora and Fauna*. Rome: Italian Ministry of Environment Land and Sea, Municipality of Rome.

Del Ponte, R. (1992). *La religione dei romani*. Milan: Rusconi.

Deric, G. (1847). *Histoire ecclésiastique de Bretagne: dédiée aux seigneurs éveques de cette province*. Saint-Brieuc: Prud'homme.

Doyle, E. (1980). *St. Francis and the Song of Brotherhood*. London: Allen & Unwin.

Eliade, M. (ed.) (1987). *Encyclopedia of Religion*. New York, NY: Collier Macmillan.

Ennius, Quintus, *Annals of Quintus Enniss*, ed. O. Skutch (1985). Oxford: Clarendon Press.

Eusebius, *Life of Constantine*: ed. A. Cameron and S. G. Hall (1999). Oxford: Clarendon Press.

Fontana, F., Lodari, R. and Sorrenti, P. (2004). *Luoghi e vie di pellegrinaggio. I Sacri Monti del Piemonte e della Lombardia*. Ponzano Monferrato: The Documentation Centre of the European Sacred Mounts, Calvaries and Devotional Complexes.

Golan, A. (2003). *Prehistoric Religion: Mythology, Symbolism*. Jerusalem: Ariel Golan.

Gosse, P. H. (1877). *Sacred Streams: The Ancient and Modern History of the Rivers of the Bible*. London.

Gout, P. (1910). *Le Mont-Saint-Michel. Histoire de l'abbaye et de la ville. Étude archéologique et architecturale des monuments*. Paris: Armand Colin.

Gregory, *Dialogues*, trans. O. J. Zimmerman (2002). Washington, DC: Catholic University of America Press.

Harrison, P. (2004). *Castles of God: Fortified Religious Buildings of the World*. Woodbridge: Boydell Press.

ICOMOS. (1979). *The Mount Saint Michel and its Bay*, Advisory Body Evaluation No. 80. Paris: ICOMOS.

ICOMOS. (1980). *Historical Centre of Rome*. Advisory Body Evaluation No. 91. Paris: ICOMOS.

ICOMOS. (1990). *'Extra-territorial' Properties of the Holy See Situated in the Historic Centre of Rome and Basilica of St Paul's Outside the Walls*. Advisory Body Evaluation No. 91/bis. Paris: ICOMOS.

ICOMOS. (1998). *Cilento and Vallo di Diano National Park with the Archeological Sites of Paestum and Velia, and the Certosa di Padula*. Advisory Body Evaluation No. 842. Paris: ICOMOS.

ICOMOS. (2000a). *Assisi, Italy*. Advisory Body Evaluation No. 990. Paris: ICOMOS.

ICOMOS. (2000b). *Sacri Monti*. Advisory Body Evaluation No. 1068. Paris: ICOMOS.

Ileana (Princess of Romania). (1952). *I Live Again*. London: Gollancz.

Indelli, G. (1999). *Cilento: The National Park's Nature and Landscape*. Milan: Giorgio Mondadori.

Italian Ministry for the Environment, Land and Sea, and Free Iraq Foundation. (2004). *The New Eden Project, Final Report*. Rome and Washington, DC: Italian Ministry for the Environment and Territory, and Free Iraq Foundation.

Laing, L. R. (2006). *The Archaeology of Celtic Britain and Ireland, c. 400–1200 AD*. London: Methuen.

Leontidou, L., Gentileschi M. L., Aru A., *et al.* (1997). Urban expansion and littoralisation. In *Atlas of Mediterranean Environments in Europe*, ed. P. Mairota, J. B. Thornes and N. Geeson. Chichester: John Wiley & Sons, pp. 92–7.

Melis, G. (2005). *Dalle aree naturali protette al patrimonio UNESCO: il paesaggio culturale dei sacri monti del piemonte e della lombardia. Politiche di tutela e di gestione*. Unpublished First Degree thesis, Polytechnic of Turin.

Micati, E. (2000). *Eremi d'Abruzzo*. Pescara: Carsa Edizioni.

Morris, R. (1989). *Churches in the Landscape*. London: Dent.

Ovid, *Metamorphoses, in Fifteen Books*, trans. Dryden, Addision *et al.* (1717). London: Sir Samuel Garth.

Palmer, M. and Finlay, V. (2003). *Faith in Conservation: New Approaches to Religions and the Environment*. Washington, DC: World Bank Publications.

Pampaloni, G. (1995). *Francesco nella Valle Santa di Rieti*. Novara: Istituto Geografico De Agostini.

Pelgrom, J. and Stek, T. D. (2006). *Paesaggi del Sacro: Ricognizione archeologica delle terre intorno i santuari sannitici di San Giovanni in Galdo (loc. Colle Rimontato) e Gildone (loc. Cupa)*. Rome: Istituto Olandese.

Petronio, Alessandro Trajano. (1552). *De aqua tiberina. Opus quidem novus, sed ut omnibus qui hac aqua utuntur utile, ita et necessarium*. Rome: Romae editors: apud Valerium et Aloisium Doricos fratres Brixienses.

Pungetti, G. (1996). *Landscape in Sardinia: History, Features, Policies*. Cagliari: CUEC.

Pungetti, G. and Romano, B. (2004). Planning the future landscape in between nature and culture. In *Ecological Networks and Greenways: Concept, Design, Implementation*, ed. R. H. G. Jongman and G. Pungetti. Cambridge: Cambridge University Press, pp. 107–27.

Rackham, O., trans. (2007). *Transitus Beati Fursei*. Norwich: Fursey Pilgrims.

Ramsar Convention. (2005). *9th Conference of the Parties Final Report*. Gland: Ramsar.

Ruggero, I. (1997). *I luoghi di culto*. Rome: Quasar.

Ruggero, I. (2003). *Roma archeologica 20° itinerario: Le dimore degli dei*. Rome: De Rosa.

Stek, T. D. (2005). Sacred landscape and the construction of identity: Samnium and the Roman world. In *SOMA 2003: Symposium on Mediterranean Archaeology*, Proceedings of Conference held in London, 21–23 February 2003, ed. C. Briault, J. Green, A. Kaldelis and A. Stellatou. British Archaeological Reports, International Series 1391, pp. 147–50.

Wyke, N. (2005). The gentle saint leads pilgrims on path to nature. *Times on Line*, 30 July 2005, 1–2.

PART II SACRED LANDSCAPES

5

Ecological and spiritual values of landscape: a reciprocal heritage and custody

GLORIA PUNGETTI, FATHER PETER HUGHES and OLIVER RACKHAM

Introduction: monks, mountains and forests

From antiquity, the landscape of mountains and forests has been associated with the sacred because it provided a natural sanctuary where human beings have felt they could approach the divine. The landscape came to have a symbolic significance favourable to a specific spiritual vocation, and in particular that of hermits.

Christian monasticism began in the deserts of Palestine and Egypt with the hermits (solitary monks) and the organisation of the earliest monastic communities. Although there are desert monasteries in the driest parts of Europe, e.g. Panayia Akrotiriani, Our Lady of the Cape, in Crete, mountains and forests were regarded as equivalent to the desert; indeed, they were sometimes called 'deserts', for example in the Cistercian and Carthusian traditions in western Europe and on Mount Athos, the holy mountain of Greece (Rackham, 2002). The same idea is present in other religions, for example Mount Hiei, the monastic mountain in Japan.

The forest, once thought of as a 'natural', uncontrollable, inhospitable space evoking fear of the unknown, came to be seen as the place best suited to an ascetic vocation because it offered the seclusion and silence that allow for listening, prayer and meditation. This is the practice that underpins the possibility of a balanced and ordered existence in harmony with nature and, according to religious tradition, oriented towards God.

This chapter aims to illustrate the ecological and spiritual values of a particular sacred landscape – the Casentino forests in the Italian Apennines – noting the importance of its heritage and custody. The natural and ecological, with the

Sacred Species and Sites: Advances in Biocultural Conservation, ed. Gloria Pungetti, Gonzalo Oviedo and Della Hooke. Published by Cambridge University Press. © Cambridge University Press 2012.

cultural and spiritual values of landscape, are explored, pointing out threats and benefits for conservation of biological and cultural diversity, and proposing ways of achieving a more sustainable future.

Sacred landscapes and protected areas

The Casentino, the upper valley of the River Arno north of Arezzo and east of Florence, has been inhabited from antiquity. High in the mountains above are several landscapes with ancient sacred associations. An Etruscan (Iron Age) presence has been identified, for example, at the so-called Idols' Lake of Mount Falterona. Other sites include the Holy Hermitage of Camaldoli (altitude 1104 m), where St Romuald (*c.* 951–1027) founded a hermitage for monks in 1024, and a hospice below it at Fonte Buona, the Monastery of Camaldoli (816 m). The Camaldolese monks, like their founder, hold in tension the eremitic and the communal traditions of monasticism; they have a group of hermitages, in the form of a *laura*, where monks live a solitary dimension in their separate small houses (cells) and walled gardens, alongside the communal dimension of shared worship and meals, whereas the monastery below is a *cœnobium* based on the Benedictine model (Frigerio, 1991). The Sanctuary of La Verna (1128 m) is a house of Franciscan friars on the site where St Francis himself lived long periods as a hermit from 1213 to 1224 (Cetoloni *et al.*, 2003). These sites were chosen by their founders because of their remoteness, silence and seclusion amid mountains and forests.

These sacred landscapes are located in the National Park of the Casentino Forests, Monte Falterona and Campigna, that covers around 360 km^2 (Figure 5.1) on the main divide of the Apennines between Romagna and Tuscany, south-east of the source of the Arno (Cavagna and Cian, 2003). This includes one of the most valuable European forests, not only for nature conservation, but also for its cultural, spiritual, historic and artistic heritage (Figure 5.2).

The Park attracts large numbers of tourists on foot, cycle, horseback and cross-country skis, along some 600 km of paths (Vianelli, 2003). About 30% of the Park is privately owned; the rest belongs either to the State or to the Regional Forestry Services. The National Park authority is mainly responsible for the natural, cultural and spiritual heritage, in cooperation with the Sanctuary of La Verna and the Hermitage and the Monastery of Camaldoli. The Casentino State Forests form the core of the Park, which includes the Integral Nature Reserve of Sasso Fratino.

Ecological and natural values of the Casentino forests

The landscape of the Casentino forests is characterised by sandstones and marls of Miocene age. On the Romagna side (north-east) of the divide these form

Figure 5.1 Sacred landscapes in the National Park of the Casentino Forests, Monte Falterona and Campigna.

Figure 5.2 The *borgo* (village) of Fiume d'Isola, Arezzo, in the middle of the forests of the National Park of the Casentino Forests, Monte Falterona and Campigna (© Italian Ministry for the Environment, Land and Sea – L. Manieri). See colour plate section.

rugged escarpments. On the Tuscan side (south-west), a forested landscape of broad hills is interrupted by ravines and badland gullies in clays and crumbly schists, out of which rise the cliffs around the hard limestone bluff of Monte La Verna.

The area is a mosaic of natural and ancient forests, artificial plantations and grasslands. The forests, partly on rugged badland gullies, include beech (*Fagus sylvatica*), oak (*Quercus* species), hornbeam (*Carpinus betulus*), sycamore (*Acer pseudo-platanus*), maple (*A. spicatum*), ash (*Fraxinus excelsior*), lime (*Tilia* species), whitebeam

(*Sorbus aria*) and cherry (*Prunus avium*). Fir (*Abies alba*) is widely dominant on the Tuscany side. Big coppice stools of beech and hornbeam testify to a long history of woodcutting, as giant chestnut trees (*Castanea sativa*) do to a history of growing nuts for food (cf. Moreno, 1990a). Plantations are of fir, pine and exotic conifers such as the Douglas Fir (*Pseudotsuga menziesii*). Grasslands nowadays remain mainly on the tops of ridges: place-names such as Prato alla Penna, now mainly forest, show that they were once much more extensive (cf. Moreno, 1990b). In the nineteenth century Camaldoli itself was in a 'grassy valley surrounded by forest', rather than situated as it is now, immediately surrounded by the forest itself (Baedeker, 1877). Between the Hermitage and the Monastery, and sloping away from the Monastery at lower altitudes, there are abandoned terraces of former cultivation and pasture.

The particular natural and human characteristics of the area have encouraged the persistence of wildlife. The Park has an extensive flora for its area, including over 1000 species of flowering plants with 48 trees and shrubs (Cavagna and Cian, 2003). The greatest richness is to be found above the forests, on the cliffs, ledges and grasslands of the Monte Falco-Falterona massif (1658 m). Notable species include *Viola eugeniae*, peculiar to the Apennines and the national flower of Italy, and outliers from the Alps such as *Anemone narcissiflora*, purple saxifrage (*Saxifraga oppositifolia*), mossy saxifrage (*S. moschata*), *S. alpina* and bilberries (*Vaccinium myrtillus* and *V. vitis-idaea*). In spring species of snowdrop (*Galanthus*) (Figure 5.3) *Cardamine*, *Scilla*, and *Corydalis* flower under the beech trees.

The wolf (*Canis lupus italicus*), considered sacred for its link with St Francis (Figure 4.4), is the most significant predator in the area. There are three native ungulates – wild pig (*Sus scrofa*) (Figure 5.4), roe deer (*Capreolus capreolus*) and red deer (*Cervus elaphus*) (Figure 13.4), and two introduced – fallow deer (*Dama dama*) and wild sheep (*Ovis ammon*).

Nearly a hundred species of birds are reported. They are typical of central Europe: alpine tree-creeper (*Certhia familiaris*), bullfinch (*Pyrrhula pyrrhula*) and ring ouzel (*Turdus torquatus*); or of the Mediterranean: Sardinian warbler (*Sylvia melanocephala*), whitethroat (*S. communis*) and black-headed bunting (*Emberiza melanocephala*). Many birds, such as eagle owl (*Bubo bubo*), brown tit-babbler (*Macronous striaticeps*), marsh tit (*Parus palustris*), blue tit (*P. caeruleus*), nuthatch (*Sitta europaea*), lesser spotted woodpecker (*Dendrocopos minor*) and green woodpecker (*Picus viridis*) nest in holes in old trees. Open areas host tawny pipit (*Anthus campestris*), wheatear (*Oenanthe oenanthe*), redstart (*Phoenicurus phoenicurus*), lesser shrike (*Lanius collurio*) and woodlark (*Lullula arborea*). Birds of prey include honey buzzard (*Pernis apivorus*) and hobby (*Falco subbuteo*), as well as woodland species, e.g. sparrowhawk (*Accipiter nisus*) and goshawk (*Accipiter gentilis*). Golden eagle (*Aquila*

Figure 5.3 Snowdrops (*Galanthus*) (© Gloria Pungetti).

Figure 5.4 Wild pig (*Sus scrofa*) (© Italian Ministry for the Environment, Land and Sea.

Figure 5.5 Peregrine falcon (*Falco peregrinus*) (© Italian Ministry for the Environment, Land and Sea – F. Bertrando).

chrysaetos) (Figure 13.5), eagle owl (*Bubo bubo*) and peregrine falcon (*Falco peregrinus*) (Figure 5.5) nest on the cliffs of the Romagna side.

Thirteen species of amphibian and 12 reptiles live in the park, including spectacled salamander (*Salamandrina terdigitata*), alpine newt (*Mesotriton alpestris alpestris*), spotted salamander (*Ambystoma maculatum*) and an adder (*Vipera aspis*).

Cultural and spiritual values of the Casentino landscape

There is evidence of Etruscan cultic activity. The 'Pilgrims' Way' from Germany to Rome crosses the Apennines at the Serra Pass, continuing through the Casentino. In Dante's *Inferno*, Buonconte da Montefeltro declares how, fleeing from the battlefield of Campaldino (in 1289), he died of his wounds at the place where:

> At the bottom of the Casentino there crosses a water named the
> Archiano, which rises in the Apennines above the Hermitage (*Purgatorio*
> V. 94–6)

Figure 5.6 The Hermitage of Camaldoli (© Gloria Pungetti).

Figure 5.7 The Convent and Sanctuary of La Verna (© Italian Ministry for the Environment, Land and Sea).

Acquacheta waterfall and the plateau of San Paolo in Alpe are, among the areas mentioned in literature (cf. Dante Alighieri, 1994) those most frequented today by hikers and naturalists. Other ancient features are hamlets and scattered houses, abandoned and ruined castles and strongholds, and stone-built shrines (Prezzolini, 2007). Stone footbridges lead to towns, villages, hermitages and monasteries. Ancient roads and hollow lanes, rich in history and art, have brought men of war to fight epic battles and duels, and to besiege castles (Piroci Branciaroli, 2008), as well as men of faith such as St Romuald and St Francis who, fascinated by the mystique of these forests, have spent long periods here. Indeed, history has witnessed the co-existence of very different people: humble and powerful, holy men and knights, merchants and pilgrims.

At Camaldoli, St Romuald withdrew from the world to found one of his hermitages. The earliest Rules of the Hermitage established the conservation and management of the surrounding forests as a priority. At La Verna, Francis – now patron saint of ecology – after spending long periods of solitude and prayer in the beech forest clinging to the rough crags, in 1213 received the stigmata and left the green slopes in the custody of his brother friars, who with ecological foresight maintained the woods intact and favoured their natural evolution. The relationship between spiritual values and ecological sensitivity clearly has an ancient origin in the region.

The forests themselves survive as an eloquent testimony to this relationship between spiritual values, a specific faith lived out in a specific environment for reciprocal benefit, and traceable in the long history of the Hermitage and Monastery of Camaldoli (Figure 5.6), and of the Franciscan Sanctuary of La Verna (Figure 5.7). The spiritual values of such religious communities and of the pilgrims they attract are often indicators of a profound respect for ecological values. A similar sensitivity is now emerging in other groups, including tourists and naturalists who appreciate both the spiritual and natural values of this landscape.

The sacred dimension of landscape: the spiritual significance of nature

The original buildings of the Hermitage of Camaldoli were constructed with materials from the forest, and while their orientation according to the four cardinal points was intentional, they nestled naturally into the fall of the land, following its contours, and were harmonious with the surroundings. The monastic enclosure of the Hermitage (Figure 5.8) was a simple timber palisade because the forest itself was thought of as both cloister and boundary (cf. the Bull of Pope Urban V – Pope from 1362).

Figure 5.8 The cells of the monks at the Hermitage of Camaldoli (© Gloria Pungetti).

In this relationship with nature, trees held powerful symbolic associations. The monks in their 'desert'-forest recalled the prophet Isaiah's vision of the desert transformed by God's creative activity, under the figure of seven types of tree, a text St Romuald would have known in the Vulgate:

> *Dabo in solitudinem cedrum, et spinam, et myrtum, et lignum olivæ; ponam in deserto abietem, ulmum, et buxum simul.*

> 'I shall give in the wilderness the cedar, and the thorn, and the myrtle, and the olive-tree; I shall set in the desert the pine [or fir], and the elm, together with the box.' (Isaiah 41 : 18–19, *in the Vulgate Latin translation*).

Whatever these trees may have been in Isaiah's original Hebrew, the monks associated their Latin equivalents in the forest with the seven virtues of the eremitic-monastic vocation. According to the Constitutions of 1080 (Licciardello, 2004), the fir or pine – the word *abies* then normally meant pine, but could be other conifers – was favoured at Camaldoli because its evergreen foliage and the incorruptible nature of pine resin were symbols of regeneration and immortality. The fir trunk, soaring directly heavenwards, suggested spiritual aspiration, contemplation, communication between heaven and earth. A crown of firs protects the Hermitage on the ridge to the north, and its practical purpose was given deeper significance by a symbolic association with Christ's crown of thorns and martyrdom, and the dimension of sacrifice a Christian is called to imitate.

Cedar (*Cedrus libani*) symbolised sincerity; 'thorn' was interpreted as hawthorn (*Crataegus* sp.), symbolising repentance and conversion; myrtle (*Myrtus communis*) – which is unlikely to have grown as high as Camaldoli itself – symbolised sobriety and temperance; olive (*Olea europæa*) – which also grows lower down in the Casentino – symbolised works of joy, peace and compassion; box (*Buxus sempervivens*), humility and perseverance; elm (*Ulmus* sp.), works of fraternal support and patience. In this way, the natural world, in which the same virtues without distinction were shared by trees and monks, became a tangible experience of the sacred.

Sacred sites in the landscape: the idea of the sacred

The term 'sacred sites' implies a separation from what is profane; likewise the term 'environment' implies separation between human beings and the world they live in. This distinction is recognised in the experience of the Camaldoli monks, although it is sustained without dualism; it is distinction without separation.

The 'site' of the monks, with their cells and gardens, hermitage and forest, is 'sacred' in the sense of microcosm (Figures 5.6–5.9). Through their awareness of a unity with nature drawn out in the symbolic significance they gave it, and in the sense of reciprocity that guided their stewardship of it, the monks demonstrated that their relationship to this particular place was a means by which they reached the consciousness of the universal sacred.

The paradigm is that of the Incarnation. We find the same idea symbolically represented, for example, in the vision (*c.* 1368) of Julian of Norwich. Contemplating a hazel nut in the palm of her hand and asking 'What may this be?' she was given the answer: 'It is all that is made'. Its smallness then raises for Julian the question of how it might have lasting significance. In his Life of St Romuald (*c.* 1042), St Peter Damian attributes to Romuald the desire that the entire world should become a hermitage (cf. San Pier Damiani, 1963). The hermitage is a paradigm. It represents a vision that the world might be transformed through the principle lived by the hermitage on a small scale, because what is manifested on a small scale is true for the whole.

Regulations for reciprocal heritage and custody

Hermitage and forest are more a sign of the sacred rather than being thought of as sacred and inviolable themselves. A reciprocal relationship between monks and forest was developed according to principles of protection and custody, as well as of use in securing an economic benefit. Protection, because the environment, as we have seen, guaranteed the quality of life; use, because the monks needed a source of income to live. Apart from extensive agricultural properties, the forest represented the only real wealth of this territory: its products, including fir timbers of large size, gave the mountain people a means of livelihood.

The monastic community of Camaldoli came to own and manage a large part of the forest and an extensive area of agriculture. The original feudal organisation of the agricultural system has left a negative legacy in the local population to some extent, while the spiritual and cultural contribution of monks, even those not native to the area, continues to be recognised.

The monks' stewardship of the forest began to be codified in the monastic *Constitutiones* drawn up in 1080 (Licciardello, 2004) and these with the successive regulations were expanded in 1520 into the 'Forestry Code of Camaldoli' (Frigerio, 1991). The decrees of successive Priors and Acts of Chapter at the Hermitage of Camaldoli testify to the strict policy concerning felling and renewal of the forest, regulation of the sale and transport of timber and wood, and the cultivation of medicinal herbs. Eight centuries of documents demonstrate their principles of land use, development and conservation.

The Monastery was suppressed in 1866. Local councils appealed to the Italian Parliament opposing suppression, noting the ill effects of changing the monks' forest management, and the loss of livelihood for the thousand Casentino families employed by Camaldoli monks in the forests. The appeal was unsuccessful. Although the suppression lasted only until 1873, the monks never regained the forest, which remained State property and is now a National Park administered by the State Forestry Body. However, the eight centuries of experience in forest management encapsulated in the Forestry Code of Camaldoli became the basis for the Forestry Code of the Italian State (Frigerio, 1991).

The Monastery of Camaldoli has played an important role in social and political fields. FUCI, the University Federation of Italian Catholics, began to meet at Camaldoli in the 1930s, and many of its members were subsequently involved in the post-war reconstruction and in drawing up the new Constitution for the Italian Republic. In recent years, some politicians have promoted the revival of the Camaldoli meetings to encourage debate on the question the relationship between values in politics, and on issues of spiritual significance.

For 800 years, the spiritual values of the monasteries in the area contributed to conserving the natural environment on which they depended. The conservation of the natural and cultural heritage of these landscapes now rests with the Park authority. However, a relationship of continuing dialogue between the religious institutions and the management of the forest can help to clarify policy in the interests of promoting both the spiritual and cultural values long associated with the landscape, and its conservation.

The religious communities continue to contribute. Apart from formal worship, they provide hospitality, conduct workshops and seminars on relevant religious and spiritual topics, and retreats for individuals and groups. The local municipalities organise art exhibitions, including the work of monks, and the Park authority organises nature displays and fairs. These spiritual and cultural initiatives are appreciated by the local population and by visitors.

Human impact on the ecological and spiritual systems of landscape

As in most forested regions, the archaeology of the area is little known. The Etruscans used it as a route across the Apennine mountains (Pungetti, 1986). The area was settled in Roman times, but later barbarian invasions left it in decline and neglect (Cavagna and Cian, 2003). In the Middle Ages, the Casentino became an area of large estates and powerful families (Prezzolini, 2007). Following the defeat of the Guidi (1440), it became part of the Florentine Republic, subsequently coming under the control of the Medici, and later incorporated into the Grand Duchy of Tuscany (Caselli, 2004). Accordingly, the non-monastic part of the forests was first in the feudal domain of the Guidi and later the Grand Duchy, who developed its management further, particularly in the nineteenth century (Caselli, 2004). Part of the forest belonged to the Cathedral Operations (Opera del Duomo) of Florence; it is said also to have produced the timbers of exceptional size used in rebuilding the Basilica of San Paolo Fuori le Mura in Rome after the fire of 1823.

The large extent of woodland and sparse human population helped to preserve the ecological balance and spiritual quality of the Casentino landscape. However, it has not been immune to external influences. In the nineteenth century, in Italy as in most Mediterranean countries, a period of population growth led to unsustainable over-population in the mountains. Depopulation began with the Second World War, and today just 1500 inhabitants (4 per km^2) remain inside the Park.

The previously wide variety of uses and management of forests narrowed in the nineteenth century. The idea was then growing that the only proper use of uncultivatable land was timber production, organised by the State on the model of – in this case – German modern commercial forestry (Grove and Rackham, 2001).

The Casentino did not escape this influence, which replaced much of the natural woods with monocultures of planted trees. This policy is attributed to Bavarian foresters brought in after the confiscation of 1866, although it is to be noted that the monks themselves had long favoured large-scale felling and replanting. The globalisation of plant diseases would have brought here, as elsewhere in Italy in the 1920s, the chestnut-blight fungus (*Endothia parasitica*), which for a time ravaged the chestnuts.

The spiritual and ecological values of natural woodland have been banished in the tracts of dark monotonous plantation, under which little grows. However, a policy of selective clearing is favouring the return of the more diverse woodland of the original forest. The forest has also reclaimed abandoned terraces and pasture. Coppice-woods, once felled every few years for successive crops of firewood and poles, have grown up into tall, densely shading trees, with the loss of their distinctive flora. Chestnut cultivation ceased, probably when disease struck; the chestnuts, now recovered from disease, have turned from orchard into forest trees. More subtly, withdrawal of human activity encourages beech to take over from more diverse woodland, and then fir to replace beech.

There have been pilgrims to Camaldoli and La Verna since their foundation. The area was at first remote and little visited by secular tourists, but the railway, arriving at Poppi in 1888, opened it up on a larger scale. This in turn led to the publication of guidebooks containing maps of the Casentino. The area was recommended mainly for walking tours, although there was a carriage road to Camaldoli at least by 1877 and to the Hermitage by 1899 (Kalle-Bishop, 1971; Baedeker 1877, 1892, 1899). Since World War II, tourism has become the driving force, and the National Park has promoted facilities that have taken precedence over pilgrimage and forest management (Pungetti, 2008).

Tourism here is of three types. First, the secular and/or religious pilgrimage, to La Verna or to the Hermitage of Camaldoli, where it is mainly a day outing with a visit to the pharmacy and the site, possible attendance at a service in the church, and a short walk into the forest. Second, mass tourism, driven by historical and cultural interest, that brings many more cars and adds to the number of buses. Large groups of people have mostly unrestricted access to the Hermitage, which current practice allows, but the impact is heavy, especially in the summer months, and makes it difficult for the community at the Hermitage – and the guests who come for religious purposes – to conserve a degree of silence important to the quality of the site, and to promote understanding and respect in the general public for the significance of the place. This invasive mass tourism and the associated problems of traffic impact, parking and the balance between use and conservation of the forest creates tension, and potential conflict arises between the conservation of the natural heritage and the protection of spiritual and cultural values. Third, 'green' tourism – agro-tourism, camping, refuges, walking and horseback tours – has been promoted in recent years.

Working with nature, culture and the spirit of the place

Nowhere else in the region are the naturally and culturally related values of the site so strongly linked with the spirit of the place and the history of the people who have lived here. Towns, villages and hamlets rich in historical, artistic and architectural heritage are scattered across the territory.

The National Park is marked by centuries of human activity and human decline in the shaping of the landscape. The relations between the ancient forestry practices of Camaldoli and the Forestry Code of the Italian State reaffirm synergies between the conservation of the natural heritage and the protection of natural, cultural and spiritual values. For centuries the two monastic orders have been champions for this cause. Future champions for an integrated approach will be those who promote the indispensable cooperation between these monastic orders, the Park, the local authorities and the local population.

Although, in general, local people and visitors appreciate natural values with a common sense of respect and protection, the practical consequences are ambivalent. The Park conserves nature and permits public access; but roads and fences create ecological barriers, and forest animals such as wild pig and deer damage the remaining cultivated fields. Nevertheless, local communities live in symbiosis with their multiple heritages, and their landscape continues to convey the spirit of the place, the *genius loci* (see Norberg-Schultz, 1979).

Tensions between tourism, monasticism, forestry and conservation need to be considered in the proposed management plan for the Park. However, the difficulty of administering the complex relationship between Park and tourism is already evident. This involves careful management of mass tourism, clear and effective regulations, and also environmental education for the public and schools, to improve scientific and cultural knowledge. There is room for improvement in the synergies between the Park authority, the monastic communities, the state forest organisation, local authorities, and other groups with interests and responsibilities, who so far have tended to work too much in isolation from each other.

The Benedictines and Franciscans were the primordial local champions in conservation and development of the landscape. They still contribute: they offer advice on nature conservation and development of the Park, but have no legal responsibility, and are not part of the official administration of the National Park. They play only a secondary and unofficial role at the margins (Figure 5.9).

Figure 5.9 Novice friars at the Sanctuary of La Verna (© Italian Ministry for the Environment, Land and Sea).

Conclusions: towards sustainability in sacred sites and landscapes

Nearly a millennium ago, when the monks came to Camaldoli, the firs were to be the columns of their natural temple. St Francis called animals and plants his 'brothers', and at La Verna he taught his followers to use the woods, and treat nature with care and respect. This spiritual heritage, inseparable from the natural heritage of the forest, has been venerated, valued, protected and respected for centuries by both the monastic and the secular communities in the area, which continue to play a part in conserving the natural, cultural and spiritual heritage of the site.

The potential contribution of well-preserved natural, cultural and spiritual wealth to the balanced socioeconomic development of the area is tied to the trends of population and visitors, and above all to tourism.

It is therefore necessary to work in the direction of exploring possible avenues for a sustainable development of the area in harmony with the natural, cultural and spiritual assets. However, better planning and management are necessary to resolve conflicts between the needs of the religious communities, the natural and spiritual qualities of the site, and the needs of the visitors. All the custodians of the sites, whether monastic or lay communities, should be consulted and involved in the planning and management deliberations of the State Forest Body and the Park Authority, because they are key collaborators and have a wealth of wisdom to draw on. Furthermore, all these communities and bodies share an educational responsibility, and much advantage could be drawn from their cooperation in educating the public, especially the young and the visitors, concerning the relationship between the natural, cultural and spiritual values of the Casentino forests. With such a policy, it would be possible to promote a holistic view of the whole area, combining natural, cultural and spiritual heritage, with the aim of fostering a more sustainable development of the Casentino forests in harmony with both the natural and spiritual values of place, and in continuity with centuries of responsible custody.

References

Baedeker, K. (1877, 1892, 1899). *Handbook for Travellers: Northern Italy*. Leipzig.

Caselli, G. (2004). *Casentino: Its History and Environment*. Montepulciano: Le Balze.

Cavagna, S. and Cian, S. (eds). (2003). *The National Park of the Casentine Forests: Where the Trees Touch The sky*. Florence-Milan: Giunti.

Cetoloni, R., Bernacchi, F. and Locatelli, F. (eds). (2003). *The Sanctuary of La Verna*. Villa Verucchio: La Verna-Pazzini Editore.

Cf. San Pier Damiani. (1963). *Vita di San Romualdo*. Camaldoli: Edizioni Camaldoli.

Frigerio, S. (1991). *Camaldoli: Historical, Spiritual and Artistic Notes*. Villa Verucchio: Edizioni Camaldoli-Pazzini Editore.

Grove, A. T. and Rackham, O. (2001). *The Nature of Southern Europe: An Ecological History*. Yale, CT: Yale University Press.

Kalle-Bishop, P. M. (1971). *Italian Railways*. Newton Abbot: David and Charles.

Licciardello, P. (ed.) (2004). *Consuetudo Camaldulensis. Rodulphi Constitutiones. Liber Eremiticae Regulae*. Florence: Edizione Nazionale dei Testi Mediolatini.

Moreno, D. (1990a). *Dal Documento al Terreno: storia e archeologia dei sistemi agro-silvo-pastorali*. Bologna: Il Mulino.

Moreno, D. (1990b). The making and fall of an intensive pastoral land-use-system. Eastern Liguria, 16–19th centuries. *Rivista di Studi Liguri*, **A56**, 193–217.

Norberg-Schultz, C. (1979). *Genius Loci: Towards a Phenomenology of Architecture*. New York, NY: Rizzoli.

Piroci Branciaroli, A. (2008). *Casentino. Land of Saints and Knights*. Florence: Aska.

Prezzolini, P. (2007). *Storia del Casentino*. Sala Bolognese: Forni.

Pungetti, G. (1986). *Valore dell'analisi storica nella pianificazione territoriale: il caso degli insediamenti Etruschi in Emilia*. Unpublished First Degree thesis. Florence: University of Florence.

Pungetti, G. (2008). Cultural and spiritual values in landscape conservation and management. In *Riconquistare il paesaggio: La convenzione Europea del paesaggio e la conservazione della biodiversità in Italia*, ed. C. Teofili and R. Clarino. Rome: WWF, pp. 360–6.

Rackham, O. (2002). 'The Holy Mountain' [Athos]. *Plant Talk*, **27**, 19–23.

Vianelli, M. (2003). *The National Park of the Forests of Casentino, Monte Falterona and Campigna*. Florence: Aska.

6

Sacred mountains and national parks: spiritual and cultural values as a foundation for environmental conservation

EDWIN BERNBAUM

Introduction

The reverence and awe evoked by sacred natural sites and species provide a powerful motivation for environmental conservation. If people revere or fear a place, plant, or animal, that sets it apart from everything else as something to treat with special care and respect. In many cases, it makes the object of reverence priceless, so that putting a monetary value on it can even appear to be a form of desecration. Programmes of environmental conservation that seek to be sustainable will find it helpful to elicit the kind of deep-seated meanings and values that sacred sites and species highlight in bold relief. Otherwise, they risk failing to win the support of the stakeholders most concerned, especially if those stakeholders belong to traditional cultures. This is true not only of indigenous peoples and traditions; it also applies to modern, secular societies. To gain lasting support of the general public as well as local communities, programmes of environmental conservation need to be grounded not only in solid scientific research and practice, but also in deeply held spiritual, cultural, and aesthetic values and ideas that will engage and inspire people to care for nature over the long term and make the sacrifices necessary to protect the environment.

Sacred mountains: views and metaphors

Of all the various kinds of natural sacred sites, the largest and most comprehensive are sacred mountains. If we consider a mountain from its base to

Sacred Species and Sites: Advances in Biocultural Conservation, ed. Gloria Pungetti, Gonzalo Oviedo and Della Hooke. Published by Cambridge University Press. © Cambridge University Press 2012.

Figure 6.1 Mount Kailas through ceremonial structure (© Edwin Bernbaum).

its summit, it can include representatives of all environments and ecosystems –
from jungle and deserts to tundra and glaciers. In the case of Hawaiian volcanoes, such as Mauna Loa and Kilauea, they even incorporate underwater systems
extending into the depths of the world's deepest ocean. This means that sacred
mountains have the potential to reveal the diverse ways that people revere features
of nature found not only in mountain landscapes, but elsewhere in the environment, such as plains and forests. Knowledge of these ways can be key to inspiring
people of different cultures and traditions and enlisting their support for conserving biological and cultural diversity throughout the world (Bernbaum, 1997a)
(Figure 6.1).

There are three general ways in which mountains function as sacred sites. First,
certain peaks, such as Mount Kailas in Tibet and Kiluaea Volcano in Hawaii, may

be singled out as traditional sacred mountains by indigenous or religious traditions, becoming foci for well-established myths, beliefs, and practices. Second,
mountains may acquire an aura of sanctity from the sacred sites they contain,
such as temples, monasteries, stones, springs, groves, and places connected with
holy people – for example, the Hindu pilgrimage shrine of Badrinath in the Indian
Himalaya. Third, mountains without established indigenous or traditional religious significance may awaken a sense of wonder and awe that sets them apart
as places of special evocative significance. Many people in modern societies seek
out mountainous national parks such as Yosemite in the US and Huangshan in
China for spiritual and artistic inspiration, as well as renewal, often regarding
them as embodiments of values central to the character or spirit of a culture
or nation.

In whichever of these three general ways a mountain is sacred, people experience its sacredness through the particular views they have of it, such as Mount
Kailas in Tibet, which is viewed by Tibetan Buddhists as the pagoda palace of Dem-
chog, the One of Supreme Bliss, and by Hindus as the heavenly abode of Siva, one
of the three forms of the supreme deity (Bernbaum, 1997a). A number of these
views enjoy widespread distribution around the world: mountains as high places,
centres, places of power, deities or dwellings of deities (such as a temple), par-
adises or gardens, abodes of ancestors or the dead, symbols of identity, sources
of water and other blessings, and places of revelation, inspiration, or transformation (Bernbaum, 2006). Some scholars have attempted to reduce these diverse
views to a single universal view or archetype underlying them all. Mircea Eliade,
for example, viewed every sacred mountain as an expression of an *axis mundi* or
centre, such as Mount Meru or Sumeru in Hindu and Buddhist cosmology, which
links together vertically the various realms of existence, from hell to heaven, and
makes sense of the surrounding universe (Eliade, 1971). Jonathan Z. Smith, on the
other hand, argues that every sacred site (and sacred mountain, by implication)
represents originally a place of political power, exemplified by the sacred city of
Jerusalem, the capital of King David, chosen for its strategic position to unify the
northern and southern kingdoms of Israel and Judah (Smith, 1987).

However, if we look at actual examples of sacred mountains in different cultures
and traditions, we find exceptions to any of the proposed universal archetypes. For
example, the four sacred mountains of the Navajo or Dineh in the south-western
US define the perimeter of the sacred land in which the Navajo live, rather than
its centre. Mount Kailas, while definitely an *axis mundi*, lies in a remote corner
of western Tibet, far from any seat of political power. With some effort, we can
force any mountain into any one of these archetypes, but only by doing violence
to the meanings and significance they have for the people and traditions that hold
them sacred. In any case, reducing diverse views of mountains to a single theme

or archetype actually limits the evocative power of mountains as multivalent symbols that can break the bonds of preconceptions and open people to new and deeper experiences of what they take to be ultimately real and meaningful in their lives.

If anything holds across diverse views of mountains and unifies them, in fact, it is not so much an underlying theme or archetype as a process. Each view of a mountain brings together various ideas, images, and associations so that they resonate with each other to enrich and deepen people's experience of the site and awaken a sense of the sacred – of another, deeper dimension of reality that gives meaning and significance to the world and their lives. The Maori of New Zealand, for example, view their sacred mountains as the frozen bodies of divine ancestors from whom they are descended today: the association of Tongariro with the body of one of these ancestors invests the sacred volcano with life and provides the Ngati Tuwharetoa Tribe with a sense of power and identity that connects them to their ancestral lands (Lucas, 1993).

Theories of metaphor can help shed light on how this process works, because each view is in essence a metaphor in which a mountain is seen or experienced as something else. According to the interaction theory proposed by scholars such as Max Black and I. A. Richards (Black, 1981; Richards, 1981), the two terms equated or juxtaposed in a metaphor interact with each other to highlight distinctive features of each term: the view of the mountain as paradise, for example, focuses our attention on the heavenly qualities of the peak and at the same time gives concrete expression to abstract notions of heaven. In the process, our experience of both mountain and paradise are transformed so that one becomes more divine, the other more tangible.

The tension theory of metaphor, advocated by Paul Ricoeur, proposes that the differences between the two terms brought together in a metaphor break the bonds of language and create new meanings and new worlds that extend the range of experience (Ricoeur, 1981). In the metaphor of viewing a mountain as a temple, the tension involved in forcing these two different images together not only reshapes each one, but also generates a new vision of reality in which mountain and temple can be seen as the same. Whereas Ricoeur speaks of the creation of new meanings, I would go further and say that for the practitioner the process reveals a sacred dimension of reality that already exists and transcends both mountain and temple, unifying the two and imbuing them with their aura of sanctity.

A couple of analogies can help us to clarify and visualise the process. A stereoscopic viewer brings together two slightly different two-dimensional photographs of the same scene so that the third dimension inherent in each suddenly pops out and a person perceives a depth of space that was not previously visible. In a similar way, the different images brought together in a view of a mountain fuse to reveal another, sacred dimension of reality infusing, in our previous example, both peak and temple. This corresponds to the sense of depth and space, of inner luminosity, that frequently characterises people's experience of what they hold sacred.

The juxtaposition of images and associations in views of mountains also functions like different notes in a chord of music. Hearing the different tones resonate together creates a harmony that no single note can produce by itself. In a similar way, people experience the sacredness of a mountain from the juxtaposition of images and associations evoked in a view of it, not from any single image or association. Just as it would be erroneous to claim that one note stands for another, so it would be a mistake to say that the mountain simply represents or symbolises a temple. Rather, for a religious practitioner, the two images work together to awaken an awareness of a sacred dimension of reality that they each embody, but usually reveal only when they resonate with each other. And, indeed, the perception of this sacred dimension usually elicits a sense of harmony, a realisation of a unity underlying the apparent diversity and discord of the world of ordinary experience.

These diverse views and the way they function apply not only to sacred mountains, but also to other sacred sites and species, where they awaken a deeper experience of reality and inspire deep-seated commitments to respecting and preserving nature. We can see aspects of this process in the case of the mountain pilgrimage shrine of Badrinath and a project there to re-establish a sacred forest in the Himalaya.

Badrinath

Badrinath, the major Hindu pilgrimage place in the Indian Himalaya, lies in a remote valley of the Garhwal region at an altitude of 3100 m, at the foot of Nilkanth, a peak sacred to the major Hindu deity Shiva. It has been a focal point of religious devotion for thousands of years, but until recently, because of its difficulty of access, relatively few people actually managed to go there (Bhardwaj, 1973). Today 450 000 pilgrims per year come to the shrine from all over India, arriving on roads built in the early 1960s after a war with China. Under the impact of so many visitors, the extensive forest that according to ancient texts used to fill the valley has disappeared (Figure 6.2).

In 1993, at the suggestion of scientists from the G. B. Pant Institute of Himalayan Environment and Development, the Chief Priest of Badrinath agreed to use his religious authority to help restore the site. In a special ceremony he blessed tree seedlings supplied by the scientists and distributed them to pilgrims and local people to plant as an act of devotion. He also gave an inspiring talk that highlighted

Figure 6.2 Badrinath temple with pilgrims (© Edwin Bernbaum). See colour plate section.

religious beliefs and stories emphasising the importance of trees in Hinduism and other religious traditions, referring in particular to the founding myth of Badrinath which relates how the wife of Vishnu took the form of a juniper tree to shelter her divine husband, the supreme deity in the form of preserver, from falling snow. Many local people, even the beggars, responded with enthusiasm. The ceremony initiated a programme to re-establish Badrivan, the ancient sacred forest of Badrinath.

In September 1996, with the help of research grants from the American Alpine Club and the Alliance of Religions and Conservation in the UK, I went to Badrinath to study the programme and examine its implications for culturally motivated environmental conservation elsewhere in India and the world. The research included numerous discussions and interviews with the various parties involved, ranging from priests, pilgrims and villagers to scientists, government officials, and the military. At Hanumanchatti, a shrine just down the valley from Badrinath, I

Figure 6.3 Hindu swami and holy men at tree planting ceremony (© Edwin Bernbaum).

participated in a tree-planting ceremony (Figure 6.3) and gave a speech along with a swami, some scientists, a brigadier general, and a well-known yogi (Bernbaum, 1997b).

A feature of the programme at Badrinath that impressed me in particular was the way it drew pilgrims from all over India and provided an opportunity to inspire people to protect the environment throughout the country. It occurred to me that National Parks play a similar role in the United States as places of secular pilgrimage enshrining cultural and spiritual values central to the country and provide ideal places for disseminating environmental messages inspired by those values. Out of this realisation was born the idea for the Mountain Institute's

National Parks Partnership Project: 'Promoting Conservation through Cultural and Spiritual Values'.

National Parks Partnership Project

The Mountain Institute collaborated with the US National Park Service from 1998 to 2009 to develop innovative interpretive and educational materials based on the evocative associations of mountains and features of mountain environments in mainstream American, Native American, Native Hawaiian, and other cultures around the world. The National Parks Partnership Project drew on spiritual and cultural traditions from other parts of the world to connect with the heritages and interests of different cultural and ethnic groups in the US, such as Native American, Native Hawaiian, African-American, Asian American, and Latino, helping to diversify the currently limited visitor base for National Parks in the US. It also presented multiple perspectives that enrich the general public's experience of nature and motivate stewardship of the environment.

In addition, the project sought to present what indigenous peoples want known about their relationships with Parks and protected areas and to help to promote respect and protection of their sacred sites and traditions. Interpretive and educational materials – such as exhibits, interpretative trails, wayside signs, publications, and artwork – that resonate with different people and their diverse heritages and backgrounds serve to deepen visitors' experiences and give them deep-seated reasons for conserving the environment – in both the parks and back home. A couple of examples of particular projects – one completed, the other proposed – will give an idea of the aims of the National Parks Partnership Project and its implications for providing sustainable foundations for programmes of environmental conservation.

Hawai'i Volcanoes *wahi kapu* sculpture

Hawai'i Volcanoes National Park preserves a host of remarkable biological and geological features found on two of the most active volcanoes in the world, Kilauea and Mauna Loa. Although the park was designated a World Heritage Site for its natural value, park management came to realise that these features also have great cultural and spiritual significance for Native Hawaiians as key components of *wahi kapu*, or sacred places, revered as the abode of Pele, the volcano goddess. In recognition of this fact, a Kupuna Committee of Native Hawaiian elders was formed to advise the park on cultural matters.

As part of their efforts to focus attention on the cultural importance of the site, park staff and the Kupuna Committee came up with the idea of commissioning a

Figure 6.4 Hawaiian elders and park superintendent with *wahi kapu* sculpture and sculptor (© Edwin Bernbaum).

major work of outdoor sculpture that would highlight the significance of Kilauea and Mauna Loa as sacred places in Native Hawaiian tradition. The Mountain Institute made it possible for the park to put out a call for proposals. Aimed at Native Hawaiians, but open to all, given the legal requirements of Hawai'i Volcanoes as a government agency, the document read: 'The park is encouraging sculpture proposals by Hawai'i artists who, by virtue of their whole life experience, feel able to produce an appropriate and meaningful sculpture depicting the important Native Hawaiian concept of *wahi kapu* as it relates to Mauna Loa and Kīlauea. Anyone who feels so qualified may submit a proposal' (Figure 6.4).

The call received widespread media attention and 18 sculptors submitted proposals consisting of models and detailed diagrams. However, none of the submissions met the criteria of the Kupuna Committee and they turned them all down. To the surprise of some, the Superintendent backed the elders on their decision, which enhanced the standing and authority of the Committee in the eyes of the Hawaiian community and the general public.

One of the elders, Emma Kauhii, had a dream in which she envisioned the sculpture. Such visions play an important role in Native Hawaiian tradition, keeping the culture fresh and alive. Accordingly, the park and the Kupuna Committee incorporated Emma Kauhii's description of her dream in a second call:

Figure 6.5 *Wahi kapu* sculpture panel of Pele riding a lava flow (© Edwin Bernbaum).

Lava is flowing from Mauna Loa like a river. The upper part of a woman's body is visible in the lava flow – it's Pele riding down the flow, her eyes staring in anticipation, looking in the direction she's going to go. The body of Pele is not the whole body or like we think of a body. It's the upper torso only. Her hair is filling in behind her, also riding the flow, and she's looking out at the ocean. The lava flow, the image of the woman, is the volcano goddess who has come to show us, the people, her power.

The document asked applicants to take this dream into consideration as they developed proposals for their works of art.

The second call produced more satisfactory results, and the Kupuna Committee selected from among three finalists a proposal by John Kalewa Matsushita, a Hawaiian-born artist, and over the course of two years he carved a seven-ton sculpture of volcanic rock 3.35 m high in the shape of a mountain with the face of Pele inscribed lightly on one side and a trickle of red representing a lava flow winding down the other side. Four wood panels around the base depict Pele's past, present, and future.

A large crowd, including all the members of the Kupuna Committee, turned out for the ceremonial dedication; this received publicity throughout the Hawaiian

Islands (Honolulu Advertiser, 2007). The sculpture and the project to create it helped to strengthen the role of Native Hawaiian culture in the National Park and to instil a sense of awe, reverence and respect that connects people to the sacred volcanoes and inspires them to care for the natural environment (Figure 6.5).

Yosemite and Huangshan: sister sources of inspiration

In May 2006 an agreement was signed forming a sister park relationship between Huangshan National Park in the People's Republic of China and Yosemite National Park in the US (www.nps.gov/archive/yose/news/2006/huan0515.htm). The Chief of Interpretation at Yosemite asked the Mountain Institute to work with the park to develop an evocative exhibit that would highlight the inspirational significance the remarkable mountain scenery of the two parks has had for generations of poets, writers, artists, photographers, and conservationists.

Huangshan is the place most renowned in China for its mountain landscapes of peaks and pines, while Yosemite is the mountain site most celebrated in the US for its impressive walls and waterfalls. In addition to their natural value and beauty, both parks have deep cultural meanings, enshrined in stories and legends. The name 'Huangshan' means 'Yellow Mountain' and dates from AD 747 when the Tang Dynasty Emperor Zuangzong renamed the mountain massif in honour of the ancient Yellow Emperor, Huang Di. The name 'Yosemite' comes from a Miwok word for 'grizzly bear' and may have its origins in accounts that Tenaya, a famous chief of the Yosemite Indians, lived in a country filled with grizzlies (Scott, 2006) (Figure 6.6).

The striking ways the two sister parks blend nature and culture are reflected in the prominent roles Huangshan and Yosemite have played in poetry, literature, art, and photography. Starting in the eighth century, major Chinese poets, such as Li Bai and Qian Qianyi, have composed verse extolling the beauties of the Yellow Mountain (Chaves, 1988). The famous Chinese traveller and geographer, Xu Xiake, wrote movingly of the deep impressions Huangshan made on him (Li and Johnson, 1968). The beautiful scenery found here inspired an entire school of Chinese art – the Anhui or Huangshan School of landscape painting (Cahill, 1981). In more recent times, well-known photographers, such as Wang Wusheng and Marc Riboud, have sought to capture timeless pictures of Huangshan's misted, ever-changing landscape (Riboud, 1990; Wusheng, 2005).

Yosemite has played an equally important role in literature, art, and photography in the US. Major nature writers and conservationists such as John Muir, James Hutchings and Clarence King wrote evocative works on the natural history and scenery of the area that helped inspire the creation of the National Park and a movement to preserve the natural environment. The dramatic paintings of Albert

Figure 6.6 Half dome, Yosemite National Park (© Edwin Bernbaum).

Bierstadt, Thomas Hill and Thomas Moran created images of evocative mountains that moved people to visit Yosemite and settle in California. The photography of Ansel Adams and other well-known recent photographers, such as Galen Rowell, helped establish prominent features of the park as enduring icons of wilderness and the spirit of adventure (Scott, 2006).

Many visitors to Huangshan and Yosemite come seeking in their mountain landscapes the experience of some deeper, more enduring reality that can give meaning and vitality to their lives. The wonder and awe that such experiences awaken can be powerful motivations for protecting the beauties of nature from which they spring. The sense of meaning and beauty enshrined in works of literature, art, and photography inspired by the sister parks of Huangshan and Yosemite provides a solid and lasting foundation for promoting conservation of the natural world on which people depend for their physical and spiritual well-being.

The proposed exhibit, 'Huangshan and Yosemite: Sister Sources of Inspiration', would use evocative paintings, photographs, and quotes from poetry and prose to present the following four themes.

1. The two parks and their sister park relationship.
2. Huangshan in literature, art and photography.
3. Yosemite in literature, art and photography.
4. Mountains as sources of inspiration for conservation.

Since the sister park relationship builds on the sister city relationship between San Francisco and Shanghai, which lie not far from their respective parks, venues for the exhibit could include museums and other sites in each city, as well as at each park, thereby gaining a maximum of exposure. The exhibit in China would highlight, through a major World Heritage Site, the wealth of artistic and literary resources in Chinese culture that can foster appreciation of China's natural and cultural heritage and promote more sensitive and sustainable tourism throughout the country. The exhibit would reach out to the Chinese American community in San Francisco and northern California and encourage this key group to visit Yosemite National Park and develop even greater interest in nature and conservation in the US and China.

Conclusions

By providing multiple perspectives from mainstream American, Native American, Native Hawaiian, Native Alaskan and other cultures around the world, the National Parks Partnership Project enhanced the experience of the general public and inspired protection of the environment and respect for indigenous views of sacred sites and species. The strength of this approach lies in its inclusiveness – in the way in which it encourages a diversity of views so that everyone feels included and no one feels left out. This makes interpretive materials and exhibits focused on indigenous American, Alaskan and Hawaiian traditions and issues much more effective: people feel more inclined to appreciate and support others' views and concerns if they feel their own are being acknowledged and respected.

References

Bernbaum, E. (1997a). *Sacred Mountains of the World*. Berkeley & Los Angeles, CA: University of California Press.

Bernbaum, E. (1997b). *Pilgrimage and Conservation in the Himalayas: A Model for Environmental Action Based on Cultural and Spiritual Values*. Project report available from The Mountain Institute, Washington, DC.

Bernbaum, E. (2006). Sacred mountains: themes and teachings. *Mountain Research and Development*, **26**, 304–09.

Bhardwaj, S. M. (1973). *Hindu Places of Pilgrimage in India: A Study in Cultural Geography.* Berkeley, CA: University of California Press.

Black, M. (1981). Metaphor. In *Philosophical Perspectives on Metaphor*, ed. M. Johnson. Minneapolis, MN: University of Minnesota Press, pp. 63–82.

Cahill, J. (1981). *Shadows of Mt. Huang: Chinese Painting and Printing of the Anhui School.* Berkeley, CA: University Art Museum.

Chaves, J. (1988). The Yellow Mountain poems of Ch'ien Ch'ien-i (1582–1664): poetry as Yu-chi. *Harvard Journal of Asiatic Studies*, **48**, 465–92.

Eliade, M. (1971). *The Myth of the Eternal Return or, Cosmos and History*, trans. W. R. Trask, Bollingen Series, 46. Princeton, NJ: Princeton University Press.

Honolulu Advertiser. (2007). Massive Pele sculpture unveiled. 8 March, posted online.

Johnson, M. (ed.) (1981). *Philosophical Perspectives on Metaphor*. Minneapolis, MN: University of Minnesota Press.

Li, C. and Johnson, D. (1968). *Two Studies in Chinese Literature*. Michigan Papers in Chinese Studies no. 3. Ann Arbor, MI: Center for Chinese Studies, University of Michigan.

Lucas, P. H. C. (1993). History and rationale for mountain parks as exemplified by four mountain areas of Aotearoa (New Zealand). In *Parks, Peaks, and People*, ed. L. S. Hamilton, D. P. Bauer and H. F. Takeuchi. Honolulu, HI: East-West Center, Program on Environment, pp. 24–8.

Riboud, M. (1990). *Capital of Heaven*. New York, NY: Doubleday.

Richards, I. A. (1981). The philosophy of rhetoric. In *Philosophical Perspectives on Metaphor*, ed. M. Johnson. Minneapolis, MN: University of Minnesota Press, pp. 48–62.

Ricoeur, P. (1981). The metaphorical process as cognition, imagination, and feeling. In *Philosophical Perspectives on Metaphor*, ed. M. Johnson. Minneapolis, MN: University of Minnesota Press, pp. 228–47.

Scott, A. (ed.) (2006). *Yosemite: Art of an American Icon*. Los Angeles, CA: Autry National Center in association with University of California Press.

Smith, J. Z. (1987). *To Take Place: Toward Theory in Ritual*. Chicago, IL: University of Chicago Press.

Wusheng, Wang (2005). *Celestial Realm: The Yellow Mountains of China*. New York, NY: Abbeville Press.

7

The history of English churchyard landscapes illustrated by Rivenhall, Essex

NIGEL COOPER

Introduction

Christianity finally became the dominant religion in England after the conversion of the Anglo-Saxons. Among its sacred sites are the local churches and their curtilages, the churchyards. Most churchyards are doubly sacred on account of the burials and of the cultic building. Over the past 30 years there has been a growing recognition of their biodiversity value. These two statements are not unlinked.

This chapter explores how these sacred sites were selected in the first place and later extended. It examines how they were treated and the effect of this on biodiversity, especially plants. It concludes with a review of modern approaches to churchyard care.

Churchyards were and still are consecrated (Taylor, 1983). Church of England churchyards, along with the church buildings, thereby fall under Faculty Jurisdiction and receive 'ecclesiastical exemption' from Listed Building Consent under secular planning control. So for many purposes, although not all, planning control is maintained through Diocesan Advisory Committees (DACs) for the Care of Churches and the diocesan Consistory Courts. This means that they are sacred sites managed in a distinctly different way to other land holdings. This chapter is written from the perspective of 16 years' experience on DACs and from the perspective of 17 years as rector (parish priest) of Rivenhall. Rivenhall is about 45 miles east of London. It is remarkable for the churchyard being extensively excavated on two occasions by archaeologists (Rodwell and Rodwell, 1985; Rodwell and Rodwell,

Sacred Species and Sites: Advances in Biocultural Conservation, ed. Gloria Pungetti, Gonzalo Oviedo and Della Hooke. Published by Cambridge University Press. © Cambridge University Press 2012.

1993; Clarke, 2004). This makes it an ideal study from which more general points can be made about churchyards in England.

How churchyard sites were selected

All of England is covered by a pattern of ecclesiastical parishes. These may be somewhat arbitrary areas in towns, but in the country they are closely associated with the ancient settlement patterns. Although there have been some later alterations to parishes in the countryside, the basic pattern had been established by the twelfth century. The simplest picture is that of a village with its own church and all those who lived in the village, or parish, had rights and responsibilities to their parish church and priest, including the right of burial in the churchyard. The reality, especially in the early centuries after conversion, when the parochial structure was not fully established, was more confused and the site of a church might have been chosen on many grounds (Morris, 1983; Taylor, 1983; Rodwell, 2005).

It is often supposed that old churches were built on pagan sacred sites (Child, 1982). This is partly on account of the advice Pope Gregory gave the missionaries on how to Christianise the local religion as quoted by Bede (1955) in his *Historia ecclesiastica gentis Anglorum*. Pope Gregory advised, in his letter to Abbot Mellitus in 601,

> that the temples of the idols among that people should on no account be destroyed. The idols are to be destroyed, but the temples themselves are to be aspersed with holy water, altars set up in them, and relics deposited there. For if these temples are well-built, they must be purified from the worship of demons and dedicated to the service of the true God. In this way, we hope that the people, seeing that their temples are not destroyed, may abandon their error and, flocking more readily to their accustomed resorts, may come to know and adore the true God. (Bede, *HE*, I.30: Sherley-Price and Latham, 1955, pp. 86–7)

This may have fuelled a romantic and rebellious notion that the Church had usurped the native religion of the country. This idea is perpetuated today with the common claim that there are many ancient yews in churchyards that are much older than their churches, which evinces that a site of pagan worship at a sacred tree was converted to Christian practice in the building erected beside it. While not doubting that this adoption of a pagan yew happened in some places, its ubiquity might be doubted on the basis of the uncertainty of the dating of the trees together with the layouts of the site where the tree is by no means the focus of the churchyard. A recent study by Bevan-Jones (2002, p. 31) accepts the antiquity of some old churchyard yews, but suggests that they may have been planted by the early Christian saints of the Celtic Church. Greater confidence can be placed in a Christian takeover of a pagan site in the case of wells and springs, which were often considered holy and still receive a muted veneration in British culture today (it is traditional to make a wish while throwing a coin into the well). Apart from ancient yews and wells, there are not many examples of churchyards sited on top of pre-Roman sacred sites, such as barrows or pagan altars. Quite often, pagan burial grounds in current use at the time, which may have been at a distance from centres of occupation, were not adopted as churchyard sites, wholly new sites being selected for Christian burial – although exceptions can always be found (Morris, 1983; Morris, 1989; Taylor, 2001; see, too, the argument – unproven – presented by Yeates, 2006, pp. 71–2).

Prosaically, the majority of church sites probably owe their selection to political factors: they were established as manorial proprietary chapels. The Saxon estates can often be traced to Roman tenurial groupings (Taylor, 1983). The sole or principal manor in an area would establish a church, usually near the hall.

The Saxon manor of Rivenhall was derived from the Roman villa and its estate. In the Roman period, Rivenhall lay aside the main road from London to the Roman town of Colchester. If the estate boundaries of the villa were anything like the later medieval parish, the estate encompassed the small valley of Cressing Brook. Near the centre of this estate were two Bronze Age round barrows. The villa was built to line up on these two barrows. The villa was surrounded by an approximately rectangular space about 1 ha in extent; this might be thought of as a 'garden' (Figure 7.1). To the east was a larger area that may have been the farmyard. With the arrival of the Anglo-Saxons, the seat of the estate moved just north of the old villa. At about this time, there is evidence of burial in the north-east corner of what had been the villa's 'garden'. Later still, the seat was moved further north by 200 m across a small valley to the present location of Rivenhall Hall. By the tenth century, a wooden church had been built near the ruins of the old villa and later that century, or early in the eleventh, this was replaced by a stone church built out of the materials of the old villa and, being built over its foundations, this stone church was on the same alignment, fortuitously only slightly clockwise to the traditional eastward orientation. The site of burial gradually shifted to around the new church (Clarke, 2004). The churchyard was now defined by the original western and southern boundaries of the old 'garden', but the churchyard did not include the site of the earlier hall to the north nor a triangular plot in the north-east corner, where there was a series of houses, presumably for the priest. It is not known what physical structures marked all these boundaries, although a ditch dug in the thirteenth century demarcated the priest's garden (Clarke, 2004). From the tenth century, churchyards generally were being enclosed, as required by Canon Law, to keep out animals and to clarify ownership (Daniell, 1999).

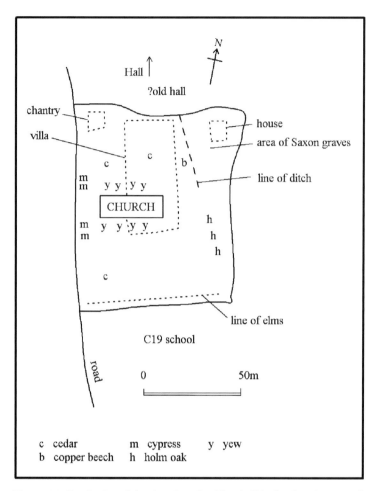

Figure 7.1 Sketch-plan of the churchyard at Rivenhall indicating the approximate locations of the features discussed (redrawn, after Rodwell and Rodwell, 1985, and Clarke, 2004).

These medieval churchyard plots were usually sufficient until the nineteenth century. By then, the increasing custom of erecting headstones over burial plots, together with a new reluctance to disturb graves, meant that churchyards could be perceived as 'full'. In towns and cities there was also a public health scandal because so many corpses were being buried in so little soil that decomposition could no longer remain discreet below ground. There was a move to create new cemeteries. In villages, where there might still be agricultural land around the churchyard, instead of establishing new sites, churchyards were often extended. Because Rivenhall churchyard was already so large there was no Victorian extension

Figure 7.2 The churchyard extension at Thorpe-le-Soken, Essex (© Nigel Cooper).

there. The parish of Brightlingsea in Essex provides an illustration of churchyard extension. The parish church of All Saints lies to the north of the small port, which was growing into a small town. This put pressure on the churchyard, which was first met by the vicar donating what had been the vicarage garden in a corner of the churchyard and incorporating it in 1871; a triangular plot was added in 1885. The twentieth century saw two further extensions, while a Consistory Court sitting in the twenty-first century has authorised a further extension (Pulman, 2004). In the case of Brightlingsea, the rate of burial was such that the new extensions did not remain unused for long. In other parishes these extensions were sometimes large by comparison with the rate of burial and remain partly unused to this day, e.g. Thorpe-le-Soken, Essex (Figure 7.2). These nineteenth-century extensions can be the richest areas for flora in churchyards. The remains of old boundary markers, such as hedges, trees, ditches and paths, are important features to be conserved, as is the change in level between old and new churchyards.

How churchyards were treated

The parish priest was the incumbent (as it were, owner) of the benefice of the parish. The benefice included rights to tithes, etc., and the benefice property: the parsonage house, the glebe farm, and the church and churchyard. The incumbent (rector or vicar) was entitled to crop from the churchyard, and to take wood from the trees. Presumably this would normally have meant either taking a hay crop or putting animals to graze (Dymond, 1999). Unscrupulous clergy sometimes took advantage of this. One glorious story from the eighteenth century is of an archdeacon (a senior cleric) making his visitation and finding turnips growing in the churchyard. He rebuked the vicar, 'I hope to see no such thing on my next visit.' 'I can assure you, Mr Archdeacon, that you will not. I plan to grow barley next season' (Greenoak, 1993). There are many records of complaints of animals disturbing graves and it seems that it was not uncommon for new graves to be protected for some years by palings or brush. Whatever the extent of this farming, and some are still grazed and many mown, it was not affected by many modern agricultural practices such as fertilising, re-seeding or the use of weedkillers and other chemicals.

From the point of view of nature conservation, this traditional-style agricultural practice is ideal for preserving meadow and pasture communities, but churchyard soils are not in the least bit typical and might be termed 'anthronecrosols' (Barker, 1972). A quick calculation suggests that a typical churchyard will contain the remains of 10 000 human corpses; village population of 500, average lifespan 50 years, age of churchyard 1000 years – so probably more than 10 000! Supposing that a typical churchyard is a quarter of a hectare, that is four corpses per square metre, which is roughly the size of a plot measuring 2 m × 0.5 m. Once asked how many bodies he dug up for a new burial, a gravedigger replied the maximum number of skulls he had removed for a new grave was eight (the common practice is to hide the old bones under the plastic 'turf' thrown over the excavated soil beside the grave). The excavations at Rivenhall demonstrate many close and overlapping graves from different periods, although not quite the density suggested by the calculations above (although one dense area had approximately five burials per square metre). The medieval graves were not dug to modern depths, more typically to about a metre (Rodwell and Rodwell, 1985).

The impact of these practices is probably significant. The soil is dug to a much greater depth than in most agricultural practices. The corpses contribute a lot of organic matter to the soil, especially adding calcium and phosphorus, and more calcium may come from limestone headstones as well. Sometimes more soil may have been brought in (Morris, 1989), but grave digging will loosen the soil so that it is less compacted than the surrounding land. The ground surface of churchyards is nearly always raised above its surroundings, as is evident at boundaries (at the north and east boundaries in the case of Rivenhall) (Figure 7.3) and in the way one steps down into the interior of churches, where the floor more nearly represents the original soil level (although there will now be a surface, of stone, tile or wood, over the original earthen floor).

Figure 7.3 The ground was lowered around Rivenhall church at the time of the 1970s excavations. This photograph shows the original soil level at a short distance from the building (© Ann Kerr).

Churchyards were dynamic building plots. Surprisingly, often secular build-ings encroached on the churchyard and nibbled away at its integrity; Great Tey in Essex is a particularly clear example. At Rivenhall all the buildings were ecclesi-astical and all have now been removed. There seem to have been three successive priest's houses in the north-east corner of the churchyard (from the twelfth to the fifteenth century), but this use is only inferred from the archaeological evidence. The triangular plot for these buildings was incorporated into the churchyard in the 1720s (Clarke, 2004). There is documentary evidence of a fifteenth-century chantry chapel, which was probably a wooden building in the north-west corner of the churchyard. There was an early bell cage and, in the seventeenth and eigh-teenth centuries, a 'herring house', which was a wooden lean-to next to the tower used for the distribution of herrings to the poor on Fridays in Lent. By the early nineteenth century there was a sexton's house in the north-west corner of the churchyard (the sexton was responsible for maintaining the churchyard); in 1839 it was demolished and rebuilt just down the road and is now occupied by the son of the last sexton of the parish (Rodwell and Rodwell, 1985).

In 1839 the church was remodelled by an architect, who may well have been John Adey Repton. By 1855 there was a re-landscaping of the churchyard, developing the previous design, perhaps of Humphrey Repton, John Adey's father (who redesigned the park of Rivenhall Place in about 1790). Many churchyards contain trees of this period in the history of landscape architecture. Churchyards do contain old trees, but usually there is not an evident plan to them apart from the majority of the trees being along the boundary. There is the added difficulty of interpretation in that many of the boundary trees were often elms and any that remained died as trees in the 1970s Dutch elm disease outbreak; now only suckers and hedges of elm remain to trace their presence. From an illustration of 1841, Rivenhall had a fine line of elms along the southern boundary of the churchyard, although these were felled many years before Dutch elm disease. They probably dated from the eighteenth century, perhaps before Repton senior (Rodwell and Rodwell, 1985). A fashion for limes seems to have replaced that for elms during the nineteenth century, along with the fashion to pollard them.

Mid-century saw two enthusiasms, both of which influenced the 1855 design at Rivenhall. One was for exotic trees; churchyards could be turned into veritable arboreta, as at Purleigh, Essex. Three cedars, one of each type: Atlantic, Indian and of Lebanon, and four holm-oaks were planted at this time. The other enthusiasm was inspired by the famous garden designer, John Claudius Loudon, who wrote *On the Laying Out, Planting and Managing of Cemeteries* in 1843. The book ends with a section on churchyards, which is a bit more flexible than his rules for the new cemeteries. To promote the right spiritual atmosphere, he advocated formal designs with a sombre tone of evergreens and a vertical theme provided by the recently discovered fastigiated Irish yew and by Monterey cypresses. The cypresses marked most of the corners and framed the main entrance at Rivenhall, while a line of Irish yews was planted down each side of the church. At the same time, all the little entrances to the churchyard from the tracks across the fields from the various farms were closed and the formal entrance was centred on the west tower of the church (Rodwell and Rodwell, 1985).

Although many of these trees have now died, enough remain to give a feel for the effect. In the twentieth century, however, principles of design were largely abandoned in favour of planting decorative trees such as Japanese cherries in rather random places in the churchyard. A lack of attention to churchyard design persists in the English Church generally.

Biodiversity in churchyards

While design may have been neglected, the value of churchyards for wildlife was recognised towards the end of the twentieth century (Cooper, 1997). There are four principal habitats of importance. Old trees are of value as characterful and, if they are sufficiently old, 'veteran trees': the centres of the trunk may be decayed, providing a specialist habitat for saproxylic insects (i.e. those that feed on standing dead wood). The grassland may be a relic of earlier agricultural meadows and pastures, and so retain a much more diverse sward of wild flowers. These may once have been common and widespread across the countryside, but are now increasingly restricted as over 80% of ancient meadows have been improved or lost in recent decades. In Norfolk, Bob Leaney (personal communication) has compiled a list of species that he reckons have 50% or more of their populations in churchyards in the county. These are Cowslip *Primula veris*, Meadow saxifrage *Saxifraga granulosa*, Ox-eye daisy *Leucanthemum vulgare*, Lady's bedstraw *Galium verum*, Pignut *Conopodium majus*, and Lesser burnet saxifrage *Pimpinella saxifraga*. Some of the more vulnerable grassland fungi are also found in churchyards. One notable example is Little Leighs churchyard in Essex, where Tony Boniface (personal communication) has found 18 species of waxcaps: *Hygrocybe pratensis*, *H. colmanniana*, *H. fornicata*, *H. irrigata*, *H. quieta*, *H. ceracea*, *H. punicea*, *H. mucronella*, *H. conica*, *H. virginea*, *H. flavipes*, *H. psittacina*, *H. reidii*, *H. coccinea*, *H. insipida*, *H. aurantiosplendens*, *H. chlorophana*, and *H. spadicea*.

The church building can provide roosting and nesting sites for bats and birds. Swifts, a species that is rapidly declining in England, are often associated with churches and there is a campaign in Ely diocese to install nest boxes in bell towers to encourage the birds to use more churches. Bats are sometimes cursed by churchgoers, especially where there is a nursery roost of the Soprano Pipistrelle *Pipistrellus pygmaeus* in which hundreds of animals may be present, leaving droppings and urine over the church interior. However, about 80% of Essex rural churches are used at some point in the year by bats as part of their portfolio of sites (John Dobson, personal communication). In many cases, only those who know to look for bat droppings on window ledges and the like will find the evidence of their presence.

Church buildings and monuments are often of stone and in a county such as Essex there are not many stone surfaces for mosses and lichens to grow on. The buildings are of very diverse materials: stone, brick and wood; the monuments are largely of stone, especially limestone, sandstone and 'granites' (the 'black granite' of stonemasons is often a gabbro to geologists). Some monuments go back to the seventeenth century, and the churches long before that, and it is usually the limestones that host the richest flora; however, the interest lies in the microhabitats of the stone, e.g. the aspect and slope, the degree water flows or collects on the stone, or if it is influenced by runoff from copper or leadwork near by. The diverse flora of the stonework includes some rarities. Three examples from Essex are *Weissia microstoma*, *Ditrichum cylindricum* and *Pottia intermedia* (Tim Pyner, personal communication). Across the country as a whole, the British Lichen Society reports on its website that members have found 160 churchyards with over 100 species in each. One particular species, *Lecanographa grumulosa*, has been nicknamed the churchyard lecanactis because it is largely restricted to churches.

The value of churchyards

Naturalists value churchyards, but there are much wider and more numerous groups of people who appreciate churchyards for other reasons (UK National Ecosystem Assessment, 2011). Chief among these are the parishioners. They have relatives buried there and they support the parish church. There is a sense in which ancestor worship is alive and well in the English countryside: come a Sunday, probably more people will visit graves in the churchyard than will enter the church building for an official service. Headstones now mark nearly all graves and many families regularly come to tend these, planting flowers or leaving cut flowers and generally tidying up. Villagers will often visit several relatives' graves, going back at least two generations. They will expect to follow their parents in due course, some even bothering to reserve plots to be near relatives. It brings a mindset quite different to that of the cosmopolitan person if one knows where one is to be buried.

Parish priests are very alert to the importance of the church and churchyard to locals. Ostensibly this is because of their Christian use, but many villagers would be hard pressed to recite the Creed or explain their faith. What seems to be going on is that the local church represents the local community, not merely as a collection of people, but with some sort of divine or sacred dimension (Lowerson, 1992; Seymour and Watkins, 1995). In the 1980s and 1990s, in Essex and elsewhere, many villages erected a village sign; most have chosen to depict the parish church on the sign. This is despite the fact that only a minority of those who choose the designs will be regular churchgoers. With fewer clergy, parishes are now amalgamated into one-priest benefices. The clergy usually arrange joint services around the villages and are disappointed that parishioners from other villages turn out in such small numbers to worship in a neighbouring village. This makes no sense in terms of Christian worship; it does make sense if the church is the cultic centre for a god of the parish.

Churchyards naturally receive all sorts of projections about death. In some villages death seems to have overcome the local community. This may be where there are a disproportionate number of incomers who are not relating to their new community, or the village population is just ageing and shrinking. Here nearly all care for the churchyard, apart from a few graves, has been abandoned, and the grassland is tumbling down to scrub. This is not good news for nature conservation, as two key interests are the meadow grassland and the headstones, both of which lose their biodiversity if they become shaded. Conversely, a community with energy

Figure 7.4 'The Real Heroes': Dot Taylor (left) leads the churchyard gang, of which Faith Murton is a member (© Ann Kerr).

but with some sense of threat, perhaps from a town culture brought by incomers, may try to dominate the wildness of a churchyard by keeping it immaculately tidy. This again leaves little room for the more uncommon wildlife.

The nature conservationist can make common cause with parishioners who are willing to put the considerable effort in to look after the churchyard in a traditional manner. Maintaining traditional management is a good rule of thumb for keeping the species that are currently living there: they must like it as it is to some extent. Rivenhall has been particularly fortunate to have had such a team of volunteers. The 'churchyard gang' (Figure 7.4) spend every Wednesday morning in the churchyard throughout the year, plus extra time when needed. They maintain the mowing (including removing the cuttings, which is so important to reduce soil eutrophication), cut the hedges, etc. Their aim is to keep a country churchyard, neither neglected nor over-manicured. They love both plants and animals, and have been very receptive to a few changes to the management regime to benefit the wildlife. This has included obvious things like attaching birdboxes to trees and leaving the grass long in some places until flowers like the cowslip ('peggles' is the Essex name) have shed their seed. They have trialled innovations such as attractive

Figure 7.5 Grasshopper strips at Rivenhall (© Nigel Cooper).

strips (Figure 7.5) – grass alternately mowed or left uncut over the summer – these strips have greatly increased the grasshopper population (Gardiner, *et al.*, 2011).

This has been part of a national movement that has popularised the phrase 'God's Acre' and promoted managing churchyards with wildlife in mind. This had begun by the 1970s when the Church of England published a booklet (Barker, 1972; Cooper, 2001). The movement has had its strength at county level, usually led by an enthusiast in either the diocese or the county wildlife trust. There has been a national organisation since the 1980s and 1990s and there is now an attempt to re-establish a national network led by the team in Herefordshire. The Church of England's national environment campaign, 'Shrinking the Footprint', includes biodiversity conservation in churchyards as part of its programme. Although only a minority of parishes actively pursue this concept of management, fortunately many country churchyards are still maintained in traditional ways and remain havens for wildlife.

Conclusions: the link between the sacred use of churchyards and their biodiversity value

The majority of English churchyards did not have a prior sacred history. They were enclosed from either the wild or from farmland, but, apart from churchyard extensions since the nineteenth century, the features of their original habitat have been overlain by subsequent treatment. As sacred sites they have had a distinctive history of management, particularly of the soil, which bequeaths an equally distinctive set of habitats. Those of greatest biodiversity significance are the grassland and the stonework, but ancient trees and roosting sites for bats are also important. Despite what is often termed the secularisation of Britain, churchyards remain as popular sacred sites, often inspiring local people to volunteer to care for them. Such local people are making common cause with nature conservationists to manage 'God's Acre' to the benefit of its fauna and flora.

References

Barker, G. M. A. (1972). *Wildlife Conservation in the Care of Churches and Churchyards*. London: CIO Publishing.

Bede. (1955). *A History of the English Church and People*, trans. L. Sherley-Price, revised R. E. Latham. Harmondsworth: Penguin Books.

Bevan-Jones, R. (2002). *The Ancient Yew*. Macclesfield: Windgather Press.

Child, M. (1982). *Discovering Churchyards*. Princes Risborough: Shire Publications.

Clarke, R. (2004). Rivenhall revisited: further excavations in the churchyard of St Mary and All Saints, 1999. *Essex Archaeology and History*, **35**, 26–77.

Cooper, N. S. (1997). A sanctuary for wildlife. *Biologist*, **44**, 417–19.

Cooper, N. S. (2001). *Wildlife in Church and Churchyard; Plants, Animals and their Management* (2nd edn). London: Church House Publishing.

Daniell, C. (1999). *Death and Burial in Medieval England 1066-1550*. London: Routledge.

Dymond, D. (1999). God's disputed acre. *The Journal of Ecclesiastical History*, **50**, 464–97.

Gardiner, T., Gardiner, M. and Cooper, N. (2011). Grasshopper strips prove effective in enhancing grasshopper abundance in Rivenhall Churchyard, Essex, England. *Conservation Evidence*, **8**, 31–7.

Greenoak, F. (1993). *Wildlife in the Churchyard: The Plants and Animals of God's Acre*. London: Little, Brown and Co.

Loudon, J. C. (1843). *On the Laying Out, Planting and Managing of Cemeteries; and on the Improvement of Churchyards*. London.

Lowerson, J. (1992). The mystical geography of the English. In *The English Rural Community: Image and Analysis*, ed. B. Short. Cambridge: Cambridge University Press.

Morris, R. (1983). *The Church in British Archaeology*. CBA Research Report 47. London: Council for British Archaeology.

Morris, R. (1989). *Churches in the Landscape*. London: JM Dent and Sons.

Pulman, G. (Chancellor). (2004). *In the Matter of Churchyard of the Parish Church of All Saints, Brightlingsea*. Judgement in the Consistory Court of the Diocese of Chelmsford.

Rodwell, W. (2005). *The Archaeology of Churches*. Stroud: Tempus Publishing.

Rodwell, W. J. and Rodwell, K. A. (1985). *Rivenhall: Investigations of a Villa, Church, and Village, 1950–1977 (Vol. I)*. CBA Research Report 55. London: Council for British Archaeology.

Rodwell, W. J and Rodwell, K. A. (1993). *Rivenhall: Investigations of a Villa, Church and Village, 1950–1977 (Vol. II)*. CBA Research Report 80. London: Council for British Archaeology.

Seymour, S. and Watkins, C. (1995). Church, landscape and community: rural life and the Church of England. *Landscape Research*, **20**, 30–44.

Taylor, A. (2001). *Burial Practice in Early England*. Stroud: Tempus Publishing.

Taylor, C. (1983). *Village and Farmstead: A History of Rural Settlement in England*. London: George Philip.

UK National Ecosystem Assessment (2011). *The UK National Ecosystem Technical Report*. Cambridge: UNEP–WCMC.

Yeates, S. J. (2006). *Religion, Community and Territory. Defining religion in the Severn Valley and adjacent hills from the Iron Age to the early medieval period*. British Archaeological Report, British series 411. Oxford: British Archaeological Reports.

8

Exmoor dreaming

PAUL SHARMAN

Introduction

'"Exmore"... is "a filthy, barren, ground"' – so said Daniel Defoe in his three-volume work *Tour through the Whole Island of Great Britain* published between 1724 and 1726, citing the comments of William Camden in his *Britannia* first published (in Latin) in 1586 (Furbank *et al.*, 1991, p. 113). Writing in the *Exmoor Official National Park Guide Book* at the beginning of the twenty-first century, Brian Pearce (2001) describes the region as 'a seemingly benign landscape in which one immediately feels at home'. In this chapter I will discuss how a barren wasteland became a sacred place in the modern English imagination. I will be focusing on Dunkery Beacon, the highest point on Exmoor, an upland region of south-west Britain.

Daniel Defoe made his dismissive report on the landscape around Dunkery Beacon prior to Exmoor's enclosure for agricultural improvement. Enclosure was never fully achieved and the modern landscape is described in the guide book as a harmony between high moorland and the 'cosy' hamlets and farms found at lower levels. It is this tension between cosy habitation and wild moorland that generates Exmoor's sacred quality or spirit of place.

The wild moorland, or in Christian Norberg-Schultz's words, 'cosmic landscape', does not offer humanity sufficient existential foothold (Norberg-Schultz, 1979, p. 45). To enable human dwelling in an ostensibly barren waste, such landscape becomes a habitat for modern imagination. The open moor has become not only a resource for biodiversity, but also a naturalised resource for the guided dreams of an urbanised population.

Sacred Species and Sites: Advances in Biocultural Conservation, ed. Gloria Pungetti, Gonzalo Oviedo and Della Hooke. Published by Cambridge University Press. © Cambridge University Press 2012.

Conservation of natural and agricultural species on Exmoor reifies the rural dreams of a modern nation. Popular support for the conservation process is autopoietic. Autopoiesis is an ecological term describing the way, in this instance, people create and are created by the world in which they live, or in a National Park, recreate. In terms of cultural ecology, the modern English man or woman is little different to their pre-modern counterparts in their desire to use selected landscapes as a spiritual resource.

Exmoor's natural heritage is built around managed moorland, beech hedges, local breeds of livestock, working ponies, common birds of prey and reintroduced deer. None of these species is considered rare or endangered, but have been conserved as cultural signifiers in an exurban vision. Grazed moorland derives its cultural and spiritual significance as a by-product of a once purely agricultural system which bred ponies for mine work, considered birds of prey vermin and conserved deer for social hunting. Michael Bell considers that the modern English nation cherishes the open countryside of Exmoor as a place for personal reflection on a crowded and industrialised island (Bell, 1994, 166). Effectively, Exmoor has become a tapestry of recreational meanings draped over certain key elements – the open moor, hedges, hamlets, farm livestock, ponies, birds of prey, managed deer and game birds. With the key elements brought together in one landscape stage, national recreation is catered for in a way reminiscent of Michel Foucault's (1967) *heterotopia*. Foucault wrote of modern places being deliberately constructed to cater for recreation away from the hum-drum of everyday life.

The conservation process implies that popular recreation on Exmoor is not simply the action of the participants' free will. As habitat of the mind, dependent on reflective space, tourist Exmoor is an imagined product of conscious social and emotional engineering through 'teleonomy' (Maturana and Varela, 1980, p. 85). Teleonomy is a term coined to describe autopoiesis or self re-creation deliberately managed towards a desired end; in this case, the desired end being a refreshed workforce to support the national economy.

As one of ten original national parks designated in mid-twentieth-century Britain, Exmoor fulfilled the basic requirement of accessibility from major urban centres. Since the Industrial Revolution, enlightened England has considered monotheist divinity inappropriate and politically questionable. In particular, the enclosure landscape of Exmoor embodies neoclassical values through the Hellenist philosophies of landscape architect Richard Payne-Knight and his landowning family's enduring 'improvements' (Ballantyne, 1997, p. 22). The Exmoor visitor is thus predisposed to re-creation through neoclassical 'spiritual' experience. Classical 'spirit of place' or *Genius loci* is most pronounced in tended landscapes, of which Exmoor is a complex example. Exmoor includes classical, cosmic and romantic landscapes in one bounded and managed region, thus making its spirit of place a very man-made entity (Norberg-Schultz, 1979, p. 58).

Having described the neoclassical origins of the *Genius loci* reified in the managed, yet natural, elements of Exmoor, I will now describe how the Spirit of Exmoor has taken almost divine meaning in a secular nation.

Bio-divinity

Bio-divinity on Exmoor began with the eighteenth-century 'scientific' philosophies of Immanuel Kant (1781), which structured experience through space and time. Kant considered tensions between space and time generated phenomenology or spirit of place. His humanist explanation for *Genius loci* resonates 200 years later in the work of Christian Norberg-Schultz. Kant suggests that entities that appear in Spirin's habitat of the mind are not things themselves, but things as they appear to the human intellect (Spirin, 1998, p. 16; Brook, 1998, p. 52).

The emergent 'Spirit of Exmoor' is revealed in the early nineteenth-century poetry of Samuel Taylor Coleridge, who considered Kant's work consonant with religion and 'capable of flowing along with it in one channel and even blending with it in one stream … it cultivates the moral sense while it clears the eye of reason; its positions are compatible with every spiritual truth, and to the spiritual are spiritual themselves' (Shaffer, 1970, p. 202). Kant had anguished over a means to provide spiritual nourishment for a scientifically enlightened nation and found an acceptable religious substitute in nature (Shaffer, 1970, p. 203). Through his poetry, Samuel Taylor Coleridge became a national guide for English visions of nature. As Noel Castree (2004) suggests, this process of moral and political guidance through nature poetry was set to become a deeply conservative process.

In his work on moorland romanticism, Ken Olwig (1984) refers to the heath and moors of north-west Europe as *Nature's Ideological Landscape*. Historically, heaths and moors have been a source of social nonconformity and political dissent, and progressively marginalised by modern states. Through disengaged vision, these communities became disempowered by 'romanticisation'.

Exmoor's fictional heroine, Lorna Doone, rises from the tension between romantic myth and local reality. The spirit of Lorna Doone has inspired a tourist industry based not on virtual reality, but on real virtuality (Fibischer, 1998, p. 21). Tension between disbelief of Exmoor as barren waste and euphoric belief as a land of romance opens a psychological crack through which the spirit appears. John Wylie (2007) advises that in order to 'see' the spirit, you must first present yourself to it (Wylie, 2007). The Exmoor 'insider' is unlikely to experience the spirit felt by the predisposed 'outsider', but may be employed to maintain the mythical invention in the interest of the local economy.

Samuel Taylor Coleridge was known for taking autopoietic walks on Exmoor with fellow Romantic, William Wordsworth. Lyrical accounts of the two poets' romantic walks inspired the later nineteenth-century visionary, John Ruskin. Ruskin subsequently sought to purchase rock, marsh and seashore for national recreation (Hoare, 2005, p. 240). In seeking recreational wild places, he was reacting against what he perceived as the rudeness and destructiveness of modern England. His Utopian dream brought him into contact with the owner of such land on Exmoor. Sir Charles Thomas Dyke Acland, inspired by Ruskin's radical romanticism, became, for a time, patron of his fundraising League of St George (Bradley, 1964). Struggling with the economic reality of agricultural depression, Acland finally leased much of the Exmoor's unviable 'barren waste' to the National Trust in 1917. Ruskin had been influential in the founding of the English National Trust in 1895, set up to preserve places of historic interest and natural beauty for the nation. At the time of the bequest, the nation was embroiled in the slaughter of the First World War. Following this modern catastrophe, historian G. M. Trevelyan proposed a network of national landscapes across England. Quoting the Christian Bible (Proverbs 29: 18), he claimed that without the vision of English countryside, the people would perish (Trevelyan, 1929, p. 19). Shared vision rather than hands-on reality was the important consideration in harmonising an industrial society. Thirty-five years later and under further economic constraint, Sir Thomas's great-nephew Richard Acland passed his family's Exmoor lands, in entirety, to the National Trust. In 1944, following the horrors of another modern war, Dunkery Hill was handed over to Professor Trevelyan, then Chairman of the Estates Committee of the National Trust (Waterson, 1994, p. 126). Through a process of personal and national tension, Dunkery Hill became a prominent and focal point in the Exmoor landscape.

Sacred site

The cairn built at the summit of Dunkery Hill marks the site of Dunkery Beacon (Figure 8.1).

Erected in 1935, the cairn commemorates national acceptance of the landscape as a recreational resource. It is not the first time such a structure has been built here. Four thousand year-old burial mounds sit close by, confirming the perception of this high place as an enduring place of spiritual power. The twentieth-century Acland benefactor followed an ancient tradition; itself followed in the early twenty-first century by an 'unofficial' cairn builder (see Figure 8.2). Freshly erected stones commemorate an individual who we can assume to have personally connected

Figure 8.1 Dunkery Beacon (© Paul Sharman).

Figure 8.2 Associate cairn building (© Paul Sharman).

Figure 8.3 Unintended consequence (© Paul Sharman).

with the spirit of this place. Unofficial commemorative cairn building has taken place as an unintended consequence of the National Trust Acland cairn, itself quite possibly an unintended consequence of Bronze Age cairn builders (see Figure 8.3). This example highlights the way landscape can make its subjects behave in ways they cannot consciously explain other than as a response to what others have done before (Pile and Keith, 1997, p. 128).

The positioning of the cairn is important. Barbara Bender (1998, p. 75) suggests that skyline monuments draw their power from visual tension between earth and sky. Christian Norberg-Schultz (1979, p. 40) describes vertical structures that pierce the horizon as the most fundamental markers of human existential space. The cairn focuses attention in the cosmic landscape; drawing English 'pilgrims of scenery' towards it (Matless, 1998, p. 84) (see Figure 8.4). Norberg-Schultz adds that such structures are essential to the development of social identity in an ever-changing natural environment (Norberg-Schultz, 1979, p. 180).

The cairn bears inscriptions slowing down the multiple trajectories and fixing memories at Dunkery Beacon. Doreen Massey (2005, p. 191) claims that such objects capture time and generate tension between past and present. Dunkery Beacon has become a place where the future is withheld and the past refused (Abram, 1996,

Figure 8.4 Pilgrims of scenery (© Paul Sharman).

p. 211). The tension between earth and sky, between nature and humanity, and between past and present contribute to the architectural tension generating *Genius loci*. Dunkery Beacon has undoubtedly become a sacred site for a modern society but as place it is held by more than stone cairns. As Pile and Keith (1997, p. 130) point out, place is held together by durable 'objects of power'. However, the 4000-year-old cairns are barely distinguishable without their interpretive notices. Although durable, heaps of stones are not everlasting and, without site management, the autopoietic spirit of place will eventually deform and disintegrate along with the cairns. Human intervention is needed to maintain both the cairns and *Genius loci* at Dunkery Beacon. As I have indicated, this can be an enduring process.

Long-distance control over the landscape and its inhabitants is a feature of Actor Network Theory (ANT). This theory evolved in the late twentieth century to explain the method by which human sociality is mediated through environmental objects. Its main proponents were French philosophers Michael Callon and Bruno Latour. A fundamental point of this theory is that socially mediating objects must be enduring. A paper notice will last a very short time, a stone cairn maybe 4000 years, but when human sociality is stabilised through self-regenerating nature, harmony can theoretically become everlasting. With biodiversity organised into an effective modern fetish ecology the effect is enduring indeed.

Sacred species

Four thousand years of agricultural grazing have created Dunkery Hill as a plagioclimax ecological community. A plagioclimax community is one where ecological succession is artificially arrested. Left unmanaged, this hilltop, at less than 900 m above sea level, would be likely to succeed to birch woodland and then on to high forest (Webb, 1986, p. 106). Plagioclimax introduces further tension into a cultural landscape where living actors are chosen rather than allowed to succeed.

Without grazing and controlled burning, the culturally important heather moorland would succeed to woodland. Farming activity is similarly constrained. Moorland reclamation is vigorously proscribed, preventing the land from reaching its agricultural potential (Blacksell, 1997, p. 100). Ecological and financial constraints all contribute to the natural and social tensions on Dunkery Hill.

In a religious context, Andrew Ballantyne remarks that the British worship the purple cloth rather than the God it represents (Ballantyne, 1997, p. 117). Considering the modern concern for conservation of heather moorland, I would argue a connection between the spiritual value of purple cloth and the conservation of purple heather. The path from the public road is designed to make walking on the heather difficult. The placing of rocks along the path edge encourages the visitor to look at, but not touch, the heather moorland (see Figure 8.5). Notices along the way request that the visitor stays on the path 'in the interest of moorland conservation'.

The *Genius loci* of moorland is a mobile spirit, residing in the imagination of the observer (Gomes, 2005, p. 76). It is encountered wherever significant moorland biological communities are to be found. Moorland is an anthropogenic landscape and its cultural importance lies in significant plant and animal replication, rather than overall biodiversity. Regardless of deterrent rocks and notices, the observation route is to a greater degree self maintaining. In an anthropogenic landscape it is always easier to follow where others have been before (Brook, 1998, p. 64). Leaving the safety of the path means entering visually unenclosed moorland. Direct encounters with moorland sublime can be fearful but viewed from the path the scene is pleasurable, leading to a Picturesque 'tickling' (Ballantyne, 1997, p. 83).

Actor Networks maintaining heather moorland involve agriculture, nature conservation, tourist information and human guides. Such exclusive networks inevitably generate their other. The very real tensions in the Exmoor farming community have meant that, economically deprived by a cultural landscape, local farmers have become radicalised to an extent. Exmoor has become a focus for hunt ban protest (Hillyard, 2007, p. 88). Another sign of radicalisation, but at a

Figure 8.5 'Look but don't touch' (© Paul Sharman).

cognitive level, has been the emergence of cryptozoology around Dunkery Beacon. At the time of the First World War, unnaturally large and ferocious wild cats were reported in the area (Dent, 1974, pp. 88, 89). In recent years, these mythical animals have re-emerged from their lairs, indicating further social troubles at the turn of the twenty-first century. The mythical Beast of Exmoor is one more actor in the heterogeneous cast making up the phenomenology of Dunkery Hill.

Sacred *Genius loci*

Christian Norberg-Schultz (1979, p. 47) acknowledges that there are many varied and complex formulae involved in constructing and recognising *Genius loci*. I consider Actor Networks vital to the process, effectively modern 'songlines' along which the spirit travels. To allow analysis to take place, both Actor Networks and *Genius loci* need to be researched within a common frame.

In an open cosmic landscape with dynamic and porous visual boundaries, the concept of framing proves problematic. Ronald Moore (2006, p. 256) suggests an answer to framing the spirit of place. Taking Tim Ingold's (1995, p. 63) concept of a tapestry of meaningful environmental objects, Moore advises that each environmental object, or collection of objects – the whole tapestry, contains the frame through which *Genius loci* emerges.

The scalar relationship between environmental objects and their place accords with the isomorphic nature of Actor Networks. Michael Callon and Bruno Latour (1981, p. 280) claim a fractal relationship for Actor Networks within a common frame. ANT suggests a formulaic pattern of environmental objects will give rise to a predictable spirit of place.

Bingham and Thrift (2000, p. 291) describe Actor Networks with a geophysical metaphor. The spirit exhibits dynamic behaviour, Dunkery Hill's phenomenology rises and falls by the hour or the season. Phenomenological contours can be experienced that vary with time of day or time of year. Visitors appear to stop and rest at lunch time and hunting takes place only in the due season. As both Lane (1988, p. 15) and Abram (1996, p. 211) remark, the ebbing and flowing of spirit of place is both centripetal and centrifugal. Metaphysical entities are equally as important as the physical and, in the example of Lorna Doone, time slows down where her spirit manifests. Mood is important to *Genius loci*. In contrast, the spirit of the Beast of Exmoor is more likely to be fleetingly encountered by marginalised locals than happy holidaymakers seeking stability and recreation through the myth of Lorna Doone.

Myths, legends and interpretive texts are cloned by the heritage industry. Long-distance control or teleonomy through spirit of place is dependent not only on the printing press, but on determined and repeated movement of appropriate mobile tokens through the landscape. Carrying a guide book suits this purpose admirably. Exmoor *Genius loci* has the potential to emerge whenever and wherever the book is opened. The centripetal nature of sacred place drew the visitor to purchase the guide book and the centrifugal nature of sacred place guides the visitor out into the landscape to open their book and raise the spirit in a new, but arguably predetermined place. The visitor drawn to or encouraged to Dunkery Beacon is unlikely to be fully aware of the guiding power behind their action. Way-markers may be obvious, managed *Genius loci* is not.

Conclusions

In arguing for sacred site and species status at Dunkery Beacon, I have based my argument on Norberg-Schultz's theory of *Genius loci* emerging from tensions between society and nature. Belden Lane (1988, p. 13) refers to the sacred effect of the clearing in the woods, the secret garden. In the classical landscape, spirit of place emerges where nature is tended, as in the managed plagioclimax of Exmoor. Mundane natural species acquire sacred status attracting the visitor to re-create in their presence and return to working life refreshed by the experience. From moorland walks to hunting and fishing, secular sacred species play an almost inestimable role in re-creating the holidaymaker. Visitor recreation services no doubt make very accurate commercial estimates of the value of the heather, ponies, hedges, deer, salmon and pheasants to the Exmoor economy.

Focused on Dunkery Beacon, the landscape of Exmoor frames both a physical and cognitive environment in which the selected actors, upon which the spirit of place depends, move around in a predetermined manner. Since the Enlightenment the secular English nation has transferred religious doctrine away from worship of a paternal deity to conservation of natural heritage. At Dunkery Beacon, the Holy Ghost has morphed into the Spirit of Exmoor.

The secular spirit flows along Actor Networks, metaphorical rhizomes emerging wherever the name Exmoor appears. Exmoor ale may appear at a distant beer festival; the tourist brochure may be posted to a far country. Exmoor hotels draw visitors to a specific place where human guides or brochures lead to Dunkery Beacon. *Genius loci* can be associated with the smallest locality to the widest region (Muir, 1999, p. 273).

As if to emphasise the sacredness of the site, the hilltop cairn suggests the classical *axis mundi* linking heaven and earth. Belden Lane advises that *axis mundi* indicates sacred place is a construction of the imagination (Lane, 1988, p. 15). Here the situation is reversed. Environmental predetermination maintains a secular spirituality through physical construction. The cairn, or *axis mundi*, at Dunkery Beacon draws its 'pilgrims' toward it; the site was not chosen by its visitors as a place for spiritual recreation. Through repeated performance, it is an ordinary place ritually made extraordinary. As remembered place, it can be trod upon but not entered, for its spirit emerges from visitor imagination or guide book. Its impulse is both local and universal. These four axioms make Dunkery Beacon a sacred site with sacred species (Lane 1988, p. 15). It is a sacred site in the secular landscape of modern England.

References

Abram, D. (1996). *The Spell of the Sensuous: Perception and Language in a More-than-human World*. New York, NY: Vintage Books.

Ballantyne, A. (1997). *Architecture, Landscape and Liberty: Richard Payne Knight and the Picturesque*. Cambridge: Cambridge University Press.

Bell, M. M. (1994). *Childerley: Nature and Morality in a Country Village*. Chicago, IL: University of Chicago Press.

Bender, B. (1998). *Stonehenge: Making Space*. Oxford: Berg.

Bingham, N. and Thrift, N. (2000). Some new instructions for travellers: the geography of Bruno Latour and Michel Serres. In *Thinking Space*, ed. M. Crang and N. Thrift. London: Routledge, pp. 281–301.

Blacksell, M. (1997). After the flood: images of Exmoor as a National Park. In *The Changing Face of Exmoor*, ed. H. Binding. Tiverton, Devon: Exmoor Books, pp. 95–102.

Bradley, J. R. (ed.) (1964). *The Letters of John Ruskin to Lord and Lady Mount-Temple*. Columbus, OH: Ohio State University Press. Available from http://www.ohiostatepress.org/index.htm?/books/book%20pages/bradley%20letters.htm (accessed 3 October 2007).

Brook, I. (1998). Goethean science as a way to read landscape. *Landscape Research*, **23**, 51–69.

Callon, M. and Latour, B. (1981). Unscrewing the Big Leviathan: how actors macro-structure reality and how sociologists help them do so. In *Advances in Social Theory and Methodology. Toward an Integration of Micro- and Macro-sociologies*, ed. K. Knorr-Cetina and A. V. Cicourel. Boston, MA: Routledge and Keegan Paul, pp. 277–303.

Camden, W. (1586). *Britannia*. See *Camden's Britannia, newly translated by E. Gibson* (1695, 4th edn 1772).

Castree, N. (2004). Commentary: nature is dead! Long live nature! *Environment and Planning A*, **36**, 191–4.

Dent, A. (1974). *Lost Beasts of Britain*. London: Harrap and Co.

Fibischer, B. (1998). Genius loci – between myth and reality. *Exhibition Catalogue*. Kunsthalle, Bern, Switzerland.

Foucault, M. (1967). *Of Other Spaces* (lecture paper). Available at: www.http://foucault.info/documents/heteroTopia/foucault.heteroTopia.en.html (accessed 16 October 2007).

Furbank, P. N., Owens, W. R. and Couldon, A. J. (eds). (1991). *Daniel Defoe. A Tour through the Whole Island of Great Britain*. New Haven, CT and London: Yale University Press.

Gomes, L. (2005). *Imagining Eden: Connecting Landscapes*. Charlottesville, VA: University of Virginia Press.

Hillyard, S. (2007). *The Sociology of Rural Life*. Oxford: Berg.

Hoare, P. (2005). *England's Lost Eden: Adventures in a Victorian Utopia*. London: Fourth Estate.

Ingold, T. (1995). Building, dwelling, living: how people and animals make themselves at home in the world. In *Shifting Contexts: Transformations in Anthropological Knowledge*, ed. M. Strathern. London: Routledge, pp. 57–80.

Kant, I. (1781). *Critique of Pure Reason*.

Lane, B. C. (1988). *Landscapes of the Sacred*. New York, NY: Paulist Press.

Massey, D. (2005). *For Space*. London: Sage Publications.

Matless, D. (1998). *Landscape and Englishness*. London: Reaktion Books.

Maturana, H. R. and Varela, F. J. (1980). *Autopoiesis and Cognition: The Realization of the Living*. Dordrecht: D. Reidel.

Moore, R. (2006). The framing paradox. *Ethics, Place and Environment*, **9**, 249–67.

Muir, R. (1999). *Approaches to Landscape*. London: Routledge.

Norberg-Schultz, C. (1979). *Genius Loci: Towards a Phenomenology of Architecture*. New York, NY: Rizzoli.

Olwig, K. (1984). *Nature's Ideological Landscape*. London: George Allen and Unwin.

Pearce, B. (2001). *Exmoor: The Official National Park Guide*. Pevensey Guides. Newton Abbot: David and Charles.

Pile, S. and Keith, M. (1997). *Geographies of Resistance*. London: Routledge.

Shaffer, E. (1970). Metaphysics of culture: Kant and Coleridge's aids to reflection. *Journal of the History of Ideas*, **31**, 199–218.

Spirin, A. W. (1998). *The Language of Landscape*. Newhaven, CT: Yale University Press.

Trevelyan, G. M. (1929). *Must England's Beauty Perish?* London: Faber and Gwyer.

Waterson, M. (1994). *The National Trust: The First Hundred Years*. London: BBC Books and National Trust (Enterprises) Ltd.

Webb, N. (1986). *Heathlands*. London: Collins.

Wylie, J. (2007). Learning to see ghosts: imperatives for spectral geographies, (unpublished paper), University of Exeter seminar, 21 February 2007.

PART III   SACRED SITES AND PEOPLE

9

The landscape in the cosmoscape, and sacred sites and species among the Tanimuka and Yukuna Amerindian tribes (north-west Amazon)

ELIZABETH REICHEL

Introduction

This chapter investigates the relevance of the Tanimuka and Yukuna notions that landscape dynamics are composed of horizontal linkages between peoples and habitats, and also of vertical linkages connecting peoples with the skies, world and underworlds through material and spiritual dynamics. It examines how sacred sites and species in rainforests and in swidden and anthropogenic landscapes are used to monitor socio-environmental well-being, and how they are used as references to shamanically negotiate and calibrate human existence with the supra-natural forces and 'Guardian Spirit/Owners' (henceforth called Guardians) of the rainforests and with other Guardians of the planet and universe. It discusses how, according to the shamanic cosmologies of the Tanimuka and Yukuna, the sacred sites and species are associated with events related to the origin, evolution and destiny of their societies, and to the rest of humanity, life, the world and the universe, and inquires how the ethno-eco-cosmic linkages pass through the sacred sites and species connecting the landscape to the cosmoscape. While indicating how this shamanic framework assesses synergies between humans and the rest of the biosphere, world and cosmos, this chapter explains how this system is applied by the Tanimuka and Yukuna to enhance socio-environmental resilience.

Sacred Species and Sites: Advances in Biocultural Conservation, ed. Gloria Pungetti, Gonzalo Oviedo and Della Hooke. Published by Cambridge University Press. © Cambridge University Press 2012.

The Colombian Amazon and indigenous peoples

The Amazon rainforest exists in nine countries, of which Colombia is one. For the last 11 000 years, indigenous peoples have inhabited Amazonia while developing a large diversity of cultures, languages and resource management strategies. During the past five centuries, the Amerindians have been impacted by genocide, ethnocide and environmental degradation accompanying the expansion of non-indigenous societies. More recently, the accrued destruction of Amazonia with deforestation, habitat degradation and unsustainable exploitation of natural resources have been threatening traditional Amerindian cultures and their sound ways of safeguarding the rainforests.

However, in the Colombian Amazon, many Amerindian societies are highly resilient. Amerindian cosmologies, worldviews and modes of life have reaped lessons for socio-environmental sustainability based on their millenarian history in the region and their profound sense of identification with the rainforests. Various traditional Amerindian cultures live in their ancestral territories and maintain their own systems of shamanism, kinship, socio-political organisation, residence, and environmental management systems that are highly adaptive to rainforest ecosystems. As such, many Amerindians achieve the well-being of their communities and a sound use and conservation of natural resources by sustaining distinctive cultures and their spiritual and pragmatic approaches to live within the Amazon rainforests (Lévi-Strauss, 1962; Reichel-Dolmatoff, 1976, 1996). It is important to recognise that these Amerindians do not make the Western-type opposition between nature and culture (Descola, 1996) because they profoundly understand how humans are part of ecosystems.

The Colombian Amazon (35% of the country) covers 477 274 km^2 (COAMA, 2010a), and is inhabited by 800 000 non-indigenous persons (in urban centres and colonisation fronts), and also by 96 261 Amerindian indigenous persons from 52 different ethno-linguistic groups belonging to 13 linguistic families and 10 language isolates (COAMA, 2010b) and this area of the north-west Amazon is characterised by high cultural diversity. During recent decades, with advances in legislation supported by the Colombian government, along with the achievements of indigenous organisations, dynamics of non-governmental organisations and civil society, and progress in national, regional and international fora concerned with the Amazon region, there has been a growing valuation of indigenous communities for the conservation of Amazon rainforests as bastions of life on earth and to mitigate climate change. At present, two-thirds of the Colombian Amazon have been legally designated for nature conservation, sustainable development, and for the protection of indigenous territories and cultures. In the area, 179 'Resguardo' (inalienable and collectively owned territories) have been titled, which cover approximately half of the Amazon region (COAMA, 2010b; Gaia Amazonas Foundation, 2010a). Some Resguardo territories overlap with official protected areas and altogether these cover 62% of the Amazon and are pivotal for the conservation of the rainforests and biocultural diversity (*ibid.*).

In Colombia, the indigenous peoples' rights and their contributions to the Colombian nation have been increasingly recognised. The Constitution of 1991 recognises the multi-ethnic and pluri-cultural composition of the nation, and acknowledges the importance of indigenous peoples' roles in sustainable development and environmental conservation. Further developments of legislation are underway along with decentralisation processes that engage indigenous participation in governance and decision-making.

The future success of countries such as Colombia to safeguard the Amazon rainforests and achieve socio-ecological sustainability, while contributing to mitigation and adaptation measures to climate change, will largely depend on protecting biocultural diversity and the diverse Amerindian modes of conserving the rainforests and biodiversity-rich anthropogenic landscapes. This is feasible in regions such as those inhabited by the Tanimuka and Yukuna Indians (Figure 9.1) who maintain well-conserved rainforests, watersheds, and high agrobiodiversity by upholding their maloca community-based modes of life and their traditional ecological knowledge as well as their resource management strategies based on a deep shamanic spirituality that has ensured the sustainability of their communities, rainforests and agroecosystems through time-proven and culturally unique ways.

The Tanimuka 'Ash People' and the Yukuna 'Story Tellers'

In the Amazon rainforests near the equatorial line, by the lower Apaporis and Caquetá rivers, live two allied inter-marrying tribes: the Tanimuka 'Ash People' (Opaina or Ufaina), numbering 400 individuals (von Hildebrand, 1975, 1984), and the Yukuna 'Story Tellers', composed of the Kemehéya, Heruriwa Peccary people, Hurumi, Imiké Herb people, Piyoti Anaconda People, and the Matapi Upichia (Reichel, 1987c, p. 197; 1997, p. 63), altogether numbering 900 persons. These two tribes numbered thousands of people a century ago (von Hildebrand and Reichel, 1987; Whiffen, 1915), but were decimated by the Rubber Boom, genocide, colonisation, epidemics, forced labour, forced relocation and ethnocide. Yet their cultural resilience is high and they are nowadays among the most traditional tribes of the Colombian Amazon.

The Tanimuka and Yukuna live in well-conserved and highly biodiverse rainforests and swidden fields. They manage these ecosystems and their ancestral territories through networks of enormous 'maloca' communal roundhouses

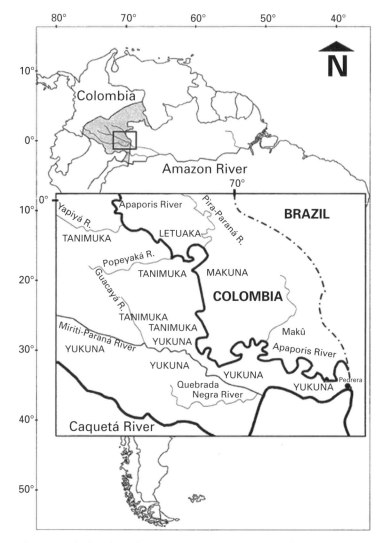

Figure 9.1 The location of Tanimuka and Yukuna Indians (© Elizabeth Reichel).

(Figure 9.2). Each maloca roundhouse (henceforth called maloca) is 30 m in diameter and 30 m high, and the symbolism of its architecture is related to the structure of the cosmos to remind its inhabitants they are part of the environment and of the dynamics of the larger world and cosmos (Reichel, 1987a, 1987c, 1997; Reichel and von Hildebrand, 1985; von Hildebrand, 1975, 1984, 1987). However, in spite of five centuries of forced acculturation to change their modes of subsistence, to live in individual permanent houses, to speak Spanish and not to speak their Amerindian languages, the Tanimuka and Yukuna have resiliently maintained their indigenous languages, maloca *habitus*, shamanism and modes of life.

Figure 9.2 A maloca communal roundhouse (© Elizabeth Reichel). See colour plate section.

The two tribes are semi-sedentary maloca dwellers with traditional modes of subsistence based on sustainable shifting cultivation and sustainable hunting, gathering and fishing. Cash, incomes and merchandises are obtained by participating in the market economy through the commercialisation of rainforest products, wage labour, and by resources received for community-based projects made in association with the central or local governments, or with non-governmental organisations (NGOs), private organisations, local traders and other entities. During recent decades, the Tanimuka and Yukuna have been involved in the Colombian government's decentralisation processes where indigenous organisations (such as Associations and Resguardos) form part of local governments with political, administrative and fiscal functions. They engage in co-governance, for example, related to the provision of public services such as health and education, and also in income-generation projects and natural resource management. These include projects that safeguard the rainforests with indigenous cultural and spiritual traditions.

The Tanimuka and Yukuna inhabit an area south of the Vaupés, a region renowned for its high cultural and linguistic diversity through the practices of multilingualism. The high biocultural diversity is linked to the diversity of languages, cultures, modes of subsistence, as well as to the ecological applications of Amerindian shamanism, modes of subsistence, cosmologies and worldviews that have ensured sustainable communities and ecosystems (Reichel-Dolmatoff, 1976, 1996).

The region that is inhabited by the Eastern Tukano-speaking Tanimuka and the Arawak-speaking Yukuna has high biocultural diversity with 10 or more different indigenous cultures and languages, in addition to the non-Amerindian populations (von Hildebrand and Reichel, 1987). Biocultural diversity is further enhanced by each Tanimuka or Yukuna tribe's own socio-ecological dynamics within its traditional territories and by their specialised stewardship of particular ecosystems and of wild and domesticated species. In addition, there are specific cultural and environmental synergies proper to each maloca's patrilineal segment who, functioning as a multi-family household, manages a particular section of their ancestral territories. Biocultural diversity is also promoted by alliances between the Tanimuka and Yukuna through marriage patterns, but also by ceremonial exchanges of food, seeds and goods, as well as by exchanges of information for joint pan-regional environmental management and maintenance of biodiversity corridors. Furthermore, biocultural diversity is enhanced by gender-based landscapes where the men and women have distinctive responsibilities, knowledge, practices and property rights to manage and conserve specific sectors of rainforests, anthropogenic landscapes and swidden plots.

Each Tanimuka and Yukuna tribe has ranked patrilineages divided into senior and junior patrilineages that manage specific territories and ecosystems (seniors upriver and juniors downriver). Patrilocal rules require that married women live in their husband's terrains. Through the preferred patterns of sister-exchange and matrilateral cross-cousin marriage, the women shuttle between the two tribes' territories. Hence a married woman adapts her ecological knowledge to her husband's territories as she creates her swidden fields. Due to principles of patrilocality and patrilinearity, the men stay in their own ancestral territories where, for generations, they upgrade their knowledge of their terrains, monitor changes in socio-ecological dynamics, and are vigilant of their communities' well-being.

A maloca household is composed of a group of brothers with their spouses and children, and it houses an agnatic patrilineal segment which is a community (ranging from 5 to 20 or more people) that owns and manages specific territories. Each maloca has mosaics of landscapes comprising the maloca residence area (a new maloca is built nearly every decade or so) surrounded by a patio with a ring of *Bactris gasipaes* peach palms and housegardens; in the jungle there are dozens of scattered women's two-hectare 'chagra' swidden fields and fallow fields; and in the rainforests the men's hunting, gathering and fishing areas. Additionally, each maloca owns river sections, ports, creeks and jungle trails. Every maloca territory has sacred sites and species that are identified to the tribe and to the specific patrilineage of the maloca, which mark their long-term co-evolution within particular ecosystems and anthropogenic landscapes.

Maloca households recreate their ethos and eidos through a solid endorsement of their shamanic cosmology, maloca *habitus*, and modes of subsistence, and each individual and community is held responsible for achieving socio-environmental well-being while respecting the sacred sites and species. The role of gender-based dynamics in this context is important, as men and women have specialised responsibilities to maintain socio-ecological sustainability and its material and spiritual dimensions.

Gender-based knowledge and practices, and gender-based landscapes

The Tanimuka and Yukuna have gender-based knowledge, practices, innovations and skills for resource management, and the men and women configure different landscapes and rainforest ecosystems. Men and women's gender-based knowledge systems (Reichel, 1987b, 1987c, 1999a, 1999b, 2005) or gender-based traditional knowledge are applied for the sustainable use and conservation of each maloca's terrains and biodiversity.

Biocultural diversity is enhanced by the production of gender-based landscapes as women manage swidden fields and housegardens and conserve the bulk of agrobiodiversity, while the men manage and conserve the rainforests and procure wild animal species and wild and semi-domesticated plant species. There is thus a complementary, but differentiated, gender-based traditional ecological knowledge held between men and women. Tanimuka and Yukuna mythology and historical memory details with encyclopaedic references the long evolutionary processes involving each gender's configuration of the rainforests and anthropogenic landscapes and agrobiodiversity for millennia.

Although, traditionally, the men use, own and conserve vast expanses of the rainforests to hunt, fish and gather, they also cultivate – and own – three types of domesticated crops in the women's swidden fields: these are the (sacred) mind-altering plants such as tobacco and coca, and also the pineapples with which men make fermented brews (Reichel, 1987b, 1987c, 1999b). Men also tend the peach palm (*Bactris gasipaes*) semi-domesticated palms near the maloca, and are also vigilant of other edible and useful species of semi-domesticated and wild fruit trees and palm groves in wetlands and rainforests.

The men are responsible for protecting the thousands of sacred species and sites within the rainforests by maintaining spiritual connections with these and by preventing over-fishing, over-hunting, over-gathering and over-exploitation of sacred sites and species. Men are the custodians of the shamanic knowledge about the function of these in the rainforest ecosystems, and also of their significance in socio-environmental co-evolution. Because patrilineal agnatic kin own and inherit their ancestral territories, along with ritual artefacts and sacred knowledge, for generations the men transmit among themselves (usually father to son) detailed knowledge and expertise of their local ecosystems and history. The men also transmit corpuses of shamanic knowledge which include the location of the Guardians of sacred sites and species within their ancestral territories and also the specific behaviours, rituals and prayers related to these.

In a maloca, each brother, according to birth order, has specialised knowledge to hold the role of being: maloca headman, senior or junior shaman, singer-chanter, ritual expert such as tobacco roller, pineapple brew maker, ceremonial leader of male initiation rituals, and intercultural mediator (von Hildebrand and Reichel, 1987; Reichel, 1999a, 1999b). Each of these roles implies specialised knowledge and responsibilities regarding the management of specific sacred sites and species as well as expertise in knowing these in their macro- and micro-biocultural dynamics. The senior 'Jaguar-Eye/Seer' shamans tend to be the encyclopaedic knowledge-holders of all the sacred sites and species of a maloca terrain, although all the men have a general shamanic knowledge and share responsibility of the sacred sites and species in their maloca teritories. On a daily basis when men hunt, gather and fish, they assess the condition of the sacred sites and species as indicators of sound shamanic management and of socio-ecological resilience, and observations of degrading sites or species are taken as a warning to redress failing socio-environmental dynamics.

Sisters, according to birth order within their families, will accumulate specialised knowledge for the roles of: maloca headwoman; expert with a 'good hand' in agriculture and in manioc processing and food preparation; pottery maker; hammock-weaver; chili pepper expert; manioc cultivar specialist; and intercultural mediator. Every married woman has two or more 'chagra' swidden plots. The women select, plant, weed, harvest and use a large diversity of root and tuber crops, and also tend fruit trees, as each woman configures her own swidden plots and agro-biodiversity. In their swidden plots, each woman 'owns' particular crop varieties, for example of bitter manioc, chili peppers, sweet potato, yams, lulo (*Solanum quitoense*), yota (*Colocasia* sp.), and they also tend fruit trees such as guama (*Inga* spp.), Amazon grape (*Pourouma cecropiifolia*), caimo (*Pouteria caimito*) and others. Women know the characteristics as well as the history and names of previous owners of their food plants. The women are also responsible for looking after the fruit trees and cultivars in the housegardens encircling the maloca. They also maintain fallowed fields where they procure firewood, fruits and other foods until the fields become secondary forests.

Although women only have usufruct rights of the swidden fields in their husband's ancestral territories, each woman controls her own swidden plot, and women own the vast majority of the cultivated plants. Women have an encyclopaedic knowledge of hundreds of domesticated plant varieties, in addition to knowledge of soil management and conservation, and of pest and disease control and women transmit among each other their expertise of sustainable shifting agriculture, agro-biodiversity and of traditional food systems (Reichel, 1987b, 1987c, 1989, 1999a, 1999b).

Co-resident women exchange knowledge about agriculture and food preparation and also negotiate access to each other's plant cultivars; in turn, women visiting other maloca also negotiate access to particular cultivars. A mother-in-law may give cultivars and associated knowledge of these to her daughter-in-law, although it is mainly mothers who transmit to their daughters their plants, seeds, tubers, roots and cuttings, and the associated plant knowledge and skills, in addition to their knowledge of the sacred female Guardians who are allies of women, reproduction, agricultural productivity, and of soil and water sustainability.

Sustainable resource use and enchanted landscapes and forests

Tanimuka and Yukuna shamanism is intent on the long-term harmonisation of human lives with the rest of nature while achieving communal and environmental well-being. Maloca people follow the shamanic ethos of a cautious use of resources that prevents, or redresses, the non-sustainable use of natural resources while respecting the sacrality of the Earth and the rainforests by maintaining the resilience of sacred sites and species that enable vital connectivities and spiritual linkages between people and the rest of nature, the world and cosmos. The respect for sacred sites and species has a high correlation with the well-conserved biodiversity of these, and the conservation of ecosystems is especially high in the sacred origin sites of each tribe and of patrilineages and also in sacred sites where animals and plants are said to be especially powerful, or vulnerable when they reproduce, migrate or develop in certain seasons, times and places. Biodiversity conservation and watershed conditions are usually optimal in the highly supervised, sacred no-go areas protected from human habitation and negative environmental impacts.

Shamans engage in 'shamanic consultations' with the Guardians of sacred sites and species in order to assess socio-environmental resilience in the short, mid and long term, and also to plan present and future changes in socio-environmental conditions. Important shamanic rituals that consult sacred sites and species are made in situations such as in carrying out foraging and swidden agriculture; in rites of passage during an individual's life cycle; in rites of affliction when people are sick or dying; and also in the large two-day (and night) chronotype rituals that celebrate the start of each yearly cycle with shamanic ceremonies/dances and also mark the start and end of dozens of seasons within the year; in addition to other rituals demarcating spatio-temporal changes in human–environmental dynamics. Rituals consulting Guardians are also made to determine important decisions such as where and when forest plots are cleared and when residential sites and swidden fields are created or abandoned, or smaller decisions concerned with obtaining clay and making pottery.

Shamans say they communicate, 'In Thought' ('Pensamiento' in Spanish) or Spirit, with the Guardians of sacred sites and species and with other Guardians in this world, the skies and underworlds. They say they negotiate with them their people's predicament and their access to resources, as they 'jointly calculate' the effects of human activities in local ecosystems. The shamans estimate the number of human lives that must optimally exist in relation to the number of the 'people' of plants and animals, and of other ecosystem dynamics, and they 'pay' Guardians with human deaths or other offerings. The shamans 'explain' to the Guardians why a resource is needed, and they request 'permission', 'pay' and 'compensate' the Guardians for the resources that humans use in a given activity and season.

Shamanic consultations with Guardians related to sacred sites and species are made throughout the year in each seasonal chronotope ritual to balance human activities with local ecosystems and with the forces of the earth, subsoils, atmosphere, weather, waters and the Amazon river. During these rituals, the shamans 'think ahead how people will live in the future' during the coming seasons, years, decades and centuries, as they estimate how the activities of their maloca people will affect future generations and ecosystems. The past, present and future socio-environmental dynamics of each maloca are considered in the context of neighbouring communities, the rest of humanity, and of the larger planet and cosmos.

These cosmological templates are used to re-create, as well as to debate, the Tanimuka and Yukuna's understanding of cosmo-eco-ethnogenesis and to explain the position of their tribe, maloca patrilineage, and individuals therein. These Amerindians hold that they have been safeguarding the rainforests and anthropogenic landscapes successfully because they 'respect the sacred' dimension of their ancestral territories, rainforests, and agro-biodiversity while adhering to the wisdom of their ancestors, respecting the ancient laws of nature, and nurturing their material and spiritual bonds with the rainforests, biosphere, world and cosmos.

The cosmoscape, and the axes and linkages of the cosmological sites and species

The Tanimuka and the Yukuna consider sacred sites and species as privileged axes that maintain the connections between their peoples and the Earth, the skies, and the underworlds, linking their landscapes to the cosmos. The cosmoscape, as a culture's overarching model and template of the shape and scope

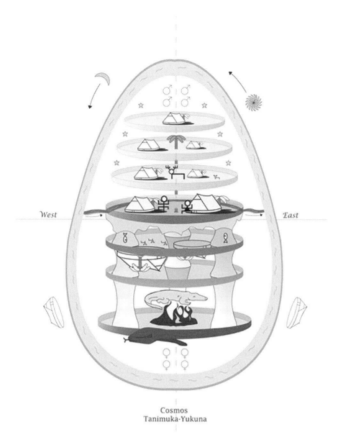

West   East

Cosmos
Tanimuka-Yukuna

Figure 9.3 Cosmos Tanimuka and Yukuna (© Elizabeth Reichel). See colour plate section.

of the cosmos, is a representation and a shared imagery of the visual form of the universe and of the structure and function of the whole universe or cosmos.

The Tanimuka and the Yukuna cosmoscape can be visualised, for the purpose of this research, as a cosmos (Figure 9.3) composed of superimposed levels that represent: six skies above, the Earth in the middle, and six underworlds below, and a surrounding cosmic river that is connected to the Amazon river and its west–east axis (inverse direction to that of the east–west 'Path of the Sun'). In the centre of all of the levels there is a sacred tree or a palm that holds the sacred centres of the Earth, skies and underworlds. All the levels of the cosmos are interconnected with special links, either permanently or seasonally. In the Tanimuka and Yukuna territories in this world/Earth, the linkages with the other levels of the cosmos are mainly through the central and cardinal axes and also through the sacred sites and species which are the axes where special flows of matter and of spirit and ancestral forces connect all the levels. The number of skies and underworlds varies slightly between the Tanimuka and the Yukuna, but the shape of the cosmos, and the cosmology, are similar, although details of the cosmo-geo-bio-ethnogenesis differs between these two tribes because they refer to different ancestral territories and ecosystems, and to particular historical trajectories (Reichel, 1987c, 1997, 1999a, 1999b; Reichel and von Hildebrand, 1985; von Hildebrand, 1975, 1984, 1987; von Hildebrand and Reichel, 1987).

The cosmoscape is a reference of the complex whole within which the Tanimuka and Yukuna define their existence; it is also a model that portrays in its structure and functioning their tribal (proto-chiefdom) social organisation, maloca *habitus*, shamanism, senior–junior patrilineal ranking, and the gender relations (Reichel, 1987c, 1999a). Each layer of the cosmos is considered to be composed of a maloca with landscape mosaics. This imagery of maloca dynamics is also applied to describe the Guardians of sacred sites and species who are considered to be maloca chiefs/senior Jaguar shamans with their own people, and the ecosystems of sacred sites are paralleled to the maloca's landscape units. As such, the cosmos and its levels are represented as networks of juxtaposed and superposed interacting maloca (Reichel, 1989).

The Tanimuka and Yukuna notion of the landscape in the cosmoscape is remarkably used as a framework for ecological awareness based on pragmatic and enchanted approaches to maintain communal and environmental well-being. These Amerindians hold that they have an ancient pact with the Guardians to respect the spiritual forces and material flows which sustain the Amazon rainforests and river which safeguard not only local but also the larger planetary and cosmic dynamics. They also hold that their society is responsible to 'well manage the world' (von Hildebrand, 1975, 1984; von Hildebrand and Reichel, 1987; van der Hammen, 1993) and the rainforests where they have been co-evolving for millennia.

Human over-consumption of plant or animal species, destruction of rainforests, erosion of river banks, and degrading sacred sites and species are deemed acts that gravely disrespect the spiritual basis of existence because they endanger life and the spiritual balance of humans with the rest of the world and cosmos. The Tanimuka and Yukuna believe that human usurpation of an ecosystem's or a species' spirit, or the unwary or unruly dispersion of the spirit of sacred ecosystems and species, not only destroys nature but also make people spiritually polluted as they become destructive, ill, or die. The mismanaged or usurped spirit is defined as 'poisonous' and is associated with ecosystem dynamics and socio-environmental systems that are inadequate or 'out of place'. Shamans seek to detect such dysfunctions and they 'gather, "send back", and "put into its rightful place" the straying poisonous' spirits by cautious shamanic intercession to detoxify and 'cure the world'. Each shaman counsels their maloca community to strive for proper conditions of healthy species, ecosystems, seasons, and of sound socio-ecological dynamics by being mindful of their spiritual and material conditions.

When people open clearings in the rainforests to make a new house or swidden field, or seek to access a key natural resource, the shaman makes detailed calculations of environmental supply and demand, and negotiates with the Guardians the advisable scale and timing of human activities. He pacts the material exchanges but also 'sends back' or 'keeps in its proper place' the spiritual forces of the resources or ecosystem dynamics, while he calculates socio-environmental dynamics needed to balance human lives with the rest of nature. In principle, not only humans but also each species is supposed to keep its own spirit within a closed circuit and only material exchanges are allowed between species. Hence, when people want to use specific flora, fauna, soils and also water resources, the shamans seek that the spirit stays with its proper Guardian so that species and ecosystem dynamics maintain their function, while the access to the material part is negotiated with the Guardians as an inter-systemic and inter-species material transaction.

Thus, when hunting particular animals such as a tapir or deer or fishing for a specific fish species, a person of a maloca, via the shaman, must ask the Guardian of that species to 'send' specific numbers of animals which can be hunted. A hunter or fisher should only take the animal's body or its 'matter', and the animal is said to 'offer' the hunter its 'shirt' which is shamanically exchanged/paid with human lives, actions and shamanic payments such as coca and tobacco. Ideally, an animal or plant should be eaten without consuming its spirit, which must stay with its 'own people' and Guardian so that a similar animal or plant can be born. This form of shamanic calculation is based on a cosmological model whereby people, ecosystems and all that exists are considered to be part of a circuit of limited energy/spirit and matter (von Hildebrand, 1975, 1984; Reichel-Dolmatoff, 1976) existing in the biosphere, world and universe and which require careful balancing. However, according to the Tanimuka and Yukuna, the matter and bodies of the humans and non-humans can be exchanged, consumed and transformed through balanced reciprocity and redistribution, while the spirit is not to be exchanged across different species (and the human/non-human units), in order to maintain essential differences and identities and also to enhance biodiversity and promote diversity within the world and universe.

The sequences of the material exchanges and of the spiritual non-exchanges are shamanically recorded specifically in relation to the networks of sacred sites and species. Because sacred sites and species are linked to circuits of matter and spirit in the other layers of the skies, underworlds, Earth, the Amazon river and the Cosmic river, the material transfers and the spiritual separations imply two systems of articulation. This shamanic awareness of the material and spiritual dynamics is significant for ecosystem management and engages a dual form of socio-environmental accounting and balancing, a double monitoring system to cross-check and assess local and regional socio-environmental conditions which are also tracked in the contexts of a grander eco-cosmic whole as the landscape is part of the cosmoscape.

Myth and oral history refer to the creation of local ecosystems by supernatural beings and ancestors with founding acts that are marked in topographical traits as well as in the trajectories of rivers, and the shapes of hills and rock formations, and are also inscribed in rocks by petroglyphs along the rivers (Reichel, 1975) and in archaeological sites rich in pottery and '*terra preta*' soils (Reichel, 1976). These marks of ancestors and Guardians are not only present in particular sacred sites and species, but also in the finer details of the characteristics of their flora and fauna, soils and waters, including features such as their shape, colour, sound, odour and taste.

Although some sacred sites refer to the origins of the Tanimuka or Yukuna as ethnic groups and patrilineages, other sites refer to the direction of human migrations and travel routes, as well as to mythical and historical ancestors' experimentations with different types of wildlife and domesticated species, and with diverse models of residence, marriage, and of demographic and resource management systems. Other sacred sites mark burial grounds, battle grounds, and places where fission or fusion between patrilineages took place. Among the Yukuna these sites are linked to the historical memory of over 10 generations of named patrilineages (Reichel, 1989, p. 198; van der Hammen, 1993) and form part of cosmological, historical, and mythic narratives which also refer to centuries of relations with the non-indigenous 'White people' and to national and international contexts.

Because the cosmoscape is an image and template used by the Tanimuka and Yukuna to concatenate, define and position their societies within the rest of humanity, life, the world and cosmos, they believe that each society is to 'take care' of its own slice of the universe that is composed of interacting dynamics of skies, the Earth and the underworlds, and also with the larger hydrological system (linked with the Amazon river) in order to maintain the rainforests and to achieve socio-environmental sustainability. However, they are aware that presently many non-indigenous societies have lost their knowledge of achieving socio-environmental sustainability. In order to maintain the wisdom of their Amerindian ancestors, heed the admonitions of the Guardians of the sacred sites and species, and also to participate in innovative forms of co-governance which the Colombian State supports, the indigenous organisations, Resguardo and Associations of traditional authorities (AATI) are articulating their cultures and spirituality within the context of intercultural dynamics for the development and conservation of the Amazon (see Gaia and COAMA, 2010b; AATI, COAMA, 2010).

Indigenous sacred species

Amerindians, across the Americas, have sacred species that are plant species and varieties as well as animal breeds and species, and they also have sacred microorganisms. These sacred species are those with whom indigenous societies have special spiritual links due to a common existence and interdependence, and also because they have been nurturing, conserving and caring for them (and they have been caring for each other). These sacred species are cosmological species because they allow humans unique connectivities with the larger spiritual and material dynamics not only of the rainforests, agrobiodiversity, life, and the biosphere, but of the world and cosmos. Sacred species of plants and animals are also used to make cosmological artefacts and shamanic paraphernalia that spiritually link their users to the wider world and cosmos.

Among the Tanimuka and Yukuna tribes, there are hundreds of sacred domesticated plant species and varieties, and also of semi-domesticated and wild plants, as well as of wild animal species. Some sacred species are related to Guardians identified to the origins of each ethnic tribe and to the mythic and historical ancestors of all Tanimuka or Yukuna, while others are linked to senior or junior patrilineages and gender-based groups. Many of these sacred species, and their location, are secret knowledge of the Tanimuka and Yukuna so they will not be considered in this chapter. Some animal and plant species associated with origins sites are considered sacred to the point that they cannot be killed or used, although other sacred species, in rainforest or anthropogenic landscapes, can be used with shamanic mediation.

There are different types of sacred animal species, ranging from highly powerful and sacred animals that are only used with extreme precaution or not consumed at all, to those which are less powerful and can be used with shamanic care and by 'asking permission', 'paying' and 'thanking' its Guardians. When identification with a sacred animal species is considered to be one of close affinity or kinship, the species cannot be consumed by that group or can only be used with special shamanic negotiations. Dietary, behavioural and sexual restrictions also accompany accessing, killing or eating sacred animals.

Jaguars, giant otters, stingrays, caimans, anaconda, dolphins, eagles, egrets and other birds, among other animals, are considered sacred animals, and special ritual attitudes are due to them. Some sacred animals are never eaten, their habitats are not to be disturbed and people must have specific behavioural and spiritual approaches to these. For example, the sacred anaconda found in origin sites, sacred headwaters, palm groves, lakes, or other places are not killed or consumed, and they involve shamanic 'caring' for the species and its habitats. In turn, some sacred animals can be eaten or used and particular fish, deer, tapirs, caimans and other edible animals with sacred attributes are accessed while observing the shamanic prohibitions to not over-fish or over-hunt them, although these norms vary according to given contexts and seasons.

Some sacred animals are used to make ritual artefacts which are cosmological artefacts that allow spiritual linkages of humans to their ancestors and to the larger forces of the world and universe. The recognition that the natural resources and living beings that humans use are part of larger systems which engage complex vertical and horizontal connectivities between the layers of the universe, that connect the landscape to the cosmoscape, is very present in the fabrication and utilisation of these artefacts. For example, when men make sacred feather crowns, they engage in shamanic negotiations with ancestors and the Guardians in the skies (and seasonally observed astronomical phenomena and meteorological conditions) and with the Guardians of the sacred birds (egrets, eagles, toucans, etc.). In two-day (and night) ritual dances, the performances and shamanic chants describe the birds' characteristics, and also refer to the synergies between people, the birds, their habitats, and to dynamics beyond tribal territories. They also refer to the capacity of birds to travel across skies, Earth and water and to have a panoptic view of landscapes and multilevel connectivities.

Sacred animals require permanent or short-term food prohibitions which also refer to norms related to specific associations between sacred animal species and people but that also imply a specialisation in resource conservation. For example, the Yukuna Matapi avoid eating caiman, anteater and certain species of lizards, whilst other Yukuna groups, and the Tanimuka, are allowed to consume them (Reichel, 1987c, p. 201). However, both the Tanimuka and Yukuna avoid consuming or killing dolphins, otters and other sacred animals, especially top predators such as jaguars, that are considered to be powerful shamans.

In turn, sacred plant species and varieties have different degrees of sacredness and prohibitions related to their use and conservation. The most sacred plants pertain to species and varieties linked to the origins of the Tanimuka or the Yukuna tribes, patrilineages and gender-based groups, and also to territorial boundaries and sacred centres. Sacred plants are also used to make cosmological artefacts such as shamanic rattles. Sacred plant species and varieties such as sacred palms, coca, tobacco and other plants mark particular linkages between the plant world and Tanimuka and Yukuna patrilineages, and also between men and women.

Sacred palm groves are located in headwater regions and wetlands, and men avoid hunting or fishing in these areas or do so with extreme shamanic care. Sacred palms and trees linked to ethnic origin sites are believed to sustain the central axis connecting the skies, Earth and underworlds. Altering the habitats or cutting the sacred palms and trees or using their fruits, leaves or wood is considered dangerous when made without shamanic precautions. Sacred trees which have red and black hardwoods are used to make shamanic cosmological artefacts, such as ritual staffs. Other sacred plant species are used in shamanism, for example to make shamanic incenses, resins, dyes, paints and other shamanic paraphernalia, as well as medicinal cures and also poisons. Some sacred plants are used to build maloca architectural features, as well as to fabricate ritual masks and clothing. Hundreds of different sacred plant species and varieties are found in the rainforests and in swidden and fallowed fields, and they are used or conserved in daily life and ceremonies. There are differences, however, within the plants, and some varieties may be considered sacred while others are not; for instance, the plant varieties employed to make gourds used in shamanic rituals are considered sacred, but not the varieties used to make the gourds for daily food and drinks.

Tobacco, coca and other mind-altering plants used for 'shamanic thinking' are sacred species, as are the plants such as pineapples used to make fermented beverages (in turn associated with sacred yeasts or microorganisms for fermentation). Sacred plants are also used for body and facial paints that convey shamanic protection. The coca plant varieties are owned and tended by men in the women's swidden fields, and the layout of the planted cloned coca plants symbolises a sacred male ancestor. Coca and tobacco are considered to have a strong spiritual power which allows spiritual communication and shamanic 'Travelling in Thought' and 'Big Thought' to communicate by 'Jaguar Thought' with the Guardians of nature as these plants are used to 'see' and communicate with the invisible but powerful forces and spirits that maintain life, the world and the universe. Significantly, coca and tobacco are among the few sacred plants whose spirit can be accessed and ingested by shamans, and by adult men and elder women. The use of these mild mind-altering plants allows people to be part of a spiritual network of powerful people–plant connectivities and give heightened awareness of the linkages of the spirit forces of people, ancestors, rainforests and Guardians. Coca and tobacco are used by shamans as offerings or spiritual foods to 'pay' Guardians for human use of resources. Adult men consume coca and tobacco on a daily basis, and during large rituals, the men of kin and allied groups exchange their coca powder to express their intent to agree joint ways of 'thinking together' to enhance regional socio-environmental well-being while respecting the balances of the cosmo-geo-bio-ethno linkages.

Sacred sites

Indigenous sacred sites are areas, spaces, places and orientations that, for indigenous peoples, have profound spiritual significance as locations that designate the spiritual and material linkages of their peoples with the natural and supernatural forces in the heavens, Earth and underworlds. There are different types of sacred sites. Some are defined as no-go zones to be managed by shamans and elders, and others can be accessed, but always with shamanic intercession and spiritual cleanliness.

For the Tanimuka and the Yukuna, at a macro level, their ancestral territories as well as the rainforests are sacred, and within each ecosystem every sacred site is considered to involve a special trajectory of spiritual and material synergies linked with specific maloca patrilineages, communities and gender-based groups who care for them and 'look after them'. The Guardians of the sacred sites are considered as ancient shamanic Guardians who are sustaining key linkages of their maloca's landscapes to the greater cosmoscape.

In turn, some sacred sites refer to orientations such as the east and west cardinal points, and to the north, south, central, nadir and zenithal points, and also to intercardinal orientations. Their shamanic symbolism refers to the beginning or end of life, and to male and female power, and each site has different types of spiritual and healing powers (von Hildebrand, 1975, 1984). These orientations or points of reference are not only located in sites in their ancestral territories and maloca territories, but are also references within the maloca house layout and concatenate each maloca community with the larger dynamics of the world and universe, (Reichel and von Hildebrand, 1985; von Hildebrand, 1984). Each of these cardinal and intercardinal orientations is identified with sacred sites believed to connect earth, skies and underworlds; they also link the rainforests and Amazon river to larger hydrological cycles and the world and cosmos, and connect the past to the present and the future. The centre of the universe passes through the apex of the heavens, the skies and the centre of the world (and the sacred origin site of each ethnic tribal group, the 'navel of the world'), the centre of every maloca, and also through the underworlds and nadir. The sacred centre of the cosmoscape is associated with a sacred tree or palm, which is a different sacred species for the Tanimuka and the Yukuna said to maintain the vertical axis across the skies, Earth and underworlds and also to organise the branching of shamanic knowledge and power.

Some sacred sites refer to a macro-shamanic territory that pertains to the whole territory of the Tanimuka or Yukuna tribes that is conceptualised as part of a larger Amazonian macro-shamanic territory (van der Hammen 1993; von Hildebrand and Reichel, 1987; von Hildebrand, 1974, 1984). Within each tribe's territory there are sacred sites that are the origin sites of the Tanimuka or of the Yukuna tribes. These are located, for the former, in the lower Apaporis river area, and, for the Yukuna, in the Mirití-paraná and lower Caquetá river areas. Access to these sites is restricted, and no habitation, habitat destruction, or desacralising acts are allowed. Shamanic knowledge and management of these sites is restricted and secret. Each maloca patrilineage has, in turn, its own sacred sites, which are looked after by the household and its shamans.

Within their ancestral lands there are hundreds of named Guardians of sacred sites in terrestrial and aquatic ecosystems. The latter, for example, are found in named river headwaters or mouths, lakes, meanders, river rapids and creeks, and their Guardians are, for example, giant otters, dolphins, stingrays and anaconda, among others. In lands and waters (as well as soils, airs and subsoils) the Guardians are identifiable with natural species, but the Guardians also exist as hundreds of fantastic beings with spiritual forces. Altogether the acknowledgement of Guardians and indigenous shamanic and spiritual practices contribute to socio-environmental well-being and sustainable resource use (Gaia Amazonas Foundation, 2010a; Reichel, 1989; van der Hammen, 1993; von Hildebrand, 1975).

Sacred sites exist at micro levels in specific habitats; for example, in sacred palm groves of *Mauritia flexuosa* in floodplains and wetlands; other sacred sites exist in ancient maloca sites; and in special 'seed ponds' and fruiting sites (*pepeadero*) where tapirs and other animals such as monkeys, fish and birds eat seasonally available fruits from specific plants in dryland or in flooded forests. Other types of sacred sites are the named salt licks used by tapirs (*Tapirus terrestris*) and other animals as well as particular sites where hunted animals seasonally reproduce, feed, migrate, or dwell. Shamans and elders have detailed knowledge of the networks of sacred sites and of *pepeaderos* and salt licks that exist in their maloca territory. Shamans know in detail the hundreds of plant/animal correlations in these sites (Reichel, 1989, p. 100). They also have an encyclopaedic knowledge of aquatic ecosystems and of fish species which are linked to sacred sites and species which have Guardians in addition to a myriad other extraordinary spiritual beings (Reichel, 1989; Rodriguez and van der Hammen, 1991; van der Hammen, 1993).

For the Tanimuka and Yukuna, their sacred sites, as such, are material and real but also spiritual and enchanted sites that people not only pragmatically use and conserve, but where they have profound spiritual linkages and responsibilities. Sacred sites connect their landscapes to the cosmoscape and give a sense of belonging to maloca communities within humanity, the rainforests, and the rest of the world and cosmos. During recent years, the Tanimuka and Yukuna have been mapping their sacred sites as part of an inventory for management plans for biodiversity conservation and for local governance systems, as well as for territorial delimitation of indigenous Resguardos and of protected areas as they apply their traditional knowledge to 'well manage the world' with shamanism while also engaging in public functions of the Colombian State (see Gaia-Amazonas; AATI, COAMA, 2010).

Shamanic 'Travelling in Thought'

To assess the condition of socio-environmental dynamics, on a daily basis the shamans and every individual makes their own observations and mental calculations and discuss these with other maloca members. However, shamans are specialists of special calculations, decisions and of sacred rituals where they contextualise human existence within the larger dynamics of the world and cosmos in material and spiritual terms. It is frequent to observe, throughout the night, the shaman sitting on his 'thinking' wooden stool/bench as he 'Travels in Thought' (Reichel, 1987c, 1989, 1999b) to the ecosystems and sites being used by maloca hunters, gatherers, fishers and shifting cultivators, in order to consider the impacts of maloca people on the sites and species and ponder how they affect the connections of the landscape with the larger cosmoscape.

For hours, the shaman will narrate to himself, and to his son or apprentice, the local ecosystems he is analysing, and the sacred sites and species related to these as he 'consults' with their Guardians and considers the specific rights and obligations of his maloca patrilineage and household over different resources and landscape units across diverse horizontal linkages. He also focuses on the vertical connectivities and travels across the airs, Earth, waters and subsoils by shamanic 'Travelling in Thought' in the guise of a jaguar, viper, eagle, anaconda, caiman, otter, stingray, or bat – the form changes if he is analysing diurnal or nocturnal dynamics (being a bat at night, for example) – to approach the dynamics from the perspectives of the Guardians of natural or supernatural forces and not only from the interest of his own maloca household (Reichel, 1989b, 1999b) as he considers the predicament of his maloca with its horizontal and vertical connectivities within the cosmoscape.

A Jaguar/Seer shaman with 'Big Thought' or 'Jaguar Thought' ascends to the skies and descends to the underworlds to consult the larger systems in order to consider the condition of a specific season or event. In order to calculate the behavioural adaptations the community or a person must make in a given season, the shaman 'Travels in Thought' to assess the situation of his maloca household and landscapes, as well as those of the neighbouring indigenous groups. Shamans also include calculations of events occurring in the non-indigenous 'White People's world' and to understand the overall state of humankind, and the Earth and the cosmos. The morning after, public advice is given after the shamanic séance and the people of a maloca, or of several allied maloca, will be informed of the shaman's analyses, and are counselled on behavioural and mental changes.

It is forbidden to desecrate sacred sites and to destroy or over-exploit sacred species. Using and consuming sacred species in undue quantities, or when they are seasonally vulnerable, allows the Guardian of sacred sites or species to 'steal' the spirit of a person in order to punish wrongdoers by making them ill. The afflicted person may be anyone in the maloca community (not just the culprit), because the Guardian seeks to give a lesson and demands compensation for the loss of the lives and spirit of its own plant or animal 'peoples' which humans have taken without asking permission, thereby disturbing the balance between their populations. The Guardians not only form networks across ecosystems but also span the skies, world and underworlds, and distinct Guardians appear in different seasons and are indicators of changes in environmental supply and demand, as they are believed to be key nodes of a greater system through which social and environmental well-being are achieved. Thus, shamans communicate with the Guardians, as *primus inter pares*, to achieve socio-environmental sustainability.

Within the annual cycle, seasonal environmental and climatic changes are reckoned across more than 20 named seasons for the Yukuna (Reichel, 1987c, 1997) and the Tanimuka (von Hildebrand, 1987). The beginning and end of each season (varying number of weeks) is ritually marked with large two-day (and night) rituals where dozens or hundreds of people from two or more allied maloca (or only of people of a same ethnic group) meet to discuss their future use of local ecosystems and their communities' dynamics and engage in collective shamanic dances proper to each season. Before and during these rituals, shamans consult the supernatural Guardian of the oncoming season, and also 'close' negotiations with those of the previous season, as they 'return' to the Guardians any residual spiritual essences straying around and cancel debts with them, in order to properly start a new season with the required socio-environmental dynamics.

For instance, important shamanic negotiations are made when the Tanimuka and Yukuna yearly cycle starts with the Dry Season, during the September equinox and a full moon. This season marks the end of the rainy season dominated by male-based hunting, fishing and gathering with high reliance on wildlife in flooded rainforests (Reichel, 1987c; von Hildebrand, 1987). As meteorological traits (rains, winds, cold spells, thunderstorms, wind devils – which have Guardians too) and environmental conditions proper to the rainy season cease, and those of the dry season set in (lower rainfall and river levels), several small 2-acre rainforest clearings are made for new maloca house sites and swidden gardens.

According to Yukuna ethnoastronomy (Reichel, 1987c), in this season at night several Guardians are observed in the skies, including the Hyades (Caiman jaw), the Pleiades (Orphans Crickets) Orion's Belt (Heron's neck), while the C-shaped constellation of Corona Australis (Cicada/Worm-Grub) descends towards the Earth. This constellation is a key Guardian of cultivated food and agriculture that will be abundant during the dry season. The Guardian of domesticated plants and foods, and other Guardians of this season, such as the female Guardians of soils and subsoils and of cultivated foods, as well as the Guardians of seasonally migrating fish and of seasonally abundant species used for hunting and gathering, are consulted. They are asked permission and compensated, in shamanic calculations, for allowing agricultural productivity, swidden gardens and house sites, and for allowing foraging in the rainforests. People observe the position of the Milky Way and other Guardians in stars and planets, and Guardians in dark interstellar spaces. These, among other (male) Guardian Spirits in the skies, are present, along with the male and female Guardians of plants, animals, microorganisms, waters, soils and sub-soils. All these Guardians are deemed to be vigilant in this season, seeking that people achieve healthy lives based on sustainable swidden cultivation and wildlife use.

In this season the Tanimuka make large chronotope rituals, with sacred earth-drum dances held in the centre of the maloca. Men dance and sing as they stamp on a wooden plank that resonates with the hollowed orifices underground. In the maloca's centre a vertical 30-m staff is ritually shaken. This shamanic staff is said to connect the skies, Earth and underworlds for the start of a new agricultural season and the time to make new maloca constructions. Calculations are made to 'manage' and 'fix the world' (von Hildebrand, 1987, p. 240) and to calculate the required number of human lives and deaths, the quantity of new swidden plots, the sites of new maloca, and also the levels of productivity of women's and men's work as swidden agriculture prevails over the men's foraging activities.

The earthdrum rituals last two days (and nights), although as in most chrono-tope rituals, on the first day ceremonies are made only with people of the maloca household 'to see how they will live in the oncoming year and also within the next four or more years' (Reichel, 1987c, p. 213), and on the second day the ritual is made with invited allied neighbouring maloca to plan and 'think together' how they will jointly manage resources and achieve socio-environmental well-being for the year ahead. For the rest of the year, different rituals accompany each new season. By monitoring each season while assessing changes in the links of their landscapes to their cosmoscape, the Tanimuka and Yukuna position their forms of human sustainability with the sustainability of the rainforests, biosphere, the world and beyond.

For decades in the region several processes are being pioneered by their tradi-tional and indigenous authorities, the Resguardo authorities, and Associations of Indigenous Traditional Authorities (AATI, COAMA, 2010) for the conservation of rainforest biodiversity based on local cultural traditions. Diverse projects relate to governance and to decision-making in intercultural projects dealing with health, education, livelihoods, traditional knowledge, biocultural diversity and resource management. Some of these initiatives are supported by national and local gov-ernments, NGOs and other sectors involved in local development and also with the sustainability of the Amazon rainforests and the management of indigenous territories and protected areas. Recently, the creation of protected areas involves indigenous people in conserving rainforest biodiversity and protecting their sacred sites and species as part of the management plans. For example, the recently cre-ated Yaigohé National Natural Park is based on respect for indigenous shamanic ecosystem management and recognises the importance of the sacred sites of the Tanimuka and other tribes. Innovative forms of collaboration with government agencies, NGOs, private sector, conservation agencies and indigenous communities, engage unprecedented intercultural and inter-institutional cooperation which are supportive of good governance and also of indigenous cultures, traditional knowledge and shamanic resource management systems and biocultural diversity (see COAMA, 2010a, 2010b; Gaia-Amazonas Foundation, 2010a, 2010b).

It is important to recognise that in the Amazon region, the indigenous peoples, in small but profoundly resilient cultures, such as those of the Tanimuka and Yukuna, are, up to now, the only societies who can safeguard the rainforests sustainably, recreate biological and cultural diversity, and also mitigate the impacts of climate change linked to the Amazon rainforests.

Conclusion

This chapter indicated how the Tanimuka and the Yukuna Amerindians of the Colombian Amazon consider the landscape as part of a cosmoscape, where the vertical interactions and connections between skies, earths and underworlds are as crucial as the horizontal links across and within ecosystems and peoples. These cosmological axes are mnemonically, and in daily and ceremonial practices, used to shamanically negotiate human existence within the rest of nature in order to enhance social and environmental well-being, and to monitor the sustainability of their communities and ecosystems, especially by managing the optimal condition of their sacred sites and species and by respecting the spiritual and material linkages they involve with the larger world and cosmos. This sustainability has been achieved through biocultural diversity maintained within and across tribes and ethnolinguistic groups, and also with the agency of patrilineal, gender-based, and maloca household dynamics which endorse the landscape within the cosmoscape approach. Their applied 'barefoot cosmologies' are pivotal to regional socio-environmental policies. The high biocultural diversity and socio-environmental sustainability achieved by collective and individual agency through ethnic maloca household, patrilineage and gender-based activities, as well as the significance of Amerindian shamanism for landscape management, along with the innovative inter-cultural and inter-institutional co-governance systems being advanced with indigenous participation in the Colombian–Amazon region, are inspiring examples for the definition of future policies and practices of development and conservation programmes for the broader Amazon region.

Without stereotyping, essentialising or idealising the Tanimuka and Yukuna Indians, it is fair to say that indigenous cultures such as these hold great lessons for our own societies and for a globalising world with complex social and environmental problems and where biodiversity is alarmingly being destroyed, while worldwide cultural and linguistic diversity is being exterminated at historically unprecedented levels (UNESCO, Terralingua and WWF, 2003; Maffi and Woodley, 2010).

The Tanimuka and Yukuna are among the last societies who still apply the lessons of their ancestors to achieve individual and collective well-being along with environmental sustainability while contributing to the socio-ecological resilience of humanity. It is significant that indigenous cultures such as the Tanimuka and Yukuna – and other Amazon Amerindians – in spite of pressure to do otherwise, are, in the twenty-first century, enhancing socio-ecological resilience and safeguarding the rainforests. However, one must also recognise that the spirits of the rainforest, and the Guardians of the world and cosmos, have also been vigilant.

References

AATI, COAMA. (2010). Documents, Acuerdos AATIs -Gobernacion. Available at: http://www.coama.org.co/english/centrodoc_interes.php (accessed June 2010).

COAMA. (2010a). COAMA 'Biological and Cultural Corridor'. Available at: http://www.coama.org.co/english/amazonia_corredor.php (accessed October 2010).

COAMA. (2010b). COAMA 'Pueblos Indigenas'. Available at: http://www.coama.org.co/english/amazonia_pueblosindigenas.php (accessed October 2010).

Descola, P. (1996). Constructing natures. In *Nature and Society: Anthropological Perspectives*, ed. P. Descola and G. Palsson. London: Routledge, pp. 82–102.

Gaia Amazonas Foundation. (2010a). Available at: http://www.gaiaamazonas.org/Estadistica.html (accessed January 2010).

Gaia Amazonas Foundation. (2010b). Available at: http://www.gaiaamazonas.org/Work%20Themes.html (accessed September 2010).

Lévi-Strauss. C. (1962). *La Pensée Sauvage*. Paris: Plon.

Maffi, L. and Woodley, E. (2010). *Biocultural Diversity Conservation: A Global Sourcebook*. Oxford: Earthscan.

Reichel, E. (1975). Levantamiento de los Petroglifos del Rio Caquetá entre La Pedrera y Araracuara. *Revista Colombiana de Antropología*, **19**, 303–70.

Reichel, E. (1976). Resultados preliminaries del reconocimiento del sitio arqueológico de La Pedrera (Comisaría Especial del Amazonas). *Revista Colombiana de Antropología*, **20**, 145–76.

Reichel, E. (1987a). Asentamientos prehispánicos en la Amazonía Colombiana. *Colombia Amazónica*. Bogotá: Universidad Nacional y Fondo Mutis FEN, pp. 129–53.

Reichel, E. (1987b). Etnografía de los grupos indígenas contemporáneos'. In *Colombia Amazónica*. Bogotá: Universidad Nacional de Colombia y Fondo Mutis FEN, pp. 237–73.

Reichel, E. (1987c). Etnoastronomía Yukuna-Matapí. In *Etnoastronomías Americanas*, ed. J. Arias de Greiff and E. Reichel. Bogotá: Universidad Nacional, pp. 193–231.

Reichel, E. (1989). La Danta y el Delfín: Manejo ambiental e intercambio entre dueños de maloca y chamanes. El caso Yukuna-Matapí (Amazonas). *Revista de Antropología*, **5**, 67–134.

Reichel, E. (1997). The Yukuna maloca roundhouse symbolism, Northwest Amazon. In *Encyclopaedia of Vernacular Architecture of the World*, ed. P. Oliver. Cambridge: Cambridge University Press, pp. 1640–2.

Reichel, E. (1999a). Cosmology, worldview and gender-based knowledge systems among the Tanimuka and Yukuna. *Worldviews: Environment, Culture and Religion*, **3**, 213–42.

Reichel, E. (1999b). Gender-based knowledge systems in the eco-politics of the Tanimuka and Yukuna of the Northwest Amazon, Colombia. In *Cultural and Spiritual Values of Biodiversity*, ed. D. Posey. London: UNEP and Intermediate Technology Publications, pp. 82–6.

Reichel, E. (2005). Cosmology. In *The Encyclopedia of Religion and Nature, Vol. 1*, ed. B. Taylor and J. Kaplan. London: Thoemmes Continuum, London, pp. 420–5.

Reichel, E. and von Hildebrand, M. (1985). Vivienda Indígena: función socio-política de la maloca. *Revista PROA*, **332**, 16–23.

Reichel-Dolmatoff, G. (1976). Cosmology as ecological analysis: a view from the rainforest (The Huxley Memorial Lecture). *MAN*, **11**, 307–18.

Reichel-Dolmatoff, G. (1996). *The Forest Within: The Worldview of the Tukano Amazonian Indians*. London: Themis Books.

Rodriguez, C. and van der Hammen, M. (1991). *Bagres, Malleros y Cuerderos en el bajo Caquetá. Programa TROPENBOS*. Bogotá: Tercer Mundo Editores.

UNESCO, Terralingua and WWF. (2003). *Sharing a World of Difference*. Paris: UNESCO Publications.

Van der Hammen, M. (1993). *El Manejo del Mundo: naturaleza y cultura entre los Yukuna del Amazonas colombiano*. Bogotá: TROPENBOS.

Von Hildebrand, M. (1975). Origen del mundo segun los Ufaina. *Revista Colombiana de Antropología*, **18**, 321–82.

Von Hildebrand, M. (1984). Notas etnográficas sobre el cosmos Ufaina y su relación con la maloca. *Revista Manguaré*, **2**, 177–210.

Von Hildebrand, M. (1987). Datos Etnográficos sobre la Astronomía de los indígenas Tanimuka del Noroeste Amazónico. In *Etnoastronomías Americanas*, ed. J. Arias de Greiff and E. Reichel. Bogotá: Universidad Nacional, pp. 233–53.

Von Hildebrand, M. and Reichel, E. (1987). Grupos étnicos del area del bajo rio Caquetá, Amazonas. In *Introducción a Colombia Amerindia*, ed. X. Pachón and F. Correa. Bogotá: Instituto Colombiano de Antropología, pp. 135–50.

Whiffen, T. (1915). *The Northwest Amazon: Notes of Some Months Spent Among Cannibal Tribes*. London: Constable and Company.

10

Sacred natural sites in zones of armed conflicts: the Sierra Nevada de Santa Marta in Colombia

GUILLERMO E. RODRIGUEZ-NAVARRO

Introduction

The Sierra Nevada de Santa Marta population includes some 32 000 members of the Kogi, Arhuaco, Wiwa and Kankuamo indigenous groups, descendants of the Tayronas and preservers of their ancient tradition. There are also approximately 150 000 peasants, and 1.5 million urban dwellers in the lowlands. Of these, the only stable populations are the indigenous groups and although each group has its own language, they all share a similar system of beliefs. Since pre-Hispanic times, the indigenous peoples of the Sierra Nevada have possessed a worldview, social organisation and living pattern which revolves around the management and conservation of this unique environment, the 'heart of the world' (Reichel-Dolmatoff, 1950, pp. 1–32).

Indigenous people believe that between man and nature there is an equilibrium, which can easily be disturbed by irresponsible human actions. This equilibrium not only refers to the management of resources, but also to the spiritual and moral balance of the individual and the group that is the basic element of peace (Arhem, 1990, pp. 105–22).

The Sierra Nevada de Santa Marta

Colombia presents perhaps the best opportunity and the greatest challenge for the conservation of biological and cultural diversity in our hemisphere. This South American country is recognised as the nation with the greatest

Sacred Species and Sites: Advances in Biocultural Conservation, ed. Gloria Pungetti, Gonzalo Oviedo and Della Hooke. Published by Cambridge University Press. © Cambridge University Press 2012.

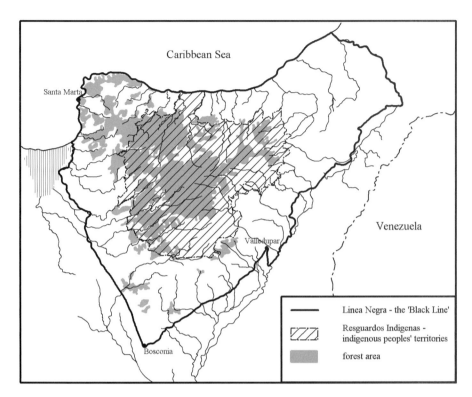

Figure 10.1 Conservation strategy in the Sierra Nevada de Santa Marta.

biological wealth per square mile and the largest number of languages. Amidst this wealth lies a national treasure: the Sierra Nevada de Santa Marta.

The Sierra Nevada de Santa Marta, a UNESCO Biosphere Reserve, is an isolated mountain set apart from the Andes mountain chain that runs through Colombia (Figure 10.1). Reaching an altitude of 5775 m above sea level in just 56 km from the Caribbean coast, Sierra Nevada is the world's highest coastal peak. Sierra Nevada encompasses about 4.2 million acres and serves as the source of 36 main rivers. The Sierra comprises two Natural National Parks (Sierra Nevada de Santa Marta and Tairona), three large indigenous reservations and five small ones. Due to its altitudinal variation, as well as its location at 11 degrees latitude north, the Sierra Nevada contains samples of all of the climatic zones that can be found in the tropical Americas.

Sierra Nevada de Santa Marta is one of the most distinctive, diverse and threatened areas in South America. Tapirs, red brocket deer and howler monkeys are among the 120 species of mammals roaming the Sierra Nevada, along with elusive cats such as the jaguar, puma and little spotted cat. The park also harbours 46 species of amphibians and reptiles; those that live above 3500 m are found

Figure 10.2 Settlement of the Arhuaco area in the Sierra Nevada de Santa Marta
(© Fundacion Pro-Sierra Nevada de Santa Marta). See colour plate section.

nowhere else on the planet, having evolved in complete isolation. An amazing 628
bird species have been recorded only in the area of the Sierra Nevada de Santa
Marta National Park (Mayr-Maldonado *et al.*, 1995, pp. 125–30)

During the last 50 years, Sierra Nevada has suffered from degradation and
deforestation. This poses a threat to the approximately 1.5 million people who
rely on its watersheds for survival, the numbers of species of this ecosystem, and
the future of its traditional indigenous cultures. At present, only 18% of the ecoregional forest remains and two of the 35 rivers have completely run out of water.

As a result of its geographic and historical characteristics, the Sierra Nevada is
shared today by a diverse set of ethnic and cultural groups, each with its own interests and values. The Sierra's population includes 32 000 members of the indigenous
cultures of the Kogi, Ijka, Wiwa and Kankuamo groups, descendants of the Tayronas who still keep their ancient traditions (Figures 10.2, 10.3 and 10.4). There are
also approximately 150 000 peasants, and 1.5 million city-dwellers in the lowlands.
Of these, the only stable populations are the indigenous groups, and although
each group has its own language they share a similar system of beliefs. Since
pre-Hispanic times, the indigenous peoples of the Sierra Nevada have possessed
a worldview, social organisations and living patterns revolving around the management and conservation of this unique environment ('the heart of the world')
(Reichel-Dolmatoff, 1982, pp. 289–96).

Figure 10.3 San Miguel: one of the bigger Kogi settlements in the Rio Ancho basin; northern slope of the Sierra Nevada de Santa Marta. (© Fundacion Pro-Sierra Nevada de Santa Marta).

Figure 10.4 Asentamiento Kogi: a family settlement (© Fundacion Pro-Sierra Nevada de Santa Marta).

The role of indigenous communities in landscape conservation

From their first moment of contact with the Western world, the indigenous communities have witnessed the incessant pillage and destruction of their territories, their sacred sites, burial grounds and customs of their ancestors. The four tribes that managed to survive are undergoing various degrees of acculturation due to outside factors. Today, few have understood the value of the philosophical store of knowledge that the indigenous people hold for humanity through their understanding of nature. The fact that some effort is now being invested in understanding the basis for indigenous natural resource management indicates that the negative attitudes commonly held about indigenous knowledge during the colonial era have begun to change (Murrilo-Sencial, 1997, pp. 139–49).

The only link between the productive sectors is through their use of water, which makes forest conservation imperative and which, in turn, requires a social accord that includes the validation of indigenous knowledge by the Colombian society, as they are controlling the conservation of the basic resources that ensure the region's well-being. As such, water, a product whose value extends beyond the forests, is a basis for dialogue between the various groups in conflict. Without social agreement between indigenous people and inhabitants of the urban and farming areas on the surrounding lowlands, conservation of the forests and of the sources of water for the future development of the region will not be possible (Figure 10.5).

This region provides an example of how local and indigenous Colombian communities can be engaged in the sustainable development and protection of mountain landscapes, revealing the complexity of interactions between culture and nature in this region and the importance of traditional indigenous practices in landscape management. For the tribal communities living here, the forests are vital, providing wildlife habitat and serving as sanctuaries for worship and religious ceremonies. The resources in the forests also provide shelter, fuel and clothing, household utensils, medicines, food and materials for their artistic expression (Balee, 1989, pp. 1–21).

Many violent conflicts are about disputes over resources between the mountain and lowland communities. Mountain communities have limited resources and their relations with the lowlands can change and rapidly deteriorate. From the time of their first contact with the Western world, indigenous peoples have suffered from plunder and the destruction of their territories, sacred sites, cemeteries and ancestral customs. The case of the Kogi people is described here in some detail to illustrate the general situation of indigenous peoples in the Sierra. They have been forcibly displaced several times, even as recently as the 1960s, and now live in the Don Diego river basin (Rodriguez-Navarro, 1999, pp. 365–74).

Figure 10.5 Arhuaco showing the excellent organic coffee produced around Nabusimake (© Corporation Caja de Herramientas).

The Law of the Mother

At present, the Kogi people are practitioners of the 'Law of the Mother'. This is a complex code of rules that regulates human behaviour in harmony with the plant and animal cycles, astral movements, climatic phenomena, and transhumance in the sacred geography of the massif. They are the best guardians of the knowledge of their ancestors (Figure 10.6).

Traditional ecological knowledge is based on observations and experience, evaluated in the light of what has been learned from the elders. The indigenous people of the Sierra Nevada de Santa Marta have relied on this detailed knowledge for their survival – they have literally staked their lives on its accuracy and repeatability that at the same time is safeguarded by their system of offerings. This knowledge is an important source of information and understanding for anyone who is interested in the natural world, the place of people in the environment, and the spiritual significance that is immersed in the sacred geography of their territory.

According to indigenous accounts of the Earth's creation, the area around the Sierra Nevada was a circular territory with high mountains at its centre and a border called the 'black line' extending to the ocean where the water cycle ends

Figure 10.6 Kogi settlement in the Rio Ancho valley (© Fundacion Pro-Sierra Nevada de Santa Marta).

(Figure 10.1). This territory is the centre of the world and home to the Mother's children who live off her and care for her water sources, lands and sacred sites.

The strict observance of this complex code of knowledge by indigenous society has enabled the native population to survive and remain self-sufficient over the course of several centuries.

However, this unique example of harmony between humans and their environment is beginning to fade due to outside intervention and the loss of fertile lands now in the hands of drug traffickers, rich banana and oil palm growers organised for international trade, and the guerrillas and paramilitary.

The indigenous groups live in a complex ranked society in which lineage plays a major role. The true power of decision in personal and community affairs is concentrated in the hands of the native priesthood (the Mama). They possess a profound knowledge of their environment such as astronomy, meteorology and ecology, and use this knowledge to plan their agronomic calendar and the distribution of lands and crops. They believe that between man and nature there is an equilibrium, which might easily be disturbed by irresponsible human actions. This equilibrium not only refers to the subsistence of resources such as water management, forest conservation and crops, but also in the spiritual and moral balance of the individual and agricultural rituals. These rituals, dances and ceremonies play a prominent role in their religion and agricultural practices, which are submitted to many ritual rules timed according to astronomically determined seasons. In other words, the ritual calendar corresponds to the agricultural cycle. This balance does not only encompass basic resources such as water, forests or crops, but extends to the moral and spiritual balance of individual community members. Kogi society, for example, is strictly hierarchical. At the top we find the Mamas, or priests, whose education is one of the most striking features of their society (Rodríguez-Navarro, 2000, pp. 455–8).

Ideally, the future priests are chosen by divination and trained from birth. The training lasts 18 years and takes place in special temples in the Sierra. When they return to society as Mamas, at around the age of 20, they may be trained to lead the community in moral and spiritual ways, but they lack all practical knowledge. Their simple but profound training prepares them for their task of preserving the universe. Practical matters are left to the Comisario or the Mayor, who works together with the Mama. Cabos are assistants to the Mamas and the Comisarios and have less authority. Mayores is a term given to elder men of good reputation whose status gives them authority over their peers and the younger generation. These Spanish names have been present since early colonial times and have been incorporated into their language to fit the Colombian concepts of authority.

Mamas, Mayores, Cabos and Comisarios are in close contact with nature and have a clear sense of how to maintain the cycles that rule the ecosystems. Their unique belief system provides the basis for indigenous biodiversity management practice. It stems from a complex offering system in which each individual holds custody of a sacred territory (Figure 10.7). An over-simplified classification of the offering system is provided here to help understand the highly complex nature of indigenous land management in the Sierra Nevada. There appear to be three distinct types of offering. The first comprises a set of rituals that maintain natural cycles. These are performed by offering stone beads, which are buried, thrown into the sea, or hidden in small caves or cracks in fields or snowy peaks. The second type of offering is made to atone for personal faults. The third type acts as payment for the use of natural resources with unpredictable yields. One example dealt with the use of trees for the construction of a bridge. In a complex ceremony, tree seedlings were cleaned, scattered in the forest, and then given spiritual nourishment (Pedro Sundenkama, Kogi community, personal communication).

While the scientific perspective differs from the traditional, both have much to offer each other. Combining the two is the best way to achieve a better understanding of nature. However, it is still difficult to establish an atmosphere of trust with the indigenous people of the Sierra Nevada de Santa Marta and to take part in their knowledge and belief systems. This can only be attained through long-standing cooperation.

Figure 10.7 Offering in the mouth of Don Diego (© Fundacion Pro-Sierra Nevada de Santa Marta).

The role of sacred sites is basically to recover the spirituality of the territory. Sacred sites also provide a way to establish a set of rules and regulations about the management and preservation of these areas, totally connected with the belief systems of the indigenous population.

The 'black line'

As already mentioned, the indigenous territory is limited by the 'black line', but what *is* the 'black line'? It is an indigenous term that has given rise to multiple interpretations. It has even been said that it refers to the paved road that surrounds the Sierra in many parts, connecting the three departments La Guajira, Cesar and Magdalena with jurisdiction in the Sierra Nevada. Nothing can be further from reality. In a general meeting celebrated in Bunkuwageka in July 1994, the traditional authorities divulged the sacred points aforementioned that constitute the 'black line', which in their own beliefs and concepts comprise their territory.

1. Kas´simuratu. Convent in Plaza Alfonso López of Vailedupar, Cesar. Place of Offerings 'Yuwangawi'.
2. Kickiaku. Bridge over Salguero from the Cesar river. Door of illness.
3. Karakui. Up Cesar river to Guacoche. Door of the illness of the left.
4. BunkwaNariwa. Up river to Badillo. Where offerings are made for illness in general.
5. BunkwaNariwa. From Badillo in direction of los Aticos. Mothers of animals and water.
6. Imakamuke. From los Aticos in direction of San Juan del Cesar. Mother of air, water, lightning and thunder.
7. Jwiamuke. From San Juan del Cesar to Fonseca. Mother of hurricanes and storms.
8. Seamuke. From Fonseca to Barrancas. Offerings for illness.
9. Kukuzha. From Barrancas to Hatonuevo. Offerings for any animal or person.
10. Unkweka. From Hatonuevo to Cuestecita. Offerings for the sap of trees.
11. Java Shikaka. From Cuestecita, in the direction of Riohacha, as far as the mouth of Rancheria river in the ocean.
12. Jaxzaka Luwen. From Riohacha to Camarones. Place to collect stones for a successful marriage.
13. Alaneia. From Camarones to Punta de los Remedios. Mother of the sun.
14. Zenisha. From Punta de los Remedios to Dibulla. Mother of the food produced in la Sierra; interchange of sea materials for offerings.
15. Mama Lujwa. From Dibulla to Mingueo, as far as the mouth of Cañas river. Mother of large pots (*tinajas*), potter.
16. Jukulwa. From the mouth of Cañas river to the mouth of Ancho river. Mother of the animals; there are three lagoons for offerings for illness.
17. Jwazeshikaka. From the mouth of Ancho river to Jwazeshikaka hill, just to the Palomino river mouth. Mother of the stone beads.
18. Java Kumekun Shikaka. From Jwazeshikaka hill to the mouth of Palomino river. Mother of all the flowers.
19. Jate Mixtendwe Lwen. From the mouth of Palomino river to Jate Mixtendwe Lwen hill. Mother of the dances.
20. From Jate Mixtendwe Lwen hill to the mouth of Don Diego river, Java Mitasma. Mother of the pigeons.
21. Java Mutanni. From the mouth of Buritaca river to the mouth of Guachaca river. Mother of all the four-legged animals.
22. Jate Telugama. From Guachaca river to Tayrona Nacional Park. Mother of gold.

23.   Java Nakumake. From Tayrona Nacional Park to Chengue. Mother of the salt.
24.   Java Julekun. From Tayrona Nacional Park as far as Taganga. Mother of Zirichu.
25.   Java Nekun. From Taganga to Santa Marta in the docks. Mother of all spiritual authorities.
26.   Java Siñigala. From Santa Marta to Ciénaga. Mother of Sokunu nego.
27.   Java Ňinawi. From Ciénaga to the mouth of Frío river. Mother of the lions.
28.   Java Waskañi Shikaka. From the mouth of Frío river to the mouth of Sevilla river.
29.   Java Katakaiwman. From Sevilla river to the mouth of Tucurinca river. Mother of everything that exists in the world.
30.   Kwarewmun. From Tucurinca to town of Aracataca. Mother of the clay.
31.   Seynewmun. From Aracataca to Fundación. Mother of the mortuary of all beings.
32.   Mama Neyumun. From Fundación to Ariguaní river. Mother of earth.
33.   Ugeka. From Ariguaní river to El Copey. Offering to avoid war.
34.   Miakun. From El Copey to Bosconia (Camperucho). Mother of fertility.
35.   Ku¨riwa. From Bosconia to Caracoli. Door where wild animals are controlled.
36.   Gunkanu. From Caracoli to Mariangola. Offerings for the spiritual pathways.
37.   Gwi´kanu. From Mariangola to Aguas Blancas. Offerings to control illness.
38.   Ka´aka. From Aguas Blancas to Valencia de Jesús. Offering site to control death.
39.   From Valencia de Jesús to Valledupar. The starting point.

These 39 references give the limits to the Sierra's indigenous territory, which were agreed by the four indigenous groups, as the main points that can be identified to surround la Sierra. The need to be permanently making offerings in these sites warrants the integrity of the Sierra's ecosystem as a whole. This territory is seen as a body, the mother's body that has to be taken care of.

Conclusions: the conflict

The situation of the indigenous people is critical, more so now than ever before. The intense territorial dispute between guerrillas and paramilitary groups has a disruptive impact on ancestral culture. Traditionally, communities had access to a variety of ecosystems of different temperature and altitude. This enabled them to build a self-sufficient economy that supplied products ranging from salt and fish from the lowlands, to potatoes and medicinal plants from the cold highlands. Today the mobility of communities is severely restricted by paramilitary groups in the lowlands and foothills and by guerrillas in the mid- and highlands of the Sierra (Rodriguez-Navarro, 2004, pp. 475–88).

The conflict has intensified over the last five years and this has worsened the situation for the communities. This has not only caused a fracture in their production system, it has also restricted or even totally precluded access to vital cultural places, including sacred sites. Communities have had to abandon their lowland territories and retreat to higher ground. These displacements are ever more frequent and the obstruction of access to the lowlands has affected the capacity to build up stocks. The most isolated communities now run the risk of starvation.

Wherever the ecology is fragile, peace is fragile too. Resources must be shared to prevent conflicts. The time has arrived for our industrialised society to learn from the indigenous one, to incorporate moral values and to develop an ecological understanding that is reflected in its social and economic measures. Knowledge should become a part of our way of life and post-modern man needs a new approach to development in which basic resources are protected and the survival of our planet is assured. Participatory management, adaptive mechanisms and regulations for accessing resources, and the attainment of a new set of conditions are the most sustainable and realistic ways of reaching solutions. An aspect that gives hope to this region is the process of empowerment that these indigenous groups have gained and the environmental awareness and the popularity that they have amongst the new generation combined with the policies of democratic security today under development.

References

Arhem, K. (1990). Ecosofía Makuna. In *La selva humanizada, ecología alternativa en el trópico húmedo colombiano*, ed. F. Correa. Bogota: ICAN-FEN –CEREC, pp. 105–22 (in Spanish).

Balee, W. (1989). The culture of Amazonian forests. In *Resource Management in Amazonia: Indigenous and Folk Strategies, Advances in Economic Botany*, ed. D. A. Posey and W. Balee. New York, NY: The New York Botanical Gardens, **7**, 1–21.

Mayr-Maldonado, J., Rodríguez-Navarro, G. E., Ortiz, N., *et al.* (1995). Región de Sierra Nevada [Colombia]. In *América Latina: estrategias para el desarrollo sostenible*, ed. A. Lopez-Ornat. Gland, Switzerland: IUCN, pp. 125–30 (in Spanish).

Murrilo-Sencial, Z. (1997). La Mata de Ahuyama: sistemas anímicos y clasificaciones totémicas. In *El Pueblo de la Montaña Sagrada: tradición y cambio*, ed. A. Colajanni. Colombia: Ricerca e Cooperazione, Santa Marta, pp. 139–49 (in Spanish).

Reichel-Dolmatoff, G. (1950). Los Kogui: una tribu de la Sierra Nevada de Santa Marta, Colombia. *Revista del Instituto Etnológico Nacional (Bogotá)*, **4**, 1–32 (in Spanish).

Reichel-Dolmatoff, G. (1982). Cultural change and environmental awareness; a case study of the Sierra Nevada de Santa Marta, Colombia. *Mountain Research and Development*, **2**, 289–96.

Rodríguez-Navarro, G. E. (1999). Evidencias prehispánicas y prácticas tradicionales indígenas en las cuencas altas de los rios Guachaca y Buritaca: un estudio de caso en el establecimiento y manejo de áreas de amortiguación en la Sierra Nevada de Santa Marta, Colombia. In *Desarrollo sostenible de ecosistemas de montaña: manejo de áreas frágiles en los Andes*, ed. M. Liberman and C. Baied. La Paz, Bolivia: The United Nations University (UNU), Liga para la Defensa del Medio Ambiente LIDEMA and Instituto de Ecologia, pp. 365–74 (in Spanish).

Rodríguez-Navarro, G. E. (2000). Indigenous knowledge as an innovative contribution to the sustainable development of the Sierra Nevada of Santa Marta, Colombia. *AMBIO [Journal of the Human Environment]* **29**, 455–8.

Rodríguez-Navarro, G. E. (2004). Conflicto, significado espiritual y efecto ambiental de las ofrendas entre los indígenas de la Sierra Nevada de Santa Marta. In: *Dimensiones Territoriales de la Guerra y la Paz. Universidad Nacional de Colombia. Red de Estudios de Espacio y Territorio RET*. Editorial Unibiblos, Bogotá D.C., pp. 475–88.

11

Struggles to protect Puketapu, a sacred hill in Aotearoa

JOSEPH S. TE RITO

Introduction

This chapter aims to improve understanding and recognition of the spiritual values of Ngati Hinemanu, a kin-based group of Maori in Aotearoa (New Zealand), in relation to a sacred hill across the river from their rural village of Omahu. Originally known as Puketapu, the name means 'sacred hill'. Puketapu was the site of an ancient battle where blood was spilt on the land and people perished. It is located six miles west of Hastings in the province of Hawke's Bay (see Figure 11.1).

In 1879, Puketapu was re-named 'Fernhill' by settlers and was documented as such in the civic records, leaving the original name buried for over a century. In about 1989, local Maori set out to actively resurrect the original Maori name of Puketapu.

This chapter is written from an insider's point of view as the author is Ngati Hinemanu. It outlines some of the history of the hill, including the ancient battle, the hill's alienation from its indigenous owners in the 1800s, and contemporary contestations led by Ngati Hinemanu to protect Puketapu from sale by the local district council. Despite few resources, since 1989 Ngati Hinemanu have thwarted the Council's attempts, first to create a housing subdivision on Puketapu, and then to sell it to grape growers or other developers.

The chapter also describes current efforts by Maori to protect the hill by coopting mainstream New Zealanders onto a charitable trust, the Puketapu/Fernhill Reserve Trust, to fundraise to purchase the hill as a reserve for the general public, to re-plant it in indigenous flora, and to build walkways.

Sacred Species and Sites: Advances in Biocultural Conservation, ed. Gloria Pungetti, Gonzalo Oviedo and Della Hooke. Published by Cambridge University Press. © Cambridge University Press 2012.

Figure 11.1 View of the Puketapu hills (© J. S. Te Rito).

Threats to sacred sites in general

Most Maori communities are facing threats to their *wahi tapu* (sacred place/s) and other places of cultural significance, as so-called development progresses across the indigenous landscape. Many of these communities stand by watching helplessly as capitalism reduces land to being no more than a mere commodity for sale and purchase. The community of Omahu is no exception.

In 2000, a policy planner at the Hastings District Council (HDC) wrote that when an application is received for a Resource Consent relating to land containing a *wahi tapu* site, the 'Council will notify and consult with *tangata whenua* [the indigenous people]...It does not however ultimately stop any landowner carrying out any proposed work, and in this way the rights of landowners are protected. The inclusion of Puketapu (Fernhill) in the Plan as a Wahi Tapu site would not give the site absolute protection' (R. Stuart, HDC memorandum, 1 August 2000).

Unfortunately for Ngati Hinemanu and other *tangata whenua* of the area, they are no longer the landowners of Puketapu. The hill is part of the 19 385-acre Heretaunga Block which was alienated from the Maori as a result of questionable land deals by the early British settlers to the area. The above quotation demonstrates quite clearly the ongoing and unrelenting impacts of colonisation on the indigenous population and on their spiritual values.

A more recent report on *wahi tapu* in the Hastings district did little to help the situation. For Omahu, only four particular sites were identified as *tapu* (sacred) (M. Campbell, CFG Heritage Ltd final report, 2007). Yet, to Omahu Maori, there are untold localised sites in the area which have been rendered *tapu* through the various types of human activity over the centuries. Apart from this, the whole landscape of Papatuanuku (Mother Earth) is regarded as *tapu* in its own right.

Spiritual and cultural traditions of Ngati Hinemanu

One of the key spiritual values at the heart of Maori culture is the concept of *tapu*. There are various reasons why the hill, Puketapu, is regarded as *tapu*. Apart from being the site of an ancient battle in which blood was spilt on the land and people killed there, local Maori believe that there are bones interred in the hill.

Kaumatua (elder), Wi Hamutana gave oral evidence to the New Zealand Historic Places Trust at Omahu Marae on 9 July 1990. He told the gathering of a *tohunga* (priest) and his pet lizard living in a cave at Puketapu; of there being two *pa* (fortified hill-top villages) on the hill, named Puketapu and Pukehou, respectively; and of a battle there in which people were killed. This information had been transmitted to this elder through the oral traditions of his people. His account concurs with the following written accounts by non-Maori.

Local Hawke's Bay historian J. D. H. Buchanan provides an account about the battle on the hill. He tells of the Whatumamoa, alias Ngati Mamoe people, who had two *pa* on the hill, also named Puketapu and Pukehou. Another tribe, Ngati Ira under Te Whakumu, were then in possession of Otatara, a *pa* six miles away. Tara, from Cape Kidnappers, invited Ngati Mamoe to join in an attack on Otatara, but Te Whakumu, having learned of their intentions, was prepared for the attack and in turn defeated the attackers (Buchanan, 1973, p. 87). Eminent ethnologist Elsdon Best tells of Te Whakumu despatching a force of 400 men against the hill fort of Puketapu in return. The place fell and maybe as many as 70 people died (Best, 1918, p. 24).

Therefore, for Maori, Puketapu is extremely *tapu*. To build houses upon it, or to grow food upon it such as grapes for wine, is simply out of the question. To do so would be to breach the *tapu* or to trample on Maori spiritual values. Yet, despite the cultural and spiritual inappropriateness of building on Puketapu, the local district council has still allowed two new houses to be built there since 2003.

In 1990 the Hawke's Bay Regional Filekeeper of the NZ Archaeological Association, Mary Jeal, carried out a site visit over the hill at the request of the Omahu Maori Committee (OMC). In her follow-up letter she writes of three possible house

Figure 11.2 Reconstructed *pa tuwatawata* (fortifications) at Otatara *pa* 10 km away (© J. S. Te Rito).

sites on the north-east slope, and of two limestone outcrops with possible abraiding grooves that she says were probably created as a result of tool or weapon dressing (M. Jeal, personal communication, 5 March 1990). So the site also has cultural significance to Maori as an old site of habitation.

Arrival of British settlers in the 1800s

A major turning point in the history of the Puketapu and indeed of the whole of Aotearoa was the arrival of mainly British settlers in the early 1800s. Along with them came muskets, as early as 1814, which resulted in widespread musket wars between the tribes. One direct result of this phenomenon was the demise of fortified hill-top *pa*. Prior to the musket the main form of combat had been man-to-man, and face-to-face, using hand weapons. Defending groups would retreat to the sanctity of their *pa*. However, the musket, with its ability to kill and maim from a distance, soon rendered palisades useless (Figure 11.2).

So a direct outcome of this new form of warfare was huge population displacement in the late 1820s. Ngati Hinemanu had lived at Puketapu. They had large areas of cultivation on the flats at the base of the western and southern sides of the hill, and a lagoon rich in freshwater eels and other fish life. The resources and land were abandoned by all but a handful of their members as the majority fled for safety under the mantle of other friendly tribes. It was not until 30–40 years later that the majority of Ngati Hinemanu returned to these lands.

Meanwhile the Treaty of Waitangi had been signed between Maori chiefs and Queen Victoria of Great Britain in 1840. What the Treaty promised for Maori was the protection of their lands, forests and fisheries. The land was protected by a particular mechanism whereby only the Crown could purchase land from the 'native' owners who owned the land collectively. However, by the 1860s the settlers had begun to make major inroads into this covenant.

Puketapu was part of the Heretaunga Block alienated in 1867, to later become the site of Hastings city. The block was alienated initially through a system of allocating Crown Grants in the land to 10 selected indigenous chiefs. They would become 'owners' in common of the whole area on behalf of their respective kin groups. This action hailed the commencement of a catastrophic change for Maori, from their traditional collective ownership of land to individualised title. The action ultimately cleared the way for capitalists like Thomas Tanner to become the owners of the land. How Tanner came to purchase the land from the 10 Crown Grantees was by haranguing these owners individually until the majority eventually signed their shares to him. He threatened seizure of their chattels and the like.

Tanner's next step was to divide the land amongst a group of other capitalists like himself, who later became known as the 'Twelve Disciples'. In 1873 a Royal Commission was established to investigate the alienation of the Heretaunga Block. However, while the process showed up a number of grave injustices, it would be to no avail: Puketapu and the rest of the Heretaunga Block still ended up in the hands of the settlers.

The use of the name 'Fernhill' for Puketapu after 1879 is attributed to Elizabeth Hill (P. Parsons, Historical Report on Puketapu, 2000). Angus Gordon, a descendant of one of the 'Disciples', J. G. Gordon, who acquired Fernhill and surrounds in the first instance, writes of the development by his ancestors of a homestead there in 1887. It still stands at the foot of Puketapu today on the eastern side. Angus Gordon writes, 'In 1892, Thomas [Gordon] sold his share of Fernhill to Kenrick Hill . . . In 1907 Dudley Hill sold off five 125 acre blocks . . . By 1912 he had sold off the majority of Fernhill . . . He kept 300 acres for himself. Most of the 70 acres, which his son Vyvian retained, have now been sold. Vyv's son Peter, still lives in the house' (Gordon, 2004, p. 45). Peter Hill continues to live in the same two-storey house today.

Acquisition of the hilltop by Hastings City Council in 1986

On 30 September 1986, the land on the top of the hill, amounting to 29.4 ha, was bought by the Hastings City Council from the then owners, the McLeod family. The Council decided to build a housing subdivision on the land. However, it was this action that brought Puketapu to the attention of local Maori. The name Puketapu had been long buried since the late 1870s and had been largely erased from the memories of most of the contemporary local inhabitants of Omahu village. Fortunately the elder, Wi Hamutana, was still aware of the indigenous name and of the fact that people had perished there. The outcome of this was that the people of Omahu became galvanised into action. Their actions are outlined further on in this chapter.

Efforts by Ngati Hinemanu to get the Council to be more cognisant of Maori values in regard to land have been a painful and soul-destroying process. Ideally, the Treaty of Waitangi should have automatically enshrined Maori values into the legislation from central government level right through to local body level, thus affording fuller protection of *wahi tapu*. However, this has clearly not happened.

Players in the recent struggles over Puketapu

Ngati Hinemanu and the people of Omahu have had to undergo a long struggle since 1989 to prevent the sale of the hill-top in Council ownership, in order to prevent any 'development' of this land. During this time, as part of a restructuring of local bodies, the Hastings City Council was re-named the Hastings District Council.

The ensuing course of events in this saga of the struggles to save Puketapu involves a two-pronged approach by the OMC and by Ngati Hinemanu adherents (Figure 11.3). The OMC was able to challenge the Hastings District Council by way of the Maori Community Development Act 1960 in which the OMC is recognised as a local authority, albeit unfunded. Ngati Hinemanu, as an indigenous kinship-based group, on the other hand, was able to challenge by laying a claim against the Crown for breaches against the sub-tribe's Treaty rights. Their claim was submitted to the Waitangi Tribunal which was set up to hear and deal with grievances over breaches of the 1840 Treaty of Waitangi, by the Crown.

During this struggle the Omahu people did not have only the Council to contend with, but also the local press and local historians. The saga of Puketapu has been very taxing upon the Omahu people who, despite this, have persevered for the last 20 years and now look towards the purchase of Council-owned land on Puketapu in the near future.

A 20-year saga to save Puketapu

When the people of nearby Omahu became aware of the Council's plans to build a housing subdivision on Puketapu, a Ngati Hinemanu woman, Waipa Te Rito, organised a petition and presented it to Council on 25 July 1989. The

Figure 11.3 Maori at a gathering at Omahu in about 1917 in front of the village meeting-house, Kahukuranui, a sacred site in its own right (© Te Rito family collection).

petitioners were objecting to any subdivision, development or sale of the said land. The local newspaper, *The Hawke's Bay Herald Tribune* (*HBHT*), published a story the next day with the headline stating, 'Maori land objection delays sale', and with a report of Mayor Dwyer saying, 'Every delay we have adds $60,000 a year to the cost of the land' (*HBHT*, 26 July 1989). The actions of the petitioners were being singled out and blamed for increasing costs to the ratepayer.

The Council eventually abandoned the idea of a subdivision and set about selling the land, advertising it for sale on 17 November 1989. With no time to waste, a Treaty of Waitangi Claim was prepared by Waipa Te Rito, and despatched on 27 November, 1989.

In April 1990, the zoning of Puketapu was changed to Rural 2. This meant the land lots could not be subdivided into the small residential sections the Council had originally planned, i.e. 200 residential sections. Of great concern, however, were statements to the newspaper attributed to a Council officer, that 'even in rural two zone, houses could still be built on each of the four titles . . . [and] the fact that there were sacred sites on the block would not normally be an issue when building permits were considered' (*HBHT*, 18 April 1990).

On 15 June 1990, claimant Waipa Te Rito received news from the Waitangi Tribunal that her claim was now formally registered with the Tribunal and listed as Claim WAI 127 (T. Bennion, personal communication, 15 June 1990). A fortnight later, news of the Waitangi Claim appeared in the newspaper. It listed all eight signatories to the claim as though they were criminals (*HBHT*, 29 June 1990).

On 30 November 1990, the NZ Historic Places Trust wrote to the OMC with news of a small victory, declaring Puketapu (Fernhill) to be a 'traditional site' (A. Geelan, personal communication, 30 November 1990). Unfortunately, this designation offered much less protection than the 'archaeological site' designation that had been sought.

The Trust also placed the matter of having Puketapu made a reserve under s439A of the Maori Affairs Act. The Chief Executive of Te Puni Kokiri (Ministry of Maori Development) then wrote to the Minister of Maori Affairs, recommending that an urgent negotiation be conducted with the Hastings District Council to purchase the site in order to set it aside as an s439A reservation (W. Gardiner, personal communication, 20 March 1992).

During April/May 1992, a researcher for Te Puni Kokiri, Mr Brian Bargh, sought the views of Hawke's Bay historian Mr Pat Parsons. Parsons concluded, 'Although Puketapu is directly across the river from Omahu and is mentioned in the Omahu case there is no indication as to how it got its name' (P. Parsons, personal communication, 30 April 1992). However, Puketapu is *not* located in the Omahu Block where the settlement of Omahu is. It is across the river in the neighbouring Heretaunga Block. What Parsons had 'failed' to find, in the short time he was given to respond to the request, was to become the undoing of our case. The Minister declined to proceed with the purchase as there was no written evidence of the hill being *tapu* (W. Gardiner, personal communication, 19 May 1992).

For the people of Omahu this was absurd. The name Puketapu was enough in itself. The hill was *tapu* and no further research was necessary.

On 8 July 1992, the Council then advertised for sale the remaining three lots on top of the hill, totalling over 18 ha. Under its legal obligations to the Maori, the Council had a Maori Advisory Standing Committee. However, the Council ignored its Committee's recommendations of 1 July 1992, i.e. that the Council designate Puketapu a *wahi tapu* and that Puketapu should not be sold. Despite this, on 10 July 1992, the Council sold the 10-ha house block to the former owner, McLeod for a mere $195 000.

In 1993, the NZ Historic Places Trust designated the whole hill a *wahi tapu* and later listed it on the Trust's National Register of Wahi Tapu. Council followed the lead and designated its own three lots on Puketapu as *wahi tapu* on its District Scheme, but for some reason, excluded the lot that it had sold back to McLeod as *wahi tapu*. Then the Council offered to set aside one of the remaining three

Figure 11.4 View looking north-west across the Ngaruroro river from one of the *pa* sites where a huge pylon has been built (© Janeen Love).

lots, of approximately 4 ha, as a reservation and place of cultural and historical interest. It is Lot 1 D.P. 14007, the lot on which stands a huge electrical pylon. Their letter states, however, 'In return, the Council would want to see ... the other two lots ... put up for sale by Council without any restrictions on their sale' (HDC, personal communication, 20 October 1994). While we were pleased at the offer being made, we found it impossible to agree to the condition that the Council was imposing upon us. It was tantamount to blackmail (Figure 11.4).

The next move by the Council was to lease all the hill-top land to Mr McLeod for three years until 30 June 1999. We were elated when, on the expiry of that three-year lease, the Council rolled it over again. This was a minor victory for us, but for how long could we continue to stall the Council?

On 11 May 2000 a member of the Omahu community spotted an excavator digging holes on top of Puketapu. The Council's and McLeod's portions of Puketapu were being put up for sale to an international wine company for grape-growing. For Maori, the growing of 'food' for human consumption on a sacred place was totally inappropriate.

The Council then engaged the services of an 'archaeologist', Elizabeth Pishief; an historian, Patrick Parsons; and a local elder, to research the history and

Figure 11.5 Protestors call for land to be returned (© Janeen Love).

Figure 11.6 View westwards from the upper *pa* showing protesters and vehicles
(© Janeen Love).

archaeology of Puketapu. The newspaper then reported, 'Historian finds no proof of pa site' (*Hawke's Bay Today*, 1 September 2000). Of course, this was exactly what Omahu Maori had predicted would happen.

There are issues with the 'archaeologist', Elizabeth Pishief, who walked over the 75-acre hill in a 2–3 hour site visit and concluded that there were no middens on the hill – thus leading Council members and public alike to believe that there had never been a *pa* there at all. It is notable that Pishief's scientific methodology comprised of auger drills into the soil of up to 600 mm depth at six spots on the whole hill. It is notable, too, that Pishief's formal qualifications make no mention of archaeology (E. Pishief, Report for HDC, 25 August 2000).

An unprecedented large gathering of Maori attended the September 2000 Council meeting. The outcome of the meeting was fortuitous. The land was not sold. The inaction by the Council was to last another three years until 2003, when glossy 'for sale' advertisements appeared in local newspapers. The publicity won support for us from two district council members.

To further help stymie the sale, a *hikoi* (peaceful march) was organised for 10 August 2003. Over 500 people turned up over the course of the day. It was a very moving occasion attended by a wide cross-section of the community including a Member of Parliament. For most people, it was the first time they had ever been up the hill. Some 400 petition signatures were gathered that day in preparation for the meeting of the Council four days later (Figure 11.5 and 11.6).

On 14 August 2003, over 200 people, Maori and non-Maori alike, turned up to Council Chambers to silently protest over the pending sale of two of the land lots. After lengthy discussions, the Council unexpectedly announced that it would set aside the one land lot it had promised Omahu Maori years before, and that it would also give Omahu Maori the opportunity to purchase the other two lots.

The Puketapu/Fernhill Reserve Trust and its plans

Hence a new entity in the battle to save Puketapu was formed. The Puketapu/Fernhill Reserve Trust (PFRT) was formed with the intention of raising a loan to purchase the land as a reservation for use by all peoples. The PFRT would undertake a fundraising campaign to repay the loan. Particular people were targeted for the Trust in an effort to ensure it was properly established and also to give the Trust some public respectability – especially once the public fundraising campaign to repay the loan would begin. Along with myself as Chairperson of the Trust, other foundation members include a retired High Court judge, two district councillors, an environmental scientist, an indigenous educationist and an accountant.

In the meantime, the Council allowed the building of two new houses on the hill after 2003, much to the disappointment of the Omahu people. The previous owner, Mr Don McLeod, had gone bankrupt, sold the land to the Council, and

Figure 11.7 The two McLeod houses on Puketapu – the upper one built since 2003 (© J. S. Te Rito).

bought one lot back; he had then built a secondary house on it for his family. He then subdivided the land and sold a part, upon which the new owner has built a house. The OMC protested at the construction of these houses, but it was to no avail (Figure 11.7).

The longer-term plan by the PFRT for Puketapu, once it is purchased, is to replant the hill with the original species of indigenous flora that once grew there. Unfortunately, Trust member Dr Geoff Park, nationally known as an expert conservationist and ecological scientist, passed away in 2009. He will be sadly missed. He had concluded that the hill was probably once covered with totara, matai, kowhai and karaka trees. The hill-top has been ploughed so many times since 1940 that very little of the original vegetation remains. It has been replaced with pasture grasses planted for grazing sheep.

The Trust's broad aim is to form a reserve for the general public. It is envisaged that the reserve will be a site where locals, school groups and tourists will visit. Once the land has been purchased by the Trust, the focus will be on ecological restoration, developing Puketapu as a nature reserve, opening it up for public enjoyment and educating the community about the historical, cultural and archaeological significance of the area.

Conclusions

From the highest point on Puketapu, one can get a panoramic view of the mountain ranges to the west, the Heretaunga Plains proper, the meandering rivers, and the sea to the east. Even for this reason alone, Puketapu is well worth protecting. Being *wahi tapu* and a site of cultural significance makes it that much more compelling that it should be protected. An end to the saga of Puketapu is eagerly awaited by Trust members and the broader Omahu community. The struggle is not over, however, until the current purchase offer by the PFRT is accepted by the HDC. The Trust has a loan lined up to pay the cost. The Trust plans to encourage the formation of a 'Friends of the Reserve' group to help raise the funds. The 19–20-year struggle will not have been in vain as Puketapu will be better protected as a sacred site, and the public will have gained a green space with great views. The battle to save Puketapu is not over yet and will go on, just as the battle to save other sacred sites all over the world must go on.

Epilogue

After 22 years of struggle by the people of Omahu and friends to protect Puketapu/Fernhill as a sacred site, the Puketapu/Fernhill Reserve Trust gained certificate of title to the newly formed reserve on 22 February 2011, hence ensuring a safer future for the site.

References

Best, E. (1918). The Land of Tara. *Journal of the Polynesian Society*, **27** (Issue 105) (Part II), 1–26.

Buchanan, J. (1973). *The Maori History & Place Names of Hawke's Bay*. Wellington: A. H. & A. W. Reed Ltd.

Gordon, A. (2004). *In the Shadow of the Cape: A History of the Gordon Family of Clifton*. Cape Kidnappers: A. Gordon.

12

The Roman goddess Care: a therapy for the planet

GRAZIA FRANCESCATO and DANIELA TALAMO

'The XXI Century will either be spiritual or it won't be at all'.
(André Malraux)

'Blessed be the water, blessed be the earth, blessed be the air, blessed be the forest, blessed be the cloud and the rain: protect us and make us fall in love with you'.
(Berito Kuwaru'wa, spokesperson of the UWA people of Colombia)

Introduction: principles, concepts and values

'Dea Cura', the Goddess Care, could be considered a minor deity within the superabundant Roman Pantheon. Yet she had a most peculiar and literally vital role. Her task was to give shape and mould to human beings so as to ensure the continuity of life within them. Life without shape, without an intentionally cast mould, constantly redesigned, maintained and purposely taken care of, simply could not exist. Goddess Care – and the set of concepts and principles which guided her mission in ancient Latin times – is of relevance to humankind of the third millennium as well. She might hand us the right ingredients of the most needed recipe for our era, an adequate therapy for Mother Earth, gripped in the most severe and global ecological crisis humans have ever caused.

Her very name – *Nomen omen* in Latin (name-giving is not neutral: it evokes and contains the destiny of each living being) – was thus extremely significant. 'Cura' implies a mix of concepts and feelings which involve both the mental and the physical level, the emotional as well as the rational response. 'Taking care' of

Sacred Species and Sites: Advances in Biocultural Conservation, ed. Gloria Pungetti, Gonzalo Oviedo and Della Hooke. Published by Cambridge University Press. © Cambridge University Press 2012.

something or somebody calls forth, first of all, the Principle of Responsibility, a principle that is basic to ecological wisdom and practice.

For the first time in the history of humankind, we are invited to accept and practice a global 'Principle of Responsibility', widening its scope to include not only other human beings, present and future, but also animals, plants and ecosystems at large – in short, all living creatures. The planet itself is considered to be a living, sentient organism according to the ancient Greek philosophy that looked upon the earth as a divine being: Gaia (a theory which has recently been revived and made famous worldwide by the British writer and ecologist James Lovelock in his book *Gaia* (Lovelock, 1979).

Deeply linked to the Principle of Responsibility, we can find, within the meaningful name of 'Dea Cura', another concept which represents a pillar of ecological doctrine; this is the Principle of Interdependency. *Tout se tient*, as the French motto goes; everything on earth is connected with everything else, weaving the rich and yet vulnerable web of life, the opulent and yet frail texture of Biodiversity.

All ecological texts, starting with the classical one of Eugene P. Odum, *Fundamentals of Ecology* (1953; rewritten with Howard Thomas Odum in 1959), give scientific evidence to this self-evident truth, which is the common wisdom (and common everyday practice) found in ancient communities. The disruption of the principle of interconnectedness has been widely accepted as one of the main causes of the current environmental disaster, as pointed out in books by well-known gurus of the environmental movements such as Barry Commoner (1966; 1971), Lester Brown (Brown *et al.*, 1997) or Vandana Shiva (1994).

While this second concept could have been dismissed simply as a scientific statement or a mere fact of life, carrying no built-in moral implication, the ecological crisis and the environmental movement, which was born to face it, have added an ethical side to the Principle of Interdependency, both at social and ecological level. Every human action, as circumscribed as you will, if it damages one link of the chain is bound to disrupt the whole of it. No action, however minor, goes without consequence.

If an oil tanker breaks down on a coast – as has happened too many times, as for instance in Alaska in 1989 in the *Exxon Valdes* disaster – the spill will not only damage the local ecosystem, but a vast sea area, the bottom of the ocean itself and a wide range of sea organisms for many years or even decades. Additionally, of course, it will affect local human communities, as well as the economy at large. If a fire is lit in a forest, not only will local ecosystems and communities be damaged, but CO_2 and greenhouse gases will be added to the atmosphere of the planet, thus worsening the situation at global level.

The knowledge, so widely diffused today that none can pretend to ignore it, that solution or at least mitigation of the planetary ecological problems depends upon recognising and practising these two key concepts – Responsibility and Interdependency – brings forth a third basic principle that Dea Cura would certainly add to her footprint for humankind: the Principle of Precaution. The latter involves not only a moral duty, but it is explicitly formulated in current legislation, both at the international, European, National and local level.

The Precautionary Principle was elaborated during the 1980s, when the debate on sustainable development and the need to prevent environmental damages started to gain ground. It was solemnly laid down in the Rio Declaration (at the UN Conference in Rio de Janeiro, best known as the Earth Summit, in June 1992) and formally inserted in the EU Treaties starting from Maastricht in 1992 (article 174) and from then regularly mentioned in European directives and policies, such as the Communication of the European Commission on Precautionary Principle, issued on 2 February 2002.

On the precautionary principle grounds, any product or process should not be considered harmful only after having caused environmental disasters, but should, on the contrary, be proved safe, and therefore admitted to market circulation, only when all reasonable doubts on its possible harm to health and environment have been eliminated.

The European Parliament has been particularly keen on this issue, as one can gather from the countless resolutions and legislative acts constantly calling for the correct use of this principle, both on social and environmental levels. One example for all: the Resolution on the Green Book on food legislation and policies, dated 1 March 1998. Or, more recently, the Resolution on Climate Change policies, specifically on a new energy policy, voted on 14 February 2007.

In the cosmogony of Dea Cura, however, these three basic principles and the values they imply would have carried little weight and consequence had they not been kindled by the all-pervasive and compassionate force of Love, as a basic value. Responsibility, Interdependency and Precaution can be binding and effective sources of 'good action' and 'best practices' only if 'taking care' of the planet and its inhabitants is performed, not exclusively through cold judgement, but also through warm feeling.

What is needed is the essence of Cura itself: Responsible Love.

Diffusion and acceptance of Dea Cura principles and practice, a personal account

Has the Dea Cura lesson been listened to by environmental movements and organisations around the world? Has her therapy been successfully adopted and closely followed somewhere? Have these principles – Responsibility, Interdependency and Precaution – been applied in basic policies and behaviours?

The answer can be 'yes, indeed' if we grant the status of 'forerunners of environmentalism' to indigenous peoples, at least to those whose culture, identity and cosmovision has not been altered or disconnected by the meeting/clash with so-called 'civilised society'. Although they may know nothing about the Principle of Precaution and the like, many of their cultures and communities seem to have been able to conceive and practise sustainable living well before – actually thousands of years before – this concept was even thought of or defined by the first ecological movements and organisations/institutions.

The author's experience may be quoted as an example: I first learned the lesson of 'responsible love' in the early 1970s, upon first encountering the indigenous people of Mexico and of the Amazonas in my former role of environmental journalist and activist of conservation organisations, such as WWF-Italy. I was particularly touched and involved by two experiences.

The first dates back to 1989, when the Italian nature magazine I worked for at the time, *AIRONE*, sent me to the Xingu river area of Brazil to report on a very crucial Meeting of the Indigenous Peoples of Amazonia (which made front-page news because of the raging fires in those years that were calling world attention to the plight of the rainforest and also thanks to the attendance of celebrities such as British singer Sting and various politicians). I had the opportunity to contact and interact with the Kayapò and Yanomami Tribes, getting acquainted with their culture, traditional beliefs and holistic approach to the 'Pacha Mama', Mother Earth.

After several trips to Amazonia, both in my professional role and as president of WWF-Italy, I wrote my first essay on Nature and spirituality in a book *In Viaggio con l'Arcangelo* (Francescato, 2000) which was deeply inspired by the indigenous world vision.

The second experience took place from the year 2000 onwards, when I had already become a politician and the leader of the Italian Green Party. We were asked to support the U'wa people: 7000 men, women and children living in the Colombian Andes close to the border with Venezuela (Figures 12.1 and 12.2). Their ancestral territory, where they have been residing for 3000 years, had been invaded by OXY (Occidental Petroleum Corporation), a US-based oil company that since 1995 had been trying to drill and exploit oil fields in what they considered their 'sacred land'. The frequent meetings we had with them, together with many environmentalists from all around the world, gave us the opportunity to rediscover an ancient knowledge that was once part of our own culture (as Dea Cura demonstrates), but that has been quite forgotten or discarded in our own recent history.

The core of this primeval wisdom was carefully guarded by the so-called Werjaràs, the spiritual guides, who lived on the peaks of the Sierra del Cucuy, on the border with Venezuela, and never descended into the territories *abajo* (in the plain) in order to keep their 'spiritual strength' untouched. Their basic belief was that

Figure 12.1 Colombia, January 2001: a family belonging to the U'wa indigenous people.

the Earth is our Mother, and therefore sacred; that every human being, animal or plant is part of a whole and therefore also sacred; that disrupting this interconnected web of life, which combines the visible and invisible dimensions, is not only devastating from the environmental and social point of view, but also on the spiritual level. Therefore, they believe that the oil so ravenously sought after by OXY was nothing less than 'the blood of Mother Earth' and that, by drilling it, the 'Pacha Mama' would be deeply wounded and the sky would fall upon humankind. The struggle of the U'wa, they explained, was thus led not only in the name of this small ethnic group but for the sake of the whole of humankind, both for present and future generations.

'Our ancestral territory', stated the Werjaràs, 'is the very heart of the world. Anything that affects it will also have an impact on the planet as a whole. In order to avoid this, we are ready to do anything, including collective suicide: the only thing we refuse is the use of weapons and violence, because our god Sira and Mother Earth wouldn't approve of it'.

When we asked them by which means they meant to fight, and possibly win, such an uneven dispute with a giant oil corporation, they pointed out two strategies. The first was to be taken care of by the so-called *pueblo de abajo*: the U'wa tribes that lived in the plain and were in touch with 'modern society' and

Figure 12.2 Colombia, January 2001: U'wa Children outside their shanty.

therefore capable of using social and political tools such as lobbying the Colombia and USA governments, taking OXY to Court, and mobilising solidarity among environmentalist and human rights activists all around the world. The second strategy, entrusted to the skills of the Werjaràs and of *el pueblo de arriba* (the U'wa people living up in the mountains), relied on their ancestral wisdom and on what they defined as their 'high spiritual technology'. They actually stated that they were able to send and receive dreams, feelings and thoughts. They even affirmed that they could, by the sheer strength of their mental concentration, change the surrounding reality; for example, removing objects or transporting them. They stated that they could do so thanks to the wisdom and spiritual know-how of their ancestors, which had been carefully guarded and transmitted from generation to generation. The secret of their knowledge, they confirmed, was a deep and loving contact with Mother Earth, whose safeguard they were responsible for.

Thus they felt that oil drilling was a threat to Mother Earth, the U'wa People and all humankind. Therefore: 'We are trying to move the oil, to make it sink at such depth that Oxy will give up drilling it … It is a very hard spiritual work but there are many of us involved in this task, living here on the mountains', they concluded, pointing to the vast array of peaks and mountain ranges above them, clouded by misty veils.

We environmentalists were, of course, called upon to contribute to the first strategy and obviously we considered the second at best as a dream, or a cultural tradition to be respected but not entrusted.

Seven months later, we heard from our U'wa friends and from the Colombian environmentalists that OXY had dismantled 'Gibraltar 1', the drilling and exploitation area in the heart of the indigenous territory and had left the region. For technical and political reasons, apparently – because the Werjaràs had done their job, the U'wa People replied.

In any case, it was thanks to their cultural and spiritual strength, to the deep belief that their place was the sacred heart of a sacred planet, that this small ethnic group was able to resist for almost a decade the assault of a powerful oil corporation (and the following intrusions of the national oil company), rejecting the temptation to resort to violence in a country like Colombia already filled with violence.

The story of the U'wa is, of course, an extraordinary one and it is likely to be rejected by the rational Western mind.

However, many such stories of resistance to the physical invasion of their land and to the disruption of their traditional cultures can be related by activists of environmental organisations who have carried on projects of cooperation with indigenous peoples. Quite often, the patrimony of ideas and habits, connected with a core belief of the sacredness of Mother Earth, have made a distinct contribution to the conservation of their land and of the sacred species and sites guarded within.

One of the first accounts of this peculiar brand of cooperation between indigenous peoples and conservationists can be found in the book *The Law of the Mother*, edited by Elizabeth Kemf, WWF International Conservation Editor, and compiled by WWF in collaboration with IUCN (Kempf, 1993). The book describes 30 conservation cases around the world, combining the protection of Indigenous People and Nature. It was meant to be 'a testimonial to these endangered peoples and their equally endangered native wisdom, offered in the hope that we may remember what they have not forgotten – that the earth is a sacred place' (Kempf, 1993, back cover).

The indigenous people – at least those who are still faithful to the 'Law of the Mother' and have not been forced or pushed to abandon their traditional ways of living – feel they belong to the earth, while we – Western People – feel that we are entitled to rule the land and limitlessly exploit its resources: they are stewards, we are owners.

The alliance between faiths and conservation

As far as environmental movements are concerned, the ancient indigenous wisdom has been part, since their appearance, of the ecological culture. At least, it is present in some of its mainstreams, like 'Deep Ecology', a philosophy which gives Nature a value in itself as part of the utilitarian use of its resources: 'L'ecologia profonda e il valore in sè della Natura' (Spinetti, 2007).

This philosophy can actually be considered, rather often, as a sort of homecoming, since the belief in the power of Mother Earth and the sacredness of places, sites and species is not only a patrimony of the 'officially' recognised indigenous peoples of the world (according to the Declaration of Human Rights on Indigenous Peoples, voted by the UN Assembly in September 2007), but it is also a common heritage of many Western rural cultures, at least up to a few decades ago. Today, there are more than 370 million indigenous people in some 70 countries worldwide (source: UNPFII – UN Permanent Forum of Indigenous Issues).

Above all, it still represents a cherished, well-guarded treasure within the most long-lasting and tradition-rooted of the world institutions: the faiths. To all faiths, Nature is not a neutral, passive, exclusively material 'phenomenon': it is part of God's creation; it holds the shining brand of its Author and Maker. Man is at the top of the pyramid, but he is meant to be the careful steward, not the selfish and thoughtless master of all other created beings. Although sacred and traditional texts might have been wrongfully interpreted as giving limitless license of predominance to human beings, the correct interpretation of God's words, be it Jehovah, Allah or Buddha, seems in line with the warning of Dea Cura: Respect, Love and Responsibility should be the keys of the relationship between man and Creation.

The first worldwide conservation organisation that consciously sought a strategy of alliance with religions and faiths was probably WWF-International. In the late summer of 1986, in the Umbrian hill town of Assisi, for the first time, the leaders of five major faiths (Buddhism, Christianity, Hinduism, Islam and Judaism) and representatives of WWF-International gathered in the Basilica of San Francis, in an inspiring ceremony, and issued the Assisi Declarations, authoritative statements on ecology and nature.

This event was the first step of a continuing process of reflection and action on ecological issues by each of the major faiths. In 1995 representatives of these faiths, joined by three more – Bahà'i, Jainism and Sikhism – met at Windsor Castle for a Summit of Religions and Conservation, during which each faith presented an action plan for environmental work over the next five years. A new

Figure 12.3 13–17 December 2000, in the old centre of Kathmandu. Photograph taken at a ceremony organised by ARC International and WWF International to celebrate 'Gifts to the Earth' (© Grazia Francescato). See colour plate section.

foundation – The Alliance of Religions and Conservation (ARC; www.arcworld. org) – was established to coordinate the various theoretical, practical and educational projects that each religion pledged to undertake (Figures 12.3 and 12.4). This alliance is discussed here as an example of the continuing efforts to coordinate such movements and objectives.

The strategy of ARC is twofold: to help faiths realise their potential to be proactive on environmental issues, and to help secular groups recognise this and become active partners. By drawing on holy books, sacred sites and the widespread assets of the faiths, ARC helps create environmental projects such as forest management, organic farming, educational projects and sacred nature reserves and to address climate change.

Actually, ARC is working with faith communities to set a lead in tackling climate change. Under ARC's Climate Change Partnership Initiative, several major world religions have launched schemes to press for urgent government action. They have also pledged to do their own environmental audits and recommend their followers to do the same. Good examples are the Sikh initiative in India, the Union of Liberal and Progressive Synagogues in the UK, and the Episcopal Power in the USA. ARC has also issued a booklet to advise people – whatever their religion or resources – on how to help tackle the global warming problem.

Figure 12.4 'Gifts to the Earth', Kathmandu (© Grazia Francescato). See colour plate section.

In Italy, a Committee has been established to promote the creation of an Italian branch of ARC, especially in order to build a network of Sacred Sites that will protect a very valuable patrimony of natural, historical and architectural sites, linked to Christianity. Quite a few of them fall inside Protected Areas. In Italy there are 3 500 000 protected hectares of land – more than 11% of the territory – 2565 sites of Natura 2000 which cover about 20% of the territory, 24 national parks, 128 regional parks, 145 national nature reserves, 270 regional nature reserves, 23 marine protected areas, 137 other protected areas (all those protected areas which are not included in the existing definitions), 2675 municipalities and 98 provinces.

For example, in the National Park of Cilento and Vallo di Diano, in the South of Italy, a survey has been carried by Domenico Nicoletti, President of HISPA, The High School for the Public Administration of Protected Areas, to identify traditions and cultural traits linked to Christian Faith. Of course, many of these rites and ceremonies used to take place in natural surroundings, which are now safeguarded by the institution of the National Park, but which were already considered sacred in rural cultures.

The following example describes pilgrimages to the local sacred mountains, the Cult of Stones, the Tree of Life, and the Angel Caves. Pilgrimages are meetings

Figure 12.5 29 September 1994: after 30 years of oblivion, the ancient pilgrimage from Vieste to the sacred site of Monte Sant'Angelo (Puglia, southern Italy) is restored by WWF-Italy.

of micro-cultures, sometimes quite far from each other but which offer a unique chance for cultural interactions (Figure 12.5).

Unaltered for centuries is the custom of *cénte* – typical of Cilento – votive offerings of candles. They are usually grouped in hundreds with coloured bands which keep them together to create the shape of a boat, a castle or an egg; this depends on the tradition of each individual village. The use of these gifts goes back to ancient Greek traditions celebrating Demetra, Goddess of harvests. The *cénte* are always brought by women and they are an expression of rural culture.

Usually the destinations for these offerings are sanctuaries which are located on the top of mountains or in caves. In the Cilento there are seven and they have in common the legend of the Seven Sisters of the Virgin Mary:

> Virgin Mary of Granato, Capaccio Vecchio, M. Vesole Sottano, m. 254;
> Virgin Mary of Stella, Sessa Cilento, M. della Stella, m. 1131;
> Virgin Mary of Civitella, Moio della Civitella, M. Civitella, m. 818;
> Virgin Mary of Carmine, Catona, M. del Carmine, m. 713;
> Virgin Mary of Neve, Piaggine-Sanza, M. Cervati, m. 1899;
> Virgin Mary of Pietrasanta, San Giovanni a Piro, M. Pietrasanta, m. 528;
> Virgin Mary of Sacro Monte, Novi Velia, M. Gelbison o Sacro, m. 1707.

The cult of 'The Seven Marys' is very ancient and it has its roots in pre-Christian models. Every cultural area of the south has its 'Seven Marys' and the cult sites are always in high locations which close themselves in a circle facing the sea, creating a sort of protection for the site which represents a micro-cosmos.

The Sacro Monte Pilgrimage. This happens once a year in all Cilento villages, in Basilicata and Calabria too, its cultural area is very extensive.

The Madonna della Stella Pilgrimage. This happens every Sunday after 15 August. The sanctuary is the only building surviving in Lucania on the top of the mountain that has been called Cilento since the tenth century.

The Madonna del Carmine Pilgrimage. This takes place every 16 July and celebrates the Tree of Life and the Stone of Fecundation ('a Prèta).

Further, the meaning implied in the customs of ascent and the sanctuary being located in a cave (the bowels of the earth) represents a direct recall to the underworld that permits one immediately to feel the sense of spirituality. The ritual of pilgrimage is more rural, going through the fields to show the countryside to the Saint Protector and then to come back to the centre (mother church), the place of people. These pilgrimages are expressions of peasant culture and have a clear point of reference (cultivated fields and houses close to the church). The presence of a pastoral world is represented in the evening when the shepherds light a fire on the mountain to show that the sacred time is starting.

The original idea of prehistoric cults such as 'The Cult of Stones' was that the stones would be able to fertilise women who were sterile. We can find their presence in the sacred sites of Cilento Sanctuaries or along the paths.

In the sanctuary of Sacro Monte – Sacred Mountain – there is a place called Manto ra Marònna where it is said that there are clear signs carved on a rock: scissors, needle and thimble. At the side of the rock there are two monoliths with Menhir shapes, very close to each other, between which a person can barely pass. In ancient times sterile women would try to pass between them, rubbing their belly on the faces. Still in the Sacro Monte, there is another place with the same ceremony involving a similar monolith called Ciamba re cavallo. One can find another Menhir in Monte della Stella – 'Star Mountain' – where there is a sacred site called Prèta ru Mulàcchio ('stone of illegitimate sons') where the same ritual is practised. Another sacred site not far away is Prèta Nzitàta (which means 'it can make pregnant').

Nowadays the pilgrims perform the same ceremony but it has a different meaning: it is carried out for the purity of the soul and as a good omen.

The 'Tree of Life' is, even today, represented by a pole in front of a cemetery or in the centre of the churchyard. One such pole is at San Mauro Cilento; it is always covered with sacred images with some flowers at its foot, while another one is at Carmine Chapel in Catona, with three wooden sticks for the lights.

The original idea is that the Tree represents the cosmos in its capacity for regeneration, so it is the symbol of the Universe and represents the home of divinity. The origin of life itself in Christian tradition is the Tree of life represented by the cross. Other examples of the Tree of Life are in the crosses planted in the rocks or in the mountains (Cuozzo ra Croce, 'a Croce, l'Aria ra Croce). The Tree is also used on banners for the processions as a symbol to protect each village and as a symbol of union: although a specific congregation may differ from the other, all have, as a unique symbol of faith, the Tree of Life.

Finally, the origin of the Grotte dell'Angelo – The Angel Caves (Grotte di Pertosa) – goes back 35 million years. These caves are among the most important in all southern Italy, the only ones crossed by an underground river, the Tanagro o Negro. The course of this river has been altered to produce energy and this has caused an enlargement of the entry to the caves so that it is now possible to enter by evocative little ships.

Conclusions

The interaction between traditional spiritual values and biodiversity conservation appears to be an important dimension through which to foster the safeguarding and correct management of nature sites and species. An holistic approach, capable of crossing the boundaries between different disciplines, linking the social and cultural elements to the scientific ones, is certainly useful and should be promoted in interdisciplinary researches and field projects.

According to these experiences and case studies, it can be shown that the ancient wisdom of the Indigenous Peoples who have been able to preserve the fundamental beliefs of their cultures can offer valuable guidance in management and policy making in protected areas and for the preservation of ecosystems. Moreover, formal alliances between faiths and conservation, like that promoted by ARC, can provide valuable tools and policies to create a worldwide web of Sacred Sites, officially recognised as such, where Sacred Species of animals and plants can find their ultimate sanctuary.

It could be suggested that worldwide conservation organisations and institutions might formally include in their statement and policy the dimension of spiritual values in order to open up a new avenue for future conservation and sustainable development.

References

Brown, L., with Flavin, C., French, H. F. and Starke, L. (1997). *State of the Word: a Worldwide Institute Report on Progress toward a Sustainable Society*. London: W. W. Norton & Co.

Commoner, B. (1966). *Science and Survival*. New York, NY: Viking; London: Gollancz.

Commoner, B. (1971). *The Closing Circle: Nature, Man, and Technology*. New York, NY: Knopf.

Francescato, G. (2000). *In Viaggio con l'Arcangelo*. Rimini: Idea Libri.

Kemf, E. (ed.) (1993). *The Law of the Mother: Protecting Indigenous Peoples in Protected Areas*. San Francisco, CA: Sierra Club Books.

Lovelock, J. (1979). *Gaia: A New Look at Life on Earth*. Oxford: Oxford University Press.

Odum, E. P. (1953). *Fundamentals of Ecology*. London and Philadelphia: Saunders (2nd edition with H. T. Odum, 1959).

Shiva, V. (ed) (1994). *Biodiversity Conservation: Whose Resource? Whose Knowledge?* New Delhi: Indian National Trust for Art and Cultural Heritage.

Spinetti, M. (2007). L'ecologia profonda e il valore in sè della Natura. Available at: http://www.ariannaeditrice.it

PART IV   SACRED SPECIES

13

The conservation status of sacred species: a preliminary study

ANNA McIVOR and GLORIA PUNGETTI

Introduction

Currently more than 16 000 species are considered threatened with extinction worldwide, out of 41 000 species which have so far been assessed by the IUCN Red List (2007). More than 750 species are already extinct, and 65 species are only found in captivity or cultivation. The protection and conservation of species is paramount, not only to preserve our natural heritage for future generations, but also because species form the ecosystems on which we and all life depend.

In many cultures and faiths throughout the world, certain species are held sacred. Sacredness can mean that an object is exclusively dedicated to a god or religious purpose or is made holy by religious association, or it can signify that an object is safeguarded by religion, reverence or tradition (Allen, 1990). Therefore, sacred species may be protected from human activities which threaten their survival, such as over-exploitation and habitat degradation. This has potential for contributing to a species' conservation.

In this chapter the results of a pilot study carried out by the Cambridge Centre for Landscape and People on the conservation status of sacred species are presented. This information is used to explore whether being held sacred can protect species from extinction.

A methodology for research and sacred species

A literature review of sacred species for the pilot study was conducted in 2007. As it was time-limited, it did not attempt to include all sacred species or to do

Sacred Species and Sites: Advances in Biocultural Conservation, ed. Gloria Pungetti, Gonzalo Oviedo and Della Hooke. Published by Cambridge University Press. © Cambridge University Press 2012.

an in-depth study of the species included. The criterion for inclusion of a species in the review was that it should be recorded as 'sacred' or 'holy' in the literature. The study was limited to the English-speaking literature because of the preliminary nature of the review. Only species currently held sacred were included.

For each species or group of species, the following information was collated:

(a) species name, both the scientific and local names;
(b) the Red List status of the species according to the IUCN Red List (2007);
(c) the group of people holding it sacred;
(d) the geographic location or distribution of the people holding it sacred;
(e) the reason why it is considered sacred, i.e. beliefs or stories associated with it or its symbolism or significance;
(f) behaviour towards the sacred species or reason of threats; and
(g) the consequences of being held sacred for the species, with particular reference to the conservation implications for the species and the environment.

This formed the data set for each species, which was usually only partially available. In particular, little information was found for category (g).

In many literature sources, groups of organisms were referred to rather than single species. For example, in Japan the bear is held sacred by the Ainu people of Hokkaido, Sakhalin and the Kuril islands (Kitagawa, 1961). However, no information could be found on which of the two bear species present on these islands is sacred, or if all bears are held sacred. In such cases, groups of species were included in the review under the higher-order biological taxonomic name (e.g. in the case of the bear, the family Ursidae was recorded as being sacred to the Ainu people).

A small number of species were chosen as case studies to demonstrate the potential links between sacredness and conservation. For these species, further research was conducted.

Conservation status of sacred species

A total of 75 species or groups of species were included in the pilot study, consisting of 33 animals, 36 plants and 6 fungi. The animals included mammals, birds, reptiles, amphibians, fish and insects, and the plants included conifers, the ginkgo and flowering plants. Fifty-one individual species and 24 groups of species were included.

Of the 51 individually named species, 11 are currently listed on the IUCN Red List as being threatened with extinction (i.e. they are listed as Vulnerable, Endangered or Critically Endangered; Figure 13.1). Seven species are considered Near Threatened (i.e. they are close to reaching the IUCN criteria thresholds for

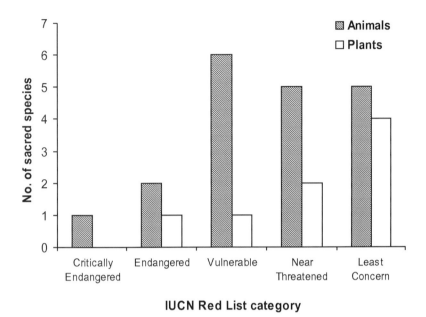

Figure 13.1 The number of sacred animals and plants included in this study are listed in each of the IUCN Red List categories.

one of the threat categories), and nine species are listed as Least Concern (i.e. they are considered in no danger of extinction). Twenty-four species have not yet been included in the IUCN Red List.

The species are held sacred by various peoples, cultures and faiths throughout the world; examples include the bowhead whale, *Balaena mysticetus*, held sacred by the Tikigaq people of north-west Alaska (Lowenstein, 1993); frogs (order Anura), sacred to the Japanese (Hyotan, 2005); and the lotus, *Nelumbo nucifera*, sacred to Buddhists and Hindus (Ward, 1952) (Figure 13.2). Some species are held sacred by members of a people, culture or faith who live in a particular area; for example: the long-tailed macaque monkey, *Macaca fascicularis*, is sacred to Hindus living in Bali (Wheatley, 1999; Dudley *et al.*, 2005). Other species are held sacred by the population of a certain area, who may be of mixed faith or ethnicity; for example, the cypress, *Cupressus sempervirens* (Figure 13.3), is sacred to the people of Turkey, including Muslims, Armenians, Christians and Jews, and is planted at the end of graves (Baker, 1974). A few deer among the *Cervidae* family are considered sacred, especially in North America and Europe (Figure 13.4).

The sacred species included here are distributed throughout the world. Several sacred species from Asia and North America have been included (31 and 19 species or groups of species, respectively). Less well represented in this study are South America (9 species), Europe (6 species), Africa (11 species) and Australasia (3 species),

Figure 13.2 The lotus is a plant sacred to Buddhists and Hindus (© Gloria Pungetti). See colour plate section.

Figure 13.3 The cypress and the olive are held sacred by populations of areas of mixed faith or ethnicity, such as in the Mediterranean (© Gloria Pungetti).

Figure 13.4 A few deer among the Cervidae family are considered sacred especially in North America and Europe (© Italian Ministry for the Environment, Land and Sea). See colour plate section.

but this may reflect the availability of literature rather than the actual number of sacred species on these continents.

Sacred species are associated with a great variety of different symbolisms. They may be believed to be incarnate deities, guardian spirits or the spirits of dead people; the species may also be the home of spirits (e.g. the kapok tree is home to spirits of nearby shrines; Van Binsbergen, 1984). Some species play a central role in the origination myths of peoples (e.g. the Mushahari clan believe they are descended from tigers; Gokhale, 2001), or they may be associated with the definition of a people (e.g. the Cuyui Ticutta are so called because they eat the cui-ui lake sucker fish, *Chasmistes cujus*; Pyramid Lake Fisheries, 2000). The species may embody desirable traits, such as the social wasps held sacred by the Bribri people of Costa Rica (Starr and Bozzoli de Wille, 1990), or may be totemic species (e.g. beetles of the family Cerambycidae are totems for certain tribes in Australia; Ratcliffe, 1990). Species may be thought to have magical powers or may be associated with good or bad luck. Sacred species are also often used in healing, to protect and cure diseases and to keep evil spirits away.

Several sacred species are associated with rituals and ceremonies, where they may be sacrificed, used as a ceremonial sacrament, used to call in the spirits or to make ritual items, or eaten to induce alternative states of consciousness (several

Figure 13.5 Eagles and their feathers are central to many religious and spiritual customs, e.g. amongst Native Americans in the United States, First Nations in Canada and many peoples of Meso-America (© Italian Ministry for the Environment, Land and Sea). See colour plate section.

plants and fungi: Schultes, 1969). Eagles, for example (Figure 13.5), are central to many religious and spiritual customs, and their feathers are used in ceremonies to honour leadership and bravery and in totem poles as heraldic crests of important clans of Native Americans, while in ancient Peru eagles were worshipped and depicted in the arts.

Behaviour towards sacred species also varies widely. Some species are protected from human contact, e.g. by taboos, curses or punishments to those who touch or harm the species. For example, among the Ashanti people of west Africa, killing a leopard is punishable by death (Olupona, 1993); and in Iraq it is believed that if someone cuts down a Christ's Thorn Jujube tree (*Ziziphus spina-christi*), he will soon fall ill and die (Dafni *et al.*, 2005). Other sacred species are used, either as part of a religious ceremony or ritual, or as part of everyday life as food, to make clothes or jewellery, or as timber in building and furniture-making. Some uses do not harm the organism; for example, the use of temple elephants to give blessings by Hindus in India. Other uses result in the death of the organism; for example, the reindeer, *Rangifer tarandus*, is used as a sacrificial animal, for food and clothes, and as a draught animal by the Nenets of north-eastern Europe and western Siberia (Niglas, 1997). A number of sacred species are also bred, fed or cultivated, including cows, elephants and doves in India, reindeer in northern Europe and western Siberia, and many plants such as rice (sacred in Japan), datura (sacred in many tropical regions), the lotus (sacred in Buddhist and Hindu areas) and the olive tree (sacred for some Jews) (Ward, 1952; Baker, 1974; Harris, 1978; Sukumar, 1989; Niglas, 1997; Leda, 2001; Sax, 2001; Hamilton, 2004; Hageneder, 2005; Finney, 1999).

For five species, being held sacred has contributed to their conservation. The black and white colobus (*Colobus vellerosus*) and the mona monkey (*Cercopithecus mona*) are sacred to the people of Boabeng and Fiema villages in Ghana; their sacred grove has become a wildlife sanctuary and is protected both by customary law and modern legislature (Dudley *et al*., 2005). In North America, the bison (*Bison bison*), grey wolf (*Canis lupus*) and cui-ui lakesucker fish (*Chamistes cujus*) are the subjects of conservation campaigns and projects, either led by or in collaboration with the people holding them sacred, i.e. the Lakota Nation, the Nez Perce people and the Paiute Tribe, respectively (Mack, 1999; Pyramid Lake Fisheries, 2000; The Buffalo War, downloaded 2007; feministing.com, downloaded 2007).

Case studies

The tiger

The tiger, *Panthera tigris*, is held sacred by the Mushahari clan of the Bodo tribe in Assam, India, who believe it to be their ancestor (Gokhale, 2001). It is listed as Endangered (IUCN, 2007); major threats include hunting and illegal poaching for skins and oriental medicine, habitat loss and decline in prey species. While it has already disappeared from the south-western part of its range, it is still widely distributed throughout Asia. Isolated populations exist in the remaining fragmented habitat (Cat Specialist Group, 2002). The area where the Mushahari clan lives is too small to ensure the survival of tigers, but could form an effective tiger reserve.

The cui-ui lakesucker

The cui-ui lakesucker fish, *Chasmistes cujus*, is listed as Critically Endangered (IUCN, 2007). It is found only in Pyramid Lake in Nevada, USA, and is sacred to the Pyramid Lake Paiute Tribe (Pyramid Lake Fisheries, 2000). It is central to their identity, and they are traditionally known as the *Cuyui Ticutta*, which translates as the cui-ui eaters. In the past, the cui-ui formed their staple food, although they currently do not eat it because of its endangered status.

It was previously found in other water bodies in the area; most recently it was lost from Winnemucca Lake when this dried up early last century due to water diversion and drought. In the years up to 1970, water diversions and a dam caused the water level of Pyramid Lake to drop by 25 m, and this prevented the cui-ui from breeding except in very wet years, as it could not reach its spawning grounds.

Pyramid Lake and the lower part of the Truckee river lie entirely within the Pyramid Lake Indian Reservation, and the Paiute Tribe have taken an active role in the conservation of this species. They have established a hatchery where young fish are reared and then returned to Pyramid Lake, so that there is recruitment into the population even when water levels prevent the fish from spawning. A combination of several wet years and this artificial rearing has resulted in an increase in population numbers, and the Paiute people look forward to a time when fish numbers have recovered sufficiently for them to be able to harvest their traditional food source (Pyramid Lake Fisheries, 2000).

The ginkgo

The ginkgo or maidenhair tree, *Ginkgo biloba*, is listed as Endangered (IUCN, 2007). Wild populations remain in only five small locations in China, although it is widely cultivated in cities around the world because it can survive well in polluted areas. It is sacred to Buddhists and Taoists in China and Japan, and is often grown in Buddhist and Taoist temple grounds (Hageneder, 2005). It also has medicinal uses, and is used like other trees for timber. Its cultivation in temple grounds over thousands of years has possibly saved this species from extinction, as even the remaining wild populations may be descendants of temple trees.

Contribution of sacredness to species conservation

In this preliminary study, 75 sacred animals, plants and mushrooms have been included. Given the time-limited nature of this study, it is likely that very many more sacred species would be identified from a more in-depth exploration of the available literature. Accordingly, for the small number of sacred species included in this review, the following discussion is offered as a first step towards the consideration of how sacredness can contribute to species conservation.

Sacredness is not enough to protect species from the threat of extinction, as several sacred species are threatened according to the IUCN Red List (Figure 13.1). In particular, nine of the 33 sacred animals species studied are threatened. By contrast, only two of the sacred plants are threatened; this could be because few of these plants have yet been evaluated by the IUCN Red List (i.e. more may be

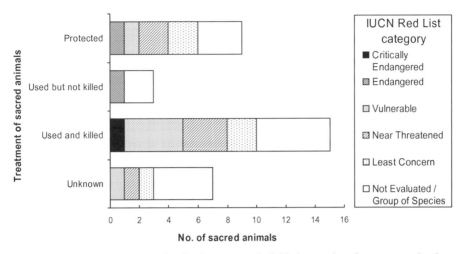

Figure 13.6 How sacred animals are treated, divided up to show how many animals are in each IUCN Red List category.

threatened with extinction), rather than because sacredness offers good protection from threats. However, the practice of cultivating sacred plants in temple grounds and burial sites may have contributed to their survival, as in the case of the ginkgo tree (see case study). None of the sacred fungi have yet been evaluated for the IUCN Red List, so the effect of sacredness on fungal conservation is unknown.

Possible reasons why sacredness has not protected some species from threats include the fact that sacredness does not always mean that species are not used, or that the people holding the species sacred are unable to give the species enough protection. These two possibilities will be discussed below.

Among sacred species included in this study, only a minority are completely protected from use by humans. The great majority are used in a variety of ways, including as foods, for healing and in ceremonies. Some societies depend on sacred species for their existence; for example, rice is sacred in Japan (Frazer, 1922; Hamilton, 2004), taro is sacred in Hawaii (Science, 2006) and reindeer are sacred to the Nenets of north-eastern Europe (Niglas, 1997). An important question is whether the use of sacred species is contributing to their decline; if so, we might expect that sacred species which are used are more likely to be threatened with extinction than those which are protected. The data shown in Figure 13.6 provide no evidence for this, with threatened species being found in both groups in similar proportions. There is also no support for the hypothesis that species which are used and killed are more likely to be threatened than those which are used but not harmed (Figure 13.6).

The main reason why many sacred species are threatened with extinction is that the threats to the species act at levels over which the people holding them sacred have no control. For example, the area where the Mushahari clan lives is very small relative to the range of the tiger (see case study). The clan cannot prevent the tiger being hunted elsewhere. In a similar way, the Inuit are unable to prevent the global warming which threatens the polar bear, one of their sacred species (Sax, 2001).

This demonstrates that being sacred is often not enough to protect species from threats. However, the high value of sacred species to these people can result in them playing an active role in the conservation of the sacred species, as shown in the case of the cui-ui lake sucker fish (see case study), where the Pyramid Lake Paiute Tribe contributed to the cui-ui's conservation by rearing young fish to supplement the lake population. This shows that even species which are not strictly protected by being sacred may be the subjects of conservation efforts by the peoples holding them sacred.

Conclusions

Sacred species form a subset of species which have spiritual value to humans. Other species of spiritual or cultural value include lucky species, magical species and taboo species. These species will also have certain behaviours associated with them that may contribute to either the protection or destruction of the species. For example, there are taboos against eating crayfish species in some villages in Madagascar, resulting in larger populations of crayfish than in villages without such taboos (Jones, 2004). In order to understand the extinction risk to a species, all these values need to be taken into account, and future work should extend its remit to include such species.

References

Allen, R. E. (ed.) (1990). *The Concise Oxford English Dictionary of Current English*. Oxford: Clarendon Press.

Baker, R. St. B. (1974). *Famous Trees of Bible Lands*. London: H. H.Greaves Ltd.

Cat Specialist Group. (2002). *Panthera tigris*. In: *IUCN 2007*. 2007 IUCN Red List of Threatened Species. URL: http://www.iucnredlist.org (accessed 19 November 2007).

Dafni, A., Levy, S. and Lev, E. (2005). The ethnobotany of Christ's Thorn Jujube (*Ziziphus spina-christi*) in Israel. *Journal of Ethnobiology and Ethnomedicine*, **1**, 1–11.

Dudley, N., Higgins-Zogib, L. and Mansourian, S. (2005). *Beyond Belief: Linking Faiths and Protected Areas to Support Biodiversity Conservation*. WWF, Equilibrium and ARC. Gland: WWF.

Feministing.com. URL: http://feministing.com/archives/006306.html (accessed 21 February 2007).

Finney, D. (1999). *The Sacred Birds*. Compiled by D. Finney. URL: http://www.greatdreams. com/alex/sacred-birds.htm (accessed 22 February 2007).

Frazer, J. (1922). *The Golden Bough*. London: Penguin Books.

Gokhale, Y. (2001). Biodiversity as a sacred space. The Hindu. Folio. Earthscapes. Special Issue, May, 2001. URL: http://www.hinduonnet.com/folio/fo0105/01050140.htm (accessed 4 March 2007).

Hageneder, F. (2005). *The Living Wisdom of Trees*. London: Duncan Baird Publishers.

Hamilton, R. W. (2004). *The Art of Rice: Spirit and Sustenance in Asia*. Los Angeles, CA: UCLA Fowler Museum of Cultural History.

Harris, M. (1978). India's sacred cow. *Human Nature*, **1**, 28–36.

Hyotan. (2005). Good luck symbols. The Frog (Kaeru). *Japanese Culture and Social Customs Part 4*. In Issue 158 (June). URL: http://www.city.hitachi.ibaraki.jp/upload/freepage/ shikatsu/hyotanhp/2005_jun/kaeru/kaeru.htm (accessed 26 February 2007).

IUCN (2007). *2007 IUCN Red List of Threatened Species*. URL: http://www.iucnredlist.org. (accessed October–November 2007).

Jones, J. P. G (2004). The sustainability of crayfish harvesting in Ranomafana National Park, Madagascar. Unpublished Ph.D. thesis, University of Cambridge.

Kitagawa, J. M. (1961). Ainu Bear Festival (Iyumante). *History of Religions*, **1**, 95–151.

Leda. (2001) URL: http://leda.lycaeum.org/?ID=16271 (accessed 21 February 2007).

Lowenstein, T. (1993). *Ancient Land: Sacred Whale. The Inuit Hunt and its Rituals*. London: Bloomsbury.

Mack, C. (1999). Restoring the Gray Wolf in Idaho. Endangered Species Bulletin, U.S. Fish and Wildlife Service (July, 1999). URL: http://findarticles.com/p/ articles/mi_m0ASV/is_4_24/ai_58505407 (accessed 1 March 2007).

Niglas, L. (1997). Reindeer in the Nenets Worldview. Pro Ethnologia, **5** (Arctic Studies 1). URL: http://www.erm.ee/?node=140 (accessed 4 March 2007).

Olupona, J. K. (1993). Some notes on animal symbolism in African religion and culture. *Anthropology and Humanism*, **18**, 3–12.

Pyramid Lake Fisheries. (2000). Dave Koch Cui-Ui Hatchery. URL: http://www. pyramidlakefisheries.org/Cui-ui.htm (accessed 1 March 2007).

Ratcliffe, B. C. (1990). The significance of scarab beetles in the ethnoentomology of non-industrial indigenous peoples. In *Ethnobiology*, ed. D. A. Posey *et al.*, Belém: Museu Paraense Emílio Goeldi, pp. 159–85.

Sax, B. (2001). *The Mythical Zoo: An Encyclopedia of Animals in World Myth, Legend and Literature*. Santa Barbara, CA: ABC-CLIO.

Schultes, R. E. (1969). Hallucinogens of plant origin. *Science*, **163**, 245–54.

Science. (21 July 2006). Universal ownership. Newsmakers, ed. Yudhijit Bhattacharjee. *Science*, **313**, 295. DOI: 10.1126/science.313.5785.295a.

Starr, C. K. and Bozzoli de Wille, M. E. (1990). Social wasps among the Bribri of Costa Rica. In *Ethnobiology*, ed. D. A. Posey *et al.*, Belém: Museu Paraense Emílio Goeldi, pp. 187–94.

Sukumar, R. (1989). *The Asian Elephant: Ecology and Management. Cambridge Studies in Applied Ecology and Resource Management Series*. Cambridge: Cambridge University Press.

The Buffalo War. URL: http://www.pbs.org/buffalowar/war.html (accessed 21 February 2007).

Ward, W. E. (1952). The lotus symbol: its meaning in Buddhist art and philosophy. *The Journal of Aesthetics and Art Criticism*, **11**(2) Special issue on Oriental Art and Aesthetics, 135–46.

Wheatley, B. P. (1999). *The Sacred Monkeys of Bali*. Long Grove, IL: Waveland Press.

Van Binsbergen, W. M. J. (1984). Socio-ritual structures and modern migration among the Manjak of Guinea Bissau: ideological reproduction in a context of peripheral capitalism. *Antropologische Verkenningen* (Utrecht), **3**(2), 11–43. URL: http://www.shikanda.net/african_religion/socio.htm (accessed 2 March 2007).

14

The role of taboos and traditional beliefs in aquatic conservation in Madagascar

MIJASOA M. ANDRIAMAROVOLOLONA and JULIA P. G. JONES

Moa raha fantatra va zalahy tsiaña fa dia fomban-drazana ka dia arahina

These are the ancestors' customs and so we follow them
(traditional saying quoted in Rahatoka, 1984)

Tsy dinin-draha ny ela

Nothing is immune to change over time
(elder from Ambalavero, Commune Tolongoina)

Introduction

Traditional Malagasy culture and religion are focused around respect and reverence for the ancestors (Sharp, 1994; Lambek, 2002). Objects or places strongly associated with the ancestors may be viewed as sacred (*masina*) and a complex system of prohibitions known as *fady* influences people's day-to-day behaviour. Although the word *fady* may be used to describe acts which are simply breaches of good manners (Lambek, 1992; Jones *et al.*, 2008), many *fady* are strict taboos which would offend the ancestors and bring supernatural punishment if broken (Ruud, 1960; Profita, 1967).

In many traditional societies, taboos have an important influence on the use of natural resources, providing protection to species or sites (McDonald, 1977; Ross, 1978; Anoliefo *et al.*, 2003; McIvor and Pungetti, Chapter 13). Colding and Folke (2001) suggest that resource and habitat taboos in many cultures play a similar role to formal institutions for conservation in contemporary society, but that the importance of this role has not been suitably recognised. In the past there has been debate between those who consider that many taboos have developed with the purpose of conserving important natural resources (McDonald, 1977; Ross, 1978) and those who consider this attitude as a return to the much-discredited 'noble savage' paradigm (Buege, 1996). It is now generally recognised that people from all societies respond similarly to incentives (Winterhalder and Smith, 2000). However, taboos and other informal institutions can play an important role in natural resource management, regardless of their origin (Colding and Folke, 2001).

There are many examples of taboos being credited with providing protection to endemic species and habitats in Madagascar (Jones et al., 2008). For example, the taboo that prevents members of the Mahafaly and Antandroy ethnic groups in southern Madagascar from touching the radiated tortoise (*Geochelonia radiata*) may have helped to prevent its extinction (Nussbaum and Raxworthy, 2000). Taboos have also protected forest patches around the country, ensuring their survival in the face of widespread clearance of natural forest (Horning, 2003; Tengo et al., 2007). Few researchers have looked explicitly at the role such taboos play in governing interactions between local people and wild species and places in Madagascar, and none have focused on aquatic habitats. Madagascar's freshwater habitats are recognised as having great significance for global biodiversity (Benstead et al., 2003), yet conservation effort, as in so much of the world, has focused overwhelmingly on terrestrial ecosystems. This chapter will discuss the role that taboos and traditional beliefs play in the management of freshwater species and habitats in Madagascar and explore potential synergies between these traditional institutions and conservation.

Background to this work

Both authors have a long interest in the role traditional institutions play in the conservation of species and habitats in Madagascar. MMA has a background in natural resource management and has carried out extensive fieldwork in the eastern rainforests. She comes from the north central region of Madagascar (Alaotra-Mangoro) and is a member of the Sihanaka ethnic group. JPGJ has worked in Madagascar since 2000, carrying out more than four years' fieldwork into the institutions governing the use of wild species, mostly in the eastern rainforests of Fianarantsoa province. She speaks fluent Malagasy. To give a broader overview than would be possible from our own geographically limited fieldwork, we have also carried out interviews with students from all over Madagascar studying in Antananarivo.

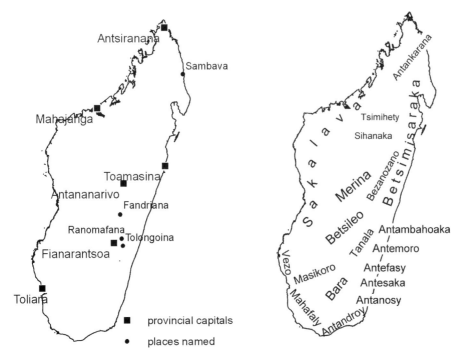

Figure 14.1 Places named in the text and the approximate distribution of the main ethnic groups in Madagascar (after Brown, 1996).

Taboos in Malagasy society

Many ethnographers have sought to dispel the concept of 'natural' tribal divisions in Madagascar, suggesting instead that the recognised ethnic groups are relatively recent constructions originating out of the expansion of a pre-colonial autocracy in the mid to late nineteenth century (Kottak, 1971). However, many Malagasy strongly self-identify with a particular ethnicity (Harper, 2002) and will report this affiliation when discussing their beliefs: we therefore refer to ethnicity in this chapter (Figure 14.1 shows the approximate distribution of the main ethnic groups and places named in the text).

The Malagasy word *fady* covers a range of prohibitions. Jones *et al.* (2008) consider three categories based on the level of prohibition and the punishment expected if the *fady* is broken. *Sandrana* are strict prohibitions from the ancestors that should not be broken under any circumstance. *Fadin-drazana* (*fady* of the ancestors) are more negotiable and people can ask their ancestors to free them in times of need. *Fadim-piarahamonina* (*fady* of the community) are a class of prohibitions based on acceptable behaviour. There is a further type of *fady* (*fadin'ody*) which refers to when a person consults a witch doctor (*ombiasa*) and is given a temporary prohibition

(Vig, 1977). Where we refer in this chapter to a species or action as taboo, we are referring to *fady* in the first two categories, i.e. where breaking the prohibition would displease the ancestors.

Although it can be difficult to uncover the origins of some taboos, others have clear and well-known stories associated with them. For example, some originate in wanting to protect a species which protected an ancestor in the past. There are a number of stories of a species protecting a clan member in the past and so being declared taboo for that clan's descendants (Toussaint, 1911; Ruud, 1960; Jones *et al.*, 2008). Other taboos originate in the characteristics of the species concerned. For example, a tenrec (a small animal like a hedgehog, *Tenrec ecudatus*) curls up in a ball when afraid and therefore is seen as cowardly and is taboo for young men to eat (Ruud, 1960). Similarly, species which resemble humans (especially lemurs in the family Indridae) may be taboo as they are seen to represent ancestors in animal form (Jones *et al.*, 2008). Sites or species may be declared taboo to protect the descendants from species or places that caused disaster to the ancestors or to protect the memory of the ancestors or their burial places (Profita, 1967). Finally, taboos may be declared for pragmatic reasons. The story given for the origin of the taboo preventing crayfish harvesting in the Ranomafana area (Jones *et al.*, 2008) is that it was placed by the ancestors to ensure that men tended to their fields first so that their family would be ensured food to eat, rather than wasting time collecting a cash crop and possibly returning empty-handed.

Taboos and conservation of aquatic habitats

Water itself is seen as sacred (Rakotoariseheno and Rakotoarimanana, 1992) and this sacred nature is reflected in the many references to water (*rano*) in religious ceremony and ritual. *Tsodrano* or *fafirano* is a benediction which Malagasy ask for before an important event (a marriage or a long journey, for example). The benediction may involve water directly (being sprinkled over the head, for example), but often the association with the purity of water is simply implied through the name. During a circumcision, the wound may be washed with strong water (*rano mahery*) which is collected from a waterfall by running men whose parents are still alive.

Many waterfalls, lakes or rivers in Madagascar are considered sacred to their local population (Decary, 1959, reported more than 30 such places), or have taboos restricting activities at the site (Figure 14.2). Places may be sacred because of the presence of taboo animals (see below) or because of their association with human burials. For example, in parts of the Sakalava region, corpses were traditionally placed in a dug-out canoe (*lakana*) and then released at sacred places in the river (Delord, 1961a). In some areas the hair, fingernails and teeth of princes were

Figure 14.2 Many waterfalls, lakes and rivers are considered sacred to local populations (© Mijasoa Andriamarovololona).

separated and placed in sacred ponds. In Fandriana, the corpses of dead babies (those who die when still too young to be placed in the family tomb) are buried close to freshwater springs. Our interviews confirmed that this is current practice; recently, the baby of a relative of one informant died abroad and the baby was brought back and buried by the village spring (MMA field notes). The areas around these springs designated as '*fasan-jaza*' (child tombs) are sacred.

Some areas are sacred for unknown reasons. In the north-west there are a number of sacred places (*doany*) in the sea or in big rivers where only spiritual ceremonies are allowed. Local people will avoid these places when fishing (MMA field notes). For example, 5 km from Sambava there are two lakes, Antohomaro and Andohabe, connected by a narrow canal. Antohomaro is fished by the local villagers. However, Andohabe is sacred and cannot be used for fishing or washing, offering full protection for anything in it (MMA field notes). In 2003 a visitor used a jetski in Andohabe lake, against local advice, and was drowned. This is reported locally as confirmation that the lake is indeed sacred.

Taboos and conservation of aquatic species

Taboos concerning eels (*Anguilla* spp; *amalona* in Malagasy) are common throughout eastern Madagascar. Poisson (1952) reports a *fady* concerning eels with ears, saying that local people avoid some eels (probably *Anguilla mossambica*) because of their large ears (probably the pectoral fins). This is still respected in many areas. People say that because they have ears, such eels are not fish but ancestors in animal form and no local people will eat them (MMA field notes). In rural Tolongoina commune, a waterfall in the area is named Besofina (big ears) because of the presence of eels with ears and is considered sacred locally. A general taboo preventing people from eating spotted eels (*amalom-badana*) is common among people from many ethnic groups (including Sihanaka, Merina, Betsimisaraka, Antakarana and Antemoro: MMA field notes). Ruud (1960) states that eating eels is taboo for Betsimisarika and Tanala women when they are pregnant as they are slippery and may cause the baby to slip out of the womb. This *fady* was still very much in evidence during our recent fieldwork in Tanala area (Jones *et al.*, 2008).

Crocodiles (*Crocodilus niloticus*; *voay* in Malagasy) are found in scattered wetlands around much of Madagascar, although their range was greatly reduced by over-exploitation, particularly during the colonial period (Kuchling *et al.*, 2003). Perhaps understandably for such a powerful and dangerous species (57 human deaths were recorded during a five-year period in the 1990s: Behra, 1996), there are many taboos governing people's interactions with crocodiles. Interestingly, many groups consider the crocodiles as sacred and have taboos which protect crocodiles and their habitat. In some areas, crocodiles are given the same funeral rites as humans (Decary, 1950; JL, 1953). One informant told us how in her area of Alaotra-Mangoro region they will wrap a dead crocodile in a cloth, as they would a dead human (MMA field notes). Both the Antandroy and the Tsimihety ethnic groups have clans that see themselves as direct descendants of crocodiles (the *zafindravoay*: Decary, 1950; Guérin, 1969; Rahatoka, 1984). Others see crocodiles as reincarnations of princes or royalty (JL, 1953; Delord, 1961b). In a number of crocodile-infested areas, local inhabitants believe that they have a contract with the crocodiles which, if respected, protects them from harm. For example, residents in Bevoahazo (near Ranomafana) would not use fishing nets in the Tsaratango river and believed that this kept them safe from crocodiles. Although crocodiles have probably not been present in this river in living memory, the taboo is still respected and has a positive effect on fishery management in the area (JPGJ field notes).

Figure 14.3 Fisherman in Alaotra: fishermen in many parts of Madagascar have taboos preventing them from attempting to land very large fish as these are seen as belonging to the spirits (© Andrea Wallace). See colour plate section.

There is a common taboo in many parts of Madagascar relating to exceptionally large fish (of any species) (Figure 14.3). People feel that particularly large fish have unnatural properties and belong to the spirits. It is strictly taboo to attempt to catch such fish and there are many stories of people dying while trying to land particularly large fish (MMA field notes).

In the Ranomafana area we found a number of Tanala villages where there were strict taboos preventing the sale of freshwater products. Hence, although crabs, crayfish and fish may be caught and eaten (Figure 14.4), they cannot be sold or exchanged for rice. For some people the taboo relates to any products of freshwater (*fady mivarotra laokan-drano*), but to others it was limited to crustaceans (*fady mivarotra orana sy foza ihany*).

Do these beliefs play a significant role in the conservation of freshwater species and habitats?

A number of freshwater species are provided at least partial protection by taboos and this may have a very real conservation benefit for some populations. For example, during the colonial period, the government of Madagascar wanted

Figure 14.4 Crayfish: although a lively trade in freshwater crayfish exists in many parts of Madagascar, many Tanala people have taboos preventing the sale of products of freshwater, particularly crabs and crayfish (© Julia Jones).

to eradicate crocodiles, which were seen as a threat to both humans and livestock (Petit, 1925). Blanc (1984) suggests that sacred lakes provided an important refuge, allowing crocodiles to persist where they may otherwise have been extirpated. Crocodiles continue to be persecuted in parts of Madagascar and our interviews suggest that taboos provide significant local protection.

Larger fish produce disproportionately more eggs and young than do smaller fish (Blueweiss *et al.*, 1978). The common taboo preventing fishermen from targeting unusually large fish is therefore likely to have beneficial effects on management of the resource as it will protect these large, highly productive individuals.

Villages that have taboos preventing the commercialisation of crayfish exploit these species at much lower levels than areas lacking the taboo (Jones *et al.*, 2008). The control of harvesting caused by this taboo plays an important role in the conservation of *Astacoides caldwelli*, a rare endemic crayfish limited to very few sites (Jones *et al.*, 2007).

We do not know of any work focused on the ecological benefits of sacred freshwater areas in Madagascar. However, by preventing fishing and other human activities, they are likely to provide refuges from the direct or indirect consequences of over-fishing. This is important, as over-fishing is one of the most significant threats to freshwater systems in Madagascar (Benstead *et al.*, 2003).

How adherence to taboos is changing

Culture is not static, but is ever-evolving. Some of the sources we quote come from early last century and although we have made every effort to check on the current relevance of what we report, all traditions and beliefs are likely to be changing over time. As Malagasy populations reflect global trends of increased movement and communication between communities, such change might be expected to accelerate. Below, we discuss a number of factors that may be influencing adherence to traditional taboos.

A number of authors have suggested that increasing movement of people around Madagascar is changing the degree to which traditional *fady* are respected (Lingard *et al.*, 2003; Lilette, 2006). Many people believe that outsiders are immune to a local taboo, but once it has been regularly broken, local adherence is also likely to reduce (MMA field notes). We have seen this in areas where tourists or researchers ask locals to help them find certain species which may be taboo, such as the aye-aye (a nocturnal lemur, *Daubentonia madagascariensis*) or chameleons. People who at first are reluctant to break the taboo soon do so willingly.

Although some Christian groups in Madagascar do not see conflict with traditional beliefs, others ask adherents to break personal *fady* or destroy sacred objects. Informants told us of a case where a group of Christians destroyed part of a sacred forest in order to demonstrate that traditional taboos have no power (MMA field notes). Some people believe that the 'power' of a *fady* can change over time and that this process can be accelerated by many people breaking a rule.

Economic need can force people to break a taboo and, if no punishment is experienced, this may result in a long-term change. For example, we found some families in areas where selling crayfish was widely taboo who happily and openly sold crayfish. Interviews revealed that an ancestor had been forced to sell crayfish to French colonists during the colonial era due to economic need. They had suffered no harm and the ancestor had subsequently declared the taboo void for his family and descendants.

Education can also influence people's adherence to a taboo. Many students we spoke to at the University of Antananarivo said that their education had diminished their belief in the importance of traditional taboos. Some parents do not pass on the knowledge of family taboos to their children. This may be especially true amongst people who have aspirations that their children will leave their natal areas.

Jorgan Ruud (a missionary who spent 20 years in Madagascar) collected information on the practice and belief system surrounding taboos from 'civil-servants, witch-doctors, labourers and employers' (Ruud, 1960). He was at pains to highlight the importance of taboos not only to people living 'traditional' lifestyles, but to people of all backgrounds and to Christians and non-Christians alike. Despite the caveats above, this remains true and taboos are clearly relevant to the cultural and religious life of many Malagasy today, particularly in the more rural areas.

Conclusions

Many of the people living closest to Madagascar's remaining biodiversity-rich habitat live in societies in which traditional beliefs are powerful, and in these areas taboos can significantly reduce pressure on some freshwater species and protect certain sites from human activities. Of course, traditional taboos alone are not going to halt Madagascar's biodiversity crisis. They do not match exactly the objectives and priorities of Western conservation, and many species of conservation concern are not covered (Jones et al., 2008). For example, one of the biggest threats to freshwater biodiversity in Madagascar is invasive fish (Benstead et al., 2003), and traditional taboos can do little to reduce or mitigate this threat. However, by attempting to understand the role that traditional beliefs play in people's interactions with wild species and their habitats, conservationists will gain a deeper understanding of the people on whom conservation of Madagascar's biodiversity depends. Authors often view rural Malagasy people in one dimension: as either the cause of Madagascar's environmental problems, or as helpless victims of circumstances (Kaufmann, 2001). Improved cultural understanding is necessary to avoid caricatures that distract from the search for shared solutions to the challenges that face all who care about the country's wild species and places.

References

Anoliefo, G. O., Isikhuemhen, O. S. and Ochije, N. R. (2003). Environmental implications of the erosion of cultural taboo practices in Awka-South local government area of Anambra State, Nigeria. *Journal of Agricultural and Environmental Ethics*, **16**, 281–96.

Behra, O. (1996). Report of crocodile attacks on people in Madagascar 1990–1995. *IUCN Crocodile Specialist Group Newsletter*, **15**, 34.

Benstead, J. P., De Rham, P. H., Gattolliat, J. L., *et al.* (2003). Conserving Madagascar's freshwater biodiversity. *Bioscience*, **53**, 1101–11.

Blanc, C. P. (1984). The reptiles. In *Madagascar (Key Environments)*, ed. A. Jolly, P. Oberle and R. Albignac. Oxford: Pergamon, pp. 104–14.

Blueweiss, L., Fox, H., Kudzma, V., *et al.* (1978). Relationships between body size and some life history parameters. *Oecologia*, **37**, 257–72.

Brown, M. (1996). *A History of Madagascar*. Colchester: Palladian Press.

Buege, D. J. (1996). The ecologically noble savage revisited. *Environmental Ethics*, **18**, 71–88.

Colding, J. and Folke, C. (2001). Social taboos: 'invisible' systems of local resource management and biological conservation. *Ecological Applications*, **11**, 584–600.

Decary, R. (1950). *La faune Malgache: son rôle dans les croyances et les usages indigènes*. Paris: Payot.

Decary, R. (1959). Les eaux douces et leurs habitants dans les traditions et industries malgaches. *Mémoire de l'Institut Scientifique de Madagascar*, Série C, Tome 5.

Delord, R. (1961a). Note sur la vénération d'un ophidien du Boina. *Bulletin de l'Académie Malgache 1961*, **39**, 28.

Delord, R. (1961b). Remarques sur des questions d'ethnographie en pays Sakalava. *Bulletin de l'Académie Malgache*, **39**, 26–7.

Guérin, M. (1969). *La transformation socio-économique de l'Androy*. Travaux de Recherche du Service de Sciences Sociales de l'Ecole Nationale Supérieure Agronomique. Antananarive, Madagascar: Université de Madagascar.

Harper, J. (2002). *Endangered Species: Health, Illness and Death among Madagascar's People of the Forest*. Durham, NC: Carolina Academic Press.

Horning, N. R. (2003). How rules affect conservation outcome. In *The Natural History of Madagascar*, ed. S. M. Goodman and J. P. Benstead. Chicago, IL: Chicago University Press, pp. 146–53.

JL (1953). Voay (le crocodile) dans la vie malgache. *Bulletin de Madagascar. Publication mensuelle du Service Général de l'Information du Haut Commissariat*.

Jones, J. P. G., Andriahajaina, F. B., Hockley, N. J., *et al.* (2007). The ecology and conservation status of Madagascar's endemic freshwater crayfish (Parastacidae; Astacoides). *Freshwater Biology*, **52**, 1820–33.

Jones, J. P. G., Andriamarovololona, M. M. and Hockley, N. J. (2008). The importance of taboos and social norms to conservation in Madagascar. *Conservation Biology*, **22**, 976–86.

Kaufmann, J. C. (2001). Introduction: recolouring the Red Island. *Ethnohistory*, **48**, 3–10.

Kottak, C. (1971). Social groups and kinship calculation among the southern Betsileo. *American Anthropologist*, **73**, 178–93.

Kuchling, G., Lippai, C. and Behra, O. (2003). Crocodylidae: *Crocodylus niloticus*, Nile Crocodile, Voay, Manba. In *The Natural History of Madagascar*, ed. S. M. Goodman and J. P. Benstead. Chicago, IL: Chicago University Press, pp. 1005–08.

Lambek, M. (1992). Taboo as cultural practice among Malagasy speakers. *Man*, **27**, 245–66.

Lambek, M. J. (2002). *The Weight of the Past: Living with History in Mahajunga, Madagascar*. New York, NY: Palgrave.

Lilette, V. (2006). Mixed results: conservation of the marine turtle and the red-tailed tropicbird by Vezo semi-nomadic fishers. *Conservation and Society*, **4**, 262–86.

Lingard, M., Raharison, N., Rabakonandrianina, E., *et al.* (2003). The role of local taboos in conservation and management of species: the radiated tortoise in Southern Madagascar. *Conservation and Society*, **1**, 223–46.

McDonald, D. (1977). Food taboos: a primitive environmental protection agency. *Anthropos: International Review of Ethnology and Linguistics*, **72**, 734–48.

Nussbaum, R. A. and Raxworthy, C. J. (2000). Commentary on conservation of 'Sokatra', the radiated tortoise (*Geochelone radiata*) of Madagascar. *Amphibian and Reptile Conservation*, **2**, 6–14.

Petit, G. (1925). Les crocodiles Malgaches, leurs moeurs, leur chasse et leur utilisation. *Revue d'Histoire Naturelle Appliquée*, **6**, 236–50.

Poisson, H. (1952). Légende de l'anguille à oreilles. *Bulletin de l'Académie Malgache*, Nouvelle Série Tome XXX.

Profita, P. (1967). Pour une révision du concept de fady. *Bulletin de l'Académie Malgache*, Nouvelle Série Tome XLV, pp. 59–64.

Rahatoka, S. (1984). Pensée religieuse et rituels Betsimisaraka. In *Ny razana tsy mba maty: cultures traditionnelles malgaches*, ed. J. P. Domenichini, J. Poirier and D. Raherisoanjato. Antananarivo. Madagascar: Librairie de Madagascar, pp. 31–92.

Rakotoariseheno, R. and Rakotoarimanana, L. (1992). Eaux et traditions. *Actes des journées de l'eau*, ed. J. -M. Elouard and M. Andriantsiferana. Antananarivo, Madagascar: IRD, pp. 225–38.

Ross, E. B. (1978). Food taboos, diet and hunting strategy: the adaptation to animals in Amazon cultural ecology. *Current Anthropology*, **19**, 1–19.

Ruud, J. (1960). *Taboo: A Study of Malagasy Customs and Beliefs*. London: Allen and Unwin.

Sharp, L. A. (1994). *The Possessed and the Dispossessed Spirits, Identity, and Power in a Madagascar Migrant Town*. Berkeley, CA: University of California Press.

Tengo, M., Johansson, K., Rakotondrasoa, F., *et al.* (2007). Taboos and forest governance: informal protection of hot spot dry forest in southern Madagascar. *Ambio*, **36**, 683–91.

Toussaint, R. (1911). Fady Tanala: les Tanala et le Railovy. *Bulletin de l'Académie Malgache*, **3**, 145–6.

Vig, L. (1977). *Croyances et mœurs des malgaches*. Antananarivo, Madagascar: Trano Printy Loterana.

Winterhalder, B. and Smith, E. A. (2000). Analyzing adaptive strategies: human behavioral ecology at twenty-five. *Evolutionary Anthropology*, **9**, 51–72.

15

Sacred species of national marine sanctuaries of the United States' West Coast

WILLIAM J. DOUROS

Introduction

In 1972, the United States Congress embarked on a grand programme to designate and protect for future generations the special areas of the United States' oceans and Great Lakes ecosystems. In passing this landmark legislation in 1972, the Congress debated at length how protective these special areas should be and also what to call them. Ultimately they chose to make resource protection the top priority, but to also promote research, education and multiple use to the extent that human use did not conflict with the mandate for resource protection.

As significantly, these new marine areas, complementary to the much-heralded national parks on land, were called 'national marine sanctuaries'. While the choice of this term has posed contradictions for many staunch environmentalists as well as advocates for ocean development and extraction, the name 'sanctuary' reflects what has been a constant through time in the US – oceans are areas of constant renewal to humans, sacred places to many and a part of our collective national identity essential to the spiritual and economic livelihoods of hundreds of millions of Americans.

There are 13 national marine sanctuaries and 1 marine national monument managed as part of the National Marine Sanctuary System. Of these, five national marine sanctuaries have been designated on the west coast of the US, offshore Washington state (Olympic Coast) and California (Cordell Bank, Gulf of the Farallones, Monterey Bay and Channel Islands; Figure 15.1). Each of these west coast sanctuaries is relatively large, ranging between 550 and 6094 square miles (1408 and 15 601 km^2) and has been designated to protect entire ecosystems. Kelp beds,

Sacred Species and Sites: Advances in Biocultural Conservation, ed. Gloria Pungetti, Gonzalo Oviedo and Della Hooke. Published by Cambridge University Press. © Cambridge University Press 2012.

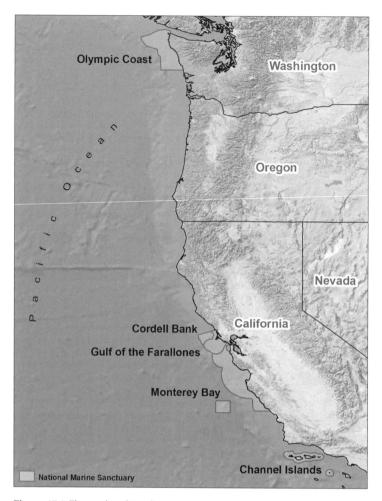

Figure 15.1 Five national marine sanctuaries on the US west coast. From north to south, Olympic Coast, Cordell Bank, Gulf of the Farallones, Monterey Bay and Channel Islands.

sandy beaches, intertidal and subtidal rocky reefs, almost 40 species of marine mammals, hundreds of bird rookeries and countless human activities that do not harm sanctuary resources are protected by these sacred sanctuaries.

Within these five sanctuaries live millions of plant and animal species as well as countless species of single-celled organisms. Scientists today find new species every year in these national marine sanctuaries. Yet the truly sacred species are few in number.

Native Americans who live today, or have lived in the past, along these coasts now protected as national marine sanctuaries have marine species they consider sacred, often in large part because those species are hunted and honoured by the native cultures by being eaten. The annual return of salmon to spawn and die in coastal rivers literally meant life (or death when they did not show up) to many Native American tribes. Native cultures also considered other species sacred because of their ferocity or because of a tradition or lore within a particular culture, such as the Makah wolf ritual in northwestern Washington state.

Other species exist in national marine sanctuaries that native cultures may not have known about historically, or may have misunderstood. Modern scientific knowledge has expanded where we can search in the oceans and, thus, what we know about the millions of species that live there. This knowledge has helped to shape how, today, humans determine special and sacred species. A species may be unique, special because of its characteristics or size or colour or life history. A species may be charismatic, offering behaviour that humans are attracted to. A species may be a keystone to an ecosystem, either as a predator or as a prey. Or a species may be special because of its abundance, because of the value harvesting it has to humans. While all species may have been created equal, humans perceive the value of species differently. The concept of sacredness arises from our desire to set aside the special places, to protect the special species that have value above other species. For each of these key criteria, these key values (to humans or to ecosystems), one may find a sacred species in the sacred 'sanctuaries' of the west coast of the US.

Characteristics

Each year on beaches across Indonesia, a thousand or more female leatherback sea turtles (*Dermochelys coriacea*) crawl from the ocean at night to spend four, maybe eight, hours laying eggs in a shallow nest which the female digs in the beach sand. As they return to the ocean, females recommence a migration in search of food that typically takes them across the Pacific Ocean from west to east on a quest for jellyfish, the primary food for leatherback turtles. The journey across the Pacific Ocean will take between eight and ten months and can cover over 9000 miles (14 400 km) one way, the longest migration of any reptile, and one of the longest of any species in the ocean. The most significant destination for Indonesian leatherback sea turtles (Figure 15.2) is the central coast of California and its productive nearshore waters that, between August and November, can fill with jellyfish, in particular *Chrysaora fuscescens* and *C. colorata*, a preferred food for Pacific leatherback sea turtles (Benson *et al.*, 2007). Tagging studies show that leatherback sea turtles can dive to depths of 7000 feet (2000 m) in search of food.

Many native cultures, for instance in Indonesia and Mexico, consider the leatherback sea turtle to be a sacred species, representing past ancestors who come

© William J. Douros

Figure 15.2 A leatherback sea turtle, with tentacles from a *Chrysaora* sp. hanging from its mouth, resurfaces after a feeding dive in Monterey Bay (© William Douros/NOAA). See colour plates section.

'home' from the ocean and offer themselves as sustenance to villagers (Safina, 2006). This is not surprising when one considers that an adult leatherback sea turtle can grow up to 8 feet in length (2.6 m) and weigh 1800 pounds (818 kg), many times larger than the humans worshipping them.

These characteristics demonstrate why native cultures and modern cultures alike consider the leatherback sea turtle a sacred species. The role played by national marine sanctuaries on the west coast is significant for this endangered species. In the months from August until November, when ocean waters typically warm above 15 degrees centigrade, when the calmness of morning stills the ocean's surface, leatherbacks can be seen gorging in Monterey Bay and around the Farallon Islands and above Cordell Bank on jellyfish that swarm by the millions. The powerful upwelling winds that normally blow for much of the spring and early summer ignite a cycle of cold, nutrient-rich waters nourishing a food chain that turns the sun's productivity into small fish and invertebrates. Jellyfish abundance similarly soars as they feed on krill, small fish, eggs and other organisms, and in turn the leatherbacks arrive to feed on jellyfish (Benson *et al.*, 2007). The national marine sanctuaries that protect these upwelling centres and the food that is produced within them are simultaneously protecting the key forage grounds for one of the oldest living vertebrate species in the Pacific Ocean, and one of the ocean's most remarkable creatures.

Leatherback sea turtles are a global species, and are considered warm-blooded reptiles that can survive in the coldest oceans at the margin of ice and in warm tropical waters. They have survived on Earth for nearly 70 million years, yet in the past 30 years, in the Pacific Ocean, their numbers have dropped by over 90%. Today, the National Oceanic and Atmospheric Administration estimates that the Indonesian subpopulation has about 4500 breeding females (Dutton *et al.*, 2007). Intentional mortality for the turtles arises from such factors as the harvesting of adults offshore and while nesting, and the removal of eggs from nests. Incidental mortality can occur from the loss of beach habitat, from the ingestion of plastics mistaken for jellyfish, and from entanglement in fishing gear – drift gillnets and hooks in longline gear (Safina, 2006).

Many protections are in place to help halt the dramatic decline of leatherback sea turtles, with success being shown in the Atlantic Ocean. Pacific populations of the sea turtle have shown few signs of recovery and many non-governmental organisations are sounding an alarm of extinction for the Pacific leatherback sea turtle. In primitive, Pacific island, beach communities where the leatherback turtle was once sought for its food value, villagers now see the value in conserving leatherbacks for tourism and for their sacred status within coastal cultures. A large area from Oregon to Monterey Bay is closed to drift gillnet and longline fishing from August to November to eliminate US fisheries' incidental mortality of leatherback sea turtles. Unfortunately, less regulated fisheries across the Pacific Ocean still kill many leatherback sea turtles each year. In fact, the characteristic that makes these animals so remarkable – their incredibly long migration – places them in particular peril.

Charisma

The sea otter can be considered a sacred species because of its important role in the development and human colonisation of the west coast of North America, for it was one of the premier species hunted by Russian and European fur traders between 1750 and 1900 due to its thick, soft, dense fur (Figure 15.3). Its population numbers plummeted in California from a high of 30 000 individuals, and it was thought for many years to have gone extinct (Silverstein and Nunn, 1995). With the construction of a new road along Big Sur in 1938, a small colony of about 50 southern sea offers (*Enhydra lutris nereis*) was found, and the population had recovered to more than 3000 individuals by 2007 (USGS, 2007).

Many species, however, were hunted for fur and contributed to the development of west coast colonies. So its value as a fur pelt does not make the sea otter sacred.

Figure 15.3 A raft of southern sea otters, several of which have been tagged by managers, float in Elkhorn Slough, in Monterey Bay National Marine Sanctuary (© Steve Lonhart/NOAA).

Rather, the key reason the sea otter is a sacred species in the national marine sanctuaries of the west coast is because of its incredible charisma that charms humans, thrilling adult and child alike. The most popular exhibit at the Monterey Bay Aquarium is its sea otter exhibit where typically four otters cavort, feed, wrestle and sleep in a huge tank surrounded by human observers (Julie Packard, personal communication). Just offshore of the aquarium, in Monterey Bay National Marine Sanctuary, which protects about 75% of the southern sea otter population, wild otters can be seen in the nearshore beds of a brown algae, the giant kelp (*Macrocystis pyrifera*), doing much the same thing.

While wild otters can be nasty animals to both humans and to each other, and should never be approached, it is the charm of their varying behaviour that takes place so visibly that endears them to humans. Within Monterey Bay National Marine Sanctuary, sea otters can be seen from the shoreline trails and beaches. They forage for echinoderms, crustaceans and molluscs in kelp beds and in coastal estuaries making repeated dives during a foraging period. Crabs are often eaten whole, or cracked open with the sea otter's sharp teeth. However, sea otters are rare among wild animals in that they use tools – typically a small stone – to crack open clams and mussels whose shells are too hard to penetrate with an otter's teeth.

Within kelp beds, otters will wrap themselves in kelp fronds to take a nap or sleep through the night, preventing themselves from floating away. Females will typically have a single pup and mothers are very attentive, diving to find food and handing it to a noisy pup. Mothers will swim on their back with a pup on their belly. Otters must groom themselves constantly as they lack the layer of blubber or fat that other marine mammals possess. This grooming forces air into an otter's pelage, which provides a layer of warmth against cold ocean temperatures (Silverstein and Nunn, 1995). Oftentimes underwater an otter will shimmer a silvery hue to scuba divers due to the air trapped within its fur. These myriad kinds of behaviour from this very active creature, very easy for humans to observe, create an enthusiasm for this species like no other marine creature found in west coast sanctuaries.

The otter is fully protected by several laws, including the Marine Mammal Protection Act, the Endangered Species Act, various state laws, and the regulations of Monterey Bay National Marine Sanctuary. It is occasionally found in the Gulf of the Farallones and Channel Islands National Marine Sanctuaries as it slowly returns to its original range. To facilitate the sea otter's overall recovery, Alaskan sea otter subpopulations were relocated to Olympic Coast National Marine Sanctuary and that population, now about 800 animals, appears to be slowly growing within annual fluctuations (WDFW, 2005).

Various management actions have been taken to help the population recover, including the designation of Monterey Bay National Marine Sanctuary. Otter relocations have also been conducted to prevent an entire population from being wiped out due to an oil spill, probably the single greatest human threat to sea otters today. There is also growing concern that coastal pollution, including parasites from domestic animals, may be affecting the ability of sea otter populations to recover to levels found before the fur trade began.

Keystones

The concept of a keystone species was first described by Robert T. Paine based on detailed intertidal work he conducted in what is now Olympic Coast National Marine Sanctuary (Paine, 1969). His research, involving the continuous removal of a predator, the seastar *Pisaster*, showed that certain species can have an impact on the structure of the community beyond what may be expected based on that species' relative abundance. This critical ecological concept of keystone species has also been shown for other species such as the sea otter, interestingly from research conducted within other west coast national marine sanctuaries (Estes and Palmisano, 1974). A central tenet of Paine's technical determination of keystone species is that a species must have an influence on a community in a proportion greater than one would expect from its relative abundance or total biomass.

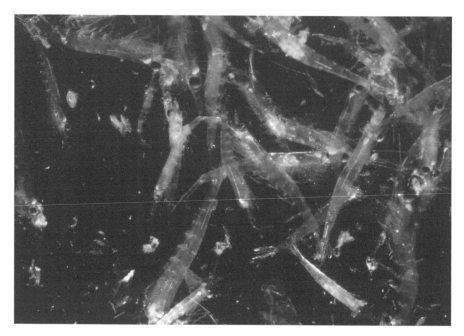

Figure 15.4 Krill are abundant in the world's oceans and form the basis of intricate food webs in national marine sanctuaries on the west coast (© NOAA/Jamie Hall).

Thriving within coastal ecosystems along the west coast, and in particular within the five west coast national marine sanctuaries, is a small shrimp-like invertebrate called krill. Krill, typically *Euphausia pacifica* and *Thysanoessa spinifera* (Figure 15.4) on the west coast, can live in huge aggregations of many billions of individuals, and while their cumulative biomass in an area can be large, the sheer diversity of organisms that depend on krill is similarly staggering. Thus, krill can be considered a keystone of a healthy, functional ecosystem within a west coast national marine sanctuary because it serves as the foundation of one of the most complex food webs on earth.

The diversity of this food web includes tiny juvenile fish and gigantic mammals. The largest animal that has ever lived, the blue whale, is commonly found feeding on krill aggregations off the four California national marine sanctuaries, making these sanctuaries probably the best place in the world to see blue whales. Shearwaters leave breeding colonies during 'their winter' in New Zealand, Chile and Argentina and fly to Monterey Bay and Cordell Bank to feed on krill, a one-way distance of nearly 12 000 miles (20 000 km). Closer to home, Cassin's Auklets that breed in the Gulf of the Farallones are dependent in their first year of life on krill for the young of the year birds to survive. Commercially important species such as squid, salmon, sardines and rockfish are critically dependent on krill, as it serves at one time or another as the main prey for these species (Croll *et al.*, 2005). Collectively, these fisheries are the main commercially viable fisheries on the west coast, valued at hundreds of millions of dollars. If krill were to disappear, so would these commercially valuable and ecologically important species, hence the growing acknowledgement of the sacredness of krill.

Because of the critical nature of krill, the Office of National Marine Sanctuaries recently proposed to regional fishery managers that the harvest of krill be banned, thereby ensuring that human harvest never affects the prey base of this complex food web. After several years of study and analysis, and with the full support of commercial fishermen, west coast states and environmental organisations, the harvest of krill in not only the five west coast sanctuaries but for the entire west coast exclusive economic zone of the United States has been banned. Therefore, this 'uncharismatic', almost unknown (to the public) species, upon which hundreds of well-known and sought-after species depend for existence, is protected and set aside from harvest. Like the massive stones that hold up the great cathedrals of Europe, the krill holds up complex food webs found in the sacred sanctuaries of the west coast.

Consumption

A major driving force behind the education programmes of the west coast national marine sanctuaries is to connect people, who live on land, with the remarkable resources that live offshore of their communities. Making this connection is challenging because oceans, while inviting to look at and walk next to, are still foreign and most people see most of the species that inhabit them only when those species are extracted from the ocean.

In Washington state, as well as in parts of central and northern California, salmon are perhaps the perfect species to assist sanctuary managers in their quest to connect people to the ocean. Pacific salmon live in both worlds during their lifetime, beginning and ending their lives in the cool fresh waters of a stream or river. In between, Pacific salmon travel to the ocean to feed and grow large, storing energy in the form of muscle and fat for their return to their native stream where they swim against the current to find calm water to mate and reproduce. After mating – laying or fertilising eggs – the adults then die (Groot and Margolis, 1991). This cycle is believed to exist for two fundamental reasons. First, the ocean is far more productive than a river and a fish can find considerably more food and grow considerably larger by feeding in the ocean. Second, the adult's dying in the stream brings carbon and other nutrients from the ocean to the river, 'feeding' the river

Figure 15.5 A recreational fisherman shows the results of a successful day's fishing for chinook salmon (© NOAA).

system in a way that provides nutrients for invertebrates that young salmon, once hatched, will feed on themselves.

All five of the Pacific salmon species (*Oncorhynchus* sp.) – the chinook, coho, pink, sockeye and chum – all display this life history strategy (Figure 15.5). The life history of each species varies slightly from the others, ranging between the chinook, which typically spends three years, and may range 2500 miles (4000 km), in the ocean, to the pink, which spends only one year in the ocean and generally stays within 150 miles (240 km) of its natal stream. Once a salmon reaches its native river, it may swim many hundreds of miles depending on the distance to natal spawning areas. In size, too, the species vary between the largest, the chinook, which today reaches a maximum size of about 50 pounds (23 kg) to the pink, which generally weighs 4 pounds (1.8 kg). Historically, salmon runs in the Pacific Northwest occurred in all seasons, as different subpopulations and different species returned to streams at different times (Groot and Margolis, 1991).

Figure 4.2 The archaeological site of Paestum was a landscape of historical and spiritual importance during Classical times (© Italian Ministry for the Environment, Land and Sea).

Figure 5.2 The *borgo* (village) of Fiume d'Isola, Arezzo, in the middle of the forests of the National Park of the Casentino Forests, Monte Falterona and Campigna (© Italian Ministry for the Environment, Land and Sea – L. Manieri).

Figure 6.2 Badrinath temple with pilgrims (© Edwin Bernbaum).

Figure 9.2 A maloca communal roundhouse (© Elizabeth Reichel).

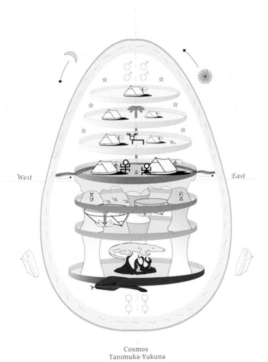

West   East

Cosmos
Tanimuka-Yukuna

Figure 9.3 Cosmos Tanimuka and Yukuna (© Elizabeth Reichel).

Figure 10.2 Settlement of the Arhuaco area in the Sierra Nevada de Santa Marta
(© Fundacion Pro-Sierra Nevada de Santa Marta).

Figure 12.3 13–17 December 2000, in the old centre of Kathmandu. Photograph taken at a ceremony organised by ARC International and WWF International to celebrate 'Gifts to the Earth' (© Grazia Francescato).

Figure 12.4 'Gifts to the Earth', Kathmandu (© Grazia Francescato).

Figure 13.2 The lotus is a plant sacred to Buddhists and Hindus (© Gloria Pungetti).

Figure 13.4 A few deer among the Cervidae family are considered sacred especially in North America and Europe (©Italian Ministry for the Environment, Land and Sea).

Figure 13.5 Eagles and their feathers are central to many religious and spiritual customs, e.g. amongst Native Americans in the United States, First Nations in Canada and many peoples of Meso-America (© Italian Ministry for the Environment, Land and Sea).

Figure 14.3 Fisherman in Alaotra: fishermen in many parts of Madagascar have taboos preventing them from attempting to land very large fish as these are seen as belonging to the spirits (© Andrea Wallace).

© William J. Douros

Figure 15.2 A leatherback sea turtle, with tentacles from a *Chrysaora* sp. hanging from its mouth, resurfaces after a feeding dive in Monterey Bay (© William Douros/NOAA).

Figure 16.2 Intangible expressions of human ecosystem relationships: magpie geese, linking sacred sites and species (© B. Verschuuren). (a) Magpie geese rock paintings, the world's oldest painting tradition and a form of intergenerational transmission of knowledge. (b) and (c) Ceremonial dance. Magpie geese can be mimicked in ceremonial dances like this to depict a creation story. [Figures are deliberately out of focus.] (d) Magpie as food source. (e) Magpie Dreaming. This site was created by an ancestral being depicted as a magpie goose called Karramala (Rose *et al*. 2002, p. 204).

Figure 17.1 A *tuatara (Sphenodon guntheri)* from Takapourewa (Stephens) Island (Photograph reproduced with permission of Susan Keal ©).

Figure 17.2 A green gecko (*Naultinus elegans*) (Photograph reproduced with permission of Rod Morris ©).

Figure 18.2 Chonggu Monastery (© Wang Nan).

Figure 18.3 Monk hand-feeding white-eared pheasants. Zhujie Monastery, Souchong, Daocheng County (© Wang Nan).

Figure 23.2 Mona monkey at Tafi Atome Monkey Sanctuary (© Michael Scace).

Figure 25.1.1 Male lion resting on Lugenda river bank (© Coleen Bragg).

Figure 26.1.1 Holy home to deities and rare species, the San Francisco Peaks are covered with snow (Photograph courtesy of Kelvin Long ©).

Figure 26.1.2 View of the Holy San Francisco Peaks: an oasis in the high desert (Photograph courtesy of Klee Benally ©).

Figure 26.2.2 Padmasambhava (Guru Rinpoche), who declared Khumbu a sacred hidden valley (*beyul*) (© Stan Stevens).

Figure 26.2.5 Himalayan Tahr, a threatened species protected by Sherpas' Buddhist values and discouragement of outsiders' poaching (© Stan Stevens).

Figure 26.4.1 Doñana, Andalusia, Spain – *sin pecado* (© Josep-Maria Mallarach).

Figure 26.4.2 Holy Island – Tibetan Buddhist rite (© Isabel Soria).

The size of the salmon runs, the diversity of the fish, and historically the near-year-round nature of the runs allowed Native Americans in the Pacific Northwest to develop stable communities with rich cultures. Understandably, the salmon was perhaps, and in some places still is, the most sacred species to native cultures. For many tribes it was the main source of sustenance and has been estimated to have provided at one time as much as 60% of the nutrients that Pacific Northwest native tribes consumed (Jones, 2005). Much of the culture of these tribes, including elaborate 'potlaches' or ceremonial feasts, was centred around salmon. The availability of salmon and other natural resources allowed a diversity of coastal tribes to develop, and within those tribes, diverse cultures and social systems arose due to the relatively easy food source in salmon (von Aderkas, 2005)

Today, salmon fishing is still a popular recreational activity and supports a sizeable commercial industry on the west coast (and moreover in Alaska). The salmon fishery is considered healthy within Olympic Coast National Marine Sanctuary; although some runs show signs of trouble, the fishery supports many commercial boats, charter boats for recreational fishing, bait and tackle shops, chandleries, as well as native sustenance harvesting.

Offshore of California, the runs of salmon have taken a dramatic drop in the past three years. First in 2006, runs to the Klamath river in northern California were very low, requiring a greatly shortened season. In 2008, fishery managers closed the entire season due to predicted poor runs into the Sacramento river in central California. Water management for agriculture and residential use is largely blamed as well as poor ocean conditions in prior years that affected the survivorship of juvenile fish.

Again, as is the case for other sacred species described previously, west coast national marine sanctuaries protect critical forage grounds for these enigmatic species. Also, they work to educate landowners, resource managers and public citizens about how their activities on watersheds may affect ocean resources such as salmon. Sanctuary managers do not make decisions about harvest levels or other aspects of fishery management for salmon. However, the public is awakening to this dramatic disappearance of salmon from the national marine sanctuaries, and their concerns highlight how a sacred species like salmon must be protected throughout its habitat and from diverse threats to its survivorship.

Conclusions

The bold action in 1972 to create the National Marine Sanctuary System allowed the United States to determine and designate the sacred places in ocean and Great Lakes waters. These sacred sites on the US west coast, home to hundreds of thousands of species and protecting huge marine ecosystems, also protect species that, for various reasons, are considered sacred species. Some of these sacred species are endangered, their populations having been exploited for generations at levels that natural reproduction cannot sustain. However, the sacred sanctuaries themselves create protective systems that will allow the threatened and the thriving sacred species to flourish.

References

Benson, S. R., Forney, K. A., Harvey, J. T., *et al.* (2007). Abundance, distribution and habitat of *Dermochelys coriacea* off California. *Fishery Bulletin*, **105**, 337–47.

Croll, D. A., Marinovic, B., Benson, S., *et al.* (2005). From wind to whales: trophic links in a coastal upwelling system. *Marine Ecology Progress Series*, **289**, 117–30.

Dutton, P. R., Hitipeuw, C., Zein, M., *et al.* (2007). Status and genetic structure of nesting populations of leatherback turtles (*Dermochelys coriacea*) in the western Pacific. *Chelonian Conservation Biology*, **6**, 47–53.

Estes, J. A. and Palmisano, J. F. (1974). Sea otters: their role in structuring nearshore communities. *Science*, **185**, 1058–60.

Groot, C. and Margolis, L. (1991). *Pacific Salmon Life Histories*. Vancouver: University of British Colombia Press.

Jones, P. (2005). Identity through fishing: a preliminary analysis of impacts to the Nez Perce as a result of the damming of the Clearwater and Snake rivers. *Cultural Dynamics*, **17**, 155–92.

Paine, R. T. (1969). A note on trophic complexity and community stability. *American Naturalist*, **103**, 91–3.

Safina, C. (2006). *Voyage of the Turtle: In Pursuit of Earth's Last Dinosaur*. New York, NY: Henry Holt & Co.

Silverstein, A. and Nunn, L. S. (1995). *The Sea Otter*. Nass, Cty Kildare, Ireland: Milbrook Press.

USGS (United States Geological Survey). (2007). Spring 2007 Mainland California Sea Otter Survey Results. Available from: http://www.werc.usgs.gov/otters/ca-surveyspr2007.htm

von Aderkas, E. (2005). *American Indians of the Pacific Northwest*. Oxford: Osprey Publishing.

WDFW (Washington Department of Fish and Wildlife). (2005). Results of the 2005 Survey of the reintroduced sea otter population in Washington State. Available from: http://www.wdfw.wa.gov/wlm/research/papers/seaotter/survey/seaotter_2005.pdf

16

Integrating biocultural values in nature conservation: perceptions of culturally significant sites and species in adaptive management

BAS VERSCHUUREN

Introduction

Ecosystems not only consist of physical attributes, they are subjected to and influenced by cultural perceptions and values. As Schama notes, 'Landscapes are culture before they are nature; constructs of the imagination projected onto wood water and rock' (1995, p. 61). Schama goes further by stating that there is an elaborate frame through which our adult eyes survey the landscape and that before landscape can ever be a response for the senses, it is the work of the mind. This leads Schama to conclude that the landscape's scenery is built up as much from strata of memory as from layers of rock. Hence, cultural perceptions and shared history of landscapes result in different and even contesting meanings of ecosystems and landscapes (Stewart and Strathern, 2003; Mainteny, 2004).

In some cultures the spiritual values of certain sites and species may be important enough for local people to conserve and protect the ecosystems that contain them. This occurs, even though an economic cost–benefit analysis may advise conversion of the ecosystem through resource development, such as mining or agriculture. To those people, the spiritual significance of rivers, mountains, or even individual tree or animal species such as the black-necked crane mentioned further on in this chapter, has led to their veneration and recognition as sacred (Verschuuren *et al.*, 2010). Those sacred sites and species are increasingly known for their significant contribution to biodiversity values (Stewart and Strathern, 2003; Dudley *et al.*, 2005; Putney, 2005; Bhagwat and Rutte, 2006; Verschuuren

Sacred Species and Sites: Advances in Biocultural Conservation, ed. Gloria Pungetti, Gonzalo Oviedo and Della Hooke. Published by Cambridge University Press. © Cambridge University Press 2012.

et al., 2010). Sacred places are often traditionally managed based on ancestral intergenerational principles that in many cases ensure cultural continuity and environmental management (Berkes, 1999; Jeanrenaud *et al.*, 2001; Verschuuren, 2006). The cultural and spiritual importance of sacred sites and species is often ignored in Western-style landscape and ecosystem management. This chapter investigates the role of sacred sites and species in new emerging biocultural approaches in nature conservation and ecosystem management.

As such, new understandings and approaches are very much needed for strengthening Western-style conservation management in biocultural diversity protection, and this chapter will discuss the potential role of integrating cultural and spiritual values into conservation management. In doing so it will focus on the potential for setting historic baselines and developing indicators for ecosystem change based on Traditional Ecological Knowledge (TEK) and cultural perceptions. Taking into account such intangible cultural values and TEK in day-to-day management is furthermore seen as a means for engaging local communities and indigenous peoples in the development of biocultural approaches and finding new ways for the management of Indigenous and Community Conserved Areas (ICCAs).

Definitions and concepts

Equitable and sustainable management is the result of decision-making processes initiated by people; their decisions are inherent constituents of social choice in any given culture. These social and cultural dimensions are also reflected in conservation management; Jepson and Canney (2003) explain them as sets of ideals and beliefs to which people individually and collectively aspire and which they desire to uphold. They structure the traditions, institutions and laws that underpin society. Thus, in line with Jepson and Canney (2003), it becomes clear that we believe certain things, not because they are logically evident, but because we live in a group where these ideas are supported and confirmed (Stark, 1996). Due to the importance of the implications of integrating cultural and spiritual values in conservation management, this chapter makes use of the following operational definition for cultural and spiritual values based on the IUCN's World Commission on Protected Areas' task force on Cultural and Spiritual Values of Protected Areas (CSVPA):

> Those qualities, both positive and negative, ascribed to nature,
> landscapes and ecosystems by different social groups, traditions, beliefs,
> or value systems that fulfil humankind's need to understand, and
> connect in meaningful ways, to the environment of its origin and to
> nature. (CSVPA, 2005)

In order to investigate such meaningful connection of humankind with nature, especially where nature is seen as venerated and held sacred, this chapter focuses on the role that people's perceptions can play in developing biocultural management approaches. In the field, all around the world, protected area managers have encountered situations in which sacred natural sites and species play a pivotal role in local people's relationship with nature (Dudley *et al.*, 2005; Verschuuren, 2006). On many occasions such cultural perceptions have proved to be invaluable in building approaches to sustainable management. Sacred sites and species are often the focal points for such approaches and for the purpose of this chapter have been defined based on Jeanrenaud: 'specific places and species recognised by people as having spiritual and religious significance or as sites and species recognised by institutionalised religions or faiths as places and species of worship and remembrance' (Jeanrenaud *et al.*, 2001).

The revitalised interest in including cultural and spiritual values as a measure of biocultural diversity offers opportunities for renewing concepts such as sacred sites and species in order to develop the dynamic nature of conservation and ecosystem management approaches. The sacred and spiritual dimensions of nature are experienced individually but also collectively, as is often the case with sacred sites. The distinct cultural perspectives associated with sacred sites and species are considered shared values amongst a group of people that have a culture clearly distinguished from others (Carmichael *et al.*, 1994; Verschuuren *et al.*, 2010). Nonetheless, the spiritual and sacred dimensions of nature can also be transcendent when sacred natural sites form a shared source of inspiration that is appreciated and recognised by a variety of social and cultural groups.

To understand the transcendental dimensions of people's relationships with the sacred in nature, it may be beneficial to extend an inquiry into people's cultural ontologies (Williams and Harvey, 2001). The concepts of worldview and cosmovision may provide a foundation for building a framework for understanding and reconciling cultural and spiritual values with Western-style conservation management in order to involve the sacred in day-to-day management in a constructive way. Haverkort and Reijntjes have emphasised that cosmovision is not something abstract, but is a reality based on concrete observation and experience. They offer the following definition:

> the way an individual or a certain population (community or cultural group) perceives the world and cosmos. It includes assumed interrelationships between the spiritual, natural and human world and provides the basis on which people relate with nature and the spiritual world and take decisions. (Haverkort and Reijntjes, 2006, p. 15)

A good example of this may be that often traditional worldviews consist of an ontology that does not contain a linear conceptualisation of time as it would be known to most Western-style conservationists. Instead, they are made up of a cyclic conceptualisation of time, based on complex and mutually constitutive cycles in which interaction and change confirm and renew relationships with nature and the sacred.

Hence, traditional cosmovisions may include the profound interferential guidance of ancestral spirits with the present natural world and encompass many generations into the present. In order to advance current management approaches this chapter suggests that new approaches derived from different worldviews are needed, rather than more information derived from conventional mindsets and accompanying monitoring systems (Mainteny, 2004).

Managing the whole spectrum: from culture to science

Most management problems are perceived when people's values are inadequately interpreted or defined. Attention is required in selecting the methodology and frameworks used in order to capture and communicate people's values to the decision-makers, especially when the people themselves are not, or cannot, be involved in the decision-making process. According to English and Lee: 'The fact of defining intangible values is not itself culturally neutral; it comes from the Western scientific tradition but if we do not define intangible values in some way, it will be virtually impossible for them to influence management' (2003, p. 45). As a possible solution it is suggested that both cultural and natural values need to be taken into account in conservation management (Figure 16.1). Of specific interest are the inextricable linkages that exist between the two value sets, as these are vital to people's unique understanding of the environment and are therefore considered of paramount importance when integrating cultural and spiritual values in conservation management.

When evolving from a biophysical to an anthropocentric sphere, the role of perception is important because if one assumes that values are merely objective then they can be managed along with the biophysical environment; if they were merely subjective, management would consist of adjustment to public preference (Harmon and Putney, 2003). In fact, this argument illustrates the dilemma of differentiating and valuing use and non-use values, tangible and intangible values, extrinsic and intrinsic values, as well as biophysical and spiritual values. Many societies and cultures place a high value on the maintenance of either historically or culturally important landscapes as well as culturally significant sacred species (Posey, 1999). Consider, for example, the maintenance of sacred groves around the world. In India, these groves are maintained despite the increasing pressure for economic

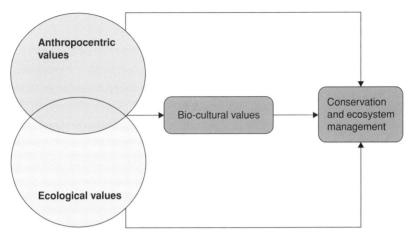

Figure 16.1 Biocultural values in nature conservation (adapted from Verschuuren, 2007a).

development at regional and national levels. They form fragmented mosaics of biodiversity havens that offer unique opportunities for conservation management to target the improvement of landscape connectivity (Bhagwat *et al.*, 2005; Bhagwat and Rutte, 2006). A good example of a sacred species is the black-necked crane (*Grus nigricollis*), whose sacred status has led to the recognition of Ramsar status in southern Tibet's Napahai wetlands (China's north-west Yunnan Province). The wetlands are under increasing population pressure, but the black-necked crane has offered opportunities for conservation, ecotourism and education based on people's traditions and beliefs (WWF, 2008). The black-necked crane is a symbol of peace and has been revered by Tibetan Buddhists for centuries because it is believed that previous incarnations of the Dalai Lama were carried from monastery to monastery on the backs of these holy birds.

A more contemporary example shows how cultural values can also hinder nature conservation and environmental management. Following people's shared nationalistic and colonial feelings rather than sacred values, this example relates to the coat of arms of Australia, which depicts an emu and a kangaroo. Both animals are hardly ever consumed by non-aboriginal Australians despite the fact that the farming of kangaroos and emu would be cost-effective and more ecologically sustainable then sheep farming. As a result, the ever-increasing populations of kangaroos, drinking from the artificial water places put in place by farmers to water their sheep and cattle, are being culled for pet meat. Sheep and cattle farming in Australia are still to be held accountable for widespread ecological problems such as soil erosion, (ground) water depletion and invasive weed infestations. Indirectly, the costs of such ecological disasters impact significantly on the nation's natural capital and are a burden to the long-term sustainability of farmers' practices and the tax payer in general.

Carter and Bramley (2002) define such values in terms of a resource's intrinsic (objectively measurable) and extrinsic (largely subjectively measurable) qualities. Both value types are significant, but they are not often integrated into the management process. This dilemma has manifested itself as a continuous status quo for managers and decision-makers, although it is generally becoming more accepted that both types of values need consideration (see Figure 16.1). In line with Berkes and Folke (1998); Folke *et al.* (1998, p. 242); Berkes (1999); Maffi (1999); English and Lee (2003, p. 347); and Cocks (2006), it is the viewpoint of the author that the interplay of cultural and biological values is of elementary importance to conservation management in which a unique role is played by sacred sites and species.

Community conservation and sacred sites and species

Integrating sacred sites, or more broadly, the perception of the sacredness of nature, into conservation planning can only be achieved by doing this across ideological, physical and institutional borders, in and outside protected areas (Verschuuren *et al.*, 2010). In short, this is a process which hinges on the integration of knowledge and wisdom. Including sacred sites in all IUCN protected area categories builds on their intercultural and cross-cutting values, which leads to equitable synergies between spiritual, cultural and natural diversity and therefore supports more holistic and often also more sustainable conservation objectives (Verschuuren *et al.*, 2007). Moving towards such conservation objectives, sacred sites are currently not effectively reflected in protected area designations and management plans, although guidance for doing so has been developed and will need to become part and parcel of the protected areas' planning domain (Dudley, 2008). Existing policy and legal frameworks do not adequately support sacred natural sites (Jeanrenaud *et al.*, 2001; Shackley, 2001; Verschuuren *et al.*, 2010). This in itself is remarkable, as there is sound and widespread evidence that sacred natural sites over the centuries have been providing, and continue to provide, effective conservation of biodiversity (Posey, 1999; Berkes, 1999; McNeely, 2000; Jeanrenaud *et al.*, 2001; Harmon and Putney, 2003; Dudley *et al.*, 2005; Bhagwat *et al.*, 2005). Recommendation 5.13 from the Fifth World Parks Congress called for management planning, zoning and training of managers, especially at the local level, in order to give balanced attention to the full spectrum of material, cultural and spiritual values; and requested the IUCN to review the 1994 Protected Area Category Guidelines with the aim of including cultural values in the planning of the management and policy guidelines of governments, non-governmental organisations (NGO)s, local communities and civil society (Dudley, 2008). The recommendation aims to ensure that protected areas approach cultural and spiritual values as co-creator for potential management objectives in categories where they are currently excluded.

Over recent decades a strong current has developed among international conservation institutions across the world demonstrating that working with people is essential in order to achieve conservation targets. It is thought that this movement, which has brought forth concepts such as Indigenous Protected Areas (IPAs) and ICCAs, may be very effective in terms of conserving desirable levels of biodiversity. When conservation targets are leading the way in endogenous development, these often result in sustainable living and land use outside protected areas boundaries (Haverkort and Reijntjes, 2006, p. 432; Verschuuuren, 2006). Sacred sites are a useful concept for setting conservation targets based on culture and endogenous development. In ecosystem management, sacred sites may be a keystone in landscape connectivity and biodiversity conservation, and they can be integrated within the concept of ICCAs and IPAs. Such synergies would be a mixture of cultural, community and conservation values (Bhagwat *et al.*, 2005; Kothari, 2007). It is therefore fundamental to empower and facilitate those communities that are key stakeholders through the co-development of ecosystem management tools and strategies in order to achieve effective biodiversity conservation. Conservation professionals should take care not to create their structures and impose a process of co-optation. A people-oriented discourse that is cognisant of conservation objectives, in and outside protected areas, is likely to provide a successful approach towards developing sustainable and equitable 'pro conservation' communities that are synchronised with conservation objectives (Beltrán, 2000; Ghosh *et al.*, 2005; Borrini-Feyerabend *et al.*, 2004; Cocks, 2006; Verschuuren, 2007a).

Sacred cultural values in nature conservation and adaptive management

According to Allaby (2005), ecosystem management is the active manipulation of an ecosystem in order to exploit its productivity or to enhance its biodiversity and conservation values. Adaptive management has been developed from the 1970s onward as a management method which is able to respond to uncertainties (Holling, 1978). Human behaviour causes anthropocentric pressures on the environment, often as a response to changing environmental conditions. Consider the adaptation to climate change or the availability of fuelwood. This chapter argues that these strategies are likely to increase the resilience of biocultural values in the face of cultural development and adaptation to uncertainties in environmental problems (Berkes, 1999; Verschuuren, 2007b).

The power of the spiritual and the sacred lies in the fact that its essence is intangible, or as Burkert (1998) puts it, 'unseen' and 'non-obvious', which cannot be verified empirically. It can only be valued adequately by those who perceive its importance; therefore, the quality of the valuation resides with those people's interpretations and ability to communicate them (Carmichael *et al.*, 1994). Communicating cultural and spiritual values to decision-makers in nature conservation is difficult because of double hermeneutics and the lack of an adequate framework or approach to capture the dynamics of culture (English and Lee, 2003; Verschuuren, 2007a). In double hermeneutics, these values become distorted or get 'lost in translation', travelling from experience and perception through the assessment and valuation approaches before they reach decision-makers (Giddens 1995). In trying to assess and value the spiritual significance of nature one finds the means to value it are complex and encompass issues like scale, perception and indicators, and in many cases require integration of scientific disciplines which may not be easy to comprehend. A possible way forward is to investigate the importance of understanding people's perceptions in relation to developing biocultural approaches in ecosystem and conservation management (Verschuuren, 2007b).

Ecological values are often based on information derived from species and ecosystem processes using biophysical methods. Over time, the use of traditional ecological knowledge has gained a foothold in ecosystem management, particularly when this knowledge has been shown to be 'Western science-proof'. Cultural values, on the other hand, are based on how people perceive ecosystems and in many cases there may not be sufficient objective scientific proof, causing management to work with additional sources of information such as photographs, drawings, artwork or poems. From these sources, indicators may be derived that can offer information on the status of natural processes. The different dimensions of the human–ecosystem relationship also become apparent in the spiritual, intellectual and physical links between human cultures and landscapes as well as ecosystems (Schama, 1995; Posey, 1999; Harmon and Putney, 2003; Cocks, 2006). The UNESCO Convention on the protection of Intangible Cultural Heritage offers a more concrete expression of the 'intangible' aspects of culture (UNESCO, 2003):

1. oral traditions and expressions, including language as a vehicle of the intangible;
2. cultural heritage;
3. performing arts;
4. social practices, rituals and festive events;
5. knowledge and practices concerning nature and the universe; and
6. traditional craftsmanship.

a

Figure 16.2 Intangible expressions of human ecosystem relationships: magpie geese,
linking sacred sites and species (© B. Verschuuren). See colour plate section. (a) Magpie
geese rock paintings, the world's oldest painting tradition and a form of
intergenerational transmission of knowledge. (b) and (c) Ceremonial dance. Magpie
geese can be mimicked in ceremonial dances like this to depict a creation story.
[Figures are deliberately out of focus.] (d) Magpie as food source. (e) Magpie Dreaming.
This site was created by an ancestral being depicted as a magpie goose called
Karramala (Rose *et al*. 2002, p. 204).

Figure 16.2 shows this biocultural connectivity by depicting the numerous ways
in which species and landscape are imbued with sacredness. The example is taken
from northern Australia, where the author has been working with various groups
of indigenous people (Verschuuren, 2006). It is intended to emphasise the critical
importance of integrating cultural and spiritual values in conservation management because cultural diversity and biological diversity are mutually interdependent (Callicot, 1994, p. 285; Posey, 1999; Berkes *et al*., 2000; Cocks, 2006). Sacred
landscapes pose a particular set of opportunities for ecosystem management, such
as the secrecy of knowledge and the transboundary nature of cultural perceptions and patterns of land use. One needs to be aware that in some indigenous
worldviews the concept of sacred is absent because its opposite, the profane, is

b

c

Figure 16.2 (*cont.*)

d

e

Figure 16.2 (*cont.*)

not recognised as real. This means that everything is perceived as sacred, a phenomenon which coincides with the non-dualistic dimensions shared by mystics of mainstream faiths (Smith, 1977).

When embracing cultural diversity, its perceptions and consciousness in relation to the sacred, particular challenges exist for establishing management objectives and related indicators to inform upon the status of these objectives. In some cases, current biophysically founded management actions will need to give way to new co-creating value sets and accept culture as a dynamic force in shaping conservation management and policies. Concurrently, including different cultural perceptions in conservation and ecosystem management demands an understanding of local and indigenous people's way of life. Their right to self-determination will need to be incorporated into ecosystem management and models for the governance of nature conservation. Within the United Nations, the Permanent Forum on Indigenous Issues also addressed the issue of indicators in relation to human well-being as it was brought forward in the Millennium Ecosystem Assessment (MA, 2005) and, through the framework of the Millennium Development Goals, indigenous experts agreed that:

> indicators must place significant emphasis on indigenous peoples' inherent values, traditions, languages, and traditional orders/systems, including laws, governance, lands, economies, etc. Indicator development should reflect true indigenous perspectives such as portraying approaches grounded in wholism and unique values. (United Nations, The Permanent Forum on Indigenous Issues, 2006, p. 22)

Indicators have been defined in literature by several authors based on their purpose. Smeets and Weterings (1999) state that communication is the primary function of indicators. According to the authors, indicators should enable or promote information exchange regarding the issue they address. This simple definition seems suitable in that it easily allows for the inclusion of perception-based indicators. For example, more often than not, people and land managers tend to incorporate 'exotic' species as part of their perception of a given landscape and as part of their ethno-botanical repertoire, particularly when economic, agricultural and aesthetic motivations are involved. In northern Australia's Kakadu National Park and World Heritage Site, this has led to a growing appreciation of the presence of wild horses in the park. In particular, the Aboriginal people that co-manage the park with the Parks and Wildlife Service insisted on this introduced (some would say pest) species being maintained in the park despite the impact it causes on the park's ecology (Lawrence, 2000). In fact, Aboriginal peoples place a cultural–historic value on horses that has simultaneously led to the species' growing spiritual significance. Because of this, Aboriginal people now recognise places in the landscape that are called 'horse dreaming' which, like other dreaming sites, are venerated and imbued with spiritual importance. Naturally, these places are an expression of human–ecosystem relationships and form focal points of cultural and spiritual values. They offer opportunities for specific management objectives that fit into the concept of sacred natural sites. Hence, protecting biological diversity and ecosystem integrity as well as cultural and spiritual diversity (sacred sites and species) poses a challenge to managers and policymakers that requires them to search for appropriate solutions beyond their conventional references and beliefs.

Conclusions

Traditional ecological knowledge concerning sacred sites and species can play a key role in understanding the broader landscape and ecosystem processes in the way they are currently perceived in Western-style conservation management. This chapter starts with the idea that the real use of TEK lies in the need to see and structure management approaches in a qualitatively new way. On the one hand, this entails the recognition that accumulating knowledge on cultural and spiritual values on sacred sites and species is indeed important in terms of documenting their cultural significance and diversity. On the other hand, it is argued that such information will always be incomplete, and that, instead of gathering more quantitative data, we might look towards the application of its qualitative aspects. For such new biocultural approaches to be applied in conservation management, the underlying values of such data need to be understood from the perspective of a different worldview or mindset, rather than by simply applying well-known conventional Western-style management approaches (Berkes and Folke, 1998, p. 459; Berkes, 1999; Berkes *et al.*, 2000; Mainteny, 2004; Verschuuren *et al.*, 2010). This suggests that investigating people's perceptions of the sacred dimensions of sites and species can contribute towards creating new approaches in adaptive management, the development of perception-based indicators, and reactive and participatory monitoring. Such approaches are thought to be of critical importance for the conservation of biocultural diversity.

References

Allaby, M. (2005). *Oxford Dictionary of Ecology*. Oxford: Oxford University Press.

Beltrán, J. (ed) (2000). *Indigenous and Traditional Peoples and Protected Areas: Principles, Guidelines and Case Studies*. Gland, Switzerland and Cambridge, UK: IUCN and WWF International.

Berkes, F. (1999). *Sacred Ecology; Traditional Ecological Knowledge and Resource Management*. Philadelphia, PA: Taylor and Francis.

Berkes, F. and Folke, C. (1998). Linking social and ecological systems for resilience and sustainability. In *Understanding Social and Ecological Systems*, ed. F. Berkes, C. Folke and J. Colding. Cambridge: Cambridge University Press, pp. 1–25.

Berkes, W., Colding, J. and Folke, C. (2000). Rediscovery of traditional ecological knowledge as adaptive management. *Ecological Application*, **10**, 1251–62.

Bhagwat, S. A., Kushalappa, C. G., William, P. H., *et al.* (2005). The role of informal protected areas in maintaining biodiversity in the Western Ghats of India. *Ecology and Society*, **10**, part 8. Available from: http://www.ecologyandsociety.org/vol10/iss1/art8/

Bhagwat, S. A. and Rutte, C. (2006). Sacred groves: potential for biodiversity management. *Ecological Society of America,* 10: *Frontiers in Ecology and the Environment,* **4**, 519–24, Available from: www.frontiersinecology.org/

Borrini-Feyerabend, G., Kothari, A. and Oviedo, G. (2004). *Indigenous and Local Communities and Protected Areas. Towards Equity and Enhanced Conservation*. Best Practice Protected Area Guidelines Series No. 11. Gland, Switzerland and Cambridge: IUCN WCPA.

Burkert, W. (1998). *Creation of the Sacred. Tracks of Biology in Early Religions*. Cambridge, MA and London: Harvard University Press.

Callicot, B. J. (1994). *Earth's Insights, A Multicultural Survey of Ecological Ethics from the Mediterranean Basin to the Australian Outback*. Berkeley, CA: University of California Press.

Carmichael, D., Hubert J., Reeves B., *et al.* (1994). *Sacred Sites, Sacred Places*. London: Routledge.

Carter, R. W. and Bramley, R. (2002). Defining heritage values and significance for improved resource management: an application to Australian tourism. *International Journal of Heritage Studies*, **8**, 175–99.

Cocks, M. L. (2006). Moving beyond the realm of 'indigenous' and 'local' people. *Human Ecology*, **34**, 185–200.

CSVPA. (2005). Quadrenial Action Plan of the Task force on Cultural and Spiritual Values of Protected Areas, World Conservation Union (IUCN), Gland, Switzerland, unpublished.

Dudley, N. (ed.) (2008). *Guidelines for Applying Protected Area Management Categories*. Gland, Switzerland: IUCN.

Dudley, N., Higgins-Zogib, L. and Mansourian, S. (2005). *Beyond Belief: Linking Faiths and Protected Areas to Support Biodiversity Conservation*. WWF, Equilibrium and the Alliance of Religions and Conservation research report. Gland, Switzerland.

English, J. A. and Lee, E. (2003). Managing the intangible, sanctuary of dreams. In *The Full Value of Parks: From Economics to the Intangible*, ed. D. Harmon and A. D. Putney, Lanham, MD: Rowman and Littlefield Publishers, pp. 43–55.

Folke, C., Berkes, F. and Colding, J. (1998). Ecological practices and social mechanisms for building resilience and sustainability. In *Understanding Social and Ecological Systems*, ed. F. Berkes, C. Folke and J. Colding. Cambridge: Cambridge University Press.

Ghosh, A., Traverse, M., Bhattacharya, D. K., *et al.* (2005). Cultural services, Chapter 14, Policy responses, in Volume 3: Global & Multiscale Assessment Report. In *Millennium Ecosystem Assessment*, ed. E. Almaco, and E. Bennet, Washington, DC: Island Press, pp. 403–19.

Giddens, A. (1995). *Politics, Sociology and Social Theory: Encounters with Classical and Contemporary Social Thought*. Cambridge: Cambridge Polity Press.

Harmon, D. and Putney, A. D. (eds) (2003). *The Full Value of Parks: From Economics to the Intangible*. Lanham, MD: Rowman and Littlefield Publishers.

Haverkort, B. and Reijntjes, C. (eds) (2006). *Moving Worldviews, Reshaping Sciences, Policies and Practices for Endogenous Sustainable Development*. Leusden, The Netherlands: Compas series on Worldviews and Sciences 4.

Holling, C. S. (ed.) (1978). *Adaptive Environmental Assessment and Management*. Chichester: Wiley.

Jeanrenaud, S., Soutter, R. and Oviedo, G. (2001). An international Initiative for the protection of sacred natural sites and other places of traditional and indigenous people with importance for biodiversity conservation, a concept paper, Draft 5. Available at www.wwf.org (accessed 7 March 2007).

Jepson, P. and Canney, S. (2003). Value-led conservation. *Global Ecology & Biogeography*, **12**, 271–4.

Kothari, A. (2007). Community conserved areas: towards ecological and livelihood security. *Parks*, **16**, 19–59.

Lawrence, D. (2000). *Kakadu: The Making of a National Park*. Melbourne: Melbourne University Press.

Mainteny, P. (2004). Perceptions of nature by indigenous communities. *Landscape and Planning*, **16**, 187–92.

Maffi, L. (1999). Linguistic diversity, language and the environment. In *Cultural and Spiritual Values of Biodiversity*, ed. D. Posey. London: Intermediate Technology Publications, pp. 19–59.

McNeely, J. A. (2000). Cultural factors in conserving biodiversity. In *Links between Cultures and Biodiversity*, ed. A. Wilkes, H. Tillman, M. Salas, T. Grinter and Y. Shaoting. Proceedings of the Cultures and Biodiversity Congress. China: Yunnan Science and Technology Press, pp. 128–42.

MA (Millennium Ecosystem Assessment). (2005). *Ecosystems and Human Wellbeing: Synthesis*. Washington, DC: Island Press.

Posey, D. (ed.) (1999). *Cultural and Spiritual Values of Biodiversity, A Comprehensive Contribution to the UNEP Global Biodiversity Assessment*. London: Intermediate Technology Publications.

Putney, A. (2005). Building cultural support for protected areas through sacred natural sites. In *Friends for Life, New Partners in Support of Protected Areas*, ed. J. McNeely. Gland, Switzerland and Cambridge: IUCN, pp. 129–41.

Rose, D. B., D'Amico, S., Daiyi, N., *et al.* (2001). *Country of the Heart. An Indigenous Australian Homeland*. Aboriginal and Torres Strait Islander Studies III. Canberra: Aboriginal Studies Press.

Schama, S. (1995). *Landscape and Memory*. London: HarperCollins Publishers.

Shackley, M. (2001). Sacred World Heritage Sites: balancing meaning with management. *Tourism Recreation Research*, **26**, 5–10.

Smeets, E. and Weterings, R. (1999). *Environmental Indicators: A Typology and Overview*. Technical Report No. 25. Copenhagen: European Environmental Agency.

Smith, H. (1977). *Forgotten Truth. The Common Vision of the World's Religions*. San Francisco, CA: HarperCollins Publishers.

Stark, R. (1996). Why religious movements succeed or fail. A revised general model. *Journal of Contemporary Religion*, **4**, 133–46.

Stewart, P. J. and Strathern, A. (2003). *Landscape, Memory and History, Anthropological Perspectives*. Anthropology Culture and Society. London: Pluto Press.

UNESCO. (2003). Convention for the safeguarding of the intangible cultural heritage. Text available at www.unesco.org (accessed 20 September 2006).

United Nations, The Permanent Forum on Indigenous Issues. (2006). Report of the meeting on Indigenous peoples and indicators of wellbeing, Ottawa, pp. 22–3.

Verschuuren, B. (2006). Socio-cultural importance of wetlands in northern Australia. In *Conserving Cultural and Biological Diversity: The Role of Sacred Natural Sites and Cultural Landscapes*, ed. T. Schaaf and C. Lee. Paris: IUCN/UNESCO. Paris: United Nations Educational Scientific and Cultural Organisation, chapter 6, pp. 141–50.

Verschuuren, B. (2007a). An overview of cultural and spiritual values in ecosystem management and conservation strategies. In *Endogenous Development and Bio-cultural Diversity, The Interplay of Worldviews, Globalisation and Locality*, ed. B. Haverkort and S. Rist. Compas/CDE, series on Worldviews and Sciences, No. 6. Leusden, The Netherlands: Compas, pp. 299–326.

Verschuuren, B. (2007b). *Seeing is Believing, Integrating Cultural and Spiritual Values in Conservation Management. Foundation for Sustainable Development*. The Netherlands and Gland Switzerland: IUCN.

Verschuuren, B., Mallarach, J. M. and Oviedo, G. (2007). *Sacred Sites and Protected Areas*. IUCN World Commission on Protected Areas, Summit on the IUCN categories in Andalusia, Spain, 7–11 May 2007. Available from www.iucn.org (accessed 11 August 2007).

Verschuuren, B., Wild, R., McNeeley, J., *et al.* (eds) (2010). *Sacred Natural Sites, Conserving Nature and Culture*. London: EarthScan.

Williams, D. R. and Harvey, D. (2001). Transcendent experience in forest environments. *Journal of Environmental Psychology*, **21**, 249–60.

WWF. (2008). Shangri-La Sustainable Community Initiative: empowering local communities to preserve their unique local cultural heritage and natural environment. Available from www.wwfchina.org (accessed 3 May 2007).

PART V SACRED ANIMALS

17

Genealogy of the sacred: Maori beliefs concerning lizards

MERE ROBERTS

Introduction

In a paper on the cultural context of resource management, Nakashima (1998) challenged scientists to accept the validity of other representations of 'reality' and acknowledge that these may offer more appropriate and sustainable ways of managing our environment. Indigenous knowledge developed over long periods of time and involving close intimacy between peoples and place contains insights and understandings that are needed today if we wish to manage and protect species and sites in ways that include rather than exclude people. Fundamental to all knowledge is the identification, naming and categorisation of all things in a particular place.

Either by uniquely creating order out of apparent disorder or, alternatively, by perceiving the order already inherent in nature (Berlin, 1992, pp. 8–13), different societies create frameworks grounded in their own metaphysical paradigm upon which to situate all known things. Among indigenous societies these frameworks reveal not only the perceived order and relationships of all things to each other and to their origins, but also the moral and spiritual 'cosmoscape' within which the place of humans is defined and their actions governed and regulated (Reichel, 2005).

At a more practical level, these mental maps can function as a 'folk taxonomy' or ethno-classification which provides insights into those natural resources and other phenomena of importance to the physical and spiritual survival of a particular culture. These taxonomies have relevance to those involved in the protection and restoration of natural resources and environments as they help to provide the

Sacred Species and Sites: Advances in Biocultural Conservation, ed. Gloria Pungetti, Gonzalo Oviedo and Della Hooke. Published by Cambridge University Press. © Cambridge University Press 2012.

cultural context and rationale for ensuring that such efforts and their outcomes are grounded in place. While it is possible for ecologists to identify species and habitats necessary for the maintenance and biological integrity of ecosystem services in a particular area, these may not always include those species and sites that are essential for the maintenance of spiritual and cultural integrity and the well-being of the people of that place. In all societies certain species of plants and animals are 'set apart' and may be referred to as sacred for a variety of reasons. Here in New Zealand, two animal species of cultural significance to Maori are known as *tuatara* and *moko kakariki*. This chapter describes a cognitive framework called *whakapapa* whereby all things, including these two animals, are classified according to their perceived celestial origins and relationships to other species and phenomena. It also describes some of the traditional beliefs concerning these species and why they are of special significance to Maori, and more recently, to all New Zealanders.

Reptiles: the scientific story

During the age of the dinosaurs, 130 million years ago, the New Zealand landmass arose from seas on the southern edge of a vast supercontinent called Gondwana. Neighbouring landmasses included Antarctica, South America and Australia, from which migrated a number of plant and animal species before New Zealand was cast adrift into the Pacific Ocean 80 million years ago. Among these 'Gondwana relics' is the *tuatara*, the only remaining member of an ancient reptilian order, Rhynchocephalia. Elsewhere in the world, members of this group and of those including its larger dinosaur relatives have become extinct (Stevens *et al.*, 1995). Because New Zealand broke away from Gondwana before mammals had time to reach it, their absence (until human arrival) played a key part in the survival of *tuatara* and of our equally unique amphibia and avifauna. Now regarded as a 'living fossil', *tuatara* was once found on all three of New Zealand's major islands. Rats and dogs introduced by Maori 800–1000 years ago were followed by more predators during European settlement 200 years ago and these, combined with habitat destruction following both colonisations, led to a serious decline in the population numbers of this species, which are now confined to a few small offshore island reserves. A further threat to survival comes from collectors and those who trade in rare and endangered species.

Taxonomically, *tuatara* (*Sphenodon guntheri* and *S. punctata*) belong to the Family Sphenodontidae, and are separate from true lizard endemics which comprise 30 species of skinks (Family Scincidae) and 29 species of geckos (Family Gekkonidae). For the purposes of this chapter, however, all will be referred to as 'lizards'. Today, many skinks and geckos are also limited to offshore islands and are equally rare,

Figure 17.1 A *tuatara* (*Sphenodon guntheri*) from Takapourewa (Stephens) Island. See colour plate section. (Photograph reproduced with permission of Susan Keal ©.)

threatened or endangered (Daugherty *et al.*, 1994). Based on their own species compilation, these authors consider 30 of 65 species as rare, vulnerable or endangered using IUCN criteria. Figures 17.1 and 17.2 show *tuatara* and *moko kakariki* (the green gecko, *Naultinus elegans*), the two species which form the focus of this chapter.

Whakapapa (genealogy) and accompanying beliefs concerning lizards

Eastern Polynesian peoples who first discovered Aotearoa (New Zealand) brought with them many things, tangible and intangible, from Hawaiki (the ancestral homelands, thought to be the Society and Cook Islands: Howe, 2003, p. 178). Among the latter are creation chants, examples of which have been recorded from the Tuamotu Islands of Anaa and Vahivahi (Stimson, 1971). Figure 17.3 depicts a cosmogonical map of the Universe from Anaa.

These creation 'mind maps' were inherited by Maori and recorded in genealogical form commencing with the origin of the universe and thence unfolding layer upon successive layer (hence *whakapapa*; literally 'to place in layers') to the object or person in question. In this way they function as genealogies, but because there is no break between the celestial and terrestrial realms, each *whakapapa* possesses spiritual as well as physical origins and descent lines, enabling all things to be

Figure 17.2 A green gecko (*Naultinus elegans*) (Photograph reproduced with permission of Rod Morris ©). See colour plate section.

located in time and space. While cosmogonical accounts were regarded as eso-teric knowledge and restricted to a select few, all other *whakapapa* of things of this world was common and essential 'everyday' knowledge. Hence for something to exist and be known, it must have a *whakapapa*; put another way, in order to 'know' about a thing (or a person), one must know its *whakapapa* (Roberts and Wills, 1998).

Plant and animal *whakapapa* typically commence with the primal parents, Rang-inui (sky father) and Papatuanuku (earth mother) and their many offspring (in some accounts, up to 70). As shown in Figure 17.4, certain of their children (*atua*, god-like deities) have procreative as well as protective responsibilities for environ-mental realms and associated phenomena.

Two of these children, Tangaroa and Tane, represent spiritual and environ-mental realms within which Maori trace the *whakapapa* of *tuatara*, skinks and geckos. One of several tribal *whakapapa* of these species is illustrated in Figure 17.5 and 17.6.

Three major groups shown in this figure, Fishes, Reptiles and Lizard gods, trace descent from their common ancestor Tangaroa and his son Punga, the god of ugly things. Accompanying narratives provide further explanations as to their

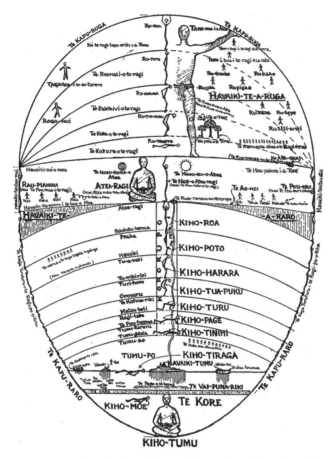

Figure 17.3 Polynesian (Anaa) chart of the universe (Reproduced from Stimson, 1933 [1971] 63).

celestial origins, earthly habitat and behaviour. According to Maori mythology, the children of Ranginui and Papatuanuku were born into darkness, so they conspired to separate their parents and let in light whence all things might grow. Led by Tane, they wrenched their father from their mother's embrace and lifted him aloft into the sky. One brother, Tawhiri-ma-tea, god of winds and storms, refused to participate and decided to wage war against his brothers in punishment for their deed. So severe were his storms that Tangaroa was forced to flee from the land to the sea. His children, Ika-tere (father of fishes) and Tu-te-wanawana (father of reptiles), argued about what they should do. Ika-tere demanded that they follow Tangaroa, but Tu-te-wanawana argued they should stay on land. Finally the brothers decided to separate and go their own ways, one to the sea and one to the land. Hence, the separation of the fishes (Ikatere) from the reptiles (Tu-te-wanawana) (Grey, 1956).

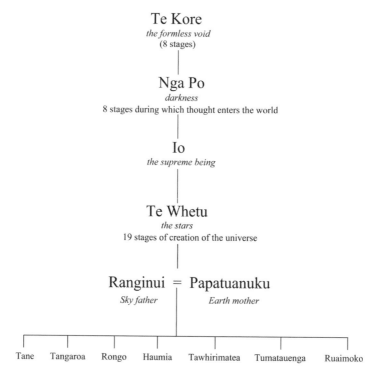

Figure 17.4 Abbreviated *whakapapa* of the children of Ranginui (sky father) and Papatuanuku (earth mother) (Adapted from Pei Te Hurinui, 1960, pp. 257–9).

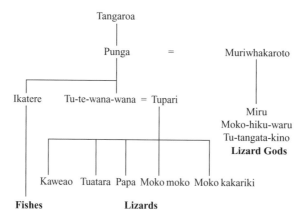

Figure 17.5 A *whakapapa* of fishes and reptiles (sourced from Anderson, 2000, pp. 159–60).

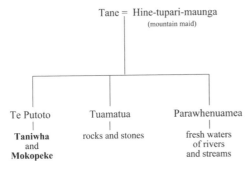

Figure 17.6 A *whakapapa* of lizards and *taniwha* (sourced from Best, 1982, p. 476).

Stories about the lizard descendants of Tu-te-wanawana and Tupari involve both historical and modern beliefs including those surrounding the *kaweau*, said by Tregear (2001) to be a large species of lizard about two feet long. Williams (1971) considers it to be the same as *tuatara* and goes on to say that Kahungunu (a tribal chief) once possessed a *kaweau*, which he kept in a special bowl, and brought out before an approaching adversary in order to instil fear. Controversy exists as to whether *kaweau* is distinct from *tuatara* and represents a mythological or a recently extinct lizard. A specimen approximately two feet long in the Natural History Museum of Marseille has been attributed to New Zealand and identified as a gecko *Hoplodactylus delcourti*. However, because the world's largest geckos are found in New Caledonia (a French protectorate) and the specimen is held in a French Museum and lacks written provenance, scientists are unconvinced that it is native to New Zealand (D. Towns, personal communication, October 2007).

Of extant reptiles, *tuatara* are the largest and are of special significance to Maori, particularly as guardians of sacred places. Because it was universally feared it was also ritualistically eaten on certain occasions. Carvings of humans about to swallow a lizard are said to symbolise a ritual test undergone by students of *makutu* (witchcraft). By overcoming their intense fear and repulsion in swallowing a lizard they attested to their courage and suitability to become a *tohunga* (priestly expert) of *makutu* and practise this evil art (Best, 1982, pp. 142, 462). Other stories tell of this act symbolising a man's *mana* (authority, prestige) and prowess. One concerns a Te Arawa chief who abducted a woman from another tribe (Tainui) and took her to Rotorua where she fretted, so they returned to her home. To help ensure his forgiveness she boasted of his prowess, saying there was nothing he could not do, whereupon the Tainui chiefs challenged him to submit to the ordeal of eating a *tuatara*. This he promptly did – and hence was re-named Ngarara-Nui ('giant lizard'; Orbell, 1995, p. 155; Sharell, 1966, p. 58). In Figure 17.7 this chief is depicted on

Figure 17.7 Carved head from the gable of a former meeting house in Whakarewara, Rotorua, now an Anglican church for people of Ngati Wahio. This carving represents Ngarara-Nui who achieved fame by swallowing a lizard (Photograph reproduced with permission of Venerable J. A. Huta, Priest, Te Ngae parish ©).

the *tekoteko* (apex) of a carved meeting house in Rotorua with a lizard in his mouth.

In addition to carvings and narratives, there are also *whakatauaki* (proverbs) which refer to the sacred status of lizards. For example, from the Ngati Awa tribe comes '*Ko Putauaki te maunga, he ngarara tona kai*', recorded by Best (1982, p. 179), meaning Putauaki is the sacred *maunga* (mountain) of Ngati Awa and hence *tona kai* (food belonging to that mountain), including *ngarara* (lizards), is also sacred, and not to be eaten. This suggests that *tuatara* bones found in middens result from their use in sacred rites such as those mentioned above. Elders from Ngati Koata of Stephens Island, Nga Puhi and Ngatiwai of Little Barrier and Mokohinau Islands (where *S. punctatus* is present) and Te Atiawa of North Brothers Island (where *S. guntheri* is found), interviewed by Ramstad *et al.* (2007, p. 460), confirm *tuatara* were not eaten but feared and respected.

Figure 17.8 Kurangaituku, the birdwoman, and her pet *tuatara*. Carved on the door of Nuku Te Apiapi, a Rotorua meeting house (Photograph reproduced with permission of the Te Arawa Lakes Trust ©).

Another story involves a folk hero, Hatupatu, who was captured and forced to cohabit with a fearsome forest dwelling bird-woman, Kurangaituku, who possessed beak-like lips with which she speared her prey. Figure 17.8 shows Kurangaituku accompanied by her *tuatara* familiars whose presence accentuates the dread this being inspired (Best, 1982, p. 208).

Other lizard offspring include *Papa* (synonym *Moko papa*, brown or rock gecko), *Moko moko* (a skink) and *Moko kakariki* (green gecko). All are representatives of Whiro (god of evil, disease and death) and can manifest as the *aria* (incarnation) of lower gods. The green gecko, personified as a lesser god Rakaiora, was particularly feared and believed capable of causing death by entering a person's body and devouring their entrails (Best, 1982, pp. 270, 600). Special ceremonies were enacted to avert calamity should one be encountered. After it was killed, a woman would step over it to remove the *makutu* (magic) and make it *noa* (free from *tapu*). A more elaborate ceremony, *whakautuutu*, involved cutting the lizard into parts, one for each person or tribe thought to have caused its appearance. Each part was then thrown into a fire along with a spell and other rituals designed to afflict those responsible for the attempted evil (Best, 1982, pp. 179, 180).

A third lineage includes the supernatural beings Mokohikuwaru (the eight-tailed lizard god) and Tutangatakino (the personification of evil humans). Both are guardians of the house of Miru, ruler of the underworld. Each are dangerous and liable to attack humans if in the employ of a human *tohunga makutu* (priestly expert of witchcraft). Tutangatakino could crawl through people's mouths while they were asleep and gnaw their stomachs causing illness (Orbell, 1995, p. 120, 233), an attribute he passed on to the green gecko *moko kakariki* (Best, 1982, p. 600).

Lizards as guardians

Because of their spiritual association with Whiro, the god of all things evil, lizards are feared and 'set apart'. These attributes also provide the basis for their role as *kaitiaki* or guardians of sacred objects and places. Live *tuatara* were often placed at the entrance to burial caves in which were hidden the bones of the dead, while charcoal drawings of lizards within the cave interior provided further spiritual enforcement (Figure 17.9). Their presence acts as a *tohu* (sign) implying that a magic spell has been cast on that place rendering it *tapu* (taboo; under sacred restriction). Transgressions were dealt with by divine retribution by an *atua ngarara* or lizard god (Best, 1982, p. 157).

Pataka (food storehouses) were also protected from unsanctioned trespass by lizard carvings such as those shown in Figure 17.10 and 17.11. Live animals might also be placed at the base of stones marking a *tuahu* (sacred place, shrine). In each case, lizard guardians provide physical as well as spiritual protection of the life force or *mauri* which sustains the vitality of all things. However, they could also be manipulated by enemy *tohunga* (priestly experts in witchcraft) seeking to destroy material representations of the *mauri*, often located in gardens or forests to ensure their fecundity. By using special *karakia* (incantations) to elicit the *kata* (chattering) of the *moko kakariki* (green gecko) guardian, the hidden *mauri* could be located and destroyed (Anderson, 2000, pp. 96, 97).

Taniwha are fearsome water monsters often found in riverside caverns and pools. As indicated in Figure 17.6, lizards and *taniwha* both descend from Putoto who lives in the heart of volcanoes and is the *pu* (source) of *toto* (blood) or red magma. His close relations Tuamatua (bed rock), Parawhenuamea (the personified form of water) and their descendants, rocks, stones and water, provide the habitat in which both *taniwha* and many lizards typically reside. One of these *taniwha*, Kataore, lived in a cave overlooking a lake from whence he devoured passing travellers. In Figure 17.11 he is carved Janus-like so as to better guard the entrance to a meeting house.

Figure 17.9 Rock drawings of *taniwha* drawn in charcoal on the roof of a limestone cave overlooking the Opihi river, Tengawai Gorge, South Canterbury (Photograph reproduced with permission of Te Runaka O Arowhenua, te tautiaki of te kaitiaki o taniwha ©).

Moko peke is a generic Maori word for lizards derived from the Polynesian cognate *moko*, while *taniwha* can possibly trace mythological descent from *moko roa*, used throughout Polynesia to refer to monster, man-destroying lizards that in former times devoured humans (Best, 1982, pp. 367, 368). *Taniwha* accompanied several founding *waka* (canoes) from Hawaiki to New Zealand, often taking the form of whales, and once here took up residence in ocean or freshwater dens. Even today, these places are subject to the restrictions of *tapu*. *Taniwha*, like lizards, might attack and kill humans, or act as guardians warning of danger, or protect a valued resource from unsanctioned exploitation. Tribal identity and *mana* (prestige) may include a *taniwha*, in addition to imposing physical features such as a mountain and river. Also, tribal chiefs who through superhuman acts in times of warfare or peace gained the fear or respect of their people might also be referred to as *taniwha*.

Figure 17.10 Carved ridgepole shown here removed from the roof of a *pataka* (storehouse) in which the valued personal property of high-ranking persons was kept. The name of the storehouse is te Puawai o Te Arawa (the flower of the Te Arawa people), so named because of its impressive carvings. It was also called Tuhua Kataore – the storepit of the *taniwha* Katore (Photograph reproduced with permission of the Auckland War Memorial Museum: B10392 ©).

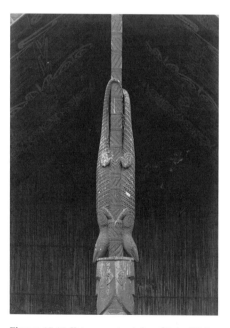

Figure 17.11 Kataore, a *taniwha* of Lake Tikitapu, Rotorua, seen here guarding the porch of a meeting house Nuku Te Apiapi (Photograph reproduced with permission of the Te Arawa Lakes Trust and the Museum of New Zealand: MA_B.007604).

Conclusions

Application of the word 'sacred' to *tuatara* and *moko kakariki* may be seen by some as problematic because of an emphasis on religious meanings which overshadow the many other ways in which species are held to be sacred. Lizards in general, and two species in particular, were 'set apart' by Maori because of the fear and dread they evoked when encountered, reactions still commonplace today. Underlying reasons for this behaviour and its associated beliefs have been traced to Polynesian origins from ancestral Lapita peoples of the West Pacific region (Howe, 2003). In the Bismarck Archipelago, crocodiles are present and are known as *moko*, and man-eating crocodiles as *moko-tolo*. Further east, a marked faunal impoverishment results in the pre-human absence of crocodiles and snakes (and any native land mammals) on the islands of Polynesia, including New Zealand. However, the name *moko* accompanied Polynesian colonisation, becoming associated with smaller reptilian fauna such as skinks and geckos. In Tonga, the Marquesas and Cook Islands, *moko* means lizard; in Samoa, *mo'o* means lizard and *mo'otai* a sea snake, while, in Hawaii, lizards and sea snakes are *moo* (Tregear, 2001). In New Zealand, the last settled island in the Pacific (and the world), the word *moko* is still present and applied to many of our endemic skinks and geckos, as illustrated above. This indicates that an unbroken (albeit attenuated) cultural legacy concerning reptiles was transported across the Pacific in the canoes of the Polynesian ancestors. Customs and beliefs pertaining to lizards were transferred by Maori to the *tuatara* and *moko kakariki*, many of which were then recorded by ethnographers such as Elsdon Best between 1895 and 1931. *Whakapapa* constructions, provided above, are but a few of those described in text form by this author and taken as a whole are but remnants of a much larger body of knowledge held by Maori about the natural world.

Apart from their interest as folk taxonomies, they are of relevance to those seeking to understand the nature of the relationship between humans and their environment, and its implications for the management of protected areas. An emphasis on the ecological impacts of this relationship has tended to overlook knowledge held by local peoples based on observation and on interaction with spiritual as well as bio-physical phenomena. Figure 17.3, along with its explanatory narrative, reveals an understanding of both realities. Maori biological, ecological and behavioural observations enable recognition of similarities as well as differences between fishes and reptiles and their presumed origins and relationship. However, Figure 17.3 also includes a spiritual dimension which provides a major distinction between the two worldviews by denying the animate : inanimate and nature : culture dichotomies of Western science. Another example based on the sweet potato (*Ipomoea batatas*) provides a more detailed comparison between the two (Roberts *et al.*, 2004). As Figure 17.4 demonstrates, the entire Maori world from cosmos to landscape constitutes a cosmoscape invested with supernatural beings who intervene in and help direct the daily affairs of humans and all other physical phenomena. Within this complex world of gods, spirits, ancestors and matter, there is a dynamic flux within and between discrete objects, 'animate' and 'inanimate'. Some sense of this can be gained from the above *whakapapa*, which on the one hand name and categorise *tuatara* and *moko kakariki* as discrete physical entities, yet on the other also perceive them as possessing supernatural powers by virtue of their origin and descent from Whiro and the lizard gods. At the other end of this spectrum are *taniwha*, supernatural entities which may in certain cir- cumstances manifest as whales or other animals. Within this spectrum are those tribal chiefs who can transform themselves from everyday physical to superhu- man roles and thereby achieve *taniwha* status. Thus landscapes and mindscapes are interwoven whereby things are not only capable of altered states but time itself is Janus-like. Hence Maori are said to be a people who walk backwards into the future, so that the past is in front of them and constantly guides future actions and decisions.

This diversity of worldviews begs the question of if, how and by whom such local knowledge should be utilised in the management of protected areas, particularly those which embrace sacred places. Answers are of critical importance in places where indigenous peoples have been marginalised or displaced by colonisation, as has happened in New Zealand. In 1840 the chiefs of most of the major Maori tribes and representatives of the British Crown signed the Treaty of Waitangi. In return for allowing Britain to govern these islands, the chiefs were guaranteed the 'full exclusive and undisturbed possession of their lands, estates, forests, fish- eries and other properties'. Subsequently, however, as a result of disease, warfare and punitive legislation, the settler Government was able to alienate Maori from their lands and sacred sites. Associated with this was the loss of cultural knowl- edge and practices necessary for maintaining the physical and spiritual well-being (*mauri*) of these places. Recent developments in New Zealand have sought legisla- tive restitution of the cultural and political rights of Maori. The State Owned Enterprises Act (1986) provides for recognition of *waahi tapu* (sacred sites) and the need for them to be returned to the appropriate tribe rather than be alien- ated by transfer to State control, and the Resource Management Act (RMA) 1991 further extends this recognition of Maori values and beliefs concerning the envi- ronment and its resources. Section 6 of the RMA requires persons to 'recognize and provide for the following matters of national importance: (e) the relation- ship of Maori, their culture and traditions with their ancestral lands, water, sites, *waahi tapu*, and other taonga'. Section 7 (a) requires all persons to 'have particular regard to Kaitiakitanga' (defined legally as the ethic of stewardship, but by Maori as the reciprocal rights and responsibilities associated with care and protection). Section 8 requires all persons to 'take into account the principles of the Treaty of Waitangi'. These requirements are being slowly implemented within the fabric of New Zealand society in different ways ranging from token representation and consultation to full and meaningful participation at all levels.

Local government is also required to consult with Maori and take account of tribal environmental management plans. Using modern technologies such as geographic information systems, such plans may contain information on sacred sites, used in discussion with developers to avoid, remedy or mitigate any adverse effects of a proposed activity on those sites and other valued resources. Conservation of endangered species comes under the mandate of the Department of Conservation (DoC), whose 1987 Act (Section 4) requires all persons 'to give effect to the principles of the Treaty of Waitangi'. Foremost among these principles is that of partnership between Maori and the Crown. Institutional as well as individual resistance to accepting the concept of partnership has slowed progress towards tangible demonstrations of this principle. A major difficulty has been the lack of knowledge of Maori traditional beliefs and practices among the majority non-Maori employees at national and local levels. Within the DoC this problem has been addressed in large part by employing Maori conservation officers and training non-Maori in a Maori worldview and Treaty of Waitangi issues. It is now usual practice for DoC (and council) employees to involve local tribal authorities in the management of parks and reserves. Conservation Boards in each conservancy have Maori membership which extends to recognition of those with traditional authority (*mana whenua*) over land in that area. According to Glenice Paine of Te Atiawa (personal communication, November 2008), her people are involved in species recovery plans for the *tuatara* on islands over which her people have *mana whenua* status, and any translocations of this species are conducted according to Maori protocol, ensuring its spiritual as well as physical well-being. By such means the customary rights and responsibilities of Maori as *kaitiaki* (caregiver and protector) are being slowly recognised and reinstated. Most Maori would agree, however, that much remains to be done in achieving true equity of participation, particularly at the highest levels of management and decision-making. Co-management between Aboriginal peoples and Parks Board representatives of several National Parks in Australia (e.g. Kakadu and Uluru) provides a vision yet to be achieved with our own National Parks here in New Zealand. It is to be hoped that progress towards realising this goal will include more understanding of the importance, not only of the underpinning science necessary for the protection of sacred species and sites, but also of the cultural and spiritual values and beliefs that have set them apart as sacred.

References

Anderson, J. C. (2000). *Maori Life in Ao-tea*. 2nd edn. Christchurch, NZ: Cadsonbury Publications.

Berlin, B. (1992). *Ethnobiological Classification: Principles of Categorizarion of Plants and Animals in Traditional Societies*. Princeton, NJ; Oxford: Princeton University Press.

Best, E. (1982). *Maori Religion and Mythology Part II*. Wellington, NZ: Government Printer.

Conservation Act. (1987). Wellington: Government Printer.

Daugherty, C. H., Patterson, G. B. and Hitchmough, R. A. (1994). Taxonomic and conservation review of the New Zealand Herpetofauna. *New Zealand Journal of Zoology*, **21**, 317–23.

Grey, Sir G. (1956). *Polynesian Mythology*. Christchurch, NZ: Whitcombe and Tombs Ltd.

Howe, K. R. (2003). *The Quest for Origins*. Auckland: Penguin.

Nakashima, D. (1998). Conceptualising nature: the cultural context of resource management. *Nature and Resources*, **34**(2), 8–22.

Orbell, M. (1995). *The Illustrated Encylopedia of Maori Myth and Legend*. Christchurch, NZ: Canterbury University Press.

Pei Te Hurinui. (1960). *King Potatau: An Account of the Life of Potataute Wherowhero the First Maori King*. The Polynesian Society, New Zealand.

Ramstad, K. M., Nelson, N. J., Paine, G., *et al.* (2007). Species and cultural conservation in New Zealand: Maori traditional ecological knowledge of tuatara. *Conservation Biology*, **21**, 455–64.

Reichel, E. (2005). Cosmology. In *The Encyclopedia of Religion and Nature*, ed. B. R. Taylor. New York, NY: Thoemmes Continuum, pp. 420–5.

Resource Management Act. (1991). Wellington: Government Printer.

Roberts, M., Haami, B., Benton, R., *et al.* (2004). Whakapapa as a Maori mental construct: some implications for the debate over genetic modification of organisms. *The Contemporary Pacific*, **16**, 1–28.

Roberts, R.M. and Wills, P. R. (1998). Understanding Maori epistemology. In *Tribal Epistemologies: Essays on the Philosophy of Anthropology*, ed. H. Wautischer. Aldershot: Ashgate, pp. 43–77.

Sharell, R. (1966). *The Tuatara, Lizards and Frogs of New Zealand*. London: Collins.

State Owned Enterprises Act. (1986). Wellington: Government Printer.

Stevens, G., McGlone, M. and McCulloch, B. (1995). *Prehistoric New Zealand*. Auckland: Reed.

Stimson, J. F. (1971, reprint). Tuamotuan religion. *Bulletin* 103. Honolulu, Hawaii: Bernice P. Bishop Museum.

Tregear, E. (2001). *The Maori–Polynesian Comparative Dictionary*. 2nd edn. Christchurch, NZ: Cadsonbury Publications.

Williams, H. W. (1971). *Dictionary of the Maori Language*. 7th edn. Wellington, NZ: Legislation Direct.

18

Pheasant conservation, sacred groves and local culture in Sichuan, China

WANG NAN, LUCY GARRETT and PHILIP McGOWAN

Introduction

Natural resources and people are intrinsically linked: religious, moral, cultural, political, economic and ecological boundaries have all shaped environmental use and perceptions (Gosling, 2001). Historically, attitudes and behaviour towards the environment and sustainable use of resources have been greatly affected and determined by nature worship and spiritual values (Khumbongmayum *et al.*, 2004; Byers *et al.*, 2001). To develop moral standards towards the community and local habitats, many cultures have formed values and beliefs to control acceptable behaviour (Goldstein and Kapstein, 1998; Laird, 1993). Conceptual traditions have, as a result, placed high values on protecting the environment and biodiversity. In this chapter we describe the relationship between cultural values (including spiritual beliefs) and nature in western Sichuan, China. Specifically, we introduce Doacheng County and its people, indicate the importance of China to global wildlife conservation and especially for pheasants, and explore the potential for traditional beliefs to play a meaningful role in conserving certain species and habitats.

Sichuan

The link between cultural and biological diversity is clearly demonstrated in south-west China with cultural and historic ties to mountain landscapes and ecosystems. With more than 30 different ethnic minority groups many landscapes are regarded as sacred, in particular those of the Tibetan people (Xu *et al.*, 2006).

Sacred Species and Sites: Advances in Biocultural Conservation, ed. Gloria Pungetti, Gonzalo Oviedo and Della Hooke. Published by Cambridge University Press. © Cambridge University Press 2012.

Tibetan society is dominated by Buddhism, which plays a central role, and its core notions of karma, reincarnation and enlightenment define the basic meaning of life and morality (Goldstein and Kapstein, 1998). Buddhism also influences daily Tibetan life, which is considered to be a non-material cycle of cause and effect, with reincarnation determined by human behaviour (Xu, 2006).

Wildlife appears in many aspects of Tibetan culture. For example, fish, birds and mammals are often found in paintings, sculptures, masks and literature (N. Wang and L. Garrett, personal observation), reflecting their importance for Tibetan people. Taboos such as the killing of wildlife have positively influenced conservation and their stewardship of other natural resources (Xie *et al.*, 2000). In addition, a local tradition of hand-feeding wildlife has encouraged some species to become habituated to humans near some settlements, particularly monasteries and sacred sites. In monasteries, monks place food offerings in front of Buddha for many days, after which the food will be dispersed outside to feed birds, mammals and fish close to the monastery.

It is believed that local people, animals and high-altitude land on the Tibetan plateau are governed by deities residing on the mountains. Buddhist lamas believe that in order to avoid disturbing and angering the spirits, expansive areas around sacred mountains should be protected from over-use (Xu, 2006; Goldstein and Kapstein, 1998). If angered, local deities may cause misfortune or illness, so preventing this is a primary concern (Goldstein and Kapstein, 1998). Consequently, logging, hunting and stone and turf collection is forbidden on sacred mountains and within sacred groves on these mountains. These groves have multiple values, representing generations of cultural and biological diversity which provide an undisturbed, rich habitat for wildlife close to human settlements.

Deeply held cultural and religious belief systems often constitute an effective means for environmental conservation, with taboos and access restrictions providing protection from degradation (Laird, 1993). In addition to providing cultural identity, the long-term conservation of sacred sites also encourages the maintenance of biodiversity within otherwise degraded environments so that they often have high conservation value.

Cultural values, however, are dynamic and evolve constantly. Rapid environmental changes, and the increasing influence of national legislation and socioeconomic development, can result in the erosion of traditional management practices, which in turn increases the vulnerability of the natural resources connected with these cultures (Xu and Wilkes, 2004). China is exhibiting rapid rates of both environmental and sociological change (Kontoleon *et al.*, 2002; Xu *et al.*, 2006). The development of roads within the region and the promotion of domestic tourism have increased tourist numbers, which greatly impacts upon rural populations. In addition, the recent commercial exploitation of non-timber forest products

(NTFPs) appears to be coinciding with a shift in aspirations for a higher standard of living, thereby altering natural resource use (Wang Nan, personal observation).

Daocheng County and its people

Daocheng County lies in Ganzi Prefecture on the Qinghai–Tibet Plateau in Sichuan Province. Given the dramatic topography, solar radiation varies substantially according to the aspect and the slope of mountainsides and, together with altitude, also determines vegetation type. Ranging between 1900 and 6032 m, the County covers 7323 km^2 of which 31.13% is covered by forest and shrub habitat (Office of Daocheng County, 2004). Traditional methods of the logging of timber by rural populations in Daocheng County have also allowed for regeneration, and as a result there are forests and shrubs of varying secondary stages of succession. In some cases, the topography has resulted in poor forest regeneration and consequently grassland and shrub, which naturally occur only in alpine areas, now exist below the tree-line. In comparison, sacred forests and remote primary forest habitats far from human settlements remain relatively unaffected by logging.

In 2002, there were 13 monasteries, 5656 families and 28 413 people living in Daocheng County, 93.81% of whom were ethnic Tibetans (Office of Daocheng County, 2004) (Figures 18.1 and 18.2). The household income of Tibetan people is predominately generated through livestock (yak herding), milk production and trade in NTFPs, such as Chinese caterpillar fungus *Cordyceps sinensis* and various mushroom species. In recent years, a small proportion has also been generated through manual labour, such as road construction and the creation of new businesses. However, income from NTFP trading can far exceed that from yak herding and many people therefore depend upon its collection for cash.

Pheasants

The potential importance of Tibetan cultural traditions for wildlife protection is vividly demonstrated by the conservation of species of pheasant. Of the world's nearly 300 species of Galliformes, 25% are threatened with extinction (see IUCN, 2007), making them one of the most threatened bird groups. Within this group, pheasants are the most threatened as 24 of the 50 species are currently on the IUCN Red List (IUCN, 2007; BirdLife International, 2005). About 20% of the world's Galliformes have been recorded within China, which is home to a greater number of pheasant species, including threatened species, than any other country (Fuller and Garson, 2000). Consequently, ensuring their survival within China is a global priority.

Figure 18.1 Distribution of monasteries in Daocheng County (3800–4400 m), Sichuan Province, China. Zhujie monastery (1), Suochong village (2), Zhalang monastery (4), Sangdui village (5), Sangdui village (6), Benbo monastery (7).

Figure 18.2 Chonggu Monastery (© Wang Nan). See colour plate section.

Conservation attention on this group of birds has, understandably, focused upon species that are found on the IUCN Red List (Fuller and Garson, 2000; BirdLife International, 2001; IUCN, 2007). Loss and degradation of forest habitats is also likely to have resulted in the fragmentation of populations of many non-threatened species. In addition to habitat reduction that affects virtually all threatened species, the large body size, protein value and colourful feathers make pheasants susceptible to hunting in most areas of China, and this is thought to have caused significant population declines in many Galliform species (Zheng and Wang, 1998). Therefore, it is important to identify and understand cultures where beliefs and traditions appear to support the long-term conservation of these species.

Sites surrounding the monasteries in Daocheng were first surveyed in 2002 (Pack-Blumenau *et al.*, 2003). The following year, surveys included sacred groves (all of which were close to villages and monasteries) and non-conserved sites (Wang, 2007). Recent research conducted in the period December 2006 to February 2007 and April to June 2007 has concentrated on seven of these sites (see Figure 18.1): Zhujie Monastery (1), Suochong (2), Zhalang monastery (3), Xiongdeng monastery (4), Sangdui village 1 (dominated by oak) (5), Sangdui village 2 (dominated by larch) (6) and Benbo monastery (7). Site selection was based on reports of areas said to benefit from various forms of traditional protection and which allowed the study to survey habitats demonstrating all levels of protection afforded to forests that still contained pheasants. Therefore, sites were either actively protected by the monks (Zhujie, Zhalang, Benbo and Xiongdeng), or by local people through cultural traditions (Suochong and Sangdui 1, Sangdui 2). In addition, a group of unprotected sites were selected as 'control sites' and these were paired with six of the above protected sites (Zhujie, Souchong, Zhalang, Xiondeng, Sangdui 1 and Sangdui 2).

Since 2002, I spent a total of 17 months living in Daocheng within monasteries and with local people, providing the opportunity to gain a detailed understanding of local traditions. Additional information was gathered during field surveys, during interviews and through direct observations and this provided further insights into the pressure on pheasant species and their habitat, the protection provided to them and attitudinal behaviours by local people towards the environment. The changing patterns of pheasant populations and habitats over time were also discussed with both monks and local people. These are described below.

Local culture and pheasant conservation

In Daocheng County, wildlife conservation is predominantly focused on the white-eared pheasant (*Crossoptilon crossoptilon*) as a result of its significance within Tibetan Buddhist beliefs (Figure 18.3). These hold that the essence of nature is seen in the colour white, and Tibetans see this in snow-capped mountains, glaciers, clouds, sheep, milk and butter, all of which surround them. The colour further symbolises life, righteousness, goodness, nobleness and holiness (Xiama, 2002). Furthermore, because of its large size and ostentatious behaviour, this species has a special affinity with local people. It is listed on the IUCN Red List as Near-threatened (IUCN, 2007).

During field surveys in 2003–2004, 13 sites were surveyed in Daocheng, 12 of which were located below the tree-line in suitable habitat for pheasant species. White-eared pheasants (*Crossoptilon crossoptilon*) were found in 11 sites (white-eared pheasants were also observed in a further site in 2006). Five further species of pheasants were surveyed within white-eared pheasant habitat including blood pheasant (*Ithaginis cruentus*), buff-throated partridge (*Tetraophasis szechenyii*), koklass (*Pucrasia macrolopha*), Tibetan partridge (*Perdix hodgsoniae*), and Chinese grouse (*Tetrastes sewerzowi*), which is Near-threatened. However, these species were not observed as frequently.

White-eared pheasant, blood pheasant, buff-throated partridge and Tibetan partridge were found in undisturbed sacred groves protected by monasteries or local culture during field surveys in 2006–2007, emphasising the importance of sacred

Figure 18.3 Monk hand-feeding white-eared pheasants. Zhujie Monastery, Souchong, Daocheng County (© Wang Nan). See colour plate section.

grove habitats for this species. Logging was also prohibited within sacred groves, providing the pheasants with undisturbed habitat. In all sites where white-eared pheasant was found, local people fed the birds and prohibited all hunting activity in the belief that this species could bring good fortune. In contrast, other pheasant species were not considered to be as important and were not specifically revered or protected. This suggests that the white-eared pheasant has the potential to act as an umbrella species for the conservation of other pheasant species which co-occur in the region.

The Tibetan cultural taboo on killing, including the killing of pest species, does not allow the use of pesticides in agricultural production in Daocheng. This also benefits white-eared pheasant and other species that forage in farmland. As a result, farmland near forests attracted large groups of white-eared pheasant and blood pheasant and farmers often allow the birds to feed inside their homes during the winter months.

Local culture and sacred groves

It has been suggested that attitudes towards the environment are strong predictors of ecological behaviour (Kaiser *et al.*, 1999) and, therefore, local people

Figure 18.4 Benbo monastery, Sangdui, Daocheng County, illustrating the placement of sacred flags within sacred groves (© Wang Nan).

would be more likely to protect a sacred grove than destroy it, on the basis of spiritual and religious connections. This has great implications for conservation. Tibetans believe that sacred mountains and sacred groves on these mountains will bring them good luck and spiritual protection. Each year, during the Tibetan Spring Festival, local people circumambulate the sacred mountain and sacred grove associated with their village to show their respect to deities residing on the mountain (Goldstein and Kapstein, 1998). During this ritual, they chant and place *Mani* stones and flags printed with prayer at the mountain top and at the sacred grove perimeter (Figures 18.4 and 18.5). Where prayer flags are placed, local people also create smoke using branches of fir. Circumambulations of sacred mountains may also occur on the 10th and 15th of the Tibetan month. These actions and beliefs are directly linked to Tibetan Buddhism and have developed into customs over many generations.

It is further believed that any activities that harm the sacred groves or wildlife within them will bring bad karma, resulting in disasters such as flooding, hail, disease, drought and other misfortune. This highlights the value of the sacred groves to local communities and their importance in traditional Tibetan culture and daily life (Xie *et al.*, 2000). The majority of the community appeared to conform to these beliefs and traditions of worshipping the sacred groves and showing

Figure 18.5 Sacred grove, Sangdui, Daocheng County. Prayer flags and *Muni* stones placed at the base of the sacred grove (© Lucy Garrett).

respect to their deities by refraining from logging, hunting and collecting within the groves and on the sacred mountain. This has the consequence of preventing forest loss and fragmentation. As a result of this limited resource use and the adherence to taboos that have existed for generations, the sacred groves have been kept in a stage of advanced secondary succession that is relatively undisturbed and which is ideal habitat for species such as white-eared pheasant.

During the Cultural Revolution (1966–1978) communities utilised the sacred groves (Goldstein and Kapstein, 1998). However, the following religious revival appears to have strengthened these traditional spiritual beliefs and the rebuilding of monasteries. This in turn has enabled the recovery of sacred groves without any formal action or legislation by government.

Changing culture and conservation

In the face of rapid development in countries such as China, great pressure is being placed upon environmental and cultural diversity (Xu *et al.*, 2006). The disintegration of traditional cultural resource management institutions have often been linked to socioeconomic factors such as market expansions and uncertainties in rural livelihoods (Chandrakanth *et al.*, 2004). Currently, rapid development of the region, improved transportation and local livelihood changes are modifying land use and weakening cultural beliefs, placing increasing pressure on sacred groves previously protected by their communities' conservation customs. South-west China is also becoming increasingly popular as a domestic tourist destination and in addition to the increased commercial NTFP markets, wealth aspirations are shifting. All of these changes impact on traditional practices and their associated conservation benefits for both sacred groves and pheasant species.

In Daocheng County, although some forests close to monasteries and villages appear to be conserved as an indirect result of religious beliefs and traditional customs, logging does occur in large areas of forest that are not protected by such sentiment. This timber is utilised in house construction, decoration, heating and cooking. Traditional Tibetan house construction requires a substantial amount of timber. As families increase their income in parallel with the commercialisation of NTFP markets, demand on the size and decoration of these houses is also increasing in order to demonstrate their wealth status. In addition, a larger amount of firewood is required to heat these larger buildings, thus placing increasing pressure on surrounding forests to meet these requirements.

Previously in Daocheng, the trapping, killing or consumption of wild animals did not occur because Tibetan beliefs were strictly adhered to. The recent growth of tourism in the region has increased the influence of external cultures of non-Tibetan visitors on rural communities, evident in Daocheng city and villages surrounding Yading, a popular pilgrimage site for tourists. Although local people are still practising Buddhists, some of them (excluding elderly individuals) have accepted that tourists wish to consume meat such as fish, chicken and rabbit and some have also begun to consume meat themselves or catch fish to sell to tourist restaurants. In contrast, rural villages far from tourist sites, such as Sangdui and Suochong, have maintained their tradition of conserving wild animals and preventing hunting or fishing. For example, monks in Zhujie monastery do not even eat eggs, believing this to be the equivalent of killing chicks.

Discussions with tourists and non-Tibetans, however, revealed that few knew of the Tibetan philosophy and its impact on wildlife conservation. They ate local meat unaware that killing birds, fish and wild animals was not permitted in Tibetan culture. Those involved in the tourist industry wished to appear affable to visitors and so did not inform them of local customs and beliefs. This lack of understanding further fuels the erosion of traditional cultural and environmental values that serve to protect natural resources and Tibetan customs. Local government efforts to conserve wildlife and the environment are attempting to encourage and employ rural people and monasteries to assist in their work, but there appears to be little evidence of direct acknowledgement of the value or incorporation of traditional beliefs for conservation of biodiversity within the region.

Conclusions

Cultural values appear highly significant in the perception and use of the wildlife and the environment in this part of western Sichuan, highlighting the necessity to consider these values when developing conservation policies whilst at the same time understanding the socioeconomic factors that influence them. The perceptions that people have of the environment are important considerations in terms of both resource value and management options (Sullivan, 2002). These values appear to have protected sacred groves, forests and pheasants in this region without the need for regulations or government control. Consequently, the cultural values and spiritual beliefs of the Tibetan people appear highly significant factors in conserving natural resources.

Ultimately there is a need to balance rural development with the complexities of these long-standing traditional cultural values, beliefs and practices. For the sacred groves to remain standing, it is necessary that the cultural values that currently protect them are maintained. Conservation policies should therefore acknowledge and incorporate these values and local practices or risk losing both cultural and biological diversity in the region.

The main threat to pheasant species and the sacred groves appears to be the potential for future decline of cultural values and traditional religious practices accentuated by the commercialisation of NTFP markets (Xu, 2006). Consequently, an interactive approach involving both local people and government is required to create effective environmental management policies to address this decline and determine the long-term viability of this environment, including alternative sources of income to NTFPs. This requires a greater understanding of the factors driving behaviour and practices in both non-sacred and sacred forests and the wildlife within them. Cultural values of the environment and appropriate economic development of natural resources can coexist if planned.

Many generations of human management and cultivation have influenced the current state of most, if not all, forest in China (Xu *et al.*, 2006). These ecosystems have contributed to human well-being, supporting a range of cultural services in addition to having spiritual, recreational and aesthetic values. China's forests can therefore be considered a product of both nature and culture. If forests and wildlife are present as a result of the actions of local people living in and around them, their future protection requires the encouragement and inclusion of the very cultural practices that have shaped them.

References

BirdLife International. (2001). *Threatened Birds of Asia*. Cambridge: Bird Life International.

BirdLife International. (2005). *Fact Sheet Summary*. Cambridge: Bird Life International.

Byers, B. A., Cunliffe, R. and Hudak, A. T. (2001). Linking the conservation of culture and nature: a case study of sacred forests in Zimbabwe. *Journal of Human Ecology*, **29**, 187–218.

Chandrakanth, M. G., Bhat, M. G. and Accavva, M. S. (2004). Socio-economic changes and sacred groves in South India: protecting a community-based resource management institution. *Natural Resources Forum*, **28**, 102–11.

Fuller, R. A. and Garson, P. J. (eds) (2000). *Pheasants: Status Survey and Conservation Action Plan 2000–2004*. IUCN, Gland, Switzerland and Cambridge, UK and World Pheasant Association, Reading, UK.

Goldstein, M. C. and Kapstein, M. T. (1998). *Buddhism in Contemporary Tibet – Religious Revival and Cultural Identity*. Berkeley, CA: University of California.

Gosling, D. L. (2001). *Religion and Ecology in India and Southeast Asia*. London: Routledge.

IUCN. (2007). *2007 IUCN Red List of Threatened Species*. [Online] Available at: www.iucnredlist.org (accessed 15 November 2007).

Kaiser, F. G., Wolfing, S. and Fuhurer, U. (1999). Environmental attitude and ecological behaviour. *Journal of Environmental Psychology*, **19**, 1–19.

Khumbongmayum, A. D., Khan, M. K. and Tripathi, R. S. (2004). Sacred groves of Manipur – ideal centres for biodiversity conservation. *Conservation Science*, **87**, 430–3.

Kontoleon, A., Swanson, T., Wang, Q., *et al.* (2002). Optimal ecotourism: the economic value of the giant panda in China. In *Valuing the Environment in Developing Countries – Case Studies*, ed. D. Pearce, C. Pearce and C. Palmer. Cheltenham: Edward Elgar Publishing Ltd, pp. 206–35.

Laird, S. A. (1993). Trees, forests and sacred groves. [Online] *The Overstory*. Available at: http://www.agroforestry.net/overstory/overstory93.html (accessed 2 April 2007).

Office of Daocheng County. (2004). Daocheng County annals 2004. Office of Daocheng County, Doacheng, Sichuan, China. [In Chinese.]

Pack-Blumenau, A. P., Wang, N. and Grabowski, K. H. (2003). White-eared pheasant, monasteries and tourist development. *Tragopan*, **18**, 18–20.

Sullivan, C. (2002). Using an income accounting framework to value non-timber forest products. In *Valuing the Environment in Developing Countries – Case Studies*, ed. D. Pearce, C. Pearce and C. Palmer, Cheltenham: Edward Elgar, pp. 377–405.

Wang, N. (2007). Cultural conservation of pheasants in Daocheng County, Sichuan Province, China. *Annual Review of the World Pheasant Association 2006–2007*, pp. 22–3.

Xiama, Z. (2002). Buddhism infection on Tibetan life, preference of numeral and colour. *China Tibet*, **94**, 51–2. [In Chinese.]

Xie, H., Wang, X. and Xu, J. (2000). The impacts of Tibetan culture on biodiversity and natural landscapes in Zhongdian, southwest China. In *Links between Cultures and*

Biodiversity: Proceedings of the Cultures and Biodiversity Congress, Yunnan Province, China, ed. J. Xu. Kunming: Yunnan Science and Technology Press.

Xu, J. (2006). The political, social, and ecological transformation of a landscape. The case of rubber in Xishuangbanna, China. *Mountain Research and Development*, **26**, 254–62.

Xu, J. and Wilkes, A. (2004). Biodiversity impact analysis in northwest Yunnan, southwest China. *Biodiversity and Conservation*, **13**, 959–83.

Xu, J., Ma, E. T., Tashi, D., *et al.* (2006). Integrating sacred knowledge for conservation: cultures and landscapes in southwest China. [Online] *Ecology and Society*, **10**(2), 7 [online only] http://www.ecologyandsociety.org/vol10/iss2/art7/ (accessed 4 August 2007).

Zheng, G. M. and Wang, Q. S. (1998). *China Red Data Book of Endangered Animals: Aves*. Beijing, Hong Kong, New York: Science Press. [In Chinese.]

19

The bear cult among the different ethnic groups of Russia (sacred Russian bear)

ROBERT E. F. SMITH

Introduction: the early history of the bear cult

Forest extended from end to end in northern Eurasia in ancient times; the bear dominated it. The bear has remained important in some Siberian cultures; and among the remnant Ainu in Hokkaido and in the Ryukyu, now Okinawa, islands into modern times. The Ainu refer to the bear as the 'spirit of the mountains' (*kimun-kamui*). Their bear cult is well known from eighteenth-century travellers' accounts and later ethnographic reports (Batchelor, 1901, p. 484). In Japan it has been claimed that shamanesses are still remarkably active in Japan as in southern Korea, among the Ainu of Hokkaido, and the Ryukyu Islands (Hori, 1974, p. 185).

From the distant pre-Russian and Russian past, there are traces of an early bear cult on the Upper and Mid-Volga from the late Fat'yanovo culture after 1500 BC: at the Volosovo site animal teeth in necklaces were often found; there were teeth from all domestic animals, but the only wild animals were dog, bear and pig (Krainov, 1964, p. 81; Gorodtsov, 1851–1918, V, 1, p. l58, ill. xxv). These were, it seems, regarded as holy, the dog and pig for their economic value, the bear for its power. Other Neolithic finds occur along the Kama and as far north as Lake Ilmen. In a ninth- to eleventh-century AD burial ground of the Mordva-Moksha, a Finno-Ugrian group on the River Tsna, several bear claws with a bronze mounting were found attached to a plait ornament. Many peoples of the Urals venerated the bear: the Komi, another Finno-Ugrian group, had a cult of the bear, known as *osha*, and one of their heroes was called Kudym-Osh. A common custom among the TransUral tribes was 'to skin the pelt with its paws and head from the dead bear, place it on a table in the sacred comer of the house with its face between its paws;

Sacred Species and Sites: Advances in Biocultural Conservation, ed. Gloria Pungetti, Gonzalo Oviedo and Della Hooke. Published by Cambridge University Press. © Cambridge University Press 2012.

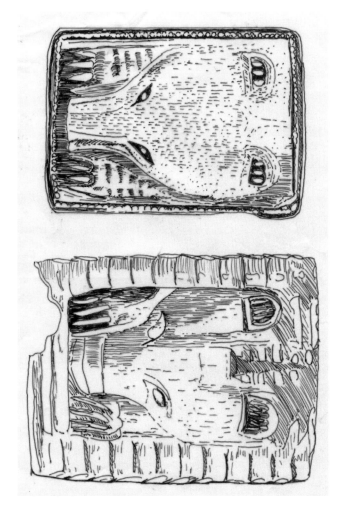

Figure 19.1 Metal plaques from north-east European Russia depicting bears (third to fourth centuries) (after Oborin, 1976, Nos. 25–28).

then the magic ritual of venerating the bear began, the bear festival' (Oborin, 1976, p. 23).[1] Metal plaques from north-east European Russia depicting bears show the same situation (Nos. 25–31, third to fourth centuries) (Figure 19.1); one (No. 30, sixth to seventh century), shows six bears (Oborin, 1976, p. 23). A modern Ainu illustration shows the bear 'at the head of the hearth' and closely resembles the bronze images, but the head is circled with a necklace and an *inau* is in its mouth

---

[1] References in Oborin, 1976, pp. 186–7 are out of order; 30–33 should be 31–34.

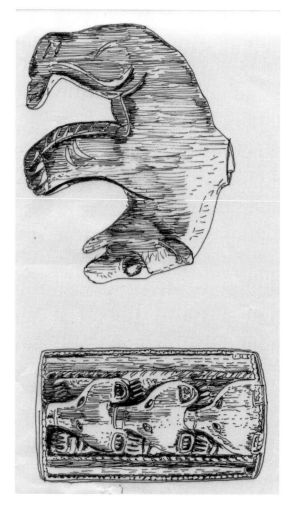

Figure 19.1 (*cont.*)

(Nakamoto, 1999, pp. 63–80, 189–210, 211). The illustration and the plaques are separated by more than 6000 miles and 1500 years.

The bear cult in Christian times

The conversion of Rus' to Christianity occurred in the late 980s, but traces of pagan cults did not fade away. Veneration of the bear has survived even into recent times. Barrow burials of the ninth to tenth centuries in the Vladimir and Rostov regions show unfired or poorly fired rough clay models of what are taken to be bear paws, sometimes associated with clay rings; these 'are not perforated

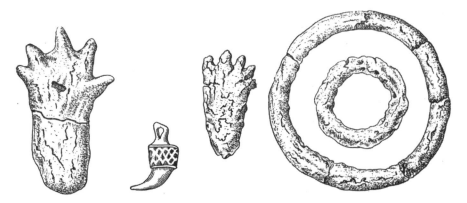

Figure 19.2 Bear artefacts from barrow burials of the late Fat'yanovo culture (after Lavrov, 1951, p. 65, fig. 12).

and so are not amulets, but were probably made for the burial ritual' (Figure 19.2) (Voronin, 1941, pp. 164–6; Lavrov, 1951, p. 65). They may have been fired in the funeral pyre. The paws, claws and rings have been interpreted as climbing gear for the soul to climb to the heavenly world; this seems to imply a close association between the human and the bear: like the shaman, both travel between the three worlds: this one, heaven and the underworld. Squirrels or water-fowl, creatures which can reach up into the tree or fly into the sky, burrow into the earth or below the water, are often associated with the shaman and convey the same implication. Slav barrow burials on the tributaries of the upper Oka also had bear claws and bones, often accompanied by bones of birds and small animals on pieces of limestone. However, in the Ladoga area only bear claws were found, and then only in the earliest barrow burials, and had not been drilled, so are not regarded as amulets. The bear here may have been sacrificed or consumed at feasts (Voronin, 1941, pp. 162, 165–6).

In the eleventh century there were a number of disturbances in a vast area in the north-east of what is now European Russia, much of which then came to be dominated by Slavs in various ways. In 1024, in the Suzdal' area, at a time of 'great disturbance and famine; all the people went along the Volga to Bolgar' for grain and so survived' (*Povest' vremennykh let*, 1950, I, pp. 99–100). The rising was led by wizards from Yaroslavl'. According to the undated Tale of the Building of Yaroslavl', the town was founded at a location called Bears' Nook (*Medvezhii ugol*) by Prince Yaroslav; he later returned to deal with people who were plundering traders along the Volga. The local people 'released from its cage a certain wild animal' (Voronin, 1941, pp. 151–7, and text 188). Probably the animal not explicitly named, perhaps deliberately so, because of its power, was a bear (cp. English bear from Latin *fera*). The prince exiled some wizards and executed others; he declared that

God sends disasters, famine, plague, drought as punishment, 'but man knows nothing' (Voronin, 1941, pp. 187–8; *Povest' vremennykh let*, 1950, I, p. 100). 'The idol they [the local people] worshipped was Volos, called the cattle god. And this Volos, with a devil living in it, supposedly, created much dread; it stood amidst the hollow named after Volos whence the cattle were customarily driven to pasture. For this wily idol, a shrine (*keremet'*) was made and a wizard was granted who kept a permanent fire for Volos and the chickens sacrificed to him' (Voronin, 1941, p. 187).

The chronicler reports a religious discussion between Yan and the wizards. Yan stated that God created man from earth and man knows nothing, 'God alone has knowledge'. The wizards, however, gave a different account. God was washing in the bathhouse, sweated and wiped himself with a bast rag which he threw down from heaven to earth. Satan argued with God as to which of them should create man. 'And the devil created man, and god put a soul in him. So when man dies his body goes to the earth and his soul to god.' Yan asked them what god they believed in and they answered 'Antichrist'. The wizards seem to treat their god and Satan as equals; the monistic Christian view is contrasted with the dualist view of the wizards. To the local people the bear was a god who could help man in times of adversity, but to the Christian powers its cult was an evil to be suppressed.

The wizards claimed that they should be taken to the prince to be tried, but Yan ordered them to be put in a boat and tied; Yan followed them. At the mouth of the Sheksna, Yan asked the boatmen whether any of them had had a relative killed by the wizards and then told them to avenge their own. 'They seized them, killed them and hung them on an oak; of a truth, they received their reward from God. Yan went home and the next night a bear climbed up, gnawed and devoured them' (*Povest' vremennykh let*, 1950, I, pp. 118–9). The wizards were given tree burial, not Christian inhumation. The account, even if not true, seems more likely to have reflected the actual view of the locals, rather than a distorted account of the chronicler. The specific mention of an oak, rather than a tree, does not confirm this view conclusively, but may show local knowledge: oaks are rare in East Slav areas and are scarcely found beyond the Urals.

We glimpse a different worldview from that of the Christians. The bear is an apt representation of the shaman travelling between the three worlds by means of the tree; the animal can climb a tree, live on the ground, but hibernate beneath its roots. The tree was of vital importance for forest dwellers, whether hunter-gatherers or slash-and-burn farmers. Tree burial was known among Siberian peoples (sometimes restricted to shamans) and traces of tree burial remained among the Mordva into recent times (Voronin, 1941, p. 158).

In early times 'the Slavs in Russia offered prayers to trees, especially hollow ones, binding their branches with lengths or pieces of cloth' (Karamzin, reprint I, 1988–9, pp. 55–6; Maksimov, 1903, pp. 288, 277; Zelenin, 1937, pp. 593–625). In the thirteenth century, Serapion, Bishop of Vladimir, wrote against the popular belief that the inhumation of persons committed to the ground (*zalozhnye*) was regarded as causing a famine in 1273; corpses were exhumed and given tree burial (Voronin, 1941, p. 159). In 1534 the Archbishop of Novgorod instructed his clergy in an extensive region to extirpate ancestor worship, including 'praying in their obscene shrines to trees and stones' (*Dopolnenie k aktam Istoricheskim*, 1846, I, no. 28, pp. 27–30). Archaeologists have argued that the fourteenth century to the fifteenth century was the period when such cults are known from the Novgorod and Kargopol' areas, in part as a result of Russian colonisation (Makarov and Chenetsov, 1988, pp. 70–90). Trees seem to have been equivalents of church and churchyard. The record of the Church Council of 1551 known as the Hundred Chapters (*Stoglav*) noted that people went to groves on the first Monday after St Peter's Day (29 June in the Orthodox calendar) to engage in devilish amusements (*Stoglav*, 1863, p. 142). 'The holy fathers equate the "Tree of Life" with Christ's Cross which they call "the new life-bearing tree"' (*Polnyi pravoslavnyi*, 1913, I, p. 773). It seems that in this phrase the Church was using a term which may have had different significance for Christians and for common folk, many of whom still practised pre-Christian customs and probably held pre-Christian beliefs (Petrukhin and Chernetsov, 1991, pp. 299–303; Zelenin, 1994, p. 222; 1933, pp. 591–629, 230). To Christians it meant the Cross of the Crucifixion, to others it was the tree linking the cosmos. For the shaman the living tree was the link in death, for the monk the dead wood was life-giving.

Other evidence shows that in the Rostov area, Veles or Volos, the god of cattle, was particularly esteemed; in the 1380s the archimandrite Avraamii (Abraham), according to tradition, reduced to dust the stone idol of Veles with a staff which he had miraculously received from Saint John the Apostle; significantly, the idol was said to have been venerated by the Chud' (i.e. Finn) ward of Rostov town. For centuries after this, the upper Volga and Rostov remained a region famed for its supply of trained bears (Karamzin, reprint II, 1988, chap. V, note 291; Afanas'ev, 1865, II, p. 268; *Polnyi pravoslavnyi*, 1913, I, p. 36; Nekrylova, 1988, pp. 42–3). In the Novgorod area, as late as 1566, Sowtham and Sparke, servants of the English Muscovy Company, noted 'a monasterie called S. Nicholas Medued', i.e. *medved* 'bear', on the River Volkhov, near its mouth on Lake Ladoga (Hakluyt, 1589, 1965, *Principall Navigations* I, p. 392; Uspenskii, 1982, 85f.; *Novgorodskaya pervaya letopis*, 1950, p. 17). Bear as a toponymic element was common in this area.

It has been pointed out that, like the Slav god 'Volos, the bear displays a special link with illness and healing, birth and death', i.e. it had both harmful and beneficial powers (Uspenskii, 1982, p. 109). *Volos* in Russian means hair and 'the hairy one' was used to indicate the bear (Uspenskii, 1982, pp. 101–2). For peasants the bear was a threat to cows. Charms to protect them have survived, but the bear was also often taken to be the god of cattle, like Veles or Volos, protector especially of pigs, probably the commonest animal in early Russian farming, or goats. The Christian saints Vlasii and Vasilii of Caesaria, too, bearing names resembling that of the pagan god, were also regarded as protectors of horned cattle among Russians, while saints Flor and Lavr protected horses. These functions were ascribed to other saints among some other Slavs (Uspenskii, 1982, pp. 85–110, 128–9, 131, 134; Ivanov and Toporov, 1974, 45f., pp. 178–9, 56–61). Vlasii was the patron saint of a Yaroslavl' church on the site of a former shrine (*keremet'*) of Volos which was associated with the bear (Voronin, 1941, pp. 160–1, 189; Fasmer I, 1964, p. 343; Jakobson, 1951, p. 190); *keremet'*, Fasmer (1967, II, p. 224) gives it as an evil spirit of the Chuvash Mari, or the place it inhabits. It also is a heathen temple in Vyatka (Uspenskii, 1982, pp. 101–2). In the Volga area (unfortunately no date is given) there were tales of Keremet, a god who appeared to man in the form of a bear (Shuklin, 1997, p. 240). The name may be cognate with Turkic *kirämät*, a word meaning both a 'healing medicine' and 'a spirit worshipped by Chuvash and also converted Tatars' (Radlov, n.d., II.2, p. 1356). A similar word, *kärämät*, means 'nobleness', 'wonder' or 'miracle' in the Turkic Kazan, Kirgiz and the Sart dialects; this suggests both a positive view of the animal and cultural links with Central Asia (Radlov, n.d., II. 2, p. 1094). The usual Turkic word for bear (*ayi*) derives from a root meaning 'wild' or 'powerful', 'lout' in Turkish, and has many negative connotations (Eyuboglu, 1988, p. 56; Hony, 1947, p. 25). In nineteenth-century Russia, the bear's curative functions were being advertised by itinerants with trained bears (Nekrylova, 1988, p. 41). At that time, the Komi, a Finnish people located east of the Northern Dvina and as far south as the steppe, had property symbols called 'small bear', 'great bear' and 'bear's ear' frequently found around the town of Oshib, which means 'Bear Field'.

Conclusions: the survival of the bear cult

The decisions of the Church Council of 1551, summoned by Ivan IV, threatened excommunication for 'those who follow pagan customs, go to wizards or wise men, or invite them home hoping to learn from them what is not to be said, and feed and keep bears or any other animal to deceive simple folk . . .' (*Stoglav*, 1911, p. 185; cp. *Stoglav*, 1971, p. 261). Here both Church and Crown united in attacking surviving pagan customs. Yet, at about the same time, or shortly after, Ivan's court had both bear hunts and bear-baiting spectacles. Fletcher noted that 'to maintaine this pastime the emperor hath certain huntsmen that are appointed for that purpose to take the wild beare' (Fletcher, 1856, p. 143). Ivan himself engaged in hunting wild bears (Karamzin, reprint III, 1989, book IX, chap. 3, pp. 97–8 (1571)). He also used them to kill people: boyars, deacons, and children (Karamzin, III, 1989, book IX, chap. 3, note 183, p. 40 (1571); chap. 4, note 398, p. 87). Later, a member of *zemshchina*, part of Muscovy not incorporated into Ivan IV's privy administration (*oprichnina*), set a bear upon a clerk in Novgorod and many other people were wounded. Then 'jolly people were taken and also bears listed for the Sovereign'; sledges took jesters and bears to Moscow (*Novgorodskie letopisi*, 1879, p. 107 (1572); Karamzin, reprint III, 1989, book IX, chap. 3, notes 183, 322). They were to provide entertainment at Ivan's third marriage. The function of the bear in this context appears comparable with that of bear-baiting in Western Europe at this period: it provided a spectacle, an entertainment. An Englishman in Muscovy in 1588 wrote about a fight between a man and a bear: 'One other speciall recreation is the fight with wilde bears which are caught in pittes or nets, and are kept in barred cages for that purpose, against the emperour be disposed to see the pastime' (Fletcher, 1856, p. 143). In 1606, the False Dmitri, a pretender with Polish support, not only had the best English dogs for bear-baiting, but also demonstrated his skill before his boyars by killing a bear with a spear and cutting the head off with a sabre (Karamzin, reprint III, 1989, book XI, chap. 4, p. 130, note 394, p. 67 (1605)). Such pastimes were not merely similar to Western bear-baiting, but were probably influenced by them. A novelty to Westerners in the 1670s was the baiting of a polar bear on the ice by English and other dogs (Reitenfels, 1905, p. 89). At least the court now engaged in such spectacles (Baron, 1967, p. 91: *The Travels of Olearius*).

Western visitors to Muscovy also noted itinerant performers with trained bears providing popular spectacles which became known in Russian as bear comedies (*medvezhie komedii*) around this time, if not before; these performances have been described as 'caricatures and in part satirical' (Zabelin, 1915, part 3, p. 306). Olearius commented on entertainers who sang of loathsome depravities in the open streets, puppeteers who depicted them and, he added, 'dancing-bear impresarios have comedians with them' (Baron, 1967, p. 142).

Churchmen, particularly reformers among them, continued to object to the bear, despite it being part of courtly and, especially in the case of the trained bear, of itinerant lower-level entertainment. In 1636 priests from Nizhnii Novgorod petitioned the Patriarch against popular festivities: 'From Christmas to the Baptism of Christ [i.e. from 25 December to 6 January] they engage in games round the houses; many men and women gather for that evil sight, they make games of every conceivable devilry with many evil images, curse God's mercy and his immaculate feast day' (Rozhdestvenskii, 1902, I, p. 24).

The jesters have been regarded as primarily professional entertainers, but were associated with paganism; the key documents about them date from 1068, 1551 and 1648. These dates approximate to those of significant urban riots: 1068 in Kiev, 1548 and 1648 in Moscow (Belkin, 1975, pp. 98, 99). The dates are also close to those of the Volga wizards (*c.* 1070), the Church Council of 1551 and the activities of the

Zealots of Piety in the 1640s. All three periods of social crisis involved religion, in a broad sense. The events around 1070 do not appear to have resulted in major changes enshrined in any formal documents, but the last two of these disturbances resulted in the *Stoglav* of 1551 and the Code of Laws of 1649. These events show a growth in the power of Orthodoxy and the state, even though there seems to have been a protective association between some state governors (*namestniki*) and jesters. There was also a corresponding decline in popular beliefs, at least formally, where Church and State power were effective. In the eleventh century the pagan–Christian struggle is in the forefront; in the 1550s Tsar and Church were prominent in surviving documents; while in the mid-seventeenth century a state Code of Laws was issued.

In Russia we see an association between bears and jesters, who may have given a voice to such popular beliefs and feelings as these, but they are only documented from around the middle of the sixteenth century, when jesters were apparently in decline. In the same century, too, court entertainments included some in which the bear featured, despite the disapproval of the Church. Such pleasures may reflect the frequent conservatism of court and nobles and may be a survival or perhaps a cultural import mediated by the need to demonstrate a Western orientation, or probably both.

Under Aleksei Mikhailovich (ruled 1645–76), courtly bear entertainments seem to have been greatly developed under early moves towards Westernisation (Zabelin, 1915, pp. 305–15). In the seventeenth century, entertainments with trained bears were also found at lower social levels: the 'bear comedies' were both festive entertainment and a means of satirical social criticism. It is not clear whether these entertainments arose as a result of court models being adapted or whether they derived from older celebrations with bears and jesters. In the eighteenth and nineteenth centuries they remained very popular until the use of bears for this purpose was prohibited in 1866, when the practice of using bears 'to amuse the people' was abolished (Zabelin, 1915, p. 315). This was only five years after the liberation of the serfs and the consequent ferment of peasant disturbances that followed and then rapidly subsided.

References to bears, however, continued to occur in some traditions. In marriage ceremonies terms for the male and the female bear (*medved'*, *medveditsa*) were used to indicate the groom and the bride, and others playing a part according to the folk poetry of these centuries (Uspenskii, 1982, pp. 95–103, 163–6). This fits with belief in the 'good' bear as bringer of health and wealth, an appropriate wish at a wedding. The bride and groom would sit on a bear skin, the rich, dense hair implying wealth and fertility. In embroideries from these centuries, the figures intended to represent lions or panthers, animals not seen by Russian peasants, were, understandably, frequently known as 'bears' (Maslova, 1978, pp. 83, 86).

Figure 19.3 Brown bears in a hunting lodge, Romania (© Sebastian Catanoiu).

Such usages and customs suggest at least an awareness of and some concern with the bear. In western Russia, even at the end of the nineteenth century, a festival called 'lump-eating' (*komoeditsa*) took place, when balls of pease-flour porridge were eaten to celebrate the bear's awakening from hibernation towards the end of April and there were celebrations and dancing with clothing worn inside out (*Slovar' russkogo yazyka*, 1912, p. 1747, citing *Pravedna Vestnik*, 1893: No. 238; Shuklin, 1997, pp. 240–1; also Collins, 1671, p. 7). The bear again features in entertainment that allows society to be mocked.

The bear also continued to be referred to in various ways in Russian and other north Eurasian languages, many of them terms of human relationship; all avoid giving the animal its proper name. 'Father, grandpa, old man, uncle, step-father, forest person, boss, bishop, lord of animals' and also 'sorcerer, knower' (*vedun, znatlivets*) have been noted (Shuklin, 1997, pp. 240–1, 23; Uspenskii, 1982, p. 109; Wilson, 2000, p. 476). Even more striking is the fact that the ordinary term for 'bear' in Russian (*medved'*), literally 'honey-knower', is itself a periphrasis. Hunters in 1885–98 were recorded as referring to the bear, as a taboo, as 'he' (*Slovar' russkikh narodnykh govorov*, 1987, 23, p. 213) (Figure 19.3). Such kenning, and similar terms used by Swedes, Lapps and Finns, indicate the animal's sacral nature: the name of the powerful animal, whether good or evil, is to be avoided (Wilson, 2000, p. 416).

However, there also often seems to be implicit a recognition that man and bear are linked in some way, almost as if they are at times interchangeable, representing dual aspects of a single entity. In European Russia in modern times the bear has sometimes been considered to be a man or a human offspring cursed by his parents; there were stories about a hunter cohabiting with a she-bear. There is also a tale, collected as recently as 1973, of a woman giving birth to a little bear cub (*Predaniya bylichki*, 1997, p. 54). A similar folk tale occurs in a mid-nineteenth-century collection (Afanas'ev 1857, I, p. 303). These tales probably derive from the suckling of bear cubs in the past. In recent times, although the bear continued to feature in aspects of ritual and tradition, it was no longer the protector and danger it had been in early times (it never had been the 'altogether lovely' animal presented by Harrison and Mirrlees, 1926), but it was altogether powerful for good as well as evil. Its survival, at least vestigially in marriage ceremonies, despite the triumph of Orthodoxy, and its contact in times of illness, seems to reflect belief in its helpfulness. In modern times it offered a chance to be entertained and to mock authority. It was present only as a ghost, its ancient significance lost in the face both of new and more threatening dangers to the safety of the community and also of more reliable social help from other sources.

The increasing industrialisation of Russia from the time of Peter the Great in the early eighteenth century involved economic and social developments. Both forest and bears became less important. The image of the bear came, quite independently it seems, to represent Russia to other countries less familiar with wild or tamed bears. Within Russia, the bear still left faint traces in surviving custom as the bringer of wealth and good health to the common people.

References

Afanas'ev, A. N. (1857, 1865). *Narodnye Russkie Shazki*, Vols. I and II. Moscow.

Baron, S. H. (ed. and trans.) (1967). *The Travels of Olearius in Seventeenth-Century Russia*. Stanford, CA: Stanford University Press.

Batchelor, J. (1901). *The Ainu and their Folk-Lore*. London: The Religious Tract Society.

Belkin, A. A. (1975). *Russkie skomorokhi*. Moscow: Nauka.

Collins, S. (1671). *The Present State of Russia*. London.

Dopolnenie k aktam Istoricheskim I. (1846). St Petersburg.

Eyuboglu, I. Z. (1988). *Türk dilinin etimoloji sözlügü*. Istanbul: Sosyal yayinlar.

Fasmer [Vasmer] M. (1964, 1967). *Russisches Etymologisches Wörterbuch*, Vols. I and II. Moscow: Progress.

Fletcher, G. (1856). Of the Russe common wealth. In *Russia at the Close of the Sixteenth Century*, ed. E. A. Bond for the Hakluyt Society, 1st series, No. 20, London.

Gorodtsov, V. A. (1851–1918). *Kul'tury bronzovoi epokhi, Zapiski Otdeleniya russkoi i slavyanskoi arkheologii Russkogo arkheologicheskogo obshchestva*. St Petersburg.

Hakluyt, R. (1589, 1965 reprint). *The Principall Navigations Voiages and Discoueries of the English Nation* (1589) London, George Bishop and Ralph Newberie. Facsimile reprint 1965 for The Hakluyt Society and the Peabody Museum of Salem, Hakluyt Society, Extra Series, No. 39 in two parts, 1. Cambridge: Cambridge University Press.

Harrison, J. and Mirrlees, H. (1926). *The Book of the Bear*. London: Nonesuch Press.

Hony, H. C. (1947). *A Turkish–English Dictionary*. Oxford: Oxford University Press.

Hori, I. (1974). *Folk Religion in Japan, Continuity and Change*. Chicago, IL: University of Chicago Press.

Ivanov, V. V. and Toporov, V. N. (1974). *Issledovaniya v oblasti slavyanskikh drevnostei*. Moscow.

Jakobson, R. (1951). *Word*, **7**, 187–91.

Karamzin, N. M. (1988-9). *Istoriya gosudarstva rossiiskogo* (1766–1826) Facsimile reprint of 5th edition, 1842–4, St Petersburg, ed. I. Dinerlingen; Facsimile reprint, 12 vols. and key in 4. Moscow: Kniga.

Krainov, D. A. (l964). Volosovo-Danilovskoi mogil'nik Fat'yanovskoi kul'tury. *Sovetskaya arkheologiya*, **4**, 68–83.

Lavrov, N. F. (1951). Religiya i tserkov (Religion and church), *Istoriya kul'tury Drevnei Rusi (History of the Culture of Ancient Russia)*, Vol. 2, Pre-Mougal period, general ancient and spiritual culture, ed. N. Voronin and M. K. Karger. Moscow and Leningrad: Academy of Science of USSR, pp. 61–113.

Makarov, N. A. and Chernetsov, A. V. (1988). K izucheniyu kul'tovykh kamnei. *Sovetskaya Arkheologiya*, **3**, 79–90.

Maksimov, S. V. (1903). *Nechistaya, nevedomaya i krestnaya sila*. St Petersburg.

Maslova, G. S. (1978). *Ornament russkoi narodnoi vyshivki kak istocheskii istochnik*. Moscow: Nauka.

Nakamoto, M. (1999). *Upaskuma* (The wisdom of the Ainu), ed. Katayama Tatsumine. Tokyo: Shina Nippon Tosho Co. Ltd.

Nekrylova, A. F. (1988). *Russkie narodnye gorodskie prazdniki, uveseleniya i zrelishcha*. Leningrad: Iskusstvo.

Novgorodskaya pervaya letopis. (1950). Moscow–Leningrad: Iskusstvo.

Novgorodskie letopisi. (1879). ed. Arkheograficheskoi kommissii. St Petersburg: Tip. Imperator akademii nauk.

Oborin, V. (1976). *Drevnee iskusstvo narodov Prikam'ia*. Perm: Permskoe knizhnoe izdatel'stvo.

Petrukhin, V. Ya. and Chernetsov, A. V. (1991). Konf erentsi ya 'Drevnerusskoe yazychestvo i ego traditsii'. *Sovetskaya Arkheologiya*, **1**, 299–303.

Polnyi pravoslavnyi bogoslovskii entsiklopedicheskii slovar'. (1913), I–II, n.p.

Povest' vremennykh let. (1950). Vols. I–II. Moscow–Leningrad: Izd-vo Moskovskogo Universiteta.

Pravedna Vestnik. (1893). No. 238.

Predaniya bylichki (Pamyatniki russkogo fol'klora Vodlozer'ya). (1997). Petrozavodsk: Izd-vo Petrozavodskogo universiteta.

Radlov, V. V. (n.d.). *Opyt slovarya tyurkskikh narechii*, 4 vols. (undated Soviet photographic reprint in 8; St Petersburg, 1893–1911: Tip. Imperatorskoi Akademii Nauk).

Reitenfels, Ya. (1905). *Skazaniya svetleishemu gertsogu toskanomu Kozme tret'emu o Moskovii*, Moscow, originally published in Padua 1680.

Rozhdestvenskii, N. V. (1902). *K istorii bor'by s tserkovnymi bezporyadkami, otgoloskami yazychestva i porokami v russkom bytu XVII v, Chteniya v imp. Obshchestve istorii i drevnostei rossiiskikh*, Bk. 1, pp. 1–31, Moscow.

Shuklin,V. (1997). *Mify russkogo naroda*. Ekaterinburg: Bank kul'turnoi informatsii.

Slovar' russkikh narodnykh govorov. (1987), 23. Leningrad.

Slovar' russkogo yazyka, sostavlennyi Vtorym otdeleniem Imp. Akademii nauk. (1912). Vol. IV, part VI, St Petersburg.

Stoglav (1863). Council of Moscow, ed. D. E. Kozhanchikova, St Petersburg. Reprint of St Petersburg edn 1911, Tip. Imperatorskaia Akademiia Nauk, 1971, Letchworth: Bradda Books Ltd.

Uspenskii, B. A. (1982). *Filologicheskie razyskaniya v oblasti slavyanskikh drevnostei*. Moscow: Izd-vo Moskovskogo universteta.

Voronin, N. N. (1941). Medvezhii kul't v verkhmem Povolzh'e v Xlv. *Materialy i issledovaniya po arkheologii SSSR*, No. 6. Moscow–Leningrad.

Wilson, S. (2000). *The Magical Universe, Everyday Ritual and Magic In Pre-modern Europe*. London–New York: Hambledon.

Zabelin, I. (1915). *Domashnii byt russkikh tsarei v XVI i XVII stoletiyakh*, part 3. Moscow, Sinodal'naya tip.

Zelenin, D. K. (1933). Totemicheskii kul't derev'ev u russkikh I belorussov, *Izvestiya AN SSSR, otdel. Obshchestvennykh nauk*.

Zelenin, D. K. (1937). *Totemy-derev'ya v skazaniyakh i obryadakh evropeiskikh narodov*. Moscow–Leningrad: Izd-vo Akademii nauk SSSR.

Zelenin, D. K. (1994). *Izbrannye trudy*. Moscow: Izd-vo 'Indrik'.

20

Specific-species taboos and biodiversity conservation in Northern Madagascar

KATE MANNLE and RICHARD J. LADLE

Introduction

In many cultures, cultural restrictions or taboos govern all aspects of life from authority within families to illness, children, death, sexual relations, place and food (Van Gennep, 1904). Significantly, taboos may also control or influence behaviour in relation to the use of natural resources, making them of great potential interest to conservationists. A systematic study of 'resource and habitat taboos' (RHTs) from around the world found that RHTs significantly contribute to the protection of a variety of species and habitats (Colding and Folke, 2001). While conservation has traditionally focused on formal institutions such as laws and protected areas to manage natural resources, informal institutions such as RHTs are being increasingly considered as potential instruments for conservation practice, either on their own or nested in more formal arrangements (Barrett *et al.*, 2001).

One type of RHT that has perhaps received less interest from conservationists are specific-species taboos (Table 20.1), possibly because their origins are not thought to derive from the sustainable use of natural resources (Lingard *et al.*, 2003; Jones *et al.*, 2008). Despite this, they may still be important for conservation because they could allow conservationists to design interventions and policies that are more sympathetic to the intrinsic and/or spiritual values of a community.

The spiritual element of specific-species taboos is particularly evident in northern Malagasy culture, where one of the central concepts of Malagasy cosmology is a strong reverence for one's ancestors. Recently deceased ancestors can influence the living, living descendants must maintain ancestral relations, and one can only do this by maintaining contact through ancestral lands and tombs (Brown, 2005).

Sacred Species and Sites: Advances in Biocultural Conservation, ed. Gloria Pungetti, Gonzalo Oviedo and Della Hooke. Published by Cambridge University Press. © Cambridge University Press 2012.

Table 20.1 *Resource and habitat taboos (RHTs) and their nature conservation and resource management functions (from Colding and Folke, 2001 and Jones et al., 2008).*

Category	Function
Segment taboos	Regulate resource withdrawal
Temporal taboos	Regulate access to resources in time
Method taboos	Regulate methods of withdrawal
Life history taboos	Regulate withdrawal of vulnerable life-history stages of species
Specific-species taboos	Total protection to species in both time and space
Habitat taboos	Restrict access and use of resources in time and space
Usage taboos	Regulate how a species can be used

One way that respect for the ancestors manifests itself in everyday life is through a complex system of taboo or *fady* to which many Malagasy people adhere. Major investigations into *fady* (Van Gennep, 1904; Ruud, 1960; Lambek, 1992; Walsh, 2002) show that *fady* are not just prescribed informal rules, but are also acts in and of themselves and, as such, people often speak of 'being' *fady* for something rather than 'having' a *fady* (Lambek, 1992). *Fady* can apply to an individual, a family lineage, a clan or a region and transpire in many aspects of life.

Fady also play an important role in regulating a number of natural resource uses in Madagascar. *Fady* can protect specific species (Lingard *et al.*, 2003), protect habitat (Horning, 2003; Tengö *et al.*, 2007), or regulate the use of a particular species (Jones *et al.*, 2008). In southern Madagascar, Lingard *et al.* (2003) found that local people were *fady* for the radiated tortoise, which may have saved it from extinction (Nussbaum and Raxworthy, 2000). However, the *fady* alone may not be effective in protecting species. Migration of people not *fady* for a certain species and market forces have been found to degrade the system of *fady* in a particular area (Horning, 2003; Lingard *et al.*, 2003).

A closer examination of specific-species *fady* and exploration of their origins may help Western conservationists working in the area to better understand local people's perceptions and interactions with their environment. Here we discuss the results of a study of specific-species taboos or *fady* in the Bay of Antsiranana area of northern Madagascar the aim of which was to explore the conservation status of species protected by *fady* in the region, the spiritual origins of specific-species *fady*, and the potential implications for conservation management in the region.

Study area: the Bay of Antsiranana

The Bay of Antsiranana is found in the province of Antsiranana in the extreme north of Madagascar. The provincial capital, Antsiranana (formerly Diego

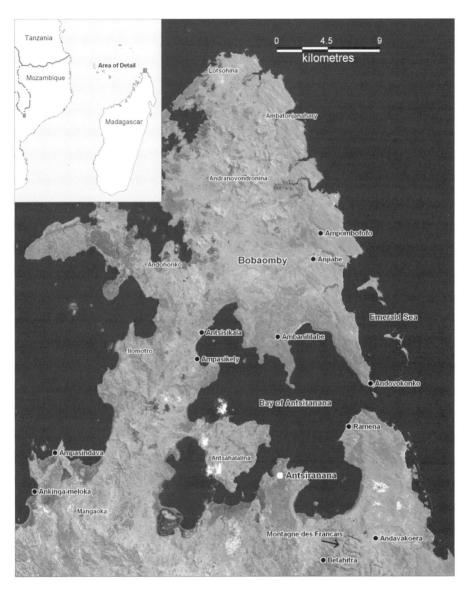

Figure 20.1 Map of the the Bay of Antsiranana Region and study villages.

Suarez and still commonly referred to as 'Diego'), sits on the south side of the Bay affording the city the use of the third largest natural harbour in the world. The bay stretches 156 km across, and is bordered to the north by a rugged triangle of land known as the Bobaomby (Rossi, 1980) and to the south-east by the Montagne des Français (Figure 20.1).

The Bay of Antsiranana region, which has not been a priority for conservationists until recent years, is rich with biodiversity. Inventories in the Bobaomby area are still incomplete; however, several known species found there are categorised as endangered or vulnerable on the IUCN Red List, mainly the Madagascan Tree Boa, the Madagascan Ground Boa and the Crowned lemur. A transfer of management from the Ministry of the Environment and Forests to a local management committee took place in July 2007, which is likely to increase conservation activities in the area. The Montagne des Français (MdF) has recently gained temporary protected area status under Malagasy law and has been much more thoroughly inventoried. The MdF forests are home to 21 species of mammal, 14 of which are endemic, and nine of which appear on the IUCN Red List. Additionally, there are at least 52 species of reptiles (50 endemic), 9 amphibians (all endemic) and 63 bird species (24 endemic) (Green *et al.*, 2007).

Communities in the area are typically made up of a diverse mix of ethnic groups including Anjoaty Sakalava, Antakarana, Tsimihety, Betsimisaraka, Antemoro, Antandroy and others. However, despite the diversity of groups represented in the area, the customs and beliefs amongst different ethnicities are quite similar, and Gezon (2006) suggests that some immigrants may even have adopted the Antakarana *fady* of their new home.

Methods

Qualitative data on specific-species *fady* were collected as part of a larger study examining the natural resource use and biodiversity knowledge in the Bay of Antsiranana area. The study was carried out over a period of two months from May to July 2007 by a team of six international researchers (two British, one American and three Malagasy) with a pilot study conducted in April 2007 ($n = 10$). A combination of research methods was employed in order to gain a comprehensive understanding of traditional ecological knowledge systems and specific-species *fady*, including a research questionnaire, key informant interviews, participant observation and a review of secondary literature.

Questionnaires were completed ($n = 220$) in nine villages in the Bobaomby and MdF areas of the Bay of Antsiranana. Villages were selected based on their proximity to forest patches, the livelihood activities of their inhabitants and proposed conservation activities in the region. Stratified purposive sampling was employed (Patton, 1990) based on livelihood activities, specifically the use of forest resources, and questionnaires were conducted at the individual level. Questionnaires were delivered orally in Malagasy and answers were translated immediately into English by the Malagasy researcher and recorded by the foreign researcher on an answer sheet. Questions regarding specific-species *fady* were open-ended and focused on, first, the animals that people are *fady* to eat; second, animals that people are *fady* to harm or kill; and third, the history and consequences of these *fady*. The researchers stayed in the villages and considerable care was taken not to raise expectations.

Semi-structured interviews were conducted with key informants from international and local conservation non-governmental organisations (NGOs) ($n = 5$), government officials ($n = 3$), and village elders ($n = 7$) in order to gain a deeper and more nuanced understanding of conservation activities in the area and familiarise the researchers to the specific customs and beliefs of each village. Grey literature, primarily sourced from local environmental NGOs, was also used to build up a broader understanding of conservation activities in the region and to help contextualise the potential role of *fady* in local conservation and natural resource management.

Results

Conservation status of 'fady *species*'

Residents surveyed in villages around the Bay of Antsiranana are *fady* for many animal taxa (species or higher taxonomic units), which include a number of IUCN Red Listed species. In one open-ended question, respondents were asked what they personally are *fady* to eat. Respondents ($n = 185$) listed 55 different animal species or families as being *fady* for eating. The most common *fady* included pork (66.5%), eel (49.2%), lemur (31.4%), goat (24.3%), turtle (15.6%), tenrec (13.5%), bat (12.4%), green pigeon (8.7%), snake (8.1%) and zebu without horns (7%). The six most frequently listed wild species were investigated further, and their conservation status was analysed (Table 20.2, Figure 20.2). In total, nine species on the IUCN Red List are *fady* to eat.

A subset of the forest users ($n = 155$) was also asked if animals were generally *fady* to harm or kill and then asked which ones were particularly *fady*. Of respondents, 94.8% listed at least one species or family of animal as being *fady* to harm or kill, and in total respondents listed 23 different species or families as being generally *fady* to harm or kill. Many respondents stated that all animals are *fady* (36.7%), while chameleons (28.6%), snakes (19.7%), boas (13.6%), fourline snake (*Dromicodryas quadralineatus*) (13.6%), lemurs (12.9%), and the Malagasy giant hognose snake (*Leioheterodon madagascariensis*) (7.48%), were the six most frequently listed as generally *fady* animals to harm or kill (Figure 20.3). In total, eight species on the IUCN Red List found in the area are *fady* to harm or kill in this area (Table 20.3) (Figure 20.3).

The origins of specific-species *fady*

While some individuals become *fady* for certain animals during their childhood or through a lived experience, most specific-species *fady* are passed

Table 20.2 *Most commonly listed wild species or orders that are given protection by being* fady *to eat.*

Common English name	Common Malagasy name	Scientific name	IUCN Red List species	Status
Eel	*Amalono*	Anguilliformes		
Lemurs	*Akomba*	Lemuriformes	*Lepilemur ankaranensis*	EN
			Eulemur coronatus	VU
			Microcebus tavaratra	EN
			Cheirogaleus major	DD
			Daubentoniidae madagascariensis	VU
Bats	*Fanihy (fany)*	Chiropteres	*Triaenops rufus*	DD
			Miniopterus manavi	DD
			Rousettus madagascariensis	LC
Turtle	*Fano*	Testudines		
Greater Hedgehog Tenrec	*Ambiko*	*Setifer setosus*		LC
Green Pigeon	*Vorono Adabo*	*Treron australis*		

IUCN threat status: EN, Endangered; VU, Vulnerable; NT, Near Threatened; LC, Least Concern; DD, Data Deficient.

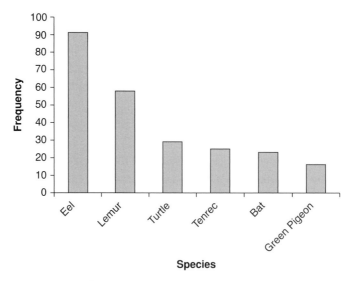

Figure 20.2 The frequency of wild species *fady* to eat ($n = 85$).

Table 20.3 *Most commonly listed wild species or orders given protection from being* fady *to harm or kill*

Common English name	Common Malagasy name	Scientific name	IUCN Red List species	Status
Chameleon	*Tarondro*	Chamaeleonidae	*Furcifer petteri*	VU
Snakes	*Bibilava*	Serpentes		
Madagascar tree boa	*Do*	*Sanzinia madagascariensis*	*Sanzinia madagascariensis*	LC
Madagascar ground boa	*Do*	*Acrantophis madagascariensis*	*Acrantophis madagascariensis*	NT
Fourline snake	*Marolongo*	*Dromicodryas quadralineatus*		
Lemurs	*Akomba*	Lemuriformes	*Lepilemur ankaranensis*	EN
			Eulemur coronatus	VU
			Microrebus tavaratra	EN
			Cheirogaleus major	DD
			Daubentoniidae madagascari	VU
Malagasy giant hognose snake	*Menalio*	*Leioheterodon madagascariensis*		
Malagasy blonde hognosed snake	*Saboa Malandy*	*Leioheterodon modestus*		

IUCN threat status: EN, Endangered; VU, Vulnerable; NT, Near Threatened; LC, Least Concern; DD, Data Deficient.

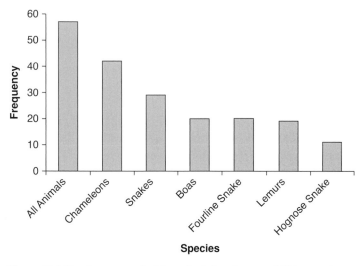

Figure 20.3 The frequency of wild species *fady* to harm or kill ($n = 155$).

on from an elder family member such as a parent or grandparent. A common narrative is that an ancestor was in danger or being chased by an enemy and an animal made noises and led the enemy astray, thereby rescuing the ancestor whose descendants were *fady* for that particular animal from that point forward. There are many variations on this theme. The following example illustrates this specific-species narrative.

> If you kill a lemur, he's 'putting his hand to his ear', which means 'Pardon me, please don't kill me'. So if you do it you will be sick because lemurs according to the story are people, they can make sounds like people. There were bandits and they made sounds like people and the bandits followed them so people don't eat them since then.

Another common narrative is that in some way the animal has harmed an ancestor or the animal now possesses the spirit of the ancestor, such as this history of turtle *fady*.

> [It came] from one of my ancestors. A turtle was laying eggs on the beach and [my ancestor] caught his leg and didn't let go. The turtle went out to sea and he was sitting on him and he disappeared. His descendants don't eat turtle.

When asked to tell the stories behind species-specific *fady*, many respondents gave explanations general to all animals. Several common themes and beliefs regarding specific-species and animal-related *fady* emerged from the open-ended responses. A number of respondents noted the connection between animals and the land as the reason that all animals are *fady*.

> All animals are *fady* because they're the spirit of the earth.

> The Bobaomby is a sacred place so it's *fady* to kill animals here.

> Lemur [are *fady*] because in our area there are lots of sacred areas so that's the reason why it's *fady* to kill them. People here don't like people who eat lemurs.

These quotations highlight a belief held by many in the Bay of Antsiranana area that land is sacred, particularly the Bobaomby to the north of the Bay. The sacred status of the land also places importance on adhering to animal-related *fady* as the spirits are stronger in this region.

Respondents also communicated a sense of 'reciprocity' with animals in that they should be left alone because they do not harm humans and that they should be treated the way humans are treated. The following excerpts express this reciprocity.

> All the animals are *fady* to kill . . . The animals that pass by, it's like people who pass by, you just say hello. They don't harm you and so you don't kill them.

> Any animals or lemurs it's *fady* to kill them. Our grandparents used to tell us it's *fady* to kill them because they don't do anything they just stay in the forest. Same with the chameleons; they just walk around.

The third major theme that emerged is that *fady* animals can be killed if they cause injury to an individual, especially if they kill chickens or cause crop damage. Snakes, especially boas, were named as frequent nuisances to livestock. Again, respondents express an attitude of reciprocity, but with negative consequences towards animals that cause harm to them.

> No animal can be killed because they have life like people. But for example, if we're raising our chickens or any kind of bird we're raising and there's a boa that kills one, we can kill it. We do a joro [prayer] that says, 'OK, we're coming here to raise chickens'. If [the boas] kill [the chickens], it is because they are not obeying the rules.

> If a boa doesn't kill your chickens you shouldn't kill it. If it did nothing to you, you should not do anything to it. The boa saliva becomes diamonds, which gives it value but I have never seen it so I don't know if it's true.

In this example, while it still remains *fady* to kill the boas, some leeway is granted to those who have been injured by the animal. In this context, animals, as well as people, are expected to adhere to a set of rules that have been handed down from the ancestors and are maintained by spirits called *tsiny*. The fear of retribution from these spirits led a couple of individuals to state that they are *fady* to kill any animal even when the animal has caused them harm.

The concept of *tsiny* and the spiritual origins of *fady*

One of the dominant themes that emerged from asking people to describe the history and consequences of their specific-species *fady* was the idea of *tsiny*. *Tsiny* was often given as a reason that animals are *fady*. Generally, *tsiny* can be described as the spirit of an animal. While other people have described *tsiny* as akin to a feeling of guilt or burden (Andriamanjato, 1957), results show a much more nuanced concept that involves distinct spirits, spirit possession, and retribution. The five major elements of *tsiny* are as follows.

First, *tsiny* is a distinctive spirit of animals and is similar to the human spirit. If a person were to harm or kill an animal, the animal's *tsiny* would then stay with the offender and seek retribution:

> All the animals that you domesticate, they have owners. Those animals in the forest they have owners too – the spirits. If you kill them they will punish you, you will get sick because of that.

Second, the origin of *tsiny* rooted in animals' defencelessness and given to them by God:

> Because God gave the crocodile and wild boar teeth to defend themselves . . . [God] said to the snakes and chameleons, 'I will give you the power. If someone will see you they will run away so you don't need the tools'. If people touch them they will be in trouble.

Third, retribution from *tsiny* can be sickness or death:

> Animals are *fady* to kill because you can have the *tsiny* from them and either you can be sick or 'kombo', sickness all your life until you die.

Fourth, *tsiny* can sometimes be appeased through ritual:

> If you kill them [boa, menarara snake and the four-line snake] and break the *fady* something bad will happen to you or your generation. To treat it you have to do the *joro* [pray]. In the *joro* you try to communicate with the spirit of the forest. In a secret place, you drop honey and ask for forgiveness.

Fifth, fear of *tsiny* offers protection to specific species:

> All the animals are *fady* because of the *tsiny*, beware of harming them. If you see a kid who is about to harm an animal we say, 'no, no, don't do that'. Snakes and chameleons are *fady*. I'm really afraid of them, I don't touch them and ask kids not to touch them.

Discussion and conclusions

A clear and sophisticated understanding of how indigenous people perceive and interact with their natural environment is crucial to the success of conservation. Traditional knowledge systems such as the one centred on specific-species *fady* in Madagascar influence interaction with landscape, species and habitat. Not only must conservationists try to understand how these systems might

Figure 20.4 Trained in biodiversity assessment, Elise Tora is not afraid of this *Furcifer paradalis*, unlike most Malagasy people for whom chameleons are some of the most *fady* or taboo animals (© Kathryn Mannle).

contribute to conservation initiatives and interventions, but also how to implement conservation programmes without contributing to the further erosion of these indigenous practices. In a broader context, given the strong influence of specific-species taboos in many of the most biodiverse countries in the world, it goes without question that conservationists could improve practice by studying the ways in which traditional knowledge systems are passed on from generation to generation. This information could also be used as a basis for the creation of a more cross-cultural conservation ethic that genuinely resonates with natural resource stakeholders in areas of immense conservation value.

In Madagascar, conservationists should take an interest in trying to understand the complexities of traditional knowledge systems such as *fady* because of the overriding affect that this poorly known social institution has on how people interact with the environment (Figure 20.4). As shown in this study and elsewhere, *fady* provides protection for a range of species and habitats at the local level, including vulnerable and threatened species such as the Madagascar tree boa, Madagascar ground boa, and Crowned lemurs. In addition, *fady* allows conservationists to better understand preferences for natural resources within the local economy (Jones *et al.*, 2008) and by doing so may allow the implementation of more sustainable practices of resource acquisition such as charcoal production and wood collection.

Figure 20.5 Brilliant day geckos are left unharmed even when they enter homes as they are considered *fady* or taboo in the Bay of Antsiranana area of northern Madagascar (© Kathryn Mannle).

Conservationists also need to be aware of specific-species taboos in order to make sure that their policies and programmes do not erode existing informal institutions for species protection and natural resource management (Horning, 2003; Jones *et al.*, 2008). For example, Jones *et al.* (2008) found some evidence that cultural norms governing the harvest of pandans have broken down near a national park where forest use has been made illegal. A solid analysis of existing informal institutions may help international conservation NGOs to target their rules and enforcement where they are most needed without endangering or weakening the cultural systems already in place.

In the Bay of Antsiranana area, understanding the knowledge, and practice and beliefs around *fady* is particularly significant given the number of ongoing conservation activities (Figure 20.5). In the Bobaomby, through the transfer of management to a local committee the government is taking important steps in acknowledging the ability of local people to manage their own resources. The system is set up so that local people first have the ability to censure transgressors of conservation rules. While the transfer of management is still a new process, it is a positive example of nesting levels of conservation management responsibilities in which there is considerable scope for effectively embedding informal institutions.

Another strong motivation for conservationists to become interested in specific-species *fady* is that it may help them to better communicate their message to important stakeholders. Some scholars have noted the importance of communicating conservation through non-scientific terms (Nadkarni, 2004), while others have called for the development of a cross-cultural conservation ethic (Berkes, 2004). Finding the common threads of respect for the land and animals may help to bridge a divide between a predominantly human-centred, functionalist perspective and one rooted in Western ecological and compositionalist traditions. Engaging local people in conservation through their own systems of knowledge, practice and beliefs may be facilitated by drawing on the rich oral traditions through which many *fady* are communicated. Stories about animals such as *fady* engage the imagination and encourage active participation between the listener and the story-teller (Nabhan and St Antoine, 1993).

In conclusion, a deeper and more sophisticated understanding of traditional ecological knowledge systems and the rich oral traditions of taboos may help conservationists plan better conservation initiatives and communicate their message more effectively.

Beliefs such as specific-species *fady* are often compatible with the wider aims of the global conservation movement and could have an important role in communicating and engaging with local stakeholders.

References

Andriamanjato, R. (1957). *Le tsiny et le tody dans la pensee malagache*. Antananarivo: Salohy.

Barrett, C. B., Brandon, K., Gibson, C., *et al.* (2001). Conserving tropical biodiversity amid weak institutions. *BioScience*, **51**, 497–502.

Berkes, F. (2004). Rethinking community-based conservation. *Conservation Biology*, **18**, 621–30.

Brown, M. L. (2005). Reclaiming lost ancestors and acknowledging slave descent: insights from Madagascar. *Comparative Studies in Society and History*, **46**, 616–45.

Colding, J. and Folke, C. (2001). Social taboos: 'invisible' systems of local resource management and biological conservation. *Ecological Applications*, **11**, 584–600.

Gezon, L. L. (2006). *Global Visions, Local Landscapes: A Political Ecology of Conservation, Conflict, and Control in Northern Madagascar*. Plymouth: Altamira.

Green, K., D'Cruze, N., Robinson, J., *et al.* (2007). *Report 14. Montagne des Français: Biodiversity Surveys and Conservation Evaluation*. Frontier-Madagascar Environmental

Research, Society for Environmental Exploration, UK, and the Institut Halieutique et des Sciences Marines.

Horning, N. R. (2003). How rules affect conservation outcome. In *The Natural History of Madagascar*, ed. S. M. Goodman and J. P. Benstead. Chicago, IL: Chicago University Press.

Jones, J. P. G., Andriamarovololona, M. M. and Hockley, N. (2008). The importance of taboos and social norms to conservation in Madagascar. *Conservation Biology*, **22**, 976–86.

Lambek, M. (1992). Taboo as cultural practice among Malagasy speakers. *Man*, **27**, 245–66.

Lingard, M., Raharison, N., Rabakonandriananina, E., *et al.* (2003). The role of local taboos in conservation and management of species: the radiated tortoise in southern Madagascar. *Conservation and Society*, **1**, 223–46.

Nabhan, G. P. and Antoine, S. St. (1993). The loss of floral and faunal story: the extinction of experience. In *The Biophilia Hypothesis*, ed. S. R. Kellert and E. O. Wilson. Washington, DC: Island Press.

Nadkarni, N. M. (2004). Conservation education not preaching to the choir: communicating the importance of forest conservation to nontraditional audiences. *Conservation Biology*, **18**, 602.

Nussbaum, R. A. and Raxworthy, C. J. (2000). Commentary on conservation of 'Sokatra', the radiated tortoise (*Geochelone radiata*) of Madagascar. *Amphibian and Reptile Conservation*, **2**, 6–14.

Patton, M. Q. (1990). *Qualitative Evaluation and Research Methods*. Newbury Park, CA: Sage.

Rossi, G. (1980). *L'extrême-nord de Madagascar*. Aix-en-Provence: Édisud.

Ruud, J. (1960). *Taboo: A Study of Malagasy Customs and Beliefs*. London: George Allen & Unwin.

Tengö, M., Johansson, K., Rakotondrasoa, F., *et al.* (2007). Taboos and forest governance: informal protection of hot spot dry forest in southern Madagascar. *Ambio*, **36**, 683–91.

Van Gennep, A. (1904). *Tabou et totémisne à Madagascar; etude descriptive et théorique*. Paris: Ernest Leroux.

Walsh, A. (2002). Responsibility, taboos and 'the freedom to do otherwise', in Ankarana, northern Madagascar. *Journal of the Royal Anthropological Institute*, **8**, 451–68.

PART VI SACRED GROVES AND PLANTS

21

The sacred tree in the belief and mythology of England

DELLA HOOKE

Introduction

Many societies throughout the world have shared the concept of the sacred tree and there were many strong beliefs of this kind across pre-Christian north-western Europe. Living or symbolical trees have sometimes been identified at ritual centres and assembly sites, their presence open to various interpretations. This chapter examines how such belief was dealt with by early Christianity in England and how, despite replacement and suppression, belief in the power of trees often persisted in folk practices and folklore, refusing entirely to disappear. Today a new respect for trees and woodland recognises once again their value, not just as an economic resource, but in the preservation of the well-being of the earth.

Archaeological evidence and early literary evidence for sacred trees and tree symbolism

Although man has constructed temples and churches in which to practise religious rites from very early times, natural objects, too, such as trees, large stones or water features, have played a prominent role in spiritual concerns, whether as the abodes of spirits or gods or as means of accessing the spirit world. In this chapter the emphasis will be upon the role of trees as sacred objects. Our earliest evidence is necessarily archaeological and in Britain one finds living or symbolical trees forming a sacred function from at least the Bronze Age. In Norfolk at Holme next the Sea, a great upturned tree which had been set deliberately with its roots

Sacred Species and Sites: Advances in Biocultural Conservation, ed. Gloria Pungetti, Gonzalo Oviedo and Della Hooke. Published by Cambridge University Press. © Cambridge University Press 2012.

upwards some 4000 years ago was a great oak, uprooted in the spring of 2050 BC just as it was bursting into life; it was surrounded by a palisade of split poles, still carrying their bark on the outer side, which must have resembled, when standing, another great tree. This may have served as a mortuary table carrying the spirit of the dead down to a hidden realm, providing a union between this earth and a perceived underworld, or represent the life force of the tree itself being returned to the earth, the source of all life (Pryor, 2001, p. 276). There is a similarity here with The Tree of Eternity of the Hindu Veda texts: it has its roots in heaven above and its branches reach down to the earth 'ancient Tree, whose roots grow upward, and whose branches grow downwards' (*Katha Upanishad*, VI, 1965, p. 65).

Some Neolithic temples, like that known as the Sanctuary on Overton Hill at Avebury, Wiltshire, must have resembled forests of trees. The continuous renewal of two of the seven circles of posts involved there must have played a relevant part of the ritual itself, even if the significance of this practice cannot now be known. It is possible that temples of wood were more to do with the living whereas stone circles may have been associated with the dead and ancestral spirits (Pitts, 2001; Pryor, 2001, p. 277). Either singly or in groups, postholes which held large posts have been identified not infrequently at Bronze Age henge sites such as Stonehenge in Wiltshire. There is a suggestion that ritual activity incorporating such features may have begun here as early as the Mesolithic period (8500–7650 BC) (Cleal *et al.*, 1995, pp. 43, 141–52; Pryor, 2001, pp. 91–5).

We later find evidence of living or symbolical trees at assembly sites such as the ceremonial Celtic centre at Navan Court in County Armagh, Ireland, the site of the legendary court of Eamhain Mhacha, where five circles of oak posts surrounded a massive central pillar of oak in about 100 BC (Green, 1993, p. 26). Ó hÓgain sees this as an example of

> a sort of 'world-tree', at the sacred centre of the community's territory
> with a ceremonial function of linking the earth with the skies. As such it
> would have been a symbol of the prosperity of the tribe or sept, and
> important ceremonies would have centred on it. (Ó hÓgain, 1999, p. 172)

Such findings are not unusual on the Continent – an enormous wooden post perhaps some 12 m high stood at the centre of an enclosure known as the Goloring in Germany built in the sixth century BC (Green, 1993, p. 66). The tradition lasted a very long time and a large posthole feature stood before the royal palace at Yeavering in Northumbria, perhaps a symbol of royal power where the highest jurisdiction might be carried out. This would have been a central place of assembly for the Anglian kingdom established there in the early seventh century, a centre which perhaps inherited strong British traditions (Semple, 2004, p. 137). The post itself may have shared the significance of the king's *staffolus* set upon, or associated with, a podium or platform designating a place of royal power as noted in a Frankish law code of the 620s, or may have resembled the *stapol* of Heorot described in a later literary source, the eighth-century poem *Beowulf*, from which the report of the slaying of Grendel was delivered (Barnwell, 2005, pp. 178–82).

Other, earlier, literary evidence also confirms the sacred association of trees: some Roman gods had their special trees and both the Romans and the Greeks had their sacred groves. Holy trees might also offer the right of asylum. In the legends of the Ancient Greeks, Hebe, perhaps the cup-bearer of the gods, was able to pardon supplicants fleeing from justice within a sacred grove of cypress trees at Phlius in the northern Peloponnese; here the trees were said to be festooned with their discarded chains. Some Gaulish tribes were identified by tree names suggesting tree veneration; these include the Eburones (possibly of Germanic origin) noted by Caesar (*De Bello Gallico* V, VI), the 'Yew tribe', whose leaders led a revolt in north-eastern Gaul in 54–53 BC, destroying the Roman *Legio XIV*, or the Lemovices, the 'People of the Elm', who gave their name to the area of the Central Massif called Limousin (*De Bello Gallico* VII, 4; Green, 1993, p. 50). The Druids are said to have carried out rites in sacred oak groves and the Irish, too, continued to have their sacred trees – such a tree was known as a *bile* – which were regarded as the source of sacred wisdom; these were usually oaks, yews, ashes or hazels (Lucas, 1963). Assemblies might be held beneath such a tree and it was taboo to damage it in any way.

Medieval sources (such as the thirteenth-century *Edda* of Snorri Sturluson: Faulkes, 1987) recount much detail, considerably embellished, of the legendary Norse Yggdrassill, often interpreted as a giant ash (although, as an evergreen, the yew has also been suggested) which held within its roots and branches many worlds – of men (Miðgarðr), gods, giants, dwarves, etc. – and which extended from the underworld (sometimes seen as the abode of the dead) to the heavens, linking the cosmos. At its roots was the serpent, Niðhöggr, and it was watered daily from the Well of Urðr (Bauschatz, 1982).

Religion and nature

Many faiths incorporated a belief in the sanctity of certain woods or groves or had a special species of tree which they held sacred. The cycle of growing and falling leaves, of the setting and sprouting of seeds, or of new growth sprouting from cut trunks, may have been seen to hold parallels to the human cycle of birth and death. Forests were often secret places, set aside for divination or religious practices (see above) and individual trees have often been regarded as the abode of a god or spirit. The 'Tree of Life' or 'World Tree' is a widespread motif in many religions worldwide, exceedingly ancient (met with in early Babylonian and Sumerian beliefs *c.* 2000–4000 BC), found not only in the Jewish Cabbala, the Koran and the Bible but in many other religious beliefs, past and present (including those of the Maya and other peoples of Central America or in Siberian shamanism). Particular species of tree have also been associated with fertility, healing or ancestor worship.

In particular, species of fig were held sacred in many religions, such as Buddhism or Hinduism. The fig or 'peepal' tree, *Ficus religiosa*, was the earliest depicted tree in the art and literature of the Indian subcontinent, while in ancient Egyptian mythology the gods were thought to sit under a sycamore fig, *Ficus sycomorus*, whose fruit was held to feed the blessed. This was thus again the 'Tree of Life', often taken as the centre of the world, binding together the world of gods and humans (Crews, 2007). However, fig species have been held sacred in many parts of the world, too, including the Polynesian islands and many parts of Africa.

Whatever one may deduce about early beliefs and legends such as these, it seems that most early 'religions' were close to nature. In Britain, the topographical siting of monuments could be significant: early burial sites were often located on high ground as if the ancestors were helping to guard their territories; stone circles, on the other hand, were often on lower-lying ground. The association of some of the Wiltshire henges with avenues leading to rivers seems to have been part of their ceremonial function. Watery places were frequently places where votive deposits were made to the spirit world – whether in the form of offerings such as swords, etc., cast into rivers and lakes or into marshes and bogs.

Christianity and the 'sacred tree'

What happened to these ideas once Christianity reached the western world and Britain in particular? The pagan tree appears to have presented a threat in many parts of continental Europe. Numerous edicts were proclaimed by the Church on the Continent from the fifth century onwards decrying worship at trees and springs, etc., seen as 'devil worship' (Rattue, 1995, pp. 78–9). There are also numerous stories of saints cutting down sacred trees, even if these stories were often written long after the supposed event. According to a *Life* of St Martin, Bishop of Tours (Skeat, 1890, pp. 244–5), the saint is said to have destroyed a heathen temple that was associated with a sacred tree. Boniface also felt compelled to cut down a particularly large sacred oak at Geismar near Frankfurt, which may have served as an assembly point for diviners and enchanters (*Life of Boniface* by Willibald VI, trans. Talbot, 1954, pp. 45–6); Charlemagne is said to have destroyed the Irminsul which may have been one of these great pillars, if not a living tree, marking a sanctuary of the Germanic tribes (*Annals of the Kingdom of the Franks*, 75, cited by Flint, 1936, p. 209). By the eighth century the Frankish kings were fining those who made vows at springs, trees or in sacred groves, and ordering that features used in this way should be removed or destroyed. From Caesarius of Arles onwards, the church leaders made increasingly hostile attacks upon what it regarded as 'pagan' practices, but what is the evidence for any such beliefs in early medieval England?

The evidence is admittedly thin. The role of Nature in Old English literature is minimal and Jennifer Neville (1999) has argued that this is partly because it had no role to play in Anglo-Saxon Christianity and, indeed, that the Christian church was actively discouraging any preoccupation with the beauties of this earth. It seems that Christianity demanded that any possibility of sacred tree worship should be expunged – it could not be allowed to compete with the 'new' tree of life, the one true cross. John Blair has argued, however, that the more rigorous edicts banning superstitious practices actually gathered force in this country only around AD 1000. He cites Wulfstan's writings in 1005 x 8:

> And it is right that every priest zealously teach the Christian faith and entirely extinguish every heathen practice; and forbid worship of wells, and necromancy, and auguries and incantations, and worship of trees and worship of stones, and that devil's craft which is performed when children are drawn through the earth, and the nonsense which is performed on New Year's day in various kinds of sorcery, and in sanctuaries (on friðsplottum) and at elder-trees, and in many various delusions in which men carry on much that they should not. (From the so-called 'Canons of Edgar' dating back to the eleventh century: Blair, 2005, pp. 481–2; Canons of Edgar, XX.16, Bodl MS. Junius 121)

Such edicts became increasingly common, repeated in the writings of Ælfric and others. They are relevant in two ways: first, they date from, as already stated, after AD 1000 but, second, they also show that many superstitions met with in English lore are not late inventions created by medieval writers or even by the Victorians. However, is there any real indication of such superstitious practices ever having been actually carried out in early medieval England? (No attempt has been made here to try to distinguish between religion and superstition, which depends upon the beliefs of the individual.)

In the Celtic world, Christianity seems to have fitted much more easily into Nature. Early Irish verse relates how the hermit brother Marban loved to dwell in his 'bothy in the wood', noting the ash, hazel, yew, 'great green oak' and the apple, etc., that surrounded him (this poem is set in the seventh century but is likely to have been written in the tenth: Jackson, 1935). Even the Mercian hermit Guthlac, who is said to have chosen a desolate fenland wilderness for his hermitage, learnt to love his secret place within a wood, filled with birdsong (Gollancz, 1895). The

Orthodox Christian Church also had few problems incorporating the biblical version of the 'Tree of Life' into its continuing symbolism (Rhodin *et al.*, 2000) and tree symbolism continued to play a part in saints' *Lives* compiled after the harsher period of the eleventh-century reforms, noted above, even within the western European Catholic Church.

If Christianity was trying to eradicate what it regarded as unhealthy superstition concerning trees it seems to have been *nearly* successful, but was early Christianity really as hostile to nature as has been implied? The Bible is not without tree imagery – witness the Cedars of Lebanon that were thought of as 'God's tree' or the trees in the Garden of Eden. The trees in the Garden of Eden may have been associated with the fall of man, but within the new Jerusalem would also be 'the tree of life, which bare twelve manner of fruits, and yielded her fruit every month: and the leaves were for the healing of the nations' (Revelations 221–2). The Tree of Jesse, too, represented in Christian art from the eleventh century, depicted the descent of the Messiah.

Sacred tree symbolism in England: the early medieval and medieval evidence

Early place-name evidence may refer to an early sacred tree or pillar at Bampton in Oxfordshire (OE *bēam* with *tūn*) where a chapel surrounded by burials going back to the seventh century AD may infer something of the sort. Only one pre-Conquest English charter, however, explicitly refers to a non-Christian practice associated with a tree. In a charter boundary clause of Taunton estates in Somerset, allegedly of AD 854, there is a reference to a 'holy ash', but a twelfth-century manuscript translates this as 'an ash which the ignorant call holy' – perhaps the way this reference should be interpreted (Sawyer, 1968, S 254; B.L Add. 15350, fos. 27v–28, fos. 60v–61). The site seems to have been a place called Cat's Ash in Fitzhead parish close to the Quantock Hills. This is admittedly flimsy evidence and there are also a number of other references in pre-Conquest boundary clauses to 'holy' oaks. It has been suggested that a place-name Holyoaks in Stockerston, Leicestershire (*Haliach* 1086), in a region of Danish influence, may take its name from a tree once sacred to Þunor (a *Þureslege* or 'grove sacred to the god Þunor' is recorded in a nearby parish) and it is highly likely that this was an attempt to Christianise the feature – a medieval hermitage was also to be established close by (Cox, 2009, p. 251). It is unclear whether the other charter oaks described as 'holy' had any pagan antecedents. It is possible that these may have been merely oaks which carried a Christian cross to mark a boundary, but there is little indication as to why one particular species should be singled out or whether there was any special reason for just a few trees being described in this way (Hooke, 2010, p. 51). 'Gospel oaks' were not uncommon as markers on later parish boundaries, places where those perambulating the bounds at Rogationtide might pause and outline their parish boundary, perhaps also seeking a blessing for the land. In medieval times such a procession was virtually obligatory for all parishioners and was accompanied by the carrying of a church cross and banners, bell-ringing and feasting, but such adjuncts were severely curtailed by the Protestant Church in Elizabeth I's reign (Hutton, 1996, pp. 277–87).

Tree symbolism reappears in many Christian saints' *Lives*. The miracle of the flowering staff is a common motif (Loomis, 1948, pp. 94–6; Hooke, 2010, pp. 37–8). These may involve stories of a saint's staff turning into a tree and of these some are genuinely early: in the *Life* of St Kenelm, which was apparently composed in the middle of the eleventh century (Love, 1996, pp. xci–xciii), but may have drawn upon existing oral tradition, it was an ash that grew when the boy-king planted his staff in the ground before his murder in the woods. Additional tree symbolism is revealed in Kenelm's vision, experienced when he was a young child, of a tree blazing with 'countless lights and lamps', from the top of which he was able to 'see everything for miles around'. But he dreamed that a friend smote the tree so that it fell and that he himself turned into a white bird – thus predicting his death as recounted in the *Life*. The brightly lit tree here recalls that other 'glorious tree ... all bedecked with gold' described in the Anglo-Saxon poem, *The Dream of the Rood* (*Vercelli Book*: Krapp, 1932), which was, of course, the tree that had been chosen for Christ's crucifixion, cut down 'at the copse's end' for this purpose.

Many trees offer cures in early Herbals, such as the *Lacnunga* (*c*. 1000: Cockayne III, 1866) or *Bald's Leechbook* (Cockayne II, 1865), whether through their leaves or bark. It is the ash which seems most often to have been used for healing and it remained associated with healing throughout the centuries.

Neither was the veneration of springs entirely eradicated – several 'holy springs' are noted in Anglo-Saxon charter boundaries (Old English *wella, wiella, wylle*), especially in the south-west, but many springs were to be dedicated (or re-dedicated) to a Christian saint; saints' cults indeed proliferated in twelfth-century England when many such 'holy wells' may have been first recognised. Interestingly, many springs were associated with trees, such as St Hawthorn's Well on the Wrekin in Shropshire (Hope, 1893, p. 141) or Ashwell at Glastonbury (Rattue, 1995, p. 38). At Hope Bagot in Shropshire an ancient yew still overhangs the spring located within the churchyard. It is as if the tree was acting as the 'guardian' of the spring, perhaps augmenting its healing power. Certain trees may have been regarded as more effective than others in offering protection against adversity or danger.

The symbolism of particular tree species

One tree, in particular, seems to have found ready acceptance with the Christians of this country – the yew. Controversy surrounds the possible age of even our most venerable churchyard yews. There have been claims that some of the oldest of these pre-date the churches they stand by or may represent trees planted by the very first Christians at a site. Even such foundations themselves remain undated, for there is a growing argument that Roman Christianity may have survived in regions like the Welsh Borderland or the western parts of Midland England. There is no English documentary source confirming this, but Bevan-Jones (2002, pp. 45–6) claims that a charter of AD 684 (source not referenced) gives instructions to the builders of a church at Peronne in Picardy that a particular yew already growing on the site there should be preserved. The oldest yew tree in Britain appears to be that at Fortingall in Perthshire, again standing within a churchyard (Bevan-Jones concedes a date of 1500 years for this tree, although others have given much older estimates, even suggesting an age of 2000–3000 years: Bevan-Jones, 2002, pp. 38–9).

Unfortunately, pre-Conquest (i.e. early medieval) charters in England which might confirm the antiquity of some of the landmarks noted in any associated boundary clause normally concern whole estates, describing features that lay along their boundaries. Even where a grant or lease concerned only part of an estate the boundary is most unlikely to have cut through a churchyard, so that any existing churchyard yew would not have been noted in such a document. Yews do occur in the boundary clauses, but rarely in such a location (Hooke, 2010, pp. 210–1). The churchyard yews themselves are now often hollow, such as that at Much Marcle in Herefordshire (with a seat inside able to accommodate seven people) (Figure 21.1). Such trees would be difficult to date by scientific means even if this were allowed (dendrochronological dating methods might carry disease into the tree). As noted above, some have claimed an age of 1500–2000 years old for certain churchyard yews, suggesting that they may have marked early saints' cells (Bevan-Jones, 2002, p. 30). Their present size can even be deceptive: Bevan-Jones notes that the present state of the yew at Church Preen in Shropshire (Figure 21.2), now tightly bound, belies its true antiquity for the rotting fragments of the base of the old trunk are now barely visible at ground level and it may have had a girth of 12 m (40 ft) or more in the past, making it 'the largest ever recorded girth in Shropshire' (*ibid.*). In the twelfth century Giraldus Cambrensis wrote of the yews found in Ireland 'in old cemeteries and sacred places, where they were planted in ancient times by the hands of holy men, to give them what orna-ment and beauty they could' (Forester, 1891, p. 125). Even if the actual date of these trees remains debatable, the strength of their legendary association

Figure 21.1 Ancient yew tree beside the thirteenth-century church of St Bartholomew at Much Marcle, Herefordshire, showing the hollow trunk (© Della Hooke).

with churchyards was obviously established very early and was strong, especially in western England and Wales, and many yews have been protected by being in such a location.

It has been suggested that the acceptance of the yew by Christianity was because it was associated with regeneration and rebirth – interestingly, the yew is the only conifer that is able to regenerate itself when ruthlessly cut back. Others have suggested that the yew was planted in churchyards because it was the nearest British equivalent available to stand in for the biblical Cedars of Lebanon, 'God's tree'.

The ash remained associated with healing, but usually only in folklore and legend. A common tradition was that children passed through a deliberately made cleft in an ash tree might be protected from rickets or other weakness in the limbs, the cleft then being bound together after the ceremony. Interestingly, the bark, leaves and fruit of the ash are now known to possess medicinal properties – diuretic and purgative. Some trees were thought to offer protection against evil, among them the rowan and the holly. The oak, the tree of Zeus, Jupiter, Hercules and the elder Irish gods, also sacred to the ancient Hebrews, remained closely associated

Figure 21.2 Ancient yew tree beside the thirteenth-century church of St John the Baptist at Church Preen, Shropshire (© Della Hooke).

with Norse and Teutonic gods and has attracted much speculation, especially concerning the role of the 'oak-king', sometimes battling with the 'holly-king' for supremacy (Frazer, 1890ff; Graves, 1997, p. 172). The role of the oak as a marker tree in Anglo-Saxon England has been briefly noted above. This tree has, however, passed into English national consciousness as a symbol of strength and steadfastness.

But what of the 'bad' trees? The elder is said to have been abhorred because it was the tree from which Christ's cross was made – although elders do not grow in Palestine. Certainly in this country it was associated with witchcraft – an association which Wulfstan's writings show to have been genuinely old. Witches were thought to turn themselves into elder trees, which were sometimes cut by Christians to 'bleed' the witch. The legend lived on until recent times in the south-east Midlands and no baby's cradle would ever be made of elder wood or its occupant would surely pine away or be pinched black and blue by the fairies; no elder logs would be brought into the house or they would carry the Devil in with them. Yet the berries of the elder are now known to possess remarkable healing properties. There may be hidden undertones here if in folklore the tree was regarded by some as 'a feminine tree used for protection, healing, exorcism and prosperity' (Paterson, 1996, pp. 276–94). The association with female benevolence has indeed lingered on in some European countries – we find the 'elder mother', considered in folklore to dwell within the tree, granting remembrance in the tales of Hans Christian Andersen, and maidens requesting the elder to send them a husband in Slovenia (Mateja Šmid, personal commentary).

Tree symbolism: its later history

Tree symbolism continued to play a large part in British folklore throughout the centuries, but was perhaps strongest in Ireland where it appears to have been less ruthlessly suppressed. Here, however, spiritual power once associated with sacred trees or *bile* became demoted to tales associated with fairies, witches and suchlike, although here again some trees became associated with particular saints or continued to be regarded as 'guardian trees' on ecclesiastical sites (Lucas, 1963).

Apart from Christian symbolism it is, therefore, through folklore and legend that a sense of 'specialness' remained associated with trees in Britain. Indeed, removed from any sacred milieu they are found increasingly associated with outstanding secular personages – kings and queens, dukes and duchesses, etc. For the 'tree symbol' represented by the maypole, there is little certain evidence from Britain before the mid-fourteenth century when Gryffydd ap Ada ap Dafydd set up a tall birch tree for a pole at Llanidloes in central Wales as the centre of festivities, although by 1400 the custom was well established across southern Britain (but not in Scotland or Ireland beyond English-speaking areas: Hutton, 1996, p. 233). Such festivities would have taken place in the month of May, a time when May flowers and foliage (*Cretaegus monogyna*) were also brought in. Some have interpreted the maypole and the gathering of the May as symbols of fertility (with obvious sexual symbolism) but there appears to be little to confirm such a view and it may be that folk were simply 'rejoicing at the returning strength of vegetation' (Hutton, 1996, p. 234). The frivolity, sometimes associated with lax sexual practices, however, drew the scorn of the evangelical Protestants during the reign of Elizabeth I and festivities were increasingly banned until the more relaxed social atmosphere of the Restoration, flourishing again in a more acceptable version in the eighteenth and nineteenth centuries.

The practice of bringing greenery in at certain festivals to decorate the church was certainly widespread from an early date, even if this had been condemned by some of the founding fathers, and by the late Middle Ages was a custom practised throughout England. The holly and the ivy were commonly chosen but yew, box, mistletoe and herbs appear in seventeenth-century accounts (Hutton, 1996, p. 34). The holly, with its sharp spines and red berries, may have symbolised the crown of thorns and Christ's blood but was not, like the ivy, without echoes of earlier pagan symbolism (Mabey, 1998, pp. 218, 225–8). The tradition continues today and at Charlton-on-Otmoor, near Oxford, for instance, a large wooden cross known as 'The Garland', solidly covered in greenery, stands on the sixteenth-century roodscreen and is redecorated twice a year (including at the May Day celebrations) with a fresh garland of yew and box foliage (Nigel Cooper, personal communication).

Although Christianity, especially after the eleventh-century reforms, was not at ease with any belief in the *power* of trees or tree spirits, tree iconography continued to figure large in medieval writings and legend. By the eighteenth century travellers and painters alike were beginning to appreciate wild scenery as God's handiwork and, by the nineteenth century, Christians were increasingly 'at home' with Nature, able to see God in living things such as woods and mountains. An exponent of this view was John Muir, the Scottish-born American naturalist who was an early advocate of the conservation of the US wilderness, especially working to conserve the Yosemite Valley and Sequoia woodlands of the Californian Sierra. Seeing the presence of the Divine in wild nature, which included the vast and ancient forests that clothed the flanks of the mountains, he believed such beauty came straight from the hand of God, 'a vast display of God's power', and he found the wilderness a place for rest, inspiration and prayer (Muir, 1911, 1992, p. 238; Nash, 1967). Others followed Muir's way of thought and found they could commune directly with God in such places, experiencing the unity of Divine purpose and human insignificance that was particularly strongly felt in the vast expanses of the American wilderness (Cosgrove, 1984, p. 185).

It has taken even longer before people have been able to see the wonders of Nature without them necessarily being the work of a single creative God-figure. We recognise today that a healthy environment is essential for man's well-being and that man has a duty to preserve the balance of Nature. Beauty can uplift the soul, remove stress and renew optimism for the future – a sense of spirituality and of our own smallness is not so far removed from Christian faith.

Figure 21.3 Old oaks at Brocton on Cannock Chase, Staffordshire (© Della Hooke).

Conclusions

Today, conservation can call upon this empathy for Nature as never before, and within any number of faiths, helping to protect natural features such as certain animals, trees, etc., as well as wider landscapes. At best, we can transcend our more mundane preoccupations and question our real needs; the natural world can awaken this deep spirituality. Among other sites of spiritual significance, the unchanging 'solace' of a woodland setting is now often actively sought out for those seeking spiritual refreshment; woodlands are also sometimes seen as appropriate places for an ecologically sound burial. Some trees, such as the ash and yew, are now known to have effective medicinal properties. Even at a more basic level of landscape appreciation, we have a growing respect for trees: many are far older than many of our most treasured historic buildings (Figure 21.3). We know that trees can help to absorb pollution in cities, play a role in stabilising the climate, and generally play a role in humanity's sense of well-being. For many, then, the value of trees approaches a significantly spiritual role. Humankind is but a small part of this much wider world of Nature which we must cherish to ensure our future.

References

Barnwell, P. (2005). Anglian Yeavering: a continental perspective. In *Yeavering. People, Power and Place*, ed. P. Frodsham and C. O'Brien. Stroud: Tempus, pp. 174–84.

Bauschatz, P. C. (1982). *The Well and the Tree*. Amherst; UMI, Ann Arbor: University of Massachusetts Press.

Bevan-Jones, R. (2002). *The Ancient Yew*. Bollington: Windgather.

Blair, J. (2005). *The Church in Anglo-Saxon Society*. Oxford: Oxford University Press.

Cleal, R. M. J., Walker, K. E. and Montague, R. (1995). *Stonehenge in its Landscape: Twentieth Century Excavations*. London: English Heritage Report No. 10.

Cockayne, Revd O. (1864-6). *Leechdoms, Wortcunning and Starcraft of Early England*, 3 vols. London: Longman, Roberts and Green.

Cosgrove, D. (1984). *Social Formation and Symbolic Landscape*. London: Croom Helm.

Cox, B. (2009). *The Place-Names of Leicestershire, Part Four: Gartree Hundred*. English Place-Name Society 84. Nottingham: English Place-Name Society.

Crews, J. (2007). Forest and tree symbolism in folklore. Available from: http://www.the-tree.org.uk/Sacred%20Grove/Articles/F&TS/f&tsymbolism.htm

Faulkes, A. (trans. and ed.) (1987). Snorri Sturluson *Edda*. London: Dent.

Flint, V. I. J. (1936). *The Rise of Magic in Early Medieval Europe*. Reprinted 1991, Princeton, NJ: Princeton University Press.

Forester, T. (trans. and ed., revised T. Wright) (1891). *The Historical Works of Giraldus Cambrensis*. London.

Frazer, Sir J. G. (1890ff). *The Golden Bough*, 13 vols.; *The Illustrated Golden Bough*, illustrated abridgement by S. MacCormack. London: Rainbird, 1978.

Gollancz, I. (ed. and trans.) (1895). *The Exeter Book, an Anthology of Anglo-Saxon Poetry, Part 1*. Poems I–VIII, Early English Text Society 104. London.

Graves, R. (1997). *The White Goddess, A Historical Grammar of Poetic Myth*, ed. G. Lindop. Manchester: Carcanet.

Green, M. (1993). *Celtic Myths*. London: British Museum Press.

Hooke, D. (2010). *Trees in Anglo-Saxon England: Literature, Lore and Landscape*. Woodbridge: Boydell Press.

Hope, R. C. (1893). *The Legendary Lore of the Holy Wells of England*. London: Elliot Stock.

Hutton, R. (1996). *The Stations of the Sun*. Oxford: Oxford University Press.

Jackson, K. (1935). *Studies in Early Celtic Nature Poetry*. Cambridge: Cambridge University Press. Reprinted 1977, Philadelphia: Richard West.

Katha Upanishad, The Upanishads. Translation from the Sanskrit with an Introduction by Juan Mascaró (1965). London/Harmondsworth: Penguin.

Krapp, G. P. (ed.) (1932). *The Vercelli Book*. Anglo-Saxon Poetic Records 2. London: Routledge.

Loomis, C. G. (1948). *White Magic*. Cambridge, MA: The Mediaeval Academy of America.

Love, R. (1996). *Three Eleventh-Century Anglo-Latin Saints' Lives. Vita S. Birini, Vita et miracula S. Kenelmi and Vita S. Rumwoldi*. Oxford: Clarendon Press.

Lucas, A. T. (1963). The sacred trees of Ireland. *Journal of the Cork Historical and Archaeological Society*, **68**, 16–54.

Mabey, R. (1998). *Flora Britannica. The Concise Edition*. London: Chatto and Windus.

Muir, J. (1911). *My First Summer in the Sierra*. Boston. Reprinted with other works as *The Eight Wilderness-Discovery Books*, 1992. London: Diadem Books.

Nash, R. F. (1967). *Wilderness and the American Mind*. New Haven, CT: Yale University Press.

Neville, J. (1999). *Representations of the Natural World in Old English Poetry*. Cambridge: Cambridge University Press.

Ó hÓgain, D. (1999). *The Sacred Isle. Belief and Religion in Pre-Christian Ireland*. Woodbridge: Boydell Press.

Paterson, J. M. (1996). *Tree Wisdom*. London and San Francisco: Thorsons.

Pitts, M. (2001). Excavating the Sanctuary: new investigations on Overton Hill, Avebury. *Wiltshire Archaeological and Natural History Magazine*, **94**, 1–23.

Pryor, F. (2001). *Seahenge. New Discoveries in Prehistoric Britain*. London: HarperCollins.

Rattue, J. (1995). *The Living Stream. Holy Wells in Historical Context*. Woodbridge: Boydell Press.

Rhodin, L., Gren, L. and Lindblom, V. (2000). Liljestenarna och Sveriges kristnande från Bysans. *Fornvännen*, **95**, 165–81.

Sawyer, P. H. (1968). *Anglo-Saxon Charters, an Annotated List and Bibliography*. London: Royal Historical Society.

Semple, S. (2004). Locations of assembly in early Anglo-Saxon England. In *Assembly Places and Practices in Medieval Europe*, ed. A. Pantos and S. Semple. Dublin: Four Courts Press, pp. 135–54.

Skeat, W. W. (ed.) (1890). *Ælfric's Lives of the Saints*, Vol. 2. Early English Text Society, Original Series 94. London.

Talbot, C. H. (ed. and trans.) (1954). *The Anglo-Saxon Missionaries in Germany*. London and New York: Sheed and Ward.

22

Sacred groves and biodiversity conservation: a case study from the Western Ghats, India

SHONIL A. BHAGWAT

Introduction

Sacred natural sites provide an apparatus for biodiversity conservation that enjoys support from local people. In addition to their cultural and spiritual significance to local people, such sites protect habitats and species that are excluded from formal protected area networks. Sacred forest groves are patches of forest that support forest-dwelling species within non-forest matrix. The focus of this chapter is particularly on sacred forest groves in the Western Ghats of India. While a network of such groves can contribute to landscape-scale conservation of biodiversity, the quality of the landscape matrix itself is important. In order to maintain the tree-covered matrix around sacred forest groves, local people's support is essential. Although sacred natural sites face challenges due to their uncertain legal ownership and changing religious and cultural values, they have the potential for biodiversity conservation because of their widespread presence across the world. I suggest that the continued conservation of sacred natural sites will require an understanding of their spatial extent, long-term approach to their management, and raising their profile to attract more conservation funding.

Sacred natural sites, protected by local people for their cultural and spiritual values, have often escaped ecological changes in the landscape surrounding them, thereby preserving elements of local and regional biodiversity. While religious places of worship – churches, mosques, temples – are also sacred sites, the definition of sacred sites adopted in this chapter is limited to 'natural' sites (IUCN, 2005). In this chapter I will focus particularly on sacred forest groves in the Western Ghats

Sacred Species and Sites: Advances in Biocultural Conservation, ed. Gloria Pungetti, Gonzalo Oviedo and Della Hooke. Published by Cambridge University Press. © Cambridge University Press 2012.

of India and discuss the importance of local communities in their management. While protected areas are considered cornerstones of biodiversity conservation, I will argue that sacred natural sites offer an alternative, but important, approach and can play a considerable role in the conservation of biodiversity.

Over 12% of the Earth's land surface is covered by protected areas today (UNEP-WCMC, 2005). These areas offer protection to 12% of the world's forests (FAO, 2007). This leaves a large proportion of forest land outside protected areas (World Conservation Union [IUCN] categories I–IV). Protected areas themselves face two major shortcomings. First, they cannot offer protection to all habitats and species. For example, in the Western Ghats of India protected areas cover mountains, but low-lying areas are excluded from protection (Ramesh et al., 1997). Second, protected areas are often resented by local people. There are many instances of 'encroachments' by local people on protected areas (Brandon et al., 1998). This demands an approach to conservation that covers landscapes outside protected areas, but one that is also welcomed by local people. Natural sacred sites provide such an approach by covering habitats and species outside protected areas, while enjoying local support (Bhagwat and Rutte, 2006).

Biodiversity in sacred sites

In a review of the published literature, Bhagwat and Rutte (2006) came across sacred sites in 33 countries, representing 10 different habitats from marshes to mountains and riparian forests to lakes (Figure 22. 1, Table 22.1). Furthermore, this was only a small sample of all sacred sites, many of which still remain undocumented. It has been suggested that 11 of the world's major religions cover over 7% of the Earth's land surface (ARC, 2007). Many of the sacred sites documented in studies reviewed by Bhagwat and Rutte (2006) belong to the less well-known faiths. One can therefore argue that sacred sites, in combination with the land owned by the world's major religions, cover a considerable proportion of the Earth's land surface and have substantial potential for biodiversity conservation.

As the examples reviewed above also suggest, sacred sites cover a wide variety of habitats and protect many species in landscapes outside protected areas (Bhagwat and Rutte, 2006). For example, sacred forest groves in the coastal part of Karnataka state in India protect swamps inhabited by a species of nutmeg, *Myristica fatua*. The surveys suggest that this species is exclusively found in coastal swamps and is outside the boundaries of the protected areas in the region, all of which cover mountain habitat (Chandran and Mesta, 2001). In Kodagu district of the Western Ghats of India, sacred groves were found to protect threatened tree species such as *Actinodaphne lawsonii*, *Hopea ponga*, *Madhuca neriifoli* and *Syzygium zeylanicum*, which are not found within protected areas (Bhagwat et al., 2005a).

Table 22.1 *Natural sacred sites protect a wide variety of habitats in 33 countries represented in a literature review conducted by Bhagwat and Rutte (2006).*

Habitat protected	Countries represented
Coastal	Australia, Guinea-Bissau, Japan, Togo
Cultivated	Indonesia, Mexico
Forest	Benin, China, Egypt, Ghana, India, Indonesia, Madagascar, Sierra-Leone
Garden	New Zealand, USA, Europe
Lakes	Egypt, India, Kenya, South Africa
Mixed landscape	Canada, Guatemala, India, Mexico, Spain, UK, USA
Montane	Chile, China, France, Greece, India, Italy, Kazakhstan, Nepal, Peru, Russia, UK, USA, European, Global
Riparian	Canada, India
Savanna	Ghana, South Africa, USA
Woodlots	Ghana, India, Israel, Senegal, Tanzania

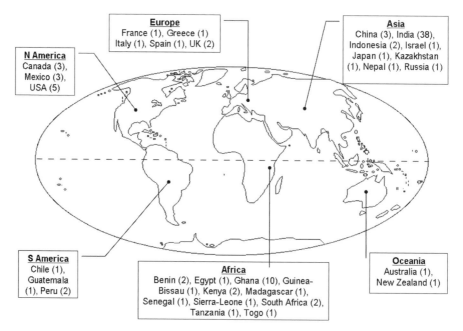

Figure 22.1 Natural sacred sites are found on all continents except Antarctica according to a review conducted by Bhagwat and Rutte (2006). The examples come from 33 different countries – 3 each from North and South America; 5 from Europe; 12 from Africa; 8 from Asia and 2 from Oceania. Numbers in parentheses following the name of each country indicate the total number of examples from that country. In addition to these examples, three others – two from Europe and one from the whole world – represented more than one country and are not shown.

The Western Ghats of India

The Kodagu district of Karnataka State in the Western Ghats of India extends between 11°56′–12°52′ N and 75°22′–76°11′ E. The formal network of protected areas (the forest reserve) in the region consists of three wildlife sanctuaries and one national park, which stretch continuously along the western and the south-western boundaries of the district, occupying about 30% of the area. Plantations of shade-grown coffee occupy much of the remaining landscape (about 60%). Here, coffee bushes are grown beneath a high tree canopy to shade the plantations. Approximately 8% of the total area is occupied by treeless land uses, such as paddy cultivation. The region has a high density of sacred groves – one grove in every 300 ha. These groves range in size from a fraction of a hectare to a few tens of hectares, and are often surrounded by shade-grown coffee cultivation. Sacred groves occupy only about 2% of the area.

Sacred groves within a landscape matrix

Ecological theory states that patches of forest that are fragmented lose species and have low biodiversity, suggesting that such patches have limited value for biodiversity conservation (Hill and Curran, 2001). However, a network of patches is known to support higher biodiversity than a single patch alone (Tabarelli and Gascon, 2005). Furthermore, if the patches are connected by corridors, they can potentially support even higher numbers of species (Wadley and Colfer, 2004). In the Kodagu district of the Western Ghats of India, more than 1200 sacred forest groves form an informal network of reserves with one grove for every 300 ha of land (Bhagwat *et al.*, 2005b). Interspersed between these patches are coffee plantations which support native trees kept in plantations for shade. In one of very few systematic inventories of tree species diversity in sacred forest groves, Bhagwat *et al.* (2005a, 2005b) compared tree diversity within sacred groves with that of sites in adjacent forest reserve (protected area) and coffee plantations. There was no significant difference in tree diversity across the three land-use types (Figure 22.2) and nearly half of the total tree species were shared among the three land-use types (Figure 22.3).

The conservation of sacred groves, therefore, is integrated within the surrounding landscape matrix (Figure 22.4). The presence of trees in the coffee agro-forestry matrix in Kodagu has been instrumental in protecting forest-dwelling biodiversity within groves. This is because the tree-covered nature of the matrix means that the patches are no longer fragmented (Bhagwat *et al.*, 2005b). Protection to the tree-covered matrix would require support from local communities, particularly coffee planters (Figure 22.5). While the local communities respect the 'spiritual

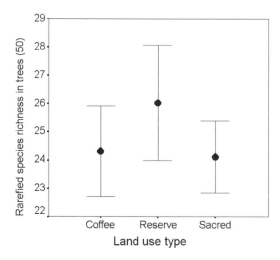

Figure 22.2 There was no significant difference in tree diversity across the three land-use types, namely forest reserves, sacred groves and coffee plantations in Kodagu, Western Ghats, India, according to Bhagwat *et al.* (2005b).

Total tree species: 215

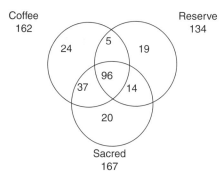

Figure 22.3 Nearly half of the total species were shared between forest reserves, sacred groves and coffee plantations in Kodagu, Western Ghats, India, according to Bhagwat *et al.* (2005a).

fence' around sacred groves, it is necessary that they also realise the importance of keeping native trees in their own plantations.

Community values of sacred grove conservation

It is believed that the tradition of sacred grove conservation began when settled agriculture started (Hughes and Chandran, 1998). The motivation behind

Figure 22.4 Sacred forest groves are patches of forest that support forest-dwelling species within non-forest landscape matrix (© Shonil Bhagwat).

keeping patches of forest may have been the ecological services that such patches provided. These include conservation of the soil and maintaining watersheds, as well as the provision of forest products. The communities may have protected groves in honour of pagan gods, animistic deities or ancestral spirits (Kosambi, 1962). In India, many of these original gods, deities and spirits underwent transformation over the years into mainstream gods and goddesses, although the tradition of conserving patches of forest has been kept up until the present day (Chandrakanth *et al.*, 2004). Traditional forest conservation practices are seen in today's society in various forms. One example comes from the Udaipur district of Rajasthan state in north-west India. The sprinkling of saffron water around a piece of land is a common practice in this area (Gandhi, 1997). The attempts of the local forest department to conserve an area of forest at a site near Udaipur were largely unsuccessful because of persistent transgressions by local people. Frustrated, the forest officers decided to sprinkle saffron water around the site, in accordance with the local tradition. This was greeted with enthusiasm by the local people and, since then, the local people have started to respect the boundaries of the conservation area (Gandhi, 1997).

Figure 22.5 In order to maintain tree-covered landscape matrix around sacred forest groves, local people's support is essential (© Shonil Bhagwat).

In order to continue the protection of sacred groves it is important, then, to consider and respect community values behind such conservation (Figure 22.6). This approach to conservation is very different to that of maintaining formal protected area networks. While formal protection is bound by legal framework, informal conservation traditions are governed by customs and taboos (Colding and Folke, 2001). The conservationists – scientists, practitioners and policy-makers – must recognise this. In recent years, integrated conservation and development

Figure 22.6 Although many sacred groves in Kodagu, Western Ghats of India, are still well preserved, conservation action needs to be taken to prevent their destruction due to changing religious and cultural values (© Shonil Bhagwat).

programmes (ICDPs) have gained popularity because they provide a basis upon which to achieve biodiversity conservation and community development simultaneously (Brandon *et al.*, 1998). However, the acceptability of such programmes among local people is questionable. An approach that is sensitive to local peoples' traditions, such as sacred grove conservation, is likely to work better than an approach that alienates local people. This is important for successful conservation programmes. Sacred natural sites are not only cultural monuments but they are also conservation vehicles and form an important apparatus in conservationists' 'tool kit'.

Challenges for sacred grove conservation

There are, however, challenges in the conservation of sacred groves that must be addressed.

First, the legal ownership of many sacred groves is still uncertain (Chandrakanth *et al.*, 2004). In Kodagu, for example, the sacred groves are owned by the forest department and managed by village temple committees. However, historically, there have been changes in the ownership of sacred groves. As a result, their management has not been consistent. This has led to confusion about their status among stakeholders. Furthermore, people are not motivated to conserve land that does not belong to them. Hardin's (1968) tragedy of the commons is very well known. Government ownership, therefore, can cause alienation of local people from their groves.

Second, a change in the society's structure and composition, as well as in economic status and religious values, poses another challenge. In Kodagu, for example, increasing urbanisation has caused dilution of religious and cultural values, often leading to the desecration of sacred groves (Kalam, 1996). In some cases, the neighbouring landowners have encroached upon groves to expand their plantations. Urbanisation has also led to the movement of rural dwellers to the cities. At the same time, immigrant plantation workers have settled into the district as permanent residents. The immigrants often do not share the same cultural and spiritual values that local people have concerning sacred groves. In some cases, this has led to further desecration of sacred groves by clearance of the forest for immigrant settlements (Bonn, 2000). While it may not be possible to reverse the immigration pattern, it may be possible to establish certain safeguards against the desecration of sacred groves. This is where the local communities and government machinery need to operate together.

The future of sacred natural sites

The lessons learnt from research on sacred groves have wider applicability to biodiversity conservation and the management of other sacred natural sites. There are a number of issues that need to be addressed for continued conservation of sacred natural sites in the future.

Spatial extent

It is important to understand the exact spatial extent of sacred natural sites across the globe (Figure 22.7). Although it is known that the 11 major faiths of the world own over 7% of the Earth's land surface, the extent of land owned or managed by minor faiths is unknown. This needs to be estimated urgently, in addition to the numbers of sacred natural sites. Recent estimates of numbers in India suggest that there are between 100 000 and 150 000 sacred groves (Malhotra et al., 2001) covering about 1% of the land. Similar estimates need to be made for other countries as a starting point. Geographical information systems can be employed for a more complete enumeration of sacred natural sites and an estimate of their extent.

Figure 22.7 Continued conservation of sacred groves will require an understanding of their spatial extent (© Shonil Bhagwat).

Long-term approach

Many sacred natural sites have a long history of conservation (e.g. the iconic sacred site of Machu Picchu since the pre-Columbian era) while protected areas are relatively recent (e.g. Yellowstone National Park since 1872). This demands a long-term approach to the conservation and management of sacred natural sites. Conservation managers need to establish the baseline conditions at those sites on which to base management principles (Willis and Birks, 2006). It must be recognised that what is seen in today's landscape is only a 'snap-shot' of what might have been there yesterday. Long-term ecological records, such as those from fossilised pollen grains and plant parts as well as charcoal, can throw light on past vegetation at sacred natural sites. Such data need to be used to inform the management of these sites.

Conservation funding

The profile of sacred natural sites and their role in conservation needs to be raised internationally. This will help attract conservation funding for their upkeep and maintenance. Conservation Internationals' Biodiversity Hotspots programme has proved successful over the last decade in setting priorities for conservation and attracting and consolidating conservation funding (CI, 2007). The conservation community interested in sacred natural sites needs to follow an effective approach for reaching the international media. The successful conservation and management of sacred natural sites will not only need their recognition on international fora, but also awareness at all levels and substantial conservation funding.

Conclusions

In conclusion, sacred natural sites present an alternative view of conservation that is led more by norms and taboos than by formal legal frameworks. They cover a substantial land surface of the Earth and hold considerable potential for biodiversity conservation. Such sites offer protection to habitats and species that are excluded from formally protected areas. This approach to conservation has found greater acceptance among local people than formally protected areas. However, sacred natural sites face a number of challenges that need to be addressed. A greater sensitivity towards these conservation traditions is necessary, as well as a long-term approach to their management. Effective conservation management of sacred natural sites will require raising their profile on the international fora in order to attract conservation funding.

References

ARC. (2007). Alliance of Religions and Conservation. Available from: http://www.arcworld.org/ (accessed October 2007).

Bhagwat, S. A., Kushalappa, C. G., Williams, P. H., *et al.* (2005a). The role of informal protected areas in maintaining biodiversity in the western Ghats of India. *Ecology and Society*, **10**, 8. Available from: www.ecologyandsociety.org/vol10/iss1/art8/ (accessed October 2007).

Bhagwat, S. A, Kushalappa, C. G., Williams, P. H., *et al.* (2005b). A landscape approach to biodiversity conservation of sacred groves in the western Ghats of India. *Conservation Biology*, **19**, 1853–62.

Bhagwat, S. A. and Rutte, C. (2006). Sacred groves: potential for biodiversity management. *Frontiers in Ecology and the Environment*, **10**, 519–24.

Bonn, E. (2000). An economic framework to land extensification. In *Mountain Biodiversity, Land Use Dynamics, and Traditional Knowledge. Man and the Biosphere Programme*, ed. P. S. Ramakrishnan, U. M. Chandrashekara, C. Elouard, *et al.* New Delhi: Oxford and India Book House.

Brandon, K., Redford, K. H. and Sanderson, S. E. (1998). *Parks in Peril: People, Politics and Protected Areas*. Washington, DC: The Nature Conservancy and Island Press.

Chandrakanth, M. G., Bhat, M. G. and Accavva, M. S. (2004). Socio-economic changes and sacred groves in south India: protecting a community-based resource management institution. *Natural Resources Forum*, **28**, 102–11.

Chandran, M. D. S. and Mesta, D. (2001). On the conservation of the Myristica swamps of the Western Ghats. In *Forest Genetic Resources: Status, Threats, and Conservation Strategies*, ed. U. R. Shaanker, K. N. Ganeshaiah and K. S. Bawa. New Delhi: Oxford and India Book House.

CI. (2007). Conservation International Biodiversity Hotspots. Available from: http://www.biodiversityhotspots.org (accessed October 2007).

Colding, J. and Folke, C. (2001). Social taboos: 'invisible' systems of local resource management and biological conservation. *Ecological Applications*, **11**, 584–600.

FAO. (2007). State of the World's Forests Food and Agriculture Organisation of the United Nations. Available from: http://www.fao.org/docrep/009/a0773e/a0773e00.htm (accessed October 2007).

Gandhi, K. (1997). Kesar Chirkav: traditional system of forest protection. Newsletter, Sevamandir. Udaipur. Available from: http://www.sevamandir.org/Newsletter.htm (accessed October 2007).

Hardin, G. (1968). The tragedy of the commons. *Science*, **162**, 1243–8.

Hill, J. L. and Curran, P. J. (2001). Species composition in fragmented forests: conservation implications of changing forest area. *Applied Geography*, **21**, 157–74.

Hughes, J. D. and Chandran, M. D. S. (1998). Sacred groves around the earth: an overview. In *Conserving the Sacred for Biodiversity Management*, ed. P. S. Ramakrishnan, K. G. Saxena and U. M. Chandrashekara. New Delhi: Oxford and India Book House.

IUCN. (2005). IUCN. The World Conservation Union Protecting the Sacred Natural sites of the World. Available from: http://www.iucn.org/themes/spg/themes_sacredsites.html (accessed October 2007).

Kalam, M. A. (1996). *Sacred Groves in Kodagu District of Karnataka (South India): A Sociohistorical Study*. Pondicherry: Institut Français de Pondicherry.

Kosambi, D. D. (1962). *Myth and Reality: Studies in the Formation of Indian Culture*. Bombay: Popular Press.

Malhotra, K. C., Gokhale, Y. and Chatterjee, S. (2001). *Cultural and Ecological Dimensions of Sacred Groves in India*. New Delhi and Bhopal: Indian National Science Academy and the Indira Gandhi Rashtriya Manav Sangrahalaya.

Ramesh, B. R., Menon, S. and Bawa, K. S. (1997). A vegetation based approach to biodiversity gap analysis in the Agastyamalai region, Western Ghats, India. *Ambio*, **26**, 529–36.

Tabarelli, M. and Gascon, C. (2005). Lessons from fragmentation research: improving management and policy guidelines for biodiversity conservation. *Conservation Biology*, **19**, 734–9.

UNEP-WCMC. (2005). World database on protected areas. Available from: http://
www.unep-wcmc.org/wdpa/ (accessed October 2007).

Wadley, R. L. and Colfer, C. J. P. (2004). Sacred forest, hunting, and conservation in
West Kalimantan, Indonesia. *Human Ecology*, **32**, 313–38.

Willis, K. J. and Birks, H. J. B. (2006). What is natural? The need for a long-term
perspective in biodiversity conservation. *Science*, **314**, 1261–5.

23

Cultural and conservation values of sacred forests in Ghana

ALISON ORMSBY

Introduction

Sacred sites, including sacred forests or sacred groves, are sites that have local cultural or spiritual significance. Sacred forests have been protected around the world for a variety of reasons, including for religious practices or ceremonies, as burial grounds, and for their watershed value (Castro, 1990; Dorm-Adzobu *et al.*, 1991; Lebbie and Freudenberger, 1996; Tiwari *et al.*, 1998; Chouin, 2002; Greene, 2002). There are often myths associated with sacred sites and taboos pertaining to the use of plants and the hunting of animals within the area. The size of groves varies greatly from very small plots (less than 1 ha) to larger tracts of several thousand hectares (Ntiamoa-Baidu, 1995).

Many places in the world have sacred natural sites, but certain countries stand out for the number and age of sites, specifically Ghana and India. Ghana, with over 1900 sacred groves, has a long history of community protection of sacred sites for cultural reasons (Ntiamoa-Baidu, 1995). These sites are commonly referred to as fetish groves and may contain a shrine or serve as burial grounds (Amoako-Atta, 1995). Local residents often believe that these forests are inhabited by ancestor spirits or a god.

Some sacred sites in Ghana, such as Boabeng–Fiema Monkey Sanctuary, are officially protected sites, but the majority of sites are culturally protected lands and vulnerable to the changing values and practices of the people living around them. Taboos on the hunting of particular species, such as certain primates, offer a form of protection from the harvest of wild meat for personal consumption or the bushmeat trade (Ntiamoa-Baidu, 1987; Lingard *et al.*, 2003). Many sacred groves

Sacred Species and Sites: Advances in Biocultural Conservation, ed. Gloria Pungetti, Gonzalo Oviedo and Della Hooke. Published by Cambridge University Press. © Cambridge University Press 2012.

Figure 23.1 Location of research sites.

are the only remaining fragments of intact forest habitat, surrounded by farms, pasture and houses, and may therefore serve an important role in biodiversity conservation (Campbell, 2005). Pressures on these forest remnants include farming, bushfires, plant and wood collection, and hunting. Both sites of this study protect monkeys, but other sacred sites in Ghana protect other species, such as the sacred crocodiles of Paga in Northern Ghana (Pleydell, 2005).

This research investigated whether traditional forest protection for cultural reasons might support a broader agenda for biodiversity conservation in Ghana. In addition, the research aimed to compare and contrast the effectiveness of community-based conservation with government management.

Figure 23.2 Mona monkey at Tafi Atome Monkey Sanctuary (© Michael Scace). See colour plate section.

Research was conducted at two sacred groves in Ghana: Tafi Atome Monkey Sanctuary and Boabeng–Fiema Monkey Sanctuary (Figure 23.1). Both sanctuaries are in a savannah woodland ecosystem type with dry, semi-deciduous forest (Fargey, 1992; Gocking, 2005). Tafi Atome is a village with over 1000 residents located on the eastern side of Lake Volta in the Volta region. Residents speak Ewe. Tafi Atome Monkey Sanctuary (TAMS) was officially established as a tourism site in 1996 to protect the subspecies of true mona monkeys (*Cercopithecus mona mona*) living there (Figure 23.2). The sanctuary is approximately 28 ha in size and is run by a community Tourism Management Committee which employs four local guides and a gift shop manager.

Boabeng–Fiema Monkey Sanctuary (BFMS) is located in the Brong-Ahafo region. There are discrepancies in the cited size of the sanctuary. According to Fargey (1992), the core forested sanctuary area is 36 ha. Saj *et al.* (2006) say the core sanctuary covers 190 ha and the larger forest is 500 ha, which is consistent with Densu (2003), who says the sanctuary is 450 ha. The larger, official sanctuary includes forest fragments in a farm matrix around the core area (Campbell, 2004). The sanctuary is named after two villages, Boabeng and Fiema, which both have associated sacred forests. Residents speak Twi. The population of Boabeng is approximately 1000 and that of Fiema is 1800. BMFS was legally recognised in 1975 to protect two species of primates, black and white colobus monkeys (*Colobus vellerosus*) (Figure 23.3) and Campbell's mona monkey (*Cercopithecus campbelli lowei*). The sanctuary is managed by employees of Ghana's Wildlife Division: an officer-in-charge,

Figure 23.3 Black and white colobus monkeys at Boabeng–Fiema Monkey Sanctuary (© Alison Ormsby).

a wildlife officer, a technical assistant and a sanctuary guide. There is also a community Sanctuary Management Committee that employs an additional sanctuary guide.

Methods

Semi-structured, open-ended interviews were conducted with residents of three communities near sacred groves to investigate:

(1)   the history of each sacred site;
(2)   the purposes for the protection of the sacred site;
(3)   the taboos relating to the grove; and
(4)   the grove management techniques.

A qualitative, ethnographic research approach was used, including interviews, participant observation, and focus groups (Bernard, 1988; Creswell, 1994; Krueger, 1994; Weiss, 1994; Morgan, 1997).

During June and July 2006, working with a local translator, 33 residents of Tafi Atome (17 men and 16 women) were interviewed. A group interview was conducted with the Tafi Atome Tourism Management Committee during and at the end of the research period to offer feedback. In addition, using the approach of participant observation, guides were viewed interacting with tourists at both research sites. A stratified sampling method (by clan) was used for interviews. In

Tafi Atome, residents generally live near their family members or clan group. An attempt was made to include in the research sample representatives of each clan and a nearly equal number of men and women.

In July and August 2006, 26 residents of Boabeng (15 men and 11 women) and 29 residents of Fiema (13 men and 16 women) were interviewed. The villages of Boabeng and Fiema are not geographically organised by clan; however, an attempt was made to interview representatives of each of the approximately eight clans in Boabeng and approximately 11 clans in Fiema. In all locations, key community members were interviewed, such as Tourism Committee members, elected officials, sanctuary employees, storeowners and religious leaders.

Results

The two research sites have contrasting management approaches and community dynamics. Boabeng–Fiema Monkey Sanctuary is older, established in 1975, whereas Tafi Atome Monkey Sanctuary was more recently established, in 1996. BFMS is government-managed and protected by a national 1975 law that prohibits the killing of monkeys and setting of fire within the sanctuary, whereas TAMS is community-managed and protected by a recent (2006) Hohoe District bylaw that forbids tree cutting, farming and hunting within the sanctuary.

Tafi Atome Monkey Sanctuary

In Tafi Atome, 33 residents were interviewed, ranging from 19 to 85 years of age. Of residents interviewed, 60.6% were born and raised in the village.

According to residents interviewed about the history of the sacred grove, approximately 200 years ago the ancestors of the residents of the Tafi Atome area migrated from Assini in central Ghana. They brought with them an idol or fetish that was placed in the sacred forest in Tafi Atome in order to keep it safe. The mona monkeys of the forest are associated with the fetish. The fetish priest of Tafi Atome acts as messenger between the village residents and the idol. Because the monkeys are associated with the idol and are sacred, it is taboo to kill them. A festival to celebrate the monkeys takes place every February, managed by the fetish priest who kills a goat and pours libations at the forest shrine.

Due to the influence of a Christian pastor in the 1980s, the tradition of protecting the monkeys was weakened and the monkeys were hunted by some of the village residents. In 1996, a representative from an Accra-based environmental organisation, the Nature Conservation Research Centre (NCRC), met with village representatives to discuss the ecotourism and conservation potential of the sacred forest. NCRC particularly stressed that the site is unique in being home to true

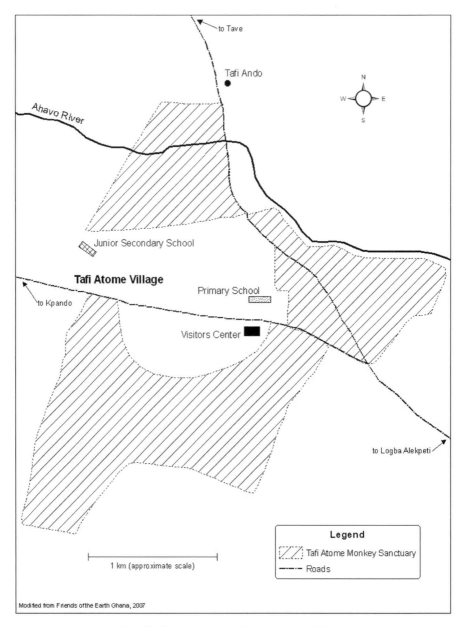

Figure 23.4 Map of Tafi Atome Monkey Sanctuary and village.

mona monkeys (*Cercopithecus mona mona*), the only intact population of this sub-species remaining in Ghana. There are numerous walking trails that traverse the sanctuary and residents use these as routes to access their farms. The core fetish grove, however, does not have clear trail access and entry is forbidden except by select persons during festival events.

Residents were asked what they believed was the purpose of the protection of the grove. The majority of respondents stated that the grove is protected for the monkeys as well as for the fetish shrine. As one Tafi Atome resident said, the grove is 'for the monkeys to live there and people can come watch the monkeys'. In addition, several residents mentioned the value that the grove serves as a windbreak and protection from storms, because the grove surrounds and shelters the village (Figure 23.4). A male Tafi Atome resident described how 'the forest is there for the monkeys. It buffers against rain and wind, protecting against storms that may hurt roofs'.

When asked about tourism, 51.5% of respondents said that they personally benefit in ways that ranged from direct employment as a guide to shop owners who sell to tourists and parents whose children's school fees are paid by visitors to the sanctuary. Tafi Atome received approximately 2850 visitors in 2005: 1820 foreign and 1030 Ghanaian. Some revenues from tourism at Tafi Atome are shared with the community; quarterly revenues are calculated and posted in the sanctuary Visitors Centre.

Interviewees were asked to explain the taboos associated with the grove. The two main activities identified as forbidden in the grove are tree cutting and hunting monkeys, both mentioned by 54.5% of respondents. Prohibition on entering the sacred fetish grove was noted by 36.4% of respondents. A taboo on collecting firewood was mentioned by 21.1% of respondents and farming was identified by 12.1% of interviewees as an activity not allowed in the grove. Interviewees were asked to try to imagine that there was no taboo on hunting monkeys. In the absence of a taboo, still only 18.2% of respondents said they would hunt monkeys.

There are two tree nursery projects underway in association with the sanctuary. A survey of plants within the sanctuary found that the flamboyant tree (*Delonix regia*) is the dominant species in several parts of the grove (Symon, 2006, unpublished data). This species is raised in the tree nursery and planted because it is a favoured food of the monkeys.

Residents were asked for their suggestions on what should happen to the grove in the future. To this open-ended question, respondents gave a wide range of answers, from forest expansion to creating a fence around the forest, which varied compared to the responses from Boabeng and Fiema to the same question (Figure 23.5). Currently, the area surrounding the Tafi Atome grove is primarily farmland or teak plantation.

Boabeng–Fiema Monkey Sanctuary

A total of 55 people in the Boabeng–Fiema area were interviewed, 26 residents in Boabeng and 21 residents in Fiema, ranging from 16 to nearly

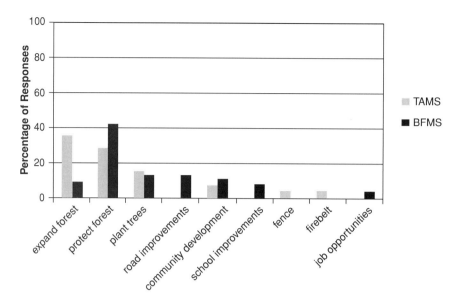

Figure 23.5 Residents' opinions of future initiatives regarding the grove.

100 years of age. The majority of residents interviewed (67.3%) were born and raised in their home village.

The core forested area of the Boabeng–Fiema Monkey Sanctuary has a well-developed trail system for use by tourists as well as researchers (Figure 23.6). The Boabeng grove contains its own sacred area, where ceremonies and rituals are performed. Both Boabeng and Fiema have separate annual yam festivals that also celebrate the monkeys, although according to some interviewees the intensity of the festivals has diminished in recent years.

Residents interviewed told a range of stories about how the monkeys came to exist in the sacred forests as well as their association with local gods. The black and white colobus monkeys are associated with a male god, Abudwo, at Fiema and the mona monkeys with a female god, Daworo, at Boabeng. According to Boabeng residents, about 200 years ago a hunter was searching for a water source and saw the forest near what is now Boabeng. In the forest, the hunter discovered a shrine – a brass pan covered with a white cloth. It was guarded by two mona monkeys and two black and white colobus monkeys. The monkeys belong to the shrine and are therefore sacred animals. It is believed that the current monkeys in the sanctuary are the offspring of Daworo and Abudwo.

According to a Queen Mother from Fiema, elders came from the Ashanti Region with a god named Abudwo. The black and white colobus monkeys followed the god and settled near Fiema. The god's shrine was put in a small forest near the village (Figure 23.7) and the Abudwo Chief guarded the shrine. Every week on Wednesday,

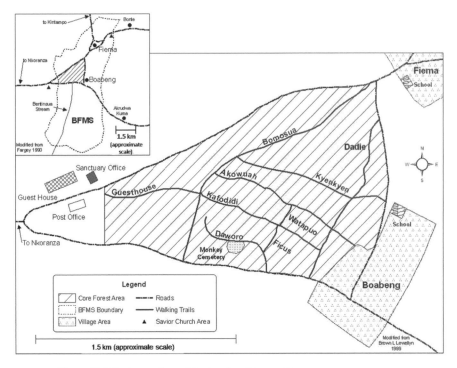

Figure 23.6 Boabeng–Fiema Monkey Sanctuary area.

Figure 23.7 Sacred forest in Fiema (© Alison Ormsby).

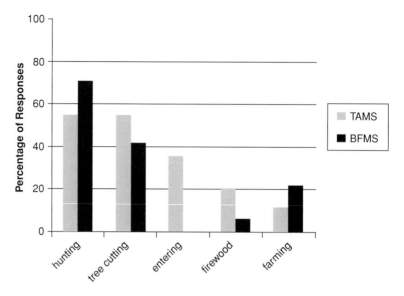

Figure 23.8 Reported taboos at sacred forests.

the Chief went to the shrine to pour libation and make sacrifice. Thus, there is a taboo in Fiema that forbids farming on Wednesdays.

Interviewees corroborated documented history that, in the 1970s, a local leader from the Savior Church said it was acceptable to kill the monkeys in the Boabeng and Fiema area. In reaction to increased hunting, some community members requested outside assistance, which led to the official government protection of the sanctuary in 1975 (Fargey, 1992; Saj et al., 2006).

Residents were asked why the forest is protected. The main reasons given were for the monkeys and for tourism. As one respondent from Boabeng said, 'When the forest is no more, the monkeys will run away. The place will turn into grassland'. Several other reasons for forest protection were given, including avoiding bushfires, the value of the forest as a windbreak and source of medicinal plants, community development (e.g. road, school, and clinic improvements), income, scientific research, future generations and local pride. As a resident expressed: the sanctuary 'serves as history for people – so young people can compare good forest to a degraded one'.

Interviewees were asked to explain the taboos associated with the grove. The main activities that residents clearly identified as forbidden are hunting monkeys and tree cutting, mentioned by 70.9% and 41.8% of respondents, respectively (Figure 23.8). Notably, prohibition on entering the sacred grove (idol shrine area) was not mentioned by any of the residents interviewed. A taboo on collecting firewood was mentioned by 5.5% of respondents and farming within the grove was identified by 21.8% of those interviewed as not allowed in the grove. Residents in Boabeng and Fiema were asked to imagine the situation if there were no taboo on hunting monkeys. In the absence of a taboo, 60% of respondents said they would hunt monkeys. This was quite a different result from the 18% of Tafi Atome residents who said they would hunt monkeys without a taboo.

Tourism rates for BFMS have dramatically increased over time, from 150 tourists in 1991 to nearly 6500 in 2002 (Fargey, 1992; Densu, 2003) and 10 000 in 2005 (Dassah, personal communication). Of residents interviewed in Boabeng and Fiema, 48.1% said that they personally benefit from tourism. As of August 2006, information about revenues from tourism at Boabeng–Fiema Monkey Sanctuary was not shared with the community, but revenues were allocated quarterly, with some tourism income given to the community. There was speculation by interviewees about what happens to income from tourism, representing a potential source of conflict regarding the sanctuary.

Due to the tourism success of the Boabeng–Fiema Monkey Sanctuary, neighbouring villages are proposing establishment of their own forest protection in the form of corridors connecting to BFMS. These villages are Bonte, Bomini, Busunya, Konkrompe, Akrudwa Kuma and Akrudwa Pinyin (Densu, 2003; Kankam, personal communication). In recent years, monkeys have been observed in increasing numbers in these villages as a result of primate population growth and dispersal. Due to the taboo on hunting, the populations of monkeys are increasing in the sanctuary (Saj et al., 2006).

The sacred forest sections in both Boabeng and Fiema are bounded on all sides by roads, houses, or farms (Figure 23.9). Boabeng and Fiema residents were asked whether they thought the forest should be expanded. When asked specifically (in contrast to an open-ended question), most residents (78.2%) did express support for expanding the forest because it would draw more tourists and provide space for the monkeys. Interviewees against forest expansion explained that there is already a shortage of farmland and, with village population growth, it would be harder for future generations to find farmland.

Monkeys frequently come into villages to steal food from residents. Tour guides respond to pressure from tourists to attract the monkeys for close viewing by feeding them bananas. Residents of Boabeng and Fiema were asked if monkeys ever come near or into their home compound and farms to steal food. In cases where the monkeys do steal food, the residents were asked how they feel about it. All of the residents surveyed said that monkeys steal food. Residents' varied emotional responses to this action included the following range of comments, each from a different Boabeng or Fiema resident: 'Since the monkeys are like children being reared, we can't do anything or feel angry'; 'I am happy when monkeys come steal food from the house'; 'I chase the monkeys away and I am

Figure 23.9 Road through Boabeng sacred forest (© Alison Ormsby).

angry'. The majority of interviewees were not mad about monkeys taking food: 61.8% felt neutral, 11.8% were happy, and 26.5% were angry.

Discussion and conclusions

The question of whether community conservation or government protection is more effective at protecting sacred groves is complex. Without the 1975 government law protecting Boabeng–Fiema, the monkeys would likely have been hunted until they were locally extirpated. However, government management and legacy in the area seems to have created a lack of initiative and feeling of ownership among village residents. When local village improvements are needed, or resource use issues arise, concerns are deferred to government representatives. The situation is further complicated by the fact that two villages are involved in the management of the sanctuary, yet these two villages have managed their own separate sacred groves in different ways. The grove near Boabeng is larger, denser and better protected than the grove near Fiema, and tourists usually visit only the Boabeng grove. Yet revenues from tourism are evenly shared between Boabeng and Fiema. This may result in Fiema having no incentive to reforest or restore local habitat areas.

Observing management challenges at Boabeng and Fiema raises questions about the Boabeng–Fiema corridor project, which is creating linkages to protected forest patches in six nearby communities. Ecologically, this corridor project is certainly advantageous. However, might this new initiative create more village rivalries or false expectations in terms of future tourism revenues?

Both Tafi Atome Monkey Sanctuary and Boabeng–Fiema Monkey Sanctuary charge an entrance fee of approximately $7 US for foreign visitors and $3 for Ghanaians. Tourism revenues at Tafi Atome are publicly posted in the sanctuary Visitors Centre, whereas at Boabeng–Fiema the fees are collected by a government employee at the sanctuary office and revenues are not made public. This leads to community speculation about the amount and allocation of revenues.

In both Tafi Atome and Boabeng–Fiema, some residents did not make the direct connection between village projects, such as electrification, road and school improvements, and the fact that these benefits are in part funded by tourism revenues or, in the case of Tafi Atome, by direct benefactors who were former visitors to the sanctuary.

Making a culturally protected sacred grove open to tourism can cause a shift in the cultural significance of the site as well as an increase in the environmental impacts on the site (Anyinam, 1999). In Tafi Atome, access to the core sacred fetish grove is still forbidden. In Boabeng–Fiema, tourists are allowed to enter the core grove. It is recommended that the core groves be kept sacred and with limited access in order to protect each grove well into the future.

Residents of both study areas expressed pride in the local sanctuaries. A Tafi Atome resident said she 'never imagined people from far places would come here to see the monkeys'. Although Tafi Atome is much newer as a tourism destination, it has a gift shop whereas Boabeng–Fiema does not. Tafi Atome has an advantage as a tourist site in that it is only three hours over well-maintained roads from Ghana's capital city, Accra. In contrast, Boabeng–Fiema requires at least nine hours of travel time from Accra. Many interviewees in Boabeng and Fiema made comments about the need to pave the road to improve access to the sanctuary.

All villages – Tafi Atome, Boabeng and Fiema – received electricity only within the last decade. In addition, all villages delayed electrification to minimise impacts on the monkeys. For example, additional efforts were made to install some of the wires underground in both sanctuaries, and also to use insulated conductors (Densu, 2003; Egbeako, personal communication).

Interviewees at both research sites voiced support for expansion of the sacred groves. However, growing human populations will surely increase demands on the land within the groves. In addition, the cultivation of cash crops near sacred groves creates pressure on sanctuary land. At Tafi Atome, there is a teak plantation on two sides of the grove. In the Boabeng–Fiema region, there is an extensive industry to grow and prepare tobacco for export. In recent years, part of the forest between Boabeng and Fiema has been cleared for new housing and a new church. Similarly, new farmland areas have been cleared near Tafi Atome. Thus, despite some community support for expansion of the sanctuary, there are never-ending pressures for use of the land up to and within the sanctuary. The Tafi Atome Monkey Sanctuary boundary was demarcated by Friends of the Earth Ghana in 2006, which should help clarify the location of the boundary and resolve any questions about whether a farm is inside or outside the sanctuary.

To facilitate positive tourism development, transparency in revenue sharing is needed. Tafi Atome is succeeding at publicising tourism revenues, but it will be an ongoing challenge, with external funding entering communities, to keep the lines of communication open and avoid speculation and misunderstandings about allocation of funds. There is a need for education and information sharing to explain how income is used in each community involved with tourist visits to sacred forests, and how funding assistance is allocated for community development projects.

The flamboyant tree (*Delonix regia*) is the dominant species in several parts of the Tafi Atome grove. This non-native species is planted because its seed pods are a favoured food of the monkeys. The problem is that the tree out-competes other species and is becoming a dominant species in the grove. Basically, the grove has been managed for the monkeys but not for habitat diversity. It is recommended that ecological studies be conducted on Ghana's sacred forests to measure current biodiversity and ensure that species representative of healthy forests are present and protected. Biological studies have been conducted at sacred groves in India and have shown that the groves are more species-rich than surrounding areas (e.g. Tiwari *et al.*, 1998; Bhagwat *et al.*, 2005).

The groves in this study have a similar history of receiving outside protection to support cultural traditions after erosion from external forces. In different decades – 1970s at Boabeng–Fiema and 1980s at Tafi Atome – each site faced pressures from religious leaders to hunt monkeys and cease idol worship. The communities at both sites responded with renewed protection and support for community conservation traditions. At Boabeng–Fiema, national government support was enlisted; Tafi Atome received support from a non-governmental organisation, regional government legislation and a community management committee.

Future research is needed – both in Ghana as well as other countries such as India with a strong tradition of sacred sites – that investigates the similarities and differences in natural resource use and management traditions at each site. This research could further evaluate the role of the preservation of sacred groves in supporting biodiversity conservation.

References

Amoako-Atta, B. (1995). Sacred groves in Ghana. In von Droste, B., *Cultural Landscapes of Universal Value*. New York, NY: Gustav Fischer Verlag, pp. 80–95.

Anyinam, C. (1999). Ethnomedicine, sacred spaces, and ecosystem preservation and conservation in Africa. In *Sacred Spaces and Public Quarrels: African Cultural & Economic Landscapes*, ed. P. T. Zeleza and E. Kalipeni. Trenton, NJ: Africa World Press, pp. 127–46.

Bernard, H. R. (1988). *Research Methods in Cultural Anthropology*. Newbury Park, CA: Sage Publications.

Bhagwat, S. A., Kushalappa, C. G., Williams, P. H., *et al.* (2005). A landscape approach to biodiversity conservation of sacred groves in the Western Ghats of India. *Conservation Biology*, **19**, 1853–62.

Campbell, M. O. (2004). Traditional forest protection and woodlots in the coastal savannah of Ghana. *Environmental Conservation*, **31**, 225–32.

Campbell, M. O. (2005). Sacred groves for forest conservation in Ghana's coastal savannas: assessing ecological and social dimensions. *Singapore Journal of Tropical Geography*, **26**, 151–69.

Castro, P. (1990). Sacred groves and social change in Kirinyaga, Kenya. In *Social Change and Applied Anthropology*, ed. M. S. Chaiken and A. K. Fleuret. Boulder, CO: Westview Press, pp. 277–89.

Chouin, G. (2002). Sacred groves as historical and archaeological markers in southern Ghana. *Ghana Studies*, **5**, 177–96.

Creswell, J. W. (1994). *Research Design: Qualitative and Quantitative Approaches*. Thousand Oaks, CA: Sage Publications.

Densu, K. A. K. (2003). Ministry treats wildlife safety as monkey business. *The Daily Dispatch*. Accra. 30 April.

Dorm-Adzobu, C., Ampadu-Agyei, O. and Veit, P. G. (1991). *Religious Beliefs and Environmental Protection: The Malshegu Sacred Grove in Northern Ghana*. Washington, DC: World Resources Institute.

Fargey, P. J. (1992). Boabeng–Fiema Monkey Sanctuary – an example of traditional conservation in Ghana. *Oryx*, **26**, 151–6.

Gocking, R. (2005). *The History of Ghana*. Westport, CT: Greenwood Press.

Greene, S. E. (2002). *Sacred Sites and the Colonial Encounter: A History of Meaning and Memory in Ghana*. Bloomington, IN: Indiana University Press.

Krueger, R. A. (1994). *Focus Groups: A Practical Guide for Applied Research*. Thousand Oaks, CA: Sage Publications.

Lebbie, A. R. and Freudenberger, M. S. (1996). Sacred groves in Africa: forest patches in transition. In *Forest Patches in Tropical Landscapes*, ed. J. Schelhas and R. S. Greenberg. Washington, DC: Island Press, pp. 300–24.

Lingard, M. N., Raharison, E., Rabakonandrianina, J., *et al.* (2003). The role of local taboos in conservation and management of species: the radiated tortoise in southern Madagascar. *Conservation and Society*, **1**, 223–46.

Morgan, D. L. (1997). *Focus Groups as Qualitative Research*. Thousand Oaks, CA: Sage Publications.

Ntiamoa-Baidu, Y. (1987). West African wildlife: a resource in jeopardy. *Unasylva*, **156**, 27–35.

Ntiamoa-Baidu, Y. (May, 1995). Indigenous vs. introduced biodiversity conservation strategies: the case of protected area systems in Ghana. *African Biodiversity Series*, **1**. Washington, DC: Biodiversity Support Program.

Pleydell, G. (2005). *Wildlife in Ghana. Publication of the Ghana Wildlife Division of the Forestry Commission*. Sussex, UK: East Sussex Press.

Saj, T. L., Mather, C. and Sicotte, P. (2006). Traditional taboos in biological conservation: the case of *Colobus vellerosus* at the Boabeng–Fiema Monkey Sanctuary, Central Ghana. *Social Science Information*, **45**, 285–310.

Tiwari, B. K., Barik, S. K. and Tripathi, R. S. (1998). Biodiversity value, status, and strategies for conservation of sacred groves of Meghalaya, India. *Ecosystem Health*, **4**, 20–32.

Weiss, R. S. (1994). *Learning from Strangers: The Art and Method of Qualitative Interview Studies*. New York, NY: The Free Press.

24

Sacred species of Kenyan sacred sites

JACOB MHANDO NYANGILA

Introduction

Sacred sites are an important component of local people's culture and history, serving as places for appeasing the spirits in the event of calamities, sacrificing for rain, peace-making and conducting certain traditional rites. In this chapter, the term *sacred sites* is used to refer to specific areas believed by the local people to be traditionally 'holy' and associated with supernatural powers; these are highly respected. These sites come in different forms, including sacred lakes, rivers, mountains, hills, caves, forests, single trees and open grounds. Sacred sites are often places that display some unnatural characteristics or appearance. They often have exaggerated features such as size (e.g. too large, too dense, unreachable or display unique formation) and are often respected by the local community.

This chapter provides a broad overview of sacred species of Kenyan sacred sites with emphasis on cultural significance, the biodiversity they support, their current conservation status and the sacred species related to them. The chapter is based on research work undertaken by the author since 1997 to the present time on sacred landscapes of Kenya (including personal communication with village elders between 1997 and 2004). The results show that most of these sites are extremely threatened and on the verge of extinction. There is a clear indication that the threats to the sites are mostly anthropogenic and include agricultural expansion and the clearance of vegetation for setting up homesteads or through the extraction of forest products. Furthermore, there has been a growing knowledge gap between generations, declining use and interest in conserving them as sacred spaces, weakening respect for them, and the gradual conversion of the

Sacred Species and Sites: Advances in Biocultural Conservation, ed. Gloria Pungetti, Gonzalo Oviedo and Della Hooke. Published by Cambridge University Press. © Cambridge University Press 2012.

usually communal land into other uses and private property. The conflict of modern religious faiths and educational ideals with traditional beliefs has had a negative impact on the sites. Several species of plants and animals found within the sites and surrounding areas are considered special and are treated differently based on their socio-cultural value. Using some of the species for construction, as firewood, or killing them is considered a taboo, which has in turn provided such species protection.

Several recommendations have come out as a result of the study, which include a review of the relevant policies and legal framework that govern protected areas, the need to enter into partnership with local communities to develop viable management strategies for them, legal protection of these sites and the need to enhance the capacity of communities to manage them through training and by supporting or revitalising their cultural practices.

The ethnic diversity of Kenya

In order to understand Kenya's sacred sites, it is important to highlight the ethnic composition of the people of Kenya. Kenya is one of the countries in Eastern Africa and has a total area of 582 646 km^2. It is a meeting point of three major groups of people, the Bantus, Nilotes and Cushites, each with a diversity of ethnic groups. There are about 55 distinct languages, most of which have a number of dialects. Some of these groups, such as the Kikuyu, Luhya and Luo, comprise many millions of people, but others, like the Suba, Segeju, Yaaku and El Molo, are small groups and their languages are on the verge of extinction. The cultural composition has been enriched significantly by later migrants from the Arabian Peninsula, India and Europe (Maundu and Tengnas, 2005).

The cultures of communities living in Kenya are complex and are deep-rooted in myths of origin featuring outer space and earthly phenomena, i.e. the sun, moon and shooting stars; talking bushes; sacred rocks, hills and groves; tattooing snakes and prophetic birds and animals. Some communities believe in the supernatural force and power of ancestors who reside in forests, water bodies, hills and huge rocks or appear in the form of snakes and animals. Most of these ethnic groups live in diverse ecosystems ranging from forests, mountains, savannah, dry lands and low lands to coastal plains, which are all linked to ancestral spirits. Therefore, culture and spiritual values are said to be inextricable and behind the preservation of the forests and ecological regions that regulate the environment.

The cultural beliefs of Kenyan ethnic groups are diverse. For example, the world is believed to be divided into three categories: human, natural and spiritual. In the human world, every person has a spirit that is able to communicate with living beings and give guidance to the people. The natural world is represented

Figure 24.1 Ramogi sacred hill in western Kenya (© Jacob Mhando Nyangila).

in sacred places, including sacred forests, single trees, animals and water bodies. The spiritual world is a combination of the two worlds (human and natural), consisting of different spirits with various responsibilities, tasks and functions, e.g. rain-making, war and health. The spirits warned the people about diseases and calamities. Ancestral support was sought in all aspects of life in the form of dreams and sacrifices through spiritual specialists. To many ethnic groups, the ancestral spirits owned humankind and were responsible for their well-being. They believed that the world is alive with spirits and gods to whom they pray, worship and make sacrifices for support.

Diversity of sacred sites in Kenya

Ramogi sacred hill (Figure 24.1)

Ramogi sacred hill, approximately 283 ha in size, is located in western Kenya. Massive rocks cover the hill, which has two small peaks overlooking Lake Victoria. The sacred forest, which derives its name from the famous Luo ancestor *Ramogi*, is said to be the first place where the Luo tribe of Eastern Africa settled as they migrated from southern Sudan in the sixteenth century and later on it was their dispersal point. Ramogi's sacred hill has a number of sacred points and cultural landmarks. The *Asumbi* rock, popularly referred to as *Agulu dhoge ariyo'* (pot with two mouths), is where Ramogi's family used to get water. It is believed that water from this rock has medicinal value. Also on the hill are several of Ramogi's former homesteads and a sacred lake that is believed to be at the top of the hill.

Loch tree is said to be the first place where Ramogi tied his livestock. Medicine men and magicians from the Luo community collect medicine from the environs. It is believed that medicinal plants growing around this site (tree) and the hill as a whole are said to have greater healing powers. *Pong'*, the grinding stone of Ramogi's two wives, is also found at the foot of the hill. *Lwanda Dhiang* is a rock believed to have been a cow, which turned into a stone upon its death. The sacred hill is rich in indigenous trees, shrubs, herbs, orchids, grasses, sedges, climbers and lianas. Plant diversity is estimated to be over 500 plant species.

Mount Kenya sacred forest

Mount Kenya (5199 m) in central Kenya is the largest sacred site and a solitary mountain of volcanic origin with a base diameter of about 120 km. Its extremely varied ecosystem is mainly due to variation in altitude and rainfall, making this mountain home to rare plant and animal species. This combination led to its recognition by UNESCO as a Biosphere Reserve and World Heritage Site.

Mt Kenya is surrounded by various cultural groups: the Agikuyu to the south and west, the Aembu to the south-east, Ameru to the east and north-east, and the Samburu to the north. In the region around Mt Kenya, the deeply religious and tradition-oriented people upheld the customs and beliefs of their forefathers, respected creation and lived in harmony with nature. Today, four ethnic groups living around Mt Kenya still uphold the cultural importance of hills, rocks, streams, trees and other plants, and they commune with nature.

Mt Kenya itself is a sacred natural site and there are other smaller sacred forests and places of unique features. These sites include caves and hills that were traditionally used for various purposes such as prayer, sacrifice, dwelling and refuge. The imposing height, its impenetrable forest and inspiring white snow at the top made most communities revere the mountain, thus developing a range of myths, folklores and beliefs. The Agikuyu believed the top was the 'house' of God and so all prayers were conducted as people faced the mountain. The original parents of the Agikuyu ethnic group, Gikuyu and Mumbi, are believed to have descended from the mountain before settling at *Mukuruwe wa Nyagathanga*, another sacred site.

Although generally unapproachable to the locals, due to beliefs and thick forest, some secret rituals were conducted in lakes on the slopes of the mountain. For instance, Thaai sacred lake, which is located on the slopes of Mt Kenya, is where the Ameru elders offered sacrifices to their gods. The word *Thaai* means peace. Lake Thaai was a conciliatory shrine and only peace sacrifices could be performed at the lake. The Ameru held the lake in awe because of the mysterious legends handed down from generation to generation. The local people believe that if one inadvertently trespassed into the lake, mysterious forces would shave their heads clean and apply oil, thus calling for heavy penalty.

Prayers and rituals were carried out in several sacred forests in time of need, for example to bring rain and to bless the community. In these, various ceremonies, including initiation rites, cleansing rituals and sacrifices, were offered. Wetlands were particularly important as they provided sanctified water and mud for ceremonies. Protection of these groves was ensured by traditional taboos and religious belief systems. Traditionally, the groves were protected and could not be exploited for other purposes apart from performing rituals and healing. Traditional healers refer to the mountain as their natural pharmacy, as they harvest herbs for traditional medicine from the sacred forest.

Mt Kenya has a wide variety of wildlife. At least five mammal species in the Red Data Book are found in the forest and six large mammals of international conservation concern occur in the Mt Kenya forests. These are the bongo, the black rhino, the leopard, the elephant, the black-fronted duiker and the giant forest hog. The mammal of greatest conservation interest in Mt Kenya is the bongo. It occurs at very low densities in only three or four areas in Kenya. The bongo is particularly endangered and very few have been sighted in the recent past. The major cause for the decline is habitat loss, hunting and susceptibility to rinderpest.

Taita skull caves (Figure 24.2)

The Taita people are found in the south-east of Kenya and have their traditional religion called *Wutasi*, which plays an important role in their lives. Each clan has set aside their own places in the forests and caves for sacrificing to their god known as *Mulungu*. The Taita believe that a person has two types of spirits – evil and good spirits. The spirits of the dead depart to a place called *Warumunyi*. These places were concealed and no one knew where this place was located. The spirits could cause trouble to those who remained on earth and therefore had to be appeased by performing ceremonies. The sacrifices in these smaller shrines included the killing of a black sheep, goat or cow and drinking special traditional beer *Njashi*. The sacrifices in these shrines were accompanied by a traditional ceremony known as *Kutasa*.

Similarly, the Taita people have a unique practice of keeping the skulls of the dead elders in caves (Figure 24.3). Such caves, locally known as *pango*, are scattered all over Taita land and are revered and thus conserved by the local people. A dead person was buried in a sitting position on a skin in a circular grave. When the body had decomposed, the skull would be exhumed, leaving the rest of the body in the grave. A stone would be placed on the grave to guide the exhumers. The skull was only removed from the grave after the spirits of the dead person had visited a member of the family through sickness or calamity demanding that the skull

Figure 24.2 Wesa rock in Taita, Kenya, Taita skull caves are found within (© Jacob Mhando Nyangila).

Figure 24.3 Taita skull caves (© Jacob Mhando Nyangila).

Figure 24.4 Kaya kinodo sacred forest at the Kenyan coast (© Jacob Mhando Nyangila).

be removed. The skull was removed from the grave, kept on the roof for three to five days and transferred to a clan cave – *pango*, a special place where all the exhumed skulls of the clan were kept. In times of trouble, clan members would cook food and slaughter a fat sheep and take it to the skulls at the caves where prayers were performed. Occasionally, people needing favours from the diseased person took the type of food that the elder had preferred when he was still alive. Even though the food was eaten by wild animals such as rats, it was strongly believed that the dead person had consumed the food. However, women's skulls were never exhumed, nor were those of children or less important people (personal communication with Taita elders).

Mijikenda sacred forests – Kayas (Figure 24.4)

The best-known sacred sites in Kenya are the *Kaya* forests of the coastal Mijikenda people. The Mijikenda comprise nine ethnic groups – the Giriama, Digo, Rabai, Duruma, Ribe, Kauma, Chonyi, Jibana and Kambe, who have lived in coastal Kenya for about three centuries. For a long time, these communities have retained forest groves around their dwellings as burial sites and places for conducting a number of rites. The Kaya forests are residual patches measuring between 10 and 400 ha of the once extensive lowland forest of Eastern Africa. Today, these relics of forests comprise about 145 fragments spreading from the north to the south coast. The Mijikenda settled in small fortified villages within the Kaya. The Kaya was governed by a supreme council of elders whose authority was based on supernatural powers derived from oaths that they had acquired. The Mijikenda council of elders had power over the use of land and acted as spiritual mediums and healers to settle disputes and they controlled witchcraft in the society.

The traditional rules and prohibitions passed down by the elders still linger in the minds of the local community and they still revere the Kaya forests. The elders enforced the protection of the Kaya forests so that they could perform their ceremonies and rites in seclusion. The protection rules were mainly enforced through taboos, taking oaths and cursing. For example, the cutting of trees was strongly prohibited in the Kayas and no tree of any size was to be removed. Grazing cattle in the Kayas was forbidden and animals that strayed into the Kaya forest were slaughtered and eaten by the elders. The obvious reason behind this is that traditional paraphernalia and artefacts were hidden in these forests and if animals roamed freely within they would damage them. Within the Kayas are designated routes for entry and any visitor to the forest is supposed to walk within such a pathway. Some sections of the forest are out of bounds to the members of the community and only chosen elders performing a ceremony are allowed to enter.

However, the Kayas and their related traditional practices are threatened and rapidly losing their value. Several factors have contributed to this scenario and include: encroachment by farms and settlements because most of the Kaya forests are found within fertile arable land; the establishment of tourist structures – the Kayas border the coastline and are increasingly being threatened by the demand for land; and the demand for fuel wood and timber, either building poles or wood from hardwood trees for woodcarving and the tourism industry. The decline in knowledge and respect for traditional values due to economic, social, cultural and other changes in society has affected the cohesion of the Mijikenda people.

Sacred species

The belief systems, as well as their practices and rituals, have links with the natural world. The link is manifested by the presence of places considered to be sacred forests, trees, groves, as well as hills and mountains. Within this natural world are found plants and animals which have cultural, spiritual and religious connection with local people. Certain trees and animals are revered for various reasons and they may not be touched, destroyed or even eaten as food. For example, big trees that stand isolated in the neighbourhood of settled areas are often believed to have supernatural links with the ancestral spirits. Under these sacred trees, ceremonies to pray for rain or to stop epidemics and thanksgivings are held. In many communities, such trees are not harmed and cutting often attracts a heavy fine from the elders. The most important are the fig (*Ficus* sp.) trees. Figs are huge trees and are often used as places of sacrifice by most communities in Kenya and Africa as a whole. They are also revered for their huge size and the surrounding areas they occupy are often associated with spirits. Their humid nature often attracts fireflies, which may occasionally be seen as spirits flying around in the night. Figs are regarded as 'cool' plants as they are associated with 'goodness', providing food to animals and people.

In Kenya, the most important fig trees are *Ficus thonningii*, *F. sycomorus*, *F. sur and F. exasperata*. They grow to huge size; their branches are dense and arch downward, therefore providing good shelter and seclusion to people conducting rituals and ceremonies under the trees. These trees are always spared when other trees are cut. Among the Maasai of East Africa, a number of rituals are conducted under a sacred *Ficus thonningii* (Oreteti) tree. In some Maasai communities, when a person dies, a branch of this tree is cut and planted on the grave. Likewise, the Agikuyu people of central Kenya carried out their ceremonies under *F. thonningii* trees (Mugumo). An example of such an old fig tree is found on Karima sacred hill in central Kenya. The *Irungu* (name of a Kikuyu age set) would meet under the tree whenever rain would fail. They offered a sheep or a goat as a sacrifice and it is said that as soon as they had completed the ceremony, rain would fall. The slaughtered animal would be eaten by *Irungu* and was not taken home. All bones and other remains were burnt to ashes. The Agikuyu respected huge trees because they resembled the house of God (Ngai). Therefore, local traditions and customs have prevented the destruction of such sacred trees and some still stand today as sacred shrines in heavily populated settlements. All of the 32 Kenyan fig tree species, with an exception of three shrubby ones, are used by Kenyan communities for one ceremony or another.

Moreover, the Luo community of western Kenya have special reverence for certain trees (Ayot, 1979). If a person goes to war and dies and cannot be traced, or if a person is killed and eaten by wild animals, then traditionally the fruit of *Kigelia Africana*, commonly referred to as the 'sausage tree', is buried in place of the deceased. Therefore, *Kigelia africana* is treated as a sacred tree and never cut in any circumstances. Among the Luhya of western Kenya, *Erythrina abyssinica* (omurembe) is used in settling disputes. People suspected of having committed criminal offences are supposed to swear by the tree. The guilty avoid doing this because it is believed that whoever does this and has committed the offence dies on the spot or becomes sick and dies later. Thus, due to its sacredness, people fear to cut the tree. Generally, trees and plants associated with medicine men and witchcraft are not cut or destroyed otherwise people believe the powers of the medicine men and witchdoctors will torment them.

Among the small Suba community, found on Mfangano Island of Lake Victoria in western Kenya, there are several sacred trees and plants that are regarded as special. *Sesbania sesban* (Asao) is a tree of luck. If it grows naturally in your homestead, then you have a good chance of prospering in anything you do pertaining, mainly, to fishing, farming and livestock keeping. It is forbidden to cut this tree, because when cut it sheds sap which drips for a very long time and is hence associated with weeping at being hurt. *Synadenium grantii* (Ofangafa or Fangafa) has protective powers that result in the ultimate punitive death of offenders. It is usually left on agricultural plots and is believed to protect the crops from thieves. However, the tree must not be allowed to grow in homesteads. *Brachylaena huillensis* (Omugezi) is associated with magical powers and if aimed at you, then evil is likely to befall you (Ogol *et al.*, 2004).

Most of the Kenyan communities such as the Luhya and Mijikenda regard the owl as the omen of bad news. If it whoops near a homestead, then it is a sign that bad things will befall the homestead. The people are therefore scared of the owl and will not harm it. Among the Mijikenda, they avoid stepping on certain species of caterpillars as they believe that, if you do so, you lose your direction. This myth ensured that people walked carefully and did not step on the caterpillars, thus ensuring their survival.

However, as much as these practices help to conserve biodiversity, they are also counter-conservation. Some communities fear, or are reluctant to conserve, certain plant and animal species for fear of death or natural calamities associated with them. For example, among the Luhya community of western Kenya, *Croton megalocarpus* (Omusutswi) is viewed with great suspicion as it is believed that it causes people to quarrel within the family with the subsequent fallout of the family unit. Similarly, it is believed that if the roots of this tree reach the foundation of a house then the occupants will die; therefore, the people do not like to be associated with the tree or plant in the homestead. Also among Luhya clans, *Erythrina abyssinica* (Omurembe) is widely revered because it is associated with evil spirits. It is said to cause lightning to strike a house if planted within the homestead. The Luo people of western Kenya associate the exotic species of *Terminalia* sp. with a myth that 'it causes people to plan their families' and also causes bad luck. This myth has caused the widespread cutting down of the tree species in the region.

The importance of sacred sites

As indicated earlier, sacred sites come in different forms and are found in a wide range of habitats. These sites are preserved for various reasons which include the following.

Historical significance

A number of sites are preserved for historical reasons. A sacred site might be where an important village elder was buried, or where his home stood, thereafter turning into a forest. A site could also represent a place where an ancient

Figure 24.5 The three-horned chameleon is regarded as a sacred species by some communities in Kenya (© Jacob Mhando Nyangila).

founder of a community first put his homestead in the land they currently occupy, or where he planted a tree upon settlement. Some of these sites may represent dispersal points and a good example is Ramogi sacred hill of the Luo community in western Kenya. Ramogi hill derives its name from the famous Luo ancestor *Ramogi*. It is said to be the first place where the Luo tribe first settled as they migrated from southern Sudan in the sixteenth century. This was also their dispersal point and, as a result, they left several historical landmarks which are preserved today as sacred sites.

Conservation of biodiversity

Most of the sacred sites are respected by the entire community and usually remain undisturbed, thus the habitats (plants and animals) associated with them get protection. With increasing pressure from agricultural expansion, these sites and the surrounding forests act as a 'safe haven' for a number of wild species, some being rare. In addition, these sites provide natural shelter or hiding places for small animals such as duikers, wild pigs and bushbucks. On the other hand, rock cliffs and ragged habitats provide unique microhabitats for specialised plants and animals. For example, the extremely endangered African violets (*Saintpaulia taitensis*) are only found in Mbololo forest in the coastal region of Kenya and nowhere else in the world. The Taita rock cliffs have been preserved by the Taita people of south-east Kenya because within are found the 'Taita skull caves'. Another example is the three-horned chameleon which is endemic to sites found around Mt Kenya region (Figure 24.5). Many of the wild species occurring in these sites have both economic and cultural value for the local communities. Some sites have rare, endangered or endemic species and in some instances species that are new to science. Therefore, sacred sites stand as islands of high biological diversity in the midst of land impoverished by human activities.

Environmental and other services

The larger sacred sites in Kenya, such as mountains, provide ecological services for any ecosystem, including water catchments, modulation of the local weather and carbon sinks. Some sacred lakes and wetlands act as water catchment areas. Mountains such as Mt Kenya (central Kenya), Kiang'ombe in Mbeere and Nzaui (eastern Kenya) provide water to people living below them and increase the amount of rainfall within this area. Some mountains are used by local people as reference points for the sun and are therefore useful in telling the seasons. Farmers look out for cloud cover on the hill and, whenever the peak is covered by clouds, the community knows that it is time to prepare the land for planting.

Sources of products

Many cultures forbid the more destructive activities, especially the harvesting of timber for building, medicine and fuel wood. However, some activities, like the collection of fruit, can be tolerated. In the larger sites most uses are permitted but with some limitations, mainly concerning harvesting from the specific holy sites or trees. For instance, the Luo people of western Kenya recognise herbal medicine harvested from certain points on Ramogi hill as having more healing power. *Mwanda* sacred tree marks the place where Ramogi, the Luo ancestor, first settled on arrival from southern Sudan. The Kaya forests of the coastal Mijikenda people serve as sources of many forest products, which include firewood, herbal medicine, wild fruits and vegetables. Rivers and ponds found within the forests are the sources of water for the local community.

Cultural significance

Probably the most obvious importance of all is cultural significance. Cultural uses are varied and may range from a practical use, such as sacrificing, to intangible importance, such as myths and beliefs. An example of the latter is the Nzambani rock cliff of the Akamba people of eastern Kenya, where it is believed that a person changes into the opposite sex if he or she goes round the rock seven times, an obviously impossible task given the formation of the rock cliff (Figure 24.6). In most cases the site is associated with the presence of a supernatural power. Whatever the type of use, most cultural uses work towards the protection of the site in question. Even in situations where the site is no longer in use, it is nevertheless a symbol and living memory of a community's past cultural practices. Ceremonial uses are the most common and well known within sacred sites. These include performing certain rites such as circumcision, sacrificing for

Figure 24.6 Nzambani rock in eastern Kenya (© Jacob Mhando Nyangila).

rain or appeasing the gods in the event of calamity, or warding off a catastrophe, e.g. drought, locust invasion and diseases. Some sites were places where wrongdoers in society were taken and punishment meted out. Some communities such as the Taita of south-east Kenya threw offenders off a cliff, while the Ameru of eastern Kenya tossed them down a waterfall. Therefore, sacred sites provide cultural continuity and promote social cohesion, giving the community hope as a place to go for a solution in case of a problem within the community or a looming disaster. The sites therefore kept the communities in peace with themselves and with the gods or spirits.

Conclusions

As already mentioned, sacred sites are of cultural, biological, historical, ecological and aesthetic importance and efforts should be made to preserve them. Their cultural importance guarantees their sustainability and their loss will lead to the loss of associated cultural practices. Changing cultural values, and hence disrespect for the sites, the urge to develop tourist and commercial resorts at the sites, and the over-exploitation of resources are all threatening the existence of the sites. Local communities and particularly the Church need to be sensitised to their importance. From the survey, it is evident that sacred sites serve many functions and therefore need to be conserved, even when their cultural use and significance is diminishing. An attempt should be made to address the widespread problem of the destruction of sacred sites. This can be done in partnership with local communities.

A good example in Kenya is the collaboration between communities and the National Museums of Kenya in the conservation of the Kayas. The partnership can strengthen the weakening traditional protection systems and beliefs as a result of fast-changing lifestyles.

References

Ayot, O. H. (1979). *A History of the Luo – Abasuba of Western Kenya from A.D. 1760–1940*. Nairobi, Kenya: Kenya Literature Bureau.

Maundu, P. and Tengnas, T. (2005). *Useful Trees and Shrubs for Kenya*. Technical handbook No. 35. Nairobi, Kenya: World Agroforestry Centre – Eastern and Central Africa Regional Programme (ICRAF–ECA).

Ogol, K. P. O., Ogola, P. O. and Khayota, B. (2004). Sacred groves (Kibaga) of Mfangano Island, Lake Victoria, Kenya. *East African Journal of Life Sciences*, **5**, 49–58.

PART VII   IMPLEMENTATION AND
CONCLUSIONS

25

Sacred species and biocultural diversity: applying the principles

GLORIA PUNGETTI and SHONIL A. BHAGWAT

Introduction

Over the past 10 000 years of settled agriculture, humans have changed the Earth's landscape. We have converted forests into farmlands, reclaimed wetlands for agriculture and planted woodlots in savannas, transforming natural landscapes into cultural ones. In the process, we have also changed the habitats of 1.8 million other known species that we share this planet with (EOL, 2008). However, during this time we have also domesticated many species by creating new habitats for them. These include a wide variety of grasses that we use for cereal grains, a number of trees that yield valuable non-timber forest products and a variety of animals for milk and meat. Furthermore, in search of useful products, humans have altered the species composition of the so-called 'natural' landscapes. For example, the Kayapo Indians of the Brazilian Amazon are known to have maintained Brazil nut groves, altering the species composition of forest they inhabited (Posey, 1985). Similarly, many indigenous societies across the world have favoured a variety of other useful species, giving rise to landscape-scale heterogeneity. In Kebon Tatangkalan agroforests of West Java, Indonesia, for example, Parikesit *et al.* (2005) identified 12 different types of tree assemblages. Such traditional land-use practices have not only given rise to landscape-scale heterogeneity, but they have made a contribution to the biocultural diversity of our planet.

Although domestication has been an important driving force in creating new habitats for some species, the reasons for conservation of many others may not just be utilitarian. It can be argued that the origins of biocultural diversity have as much to do with the veneration of species as with their usefulness, as the examples below

Sacred Species and Sites: Advances in Biocultural Conservation, ed. Gloria Pungetti, Gonzalo Oviedo and Della Hooke. Published by Cambridge University Press. © Cambridge University Press 2012.

suggest. Near the town of Madurai, in the Tamilnadu state of India, tree groves provide roosting sites for colonies of the Indian flying fox (*Pteropus giganteus*). It is believed that this bat, which elsewhere is hunted for its body fat, receives protection because the trees are worshipped by the local people (Marimuthu, 1988). Christ's Thorn Jujube (*Ziziphus spina-christi*, Rhamnaceae) is a tropical evergreen tree of Sudanese origin, known to have a wide variety of medicinal uses. In Israel, however, this tree is venerated due to historical or magical events related to it, regardless of its botanical identity. In the fortieth year after planting, the saints in Israel perform a traditional ritual under this tree – a reason for its continued conservation in the Holy Land (Dafni *et al.*, 2005). Is it possible that the medicinal uses of Christ's Thorn Jujube were 'discovered' because the saints would not allow this tree to be cut until it turned 40? Alternatively, is it equally likely that the tree is venerated by people because it has medicinal uses? These questions have no simple answers. The driving forces of traditional practices, rituals and the resulting biocultural diversity might be more complex than mere cause and effect.

In this chapter, the extent of biocultural diversity across the world is illustrated through a variety of examples. We ask whether the utility of species leads to their conservation, or whether reverence for them plays a role. In answering this, we apply a framework of resource and habitat taboos suggested by Colding and Folke (2001) to these examples, and explore the role of sacred species and sites in nature conservation and resource management. Finally, some of the challenges for conservation of this biocultural diversity in the face of cultural homogenisation in the modern world are appraised.

Sacred species and biocultural diversity

What motivation do humans have for the conservation of species and protection of habitats? Do we conserve species because they are useful to us, or do we protect them out of reverence? Do we protect certain habitats because we have respect for them, or do we protect them because they provide 'ecosystem services'? The example of sacred groves in the Pindos Mountains of Greece is illustrative (Box 25.6). A large number of tree groves are found in Zagori, a group of villages in Northern Pindos National Park, Greece. It has been suggested that the motivation behind protection of these groves is not only their strategic location, but also their 'supply' function to the local community as well as their role as offering 'security' in difficult times. The groves may protect village aquifer and prevent landslides or torrents, or, indeed, provide fodder for livestock in hard winters or famines. It can be argued, therefore, that they provide certain 'services' to the local community, and this has been an important factor in their protection. Similarly, a number of domesticated species happen to be conserved because of their use. In an example of ritual from the Russian North, a newborn baby on its first day is wrapped in a special type of sheepskin and fleece. This variety of sheep is traditionally protected in order to perform the ritual (Box 25.2). Without this ritual, perhaps, the local variety would soon be replaced by a high-yielding, exotic, hybrid variety. These two examples, as also illustrated in Chapter 13, make a strong case that 'utility' is an important driver for conservation.

A number of other examples, however, suggest that this may not be a complete picture. Many 'wild', as opposed to domesticated, species around the world have also been given protection by traditional societies, where taboos frequently guide human conduct towards the natural environment. These taboos have been instrumental in attributing 'sacred' status to many species and habitats where they live. Such status is considered important for regulating the use of species, resources or habitats, and for ensuring their conservation. Termed 'resource and habitat taboos', these practices are argued to have functions similar to those of formal institutions for nature conservation in contemporary society (Colding and Folke, 2001). Six categories of resource and habitat taboos have been suggested: (1) segment taboos: these regulate resource withdrawal; (2) temporal taboos: these regulate access to resources in time; (3) method taboos: these regulate methods of resource withdrawal; (4) life history taboos: these regulate the withdrawal of a species at vulnerable stages in its life history; (5) specific-species taboos: these provide total protection to species in time and space; and (6) habitat taboos: these restrict access and the use of resources in time and space. Here examples in each of these categories are appraised.

(1) Segment taboos: in many tribal societies, there are gender- or age-based restrictions on the use of natural resources. For example, in the Jharkhand state of India the Oraon tribe conducts a ritual twice a year for acquiring procreative vigour, in which only young boys are allowed to participate (Box 25.7). The ritual uses parts of the Sal tree (*Shorea robusta*) and is performed in secrecy. Such a segment taboo possibly restricts the use of the Sal tree, considered sacred by the Oraon tribe. This tree, which happens to be a valuable timber tree, is endemic to central India and, without traditional restriction on its use, the tree might have become extinct a long time ago.

(2) Temporal taboos: this is where the harvest of a resource is restricted at certain times of the year. The brown bear (*Ursus arctos*) was widespread in Europe before the industrial revolution. Its populations have dramatically declined in the last century. However, in the Romanian Carpathians certain days of the year are referred to as 'days of the bear' (Box 25.3). On some of these days, feasts of meat and honey are left in the

forest near bear tracks. Such practices may have made a significant contribution to the conservation of brown bear populations in the Romanian Carpathians, whereas in the rest of Europe this species has been wiped out due to habitat destruction and hunting.

(3)   Method taboos: this is when restrictions are placed on the method of resource extraction. For example, hunting with bows and arrows only may be allowed while guns are prohibited. For example, Lamap people in Vanuatu are not allowed to use any weapon other than bow and arrow for hunting (Johannes, 1998). Such practices prevent large-scale hunting and conserve populations of the animal in question.

(4)   Life history taboos: this is when hunting is prohibited at certain stages of an animal's life cycle. For example, Phasepardhis of the Ahmadnagar district in Maharashtra, India, are prohibited by social conventions from hunting calves or pregnant does of deer (Gadgil, 1987). Such practices ensure that the breeding cycle of the animal in question remains intact, ensuring conservation of that species.

(5)   Specific-species taboos: a large number of examples of such restrictions exist. In Pemba Island, Tanzania, the critically endangered Pemba flying fox is protected in sacred sites, while in Sapo National Park, Liberia, the western chimpanzee and the pygmy hippopotamus have received similar protection. Similarly, in Cambodia, the Por community is actively helping to protect critically endangered Siamese crocodiles and other important wildlife and habitats that share their environment. The informal traditions, therefore, have helped to protect species of conservation importance (Box 25.1). On the other hand, the Lebanese cedar, *Cedrus libani*, which was once a sacred tree protected through tradition, has emerged as the symbol of national unity and twentieth-century nature conservation movement in Lebanon (Box 25.4). Therefore, in many cases, the 'sacred' status of species might even have triggered their modern-day conservation.

(6)   Habitat taboos: this is when certain habitats, traditionally considered 'sacred', receive protection. These include forests, groves, lakes and rivers (Bhagwat and Rutte, 2006). In the Russian North, 45 sacred groves have been documented around Lake Kenozero (Box 25.5). Sacred groves are considered unusual in the Russian landscape; however, it is suggested that these groves had been in existence before the Orthodox Church gained prominence. Because of their biocultural significance, all groves have now been incorporated within the Kenozersky National Park, suggesting the role of traditional conservation practices in guiding modern-day conservation initiatives.

These examples suggest that, in addition to using a resource, a species or a habitat, societies have traditionally promoted their conservation through restrictions on use. Therefore, 'prudence' in resource use practised by traditional societies might have played an important role in conservation. The utilitarian approach on the one hand and reverence on the other are perhaps two extreme scenarios – the reality of resource use versus restriction might be somewhere in between.

Holy animals

Box 25.1   Sacred species and sites in the projects of Fauna & Flora International

STEPHEN BROWNE

Introduction

Fauna & Flora International (FFI) works to conserve threatened species and ecosystems worldwide. It chooses solutions that are sustainable, based on sound science and are compatible with human needs. Today, FFI's 200 employees work with over 180 local partners, usually local non-governmental organisations (NGOs), community-based organisations (CBOs) and, as required, government departments, in over 40 countries.

Projects

In Africa, a belief in spirit lions features in Niassa NR and is influencing future mitigation strategies to reduce human–lion conflicts (Figure 25.1.1). Lion attacks recorded in the reserve in the 1980s were believed to be the work of witchcraft and 'spirit' lions; however, they appear to have declined in the 1990s due to the death of the local powerful traditional healer (Begg *et al.*, 2007). On Pemba Island, Tanzania, the endemic and critically endangered Pemba flying fox is partly protected through a number of the bat roosts being associated with sacred sites (Bowen-Jones and Entwhistle, 2002) (Figure 25.1.2). In Liberia, in the Sapo National Park, work to protect the western chimpanzee and the pygmy hippopotamus is enhanced by the belief of local communities that the chimps are their ancestors and should not be killed and because the hippo features strongly in local folklore.

In 2006, FFI and Uganda Wildlife Authority (UWA) embarked on the Culture, Values and Conservation Project in Lake Mburo and Rwenzori

Figure 25.1.1 Male lion resting on Lugenda river bank (© Coleen Bragg). See colour plate section.

Mountains National Parks, a three-year pilot project whose main objective was to gain community support for conservation through the integration of cultural values in the management of the two parks. Of particular importance has been recognition of the cultural significance of the high mountains as the home of the gods and of specific sacred sites, acting as a focus to involve local communities within the Rwenzori Mountains National Park. This project has also focused on the importance of the Ankole cow within the local culture of Bahima pastoralists living around Lake Mburo National Park. Historically, the Ankole cow was an important aspect of the local culture, but today it is facing extinction.

In Asia, the sacred and cultural importance of the Siamese crocodile to the Por people in Cambodia has been important in helping to ensure its continued survival (Figure 25.1.3). The community is actively helping to protect critically endangered Siamese crocodiles and other important wildlife and habitats that share their environment. In spite of the recent conflicts and political problems in Cambodia, many traditional customs

Figure 25.1.2 A cluster of flying foxes (*Pteropus voeltzkowi*) on Pemba Island, Tanzania (© Evan Bowen-Jones/Fauna & Flora International).

Figure 25.1.3 Young Siamese crocodile (© Jeremy Holden/Fauna & Flora International).

have survived among the village elders. Of particular interest is the Por taboo against cutting tall forests or harming certain 'sacred' animals, especially crocodiles. If a crocodile is hurt or killed, it is said that a forest spirit will bring sickness or death to the person responsible. Also in Cambodia, FFI has worked with local religious leaders and has sometimes asked Buddhist monks to bless individual animals and trees to make them sacred, in the

Figure 25.1.4 A wild Asian elephant (© Fauna & Flora International/Jeremy Holden).

hope that no one will harm them. This tends to be specific to individual animals or trees, although one monk in Phnom Aural Wildlife Sanctuary gave a general blessing to all wildlife within an indeterminate radius of his pagoda.

Working with the Bunong, a focal group of indigenous people in Mondulkiri Province, Cambodia, FFI has integrated its work with the traditional Bunong forest management strategies to help conserve wild Asian elephants (Figure 25.1.4). Integral to the traditional livelihoods of the Bunong are their Spirit (sacred) Forests, the exploitation of which are carefully governed by religious rules, and these are important wildlife habitats and elements in conserving biodiversity in the area. In Eurasia, working with local NGO, the Community and Business Forum, FFI helped catalogue the Sacred Sites of Kyrgyzstan, in a similarly entitled book (Dyikanova *et al.*, 2004). The aim of the publication was not only to detail the country's sacred sites before much of the knowledge was lost to future generations, this having already been eroded under the Soviet system, but also to develop a strategy and action plan for the sites. The main goal of the plan is the 'Preservation and rational use of sacred sites and landscapes of Kyrgyzstan with a view to form ecological consciousness and sustainable human development'. This plan has already resulted in four projects being developed, three to enhance sacred sites and one to draft local policy in order to feed, hopefully, into national legislation for the better protection of sacred sites.

In South America, FFI works with NGO Ya'axche Conservation Trust (YCT) in the Golden Stream Watershed in southern Belize, an area where cultural associations between the indigenous Maya people and natural landscapes and Jaguars were previously very strong. The culture of these people has been eroded, but the FFI/YCT project aims to re-establish and build upon these cultural driving forces to enhance Jaguar conservation among Maya communities by improving knowledge of Mayan Jaguar symbolism, legend and traditions.

Conclusion

Through its extensive portfolio of conservation projects, FFI is inevitably working with a number of sacred species and sacred sites. Although not a central focus for our activities, the sacred and spiritual nature of various animals and their habitats is incorporated into our conservation work if appropriate.

Box 25.2 Sacralisation of sheep in the Russian North

ALEXANDER N. DAVYDOV

Introduction

The belt of taiga forests of the European part of Russia is about 1000 km wide and it extends from the Ural Mountains as far as Finland. The historic–cultural region called the Russian North is located in the north-western part of Russia between the Ural Mountains and Finland.

Natural environment: the land of the taiga

The Onega–Dvinsk–Mezensk Plain takes up the greater part of the territory, which is the northern section of the East European Plain. The relief of the historic–cultural area Russian North is mostly flat. Only a few ridge and hill formations exceed 200 m in height. The highest point is Timan

Kriazh, which is 460 m above sea level. Rivers in the region are rather long. The length of Severnaya Dvina river is 744 km. The length of Pechora is 1809 km.

The winter season lasts 200–240 days, the average January temperature being −17°C. The recorded minimum temperature is −48°C. The thickness of snow in winter in the forest zone is 40–60 cm in winter. The average July temperature is 15°C. The recorded maximum temperature is 31°C.

The region lies in three vegetation zones: the middle and northern taiga forests, the sub-arctic and arctic tundra area with permafrost and the arctic deserts with glaciers and eternal ice.

The rivers and lakes of the taiga are inhabited by various kinds of fish (cod, turbot, plaice, herring, salmon), birds (hazel-hen, capercaillie, ptarmigan) and mammals (seal, reindeer, elk, polar fox, hare, wolf, bear).

Cultural environment: the Russian North as a historical–cultural area

The culture of the Russian North developed as a result of the interaction of four different ethnic–ecological systems: the 'culture of fields' (Russians), the 'culture of woods' (Finno-Ugric peoples), the 'culture of reindeer' (Nenets, Lapps and some groups of Komi), and the 'culture of sea' (the international maritime culture of North Europe and the Arctic Ocean).

The mass settlement of the European taiga by Russians increased with the influence of the Tatar–Mongol invasion and the Tatar–Mongol yoke in the thirteenth to the fifteenth century. Russians brought to the North such values of civilisation as agriculture, literacy and Christianity. The characteristic features of the pioneers of agriculture in the taiga were a disposition to engage in ventures and enterprise.

Sheep and the total herd in the Russian North

The traditional economy of Russian peasants adapted to the taiga zone involved agriculture and domestic cattle breeding in extreme natural conditions (Figure 25.2.1). Sheep breeding is represented in the taiga, on the coasts of the Arctic Ocean, and across the Polar Circle on the boundaries of permafrost (Figure 25.2.2).

There are special terms for ram and ewe in the Russian language. The female ewe is *ovtsa* or *yarka*. The ram is *baran*. A lamb is *yagnenok*. At the same time, the names of the products of sheep breeding have common names. The meat of the ram and ewe is called *baranina*. The name for the sheepskin is *ovchina*.

Figure 25.2.1 Sheep hut at the Mezen' house (© A. N. Davydov).

Figure 25.2.2 Sheep in the village of Kimzha Mezensky district of Archangel Region, summer 2007 (© A. N. Davydov).

Figure 25.2.3 A north Russian sheep. Old photograph.

Sheep used to have no proper noun. Peasants in Archangelsk gouberny addressed sheep by calling them *byasha*. Another known local name for sheep was *boreyushko* (for instance, 'Boreyushko, boreyushko! Let you take a piece (of something)': Efimenko, 1864, p. 38). The last name gives the association of the name with Borey (God of the North and Northern wind).

Flocks of sheep in the Russian North are represented mostly by the northern short-tailed sheep. According to nineteenth-century sources, 'they were small with rude fleece' (*Pamyatnaya knizhka Arkhangel'skoy gubernii*, 1864, p. 104) (Figure 25.2.3). In the monograph 'Issledovanie sovremennogo sostoyaniya ovtsevodstva v Rossii' ('Study of contemporary conditions of sheep-farming in Russia', 1882), an interesting proposal occurs: 'According to its geographic spread, this type is one of the oldest; this is the type used by Finnish tribes and with which they migrated to Northern Europe from the mountain plains of Central Asia'.

Shuba and *tulup*: winter outer clothing

Sheepskin coats, *shuba* and *tulup*, were the typical winter outer clothing in the Russian North and were widespread in Russia. Both were always sewn with the fleece inside and had the wrap over from the right to left side.

The *shuba* had long sleeves, a big collar and flaps as far as the knees. There were several types: *belaya* (white) *shuba*, *nagol'naya shuba*, *dublenka*, *krytaya shuba*, etc.

The *tulup* had sleeves longer than the *shuba* and wide flaps reached the ankles. The collar of the *tulup* was bigger than the collar of the *shuba* and was made from pelts of fox, polar fox and sable. Peasants wear the *tulup* unbuttoned or they girdle it with a *kushak* (a type of belt). The *tulup* was made from sheepskin with fleece of a black colour, but sometimes the *tulup* was made with the pelt of bear or fox. During sleigh travels in winter, people put on the *tulup* over the *shuba* (Shangina, 2003, pp. 617–8, 637–41).

The use of clothing of sheepskin and fleece in rituals

Clothing made of sheepskin and fleece was used in some of rituals. The *shuba* was a symbol of protection and richness. A newborn baby on its first day was wrapped in a *shuba* or a *tulup*. Relatives might say: '*Shuba* is warm and hairy, may you live rich and happy'. In the wedding ceremony the mother-in-law, waiting for the just-married couple after church, stayed clothed in a *tulup* turned outwards. During *Svyatki* (Christmastide) young men and ladies arrayed themselves into outward-turned *tulup* or *shuba* and visited the houses of their village with symbolic wishes 'health to peoples and to sheep' (*zdorovya ovechja i chelovechya*). According to peasants' beliefs, a sheepskin *tulup* made the magic wishes stronger. There was also a tradition of telling fortunes on Christmastide nights. At midnight young ladies dressed in fleece stockings would run to the rivers. They would put their stockinged legs into the water through an ice-hole and then return home. They would then go to bed in their wet stockings saying: 'he who will be my promised (husband) let him awaken me' (Shangina, 2003, pp. 618–9; Efimenko, 1877, p. 196).

Conclusion: the ram on the emblem of the town of Kargopol'

The ram is represented on the emblem of Kargopol', one of the oldest towns of the Archangel region. The settlement has been known since the eleventh century. It is situated on the left bank of the Onega river, 5 km from the river source, which is Lake Lacha. In medieval times Kargopol' was, for Russian people, a very important centre of penetration to the North. The emblem of Kargopol' was affirmed by the Imperial Decree of Cartherine the Great on 16 August 1781. This emblem is a ram surrounded by a blue field (Rossii, 1994, p. 181).

Box 25.3 Different stories of two sacred species of Moldavia, Romania: the European bison and the brown bear

SEBASTIAN CATANOIU

Introduction

The location of the Carpathian Mountains in the middle of the country has shaped the history of the Romanian people, the only eastern Latin nation. After the Roman conquest, the mixed Latin population, having sought retreat in the forested mountains, although confronted with different migratory populations, succeeded in surviving and in preserving a Latin language. Due to this permanent connection with the forests and mountains, the ancient myths and beliefs about sacred animals were transmitted with little change. Nowadays, the Carpathian Chain is considered to be the biggest reservoir of biodiversity in Europe, with more than 50% of the mountain area located in Romania. The preservation of this high level of biodiversity will require a holistic approach.

Research progress

The brown bear and the European bison were examined as important species of sacred mammal. The presence of these species was followed through Romanian popular traditions and iconography in order to obtain an image of the past and present sacredness of these species. The study was located in Vanatori Neamt Nature Park, a protected area situated north-east of the Romanian Carpathians, which is a well-known sacred place because of the number and importance of the monasteries and hermitages found there. During the last years of the project, visits and interviews were conducted with elders and practitioners of traditions involving sacred animals.

Outcomes

The bull is well known as a sacred animal in Mediterranean cultures. However, for the Geto-Dacians, who inhabited the present territory of Romania, dwelling near the forest, the cultural place of the bull was replaced by the European bison. The foundation of the medieval state of Moldavia took place, according to legend, during a hunt for European bison. Since then, the head of this animal has been represented between the sun and the moon and under a star on coins, the coat of arms and blazons, as the Moldavian symbol.

Figure 25.3.1 The main door of Agapia Veche Monastery, Agapia village, Romania (© S. Catanoiu).

For centuries this model has been replicated by craftsmen, especially by wood carvers (Catanoiu and Deju, 2005). The image of European bison can be found on imperial chairs and doors inside churches and monasteries, on the external walls and main gates of monasteries (Figure 25.3.1) and also on the traditional gates of houses (Figure 25.3.2).

The brown bear, as a sacred animal, was adored from immemorial times. The main deity of the Geto-Dacians was Zamolxe, with *zelmo* meaning skin and *olxis* meaning bear. After his birth, he was blanketed in a bearskin, and he spent a part of his life living for long periods in an underground cave, only appearing and teaching the people occasionally. At that time, the brown bear was related to courage, power, death and resurrection.

In the popular calendar, which mixes phenology with pagan and Christian events, the brown bear is well represented: 24 March is the

Figure 25.3.2 The pillars of the gate of a traditional house, Nemtisor village, Romania (© S. Catanoiu).

'Saturday of bear', 31 July, 1, 2 and 13 August are the 'Days of Bear'. The most important period for the bear is 1–3 February, which is called 'Sretenie' or 'Winter Martins', during which, out of respect, different names are used for the bear, such as 'Martin the crone' and 'the elder'. Offerings consisting of meat and honey are left in the forest, near a track used by bears, on 2 February, which is called 'The big Martin' (www.muzeulastra.ro). During the winter feasts, masks are used in order to avoid the malefic spirits in the 12-day period between the old and New Year, in accordance with pagan heritage. As a sign of respect, the bear mask is the only one without coloured strings, hand bells or stained glass. The play of the bear mask, which is very spectacular in the Moldavia region, suggests the death and resurrection of nature, also demonstrating vitality, finesse and force (Gorovei, 1995). Some popular, still present, beliefs say that the bear was a man punished by God to become half beast, but still having human appendages. Many beliefs surround the function of the bear: for example, its presence alone dissipates the belial (evil spirit), a fumigation of hair of bear heals fear, and a heavy bear foot is a solution for backaches. The bear is currently abundant in Romanian forested areas, its numbers there the most important contribution, two-thirds of the total, to the European brown bear population.

Conclusion

The brown bear is currently an abundant wildlife species and is still associated with significant popular beliefs. An impressive iconography developed around the European bison, mostly in relation to Christian places of worship, but this disappeared as a wild species two centuries ago. Affirming the sacred values of endangered species is a necessary step to protect wildlife.

Holy plants

Box 25.4 Myth, legend and national emblem: the enduring legacy of the sacred cedar tree of Lebanon

JALA MAKHZOUMI

Introduction

Changing perceptions of the cedar tree of Lebanon over time reflect cultural shifts in the meaning, value and valuation of forested landscape in the eastern Mediterranean. Rooted in ancient mythology, referenced in the scriptures, the cedar tree today is a religious symbol, a national emblem and an icon spearheading twentieth-century nature conservation in Lebanon. This study is an attempt to uncover the legacy of the cedar tree as a symbol and how it evolved from the sacred and spiritual to the profane.

Myth and legend

The earliest mention of cedar trees is found in the third millennium *Epic of Gilgamesh* (about third century BC). The epic relates the journey of King Gilgamesh to the cedar forests of Lebanon, a sacred realm and the abode of the gods. It is not hard to understand why cedar forests were so closely associated with the gods. The exceptional height, stature and girth of the cedar tree embody the sacred trunk at the Centre of the World linking the Cosmic Mountain with Heaven (Eliade, 1991). At the time of Gilgamesh,

Figure 25.4.1 A Lebanese cedar forest.

mountains and valleys in Lebanon were scenes of 'surpassing sylvan beauty, with the two great mountains, deep in forest, soaring on either side' (Brown, 1969, p. 167). Tall cedar forests therefore became a symbol of ascension, inspiring a lifting of the soul and union with the gods. The universality of this mystical experience explains the persistent sacredness of cedar forests over time (Figure 25.4.1).

With the help of his friend Enkido, Gilgamesh conquers Humbaba, guardian of the forest, and claims his cedar logs. Before being slain, Humbaba warns Gilgamesh that most of what is important and necessary on the earth is encoded in the old forest, which is why cedar incense is favoured by the gods. Humbaba's warning precedes the Abrahamic religions' regard of the cedar as a 'world-tree' closely associated with Eden, the 'garden of God', which is located in Lebanon, the cutting of which was seen as 'the destruction of world-empires' – really, as the end of history (Brown, 1969). These mythical insights, argues Brown, are made explicit through 'our understanding of ecology and the dependence of human history on maintenance of the natural environment' (Brown, 1969, p. 167).

The threat to cedars grew as the demand for cedar logs increased. Commodified, cedar forests were no longer at the Centre of the World, no longer the sacred place of mythical geography. Rather, destruction of the majestic cedars became a metaphor for worldly pride as illustrated in a passage from Ezekiel (31.2–4).

Enduring legacy

Even as it lost its sacredness, the cedar tree continued to figure high in the scriptures. In Judaic mythology the cedar was the principal tree in the Garden of Eden, identifying Lebanon with the Temple of Solomon, associating cedars with the tree of the knowledge of good and evil that 'grew lofty like the cedars of Lebanon' (Brown, 1969, p. 171).

Cedar wood was used in the construction of the palaces of Assyrian kings, as in the palace of Darius at Persepolis. It was valued by Phoenicians, Greeks and Romans for shipbuilding. Cedar resin was used in mummification and medicinal remedies, cedar sawdust found in the tombs of pharaohs. Cedars of Lebanon were felled by an army of men sent and provisioned by King Solomon. Hiram, king of Tyre, entered into a treaty with Solomon, and the timber was transported as rafts to a suitable point on the coast of Palestine (Kings 5:9, quoted by Hepper, 1992) and in rebuilding Jerusalem (Nehemiah 2.7–8).

By the beginning of the twentieth century, ruthless exploitation of cedar forests had reduced them to a few remnant forests. Today, one of these forests is referred to as Cedars of the Lord (Arabic *arz er-Rab*). Gibran Khalil Gibran refers to this forest in an untitled poem:

> Standing before me as the cedar of God on Lebanon –
> I knew thee because the light was in thine
> Eyes, and the motherly smile on thine lips.
> You blessed me with a touch, and whispered to my soul these words –
> 'Follow me child, I am thy guide'
> 'I shall reveal what sorrow doth hide'

A national emblem

The mythical repute of the cedar tree, their repeated mention in the scriptures and the plethora of historical references linking them to the Lebanon, justified their use as an emblem of the modern state of Lebanon (about 1930). Today the cedar tree graces the Lebanese flag (Figure 25.4.2a), is the emblem of the national airlines and appears on various denominations of the Lebanese currency (Figure 25.4.2b). The cedar is a symbolic object, a heraldic device for land and people as demonstrated in the Lebanese national anthem *majduhu arzuhu, ramzuhu lil khulud* 'the glory [of Lebanon] lies in the cedars, its symbol of eternity'.

Circa 1914   Circa 1930   1943 to present

Figure 25.4.2 The cedar tree as a national symbol: the Lebanese flag; the cedar as commodity: emblem of the national airlines, Lebanese currency, logo for the American University of Beirut; the cedar tree as a political symbol (2006 war, cedar revolution), etc.

More recently, the cedar has lent its name to a political movement triggered by the assassination of former Lebanese Prime Minister, Rafik Hariri in February 2005 (Figure 25.4.2c). The movement, known as the 'Cedar Revolution', called for the removal of the pro-Syrian government, which was indeed disbanded. The events, however, divided the nation politically. Thus the cedar tree, an emblem for national unity, has become a symbol of confrontation. The political impasse continues.

Conclusion

The long historical association of the cedar tree, *Cedrus libani*, with the Lebanon, the extent of its destruction and the socio-cultural valuation of the cedar made it a befitting symbol for twentieth-century nature conservation in Lebanon (Talhouk *et al.*, 2001). Since the end of the civil war in 1990, four remnant cedar forests in Lebanon have been declared Protected Area, and 13 protected cedar forests (MOE, 2008). National action to protect cedar draws not only on the value of cedar forests as an ancient ecosystem and

Figure 25.4.3 Cedar: a sketch.

wildlife habitat but equally on the social and cultural valuation. Vernacular myths and stories associated with cedars, mountains and the rural landscape, and religious, spiritual and aesthetic values associated with cedar forests play an important role in relaying the mission of national conservation strategies (Makhzoumi, 2001).

The intertwining fate of the cedars, land and people of Lebanon can be seen as a continuation, whether explicit or implicit, of ancient myth, the enduring value of sacred cedar groves. A powerful symbol, myth and image, cedar trees are the very substance of the spiritual and sacred argues Mircea Eliade: 'they may become disguised, mutilated or degraded, but (they) are never extirpated' (Eliade, 1991, p. 11) (Figure 25.4.3).

Box 25.5   A birch or a pine? Sacred groves and sacred trees in the European North of Russia

ALEXANDER N. DAVYDOV

Introduction

The Russian North is a historical–cultural area which is located between the ethnic borders of Russian people with those of the Komi in the

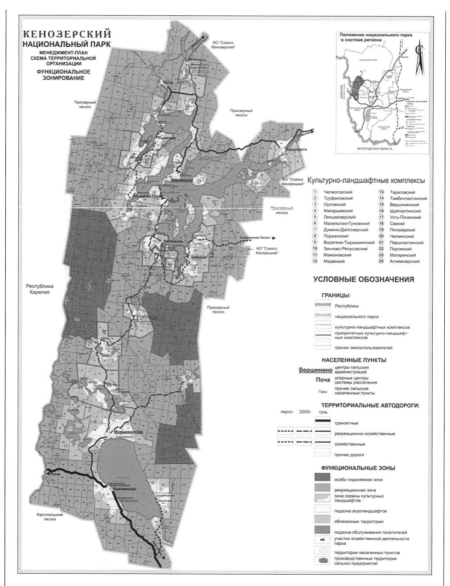

Figure 25.5.1 National Park 'Kenozersky' (Archangel region, Russia).

east, the Karelian in the west, the Nenets in the north and the Sami in the Kola Peninsula. Most of the territory of the Russian North is now the Archangel Region. The southern border of the area is located in Vologda region (Figure 25.5.1).

The culture and beliefs of the Finnish (Finno-Ugric) speaking tribes who lived here before Russians came, such as the legendary *Chud' Zavolochskaya*, form a Finnish substratum in North Russian culture.

A main characteristic of the cultural landscape of the Russian North is the relationship between Forest and Field. Legends and widespread oral tradition say that the territory of the northern taiga forests was populated by *chud'* (the word means in Russian 'queer', 'strange'). 'The chud' went underground when the white birch came' – this saying expresses the changes in cultural landscapes that occurred through the ethno-historical process, usually connected with the penetration of agriculture into the taiga forests. Chud' were the taiga forests' hunters and fishermen, who lived in mud huts. According to the oral tradition of North Russian peasants, these mud huts later became known as 'chud's pits' (from the old times 'when the white birch came and chud' went underground'). The chud' pits (*chudskie yamy*) are one of the characteristic features of the cultural landscape of the Russian North. The birch is a well-known sacred tree of the East Slavs. In the taiga forest zone the agricultural activities were connected with the cutting and burning of large areas of trees for fields. The deciduous trees penetrated first into the borders of these fire-sites, and first of all was the birch tree. A similar process of landscape change occurred with the development of the network of villages and roads. The word-combination 'a white birch' (*belaya bereza*) is very typical of the Russian North, because of the white colour of birch bark. Birch is often grown in a churchyard in Central Russia.

The sacred groves of Kenozero

Sacred groves are associated with the region of Lake Kenozero, located in the south-western part of the Archangel region. Since 1991 the territory has belonged to the Kenozersky National Park. The author of this contribution has carried out field research on this territory since 1981, with the exploratory design of the National Park, and has collected a number of stories of local people about sacred groves (the last field trip was in 1994, when the National Park had already been designated).

More than 30 villages are located within Kenozersky National Park. Most of the villages are old-type settlements with a large number of traditional wooden houses, granaries, saunas, barns, and threshing floors. There are also many monuments of the Russian Orthodox Church. Wooden churches dating from the seventeenth century are situated in the villages Porzhenskoe and Pochezero (see Figure 25.5.1). There are about 35 wooden chapels surviving in different places in the Park.

Nowadays, there are 45 sacred groves in the Kenozersky National Park. Most are located near the villages, such as at Korovya Myza, Ovechya Myza, Vershinino, Tyrnavolok, Nemyata, Zakharovo, Fedosovo, Porzhenskaya,

Ryzhkovo, Semenovo, Kositsyno, Ust' Pocha, Pochezero, etc. (Figure 25.5.1). The sacred groves of Kenozero are of coniferous trees (pine and common spruce). Local people mark out these groves in the surrounding woodland. These groves have a special name, *svataya roscha* ('sacred grove'). The presence of *coniferous* sacred groves is unusual in Russian tradition (for Russian people, the sacred tree is the birch). Analogies of the sacred groves of Kenozero can be found in the taiga forests of western Siberia. Among the Khanty and Mansy peoples there is very strong tradition of sacred groves of coniferous trees, connected with shamanism. This fact suggests that the historical roots of the sacred groves on Kenozero came with the Finno-Ugric tribes, who settled this territory before the Russians. A similar phenomenon of sacred groves was mentioned by Nikolay Kharuzin in the nineteenth century (1889) in Karelia.

Most of the sacred groves were transformed by Russian Orthodox folk tradition. In many of the sacred groves are located wooden chapels and churches or holy crosses. There is a tradition of putting on the holy cross a special shroud (*pelena*). The word *pelena* in the Russian language comes from the verb *pelenat* ('to swaddle'). A towel or an available piece of textile could also be used as a *pelena*, but the typical type has special embroidery on it. The embroidery shows the purpose for which the *pelena* was made. Typical is an embroidered image of the Holy Cross, which is next to the image of a head, an arm, a foot or a leg, a child, or even a cow! The local people claim that the images mean that the *pelena* is a special type of a prayer, which is connected with the peasants asking God to help a specific person to be healthy and to be saved from a headache (i.e. the image of a head), or from illness of his/her arms, feet or legs. An image of a child on a *pelena* often signifies a prayer for a grandchild. An image of a cow on a *pelena* is explained by the story about a cow being lost in the forest, but after a *pelena* was made and put on the Holy Cross the owner found the cow. A large number of *pelenas* are located in the Orthodox chapels which have survived in the sacred groves. Sometimes only two or three trees (pine or spruce) are located near the chapel as the remnants of a holy grove (Figure 25.5.2).

A number of stories about holy groves were collected from local peasants during field trips on Kenozero in 1981–1994. All of the stories tell about the sacred punishment of people who broke the regulations in the sacred groves. These people were rough and behaved impolitely in the sacred grove: they collected trees and tree branches from the grove for fire; they even broke the branches of a bush in the grove, collected plants or flowers from the place, or were rough in their speech while within the holy grove – sacred punishment came to all these people. There were different forms of sacred punishment:

Figure 25.5.2 The remnants of a holy grove near the chapel of St Spirit on Kenozero Lake, Kenozero, Archangel Region (© A. N. Davydov).

a sinner might become ill, or die, or lose his house by fire, or one of his cows might be killed by a bear, etc.

Conclusion

All of the examples of the sacred trees and sacred groves of the Russian North are connected with old pre-Christian tradition and often came from the ethnic groups who were settled on the territory before the Russians came. Later, these ethnic groups were assimilated by the Russian people, but their beliefs were implanted into the spiritual tradition of North Russians.

The spiritual landscape of the Russian North was formed in the process of the intercommunication of the Russian Orthodox (Byzantine) tradition with an ancient Finno-Ugric substratum.

Research for this article has been carried out within the Program of Fundamental Research of the Presidium of Russian Academy of Sciences 'Adaptation of peoples and cultures to changes of nature environment and to social and technogenous transformations'.

Box 25.6 Sacred trees and groves in Zagori, Northern Pindos National Park, Greece

KALLIOPI STARA, RIGAS TSIAKIRIS and JENNY WONG

Introduction

Veteran trees and ancient forests are an important element of cultural landscapes, their survival as symbols redolent of ancient taboos, old traditions and faiths. In modern Greece, these features are not only significant for their aesthetic and historical qualities, but also as reservoirs of biodiversity.

Methodology

The study took place in Zagori, a network of 45 villages within the newly established Northern Pindos National Park. During 2006, 145 residents in 22 villages were interviewed and the following year 220 sites were surveyed and the species, size, condition and artefacts associated with 800 trees encountered on these sites were recorded. Biodiversity importance and potential threats to each site were also recorded. A preview of the findings is presented here, as data analysis is still in progress.

Results

It was found that small chapels or shrines characteristically guard the entrances to Zagori villages. These encircle and magically guard the settlement from the external 'wilderness' and tame the forces of nature by invoking the name and hence spiritual power of particular saints (Kyriakidou-Nestoros, 1989). The trees associated with such sites were

Figure 25.6.1 Vrysochori village – Chapel of Santa Paraskevi and its associated oak belfry tree (© Kalliopi Stara).

typically evergreen or broadleaved oaks and often contained artefacts such as the chapel bell or a cross incised into the bark (see Figure 25.6.1).
Figure 25.6.1 shows Vrysochori village – the Chapel of Santa Paraskevi and its associated oak belfry tree. Santa Paraskevi is a dragon-killer and in popular belief is connected with underground water and springs.

Another important feature of Zagorian landscapes is the excommunicated forest. Excommunication was used as a punishment and deterrent by the Orthodox Church and during the time of the Ottoman occupation this was used by the Church to govern land use within the villages (see Figure 25.6.2).

Figure 25.6.2 Mikro Papigo village (© Kalliopi Stara)

This figure shows Mikro Papigo village. The excommunicated wooded steep slope 'Plai', composed of sparse formations of *Juniperus foetidissima* and *J. excelsa*, functions as a protective wood belt just below the alpine meadows. Excommunication protected the settlement from landslides and torrents at a time when wood demand was very high.

   Performing prohibited acts such as felling trees on excommunicated land not only threatened the exclusion of the wrong-doer from the church community during their lives, but also denied them an afterlife in heaven and imperilled the souls of the perpetrator's family (Mihailaris, 2004). We found forests excommunicated at that time in almost all villages. Examples

Table 25.6.1 *Examples of different reasons for which forests were excommunicated in the study area. Free pasture with prohibition of logging and cutting of trees for fodder were common management practices in all examples below.*

Village	Site	Reason of protection
Aristi	*Pournaria* (Prickly oak forest)	Last resort to be used in times of exceptional need, e.g. in hard winters or famine fodder for livestock
Kapesovo	*Gradista* (Fortress)	Trees reserved only for community use, i.e. public works
Mikro Papigo	*Plai* (Slope)	Protection of the settlement from natural disasters, such as landslides and torrents
Negades	*Livadi* (Wood pasture)	Protection of village aquifer

of different reasons for which forests were excommunicated in order to manage and control use are cited in Table 25.6.1.

Excommunication entailed ostentatious official ceremonies, which engendered a vague menace to all possible trespassers and underlined the seriousness of the protection afforded to the forest. Some of our older informants recalled narratives of ceremonies involving seven priests who announced the excommunication holding black candles. For that reason such areas were called *eftapapada* which means 'excommunicated by seven priests'.

Discussion

Fear of the supernatural successfully protected the sacred trees, groves and forests until the recent past as local people feared that felling them might cause misfortune, disease or even death to the wrong-doer, their family and animals. Many local people can relate stories in which the Virgin Maria or saints, invoked as supernatural protectors of specific places, appeared in warning, paralysing the wrong-doer until repentant, sending a snake to frighten them, or appearing in their dreams and beating them. The worst stories equate trespassing to the amputation of limbs, falling blind, becoming severely ill, or death.

Sacred sites in Zagori contain significantly more ancient trees than their surroundings and although their biodiversity has not been surveyed comprehensively, it seems likely, because the presence of mature forest vegetation with a well-developed structure and plentiful dead wood will give rise to high biodiversity importance. In addition, isolated veterans are known to represent important habitats for a range of organisms that require the special environment that only ancient trees provide (Rackham, 2006).

Conclusion

This study clearly showed that antecedent systems of local and religious restrictions have broken down and we frequently encountered sacred trees which were obviously forgotten, neglected, damaged or had even been felled. Continued protection of these sites and trees now needs something other than the fear of God and threats of spiritual punishment. Interviews with younger villagers suggest that respect for nature, local history and tradition may be more effective than fear. Thus it is hoped that drawing public attention to the cultural and biodiversity value of these 'sacred' places will reinforce their preservation by connecting modern and traditional protection systems. There is an urgent need for the conservation of these fragile cultural landscapes that, whether expressed in spiritual or secular terms, are charged with social and ecologically important values and qualities.

Box 25.7 The sacred Sal groves of the Indian Jharkhand

RADHIKA BORDE and JYOTISH KUMAR KERKETTA

Introduction

East-central India is home to several groups of people that are understood to be indigenous to the sub-Continent. The state of Jharkhand ('land of forests') in the region was formed in the year 2000 in response to a demand from these tribal groups for an administrative unit that would facilitate their own cultural expression. Among the many tribes that are represented demographically within this state, the major ones are the Santhals, Oraons, Mundas and Hos. They practise an elaborate form of localised nature worship centred around the sacred groves that are to be found adjacent to their villages. The sacred groves of the Oraons, Mundas and Hos consist almost exclusively of Sal trees or *Shorea robusta*. *Shorea robusta* has been acknowledged as sacred for many of the thousands of years of Indian history, as is testified by its mention as such in the *Atharva Veda Samhita*, an ancient Indian text (Zysk, 1985, p. 99). This tree species is endemic to the region of Jharkhand and in fact largely constitutes the

Figure 25.7.1 A sacred Sal grove in India.

middle and upper storey of its forest vegetation (classified as the dry deciduous type) (Figure 25.7.1).

Sacred Sal groves

These sacred Sal groves are known as Sarnas or Jahiras by tribal people, who believe that they form the residence of several deities. Sacred groves constitute the primary sites of the expression of tribal spirituality in India – seen most vibrantly during the annual spring festival that occurs when the Sal trees begin to blossom. Amongst the Santhals the festival is known as Baha Parab. Two sheds made of Sal branches are constructed within the sacred grove, to house spirit deities for the duration of the festival. Sal blossoms are collected and distributed among villagers to attract prosperity and health. The Oraons refer to this festival as Sarhul and celebrate it in a similar manner. Additionally, they single out a Sal tree within the grove for especial veneration – tying a thread around it thrice and sacrificing fowls to it, which along with rice and water is distributed to the people present in cups made out of Sal leaves (Figure 25.7.2).

Shorea robusta finds sacred use in several tribal rituals. On the eve of the Disom Sendra or annual hunt, which the Santhals celebrate to express their

Figure 25.7.2 Sacrifice of fowls to sal groves during the *Sarhul* festival.

relationship with the spirit world, Sal twigs are cast into a brass water vessel. If the twigs are seen to appear fresh the following morning, it is taken as a good omen for the commencement of the hunt. Sal leaves are also employed in Santhal divorce proceedings. The party seeking divorce symbolises the breaking of the conjugal bond by tearing three Sal leaves along the mid-rib in the presence of the village head-man. After the conclusion of a Santhal funeral, Sal twigs and Sal oilseed cakes are offered to the major village deities as a plea to offer the deceased spirit rest. Santhal spirit doctors divine the cause of disease or misfortune by anointing Sal leaves with oil and inspecting the pattern it forms upon them. The Oraons are documented to employ *Shorea robusta* in a ritual that is conducted twice a year for acquiring procreative vigour. This requires Oraon boys to besmear themselves with red earth and insert their genitals into a split Sal twig that is supposed to represent the female sexual organ (Sahay, 1965, p. 72).

Sal is venerated across the cultural landscape of the country. The tribals of the Indian state of West Bengal believe it to be the symbol of the sun God, Indra. Sal is mentioned in the mythology of the Baiga tribe as the marriage pole around which the Earth married the founder of the tribe. The Buddha is understood to have been born under a Sal tree, to have attained enlightenment in a Sal grove and also to have spent the last night of his life under a Sal tree (Dymock *et al.*, 1890, p. 195) A Buddhist legend reveals the Sal tree to be nothing less than a Bodhisattva – an incarnation of the Buddha.

Conclusion

Shorea robusta products also play a most vital role in the material culture of Indian tribals. The seeds are eaten and pressed for oil. Several medicinal properties are attributed to the resin of the Sal tree. It is used in the preparation of ointments, employed to fumigate rooms occupied by the sick and is ingested to cure dysentery. A list of its many curative uses can be found in a sixteenth-century medical text attributed to a member of the then Mughal court. The value of its produce being so high, it is no wonder that the logging of *Shorea robusta* in state commercial forestry operations has received trenchant criticism – it has in fact been described as nothing less than cultural genocide. In recognition of the religious–cultural value of the sacred Sal groves of Jharkhand, an attempt was made in 1993 to grant them a special status under UNESCO.

Box 25.8   The role of *Íbú ódó* sacred pools in preserving riparian forest structure and diversity along the Ouèmé and Okpara rivers of Central Benin

NATALIE CEPERLEY

Introduction

Íbú ódó are sacred pools at points in the river that are commonly found in the Ouèmé and Okpara rivers of central Benin. *Íbú ódó* are subject to rules that may influence conservation practices, including the prohibition of the use of fish poison, over-fishing and pollution, and also cover the discouragement of grazing cattle. The fact that these sacred pools are respected, not only by resident populations but also by migrants to the area, suggests their value to riparian forest and water conservation. Riparian vegetation filters nutrients and sediment from entering waterways and slows flood damage, but these and other ecological functions are dependent on the width of the riparian zone, forest structure and species composition (Piegay and Bravard, 1997). These characteristics are modified by human use of the forest and adjacent lands. Riparian buffer degradation can have serious consequences for neighbouring settlements and farms. This study examines the value of *Íbú ódó* sacred sites for riparian forest conservation and indirectly for flood and runoff buffering.

Research progress

All trees with a breast height diameter greater than 10 cm, in three circular plots of 4-m radii located along the river bank, in the centre, and on the forest edge, on 163 transects laid perpendicular to the river near three villages, Idadjo (population 1918), Monka (1128) and Djabata (692) (INSAE, 2004), were identified and measured at breast height. Transects were spaced semi-randomly 50–100 m apart and they spanned areas adjacent to the villages, sacred sites, and state-protected forests (*Foret Classé de Ouari Maro*). The sites, which are home to the Tchabé (Yoruba) ethnic group, are situated along a riverbank in the Ouèmé Basin and situated in the Guineo-Congolian vegetation zone. At least 30 elders or dignitaries were interviewed at each site concerning devotion practices, values of the forest, and land-use practices.

Outcomes

The number of sacred sites and the diversity of the riparian forest in each site were correlated. Idadjo has a specific richness of 35 tree species, Monka of 26, and Djabata of 39. Monka's position on the main Nigerian transport road and its corresponding accessibility for economic exploitation can explain its low richness, whereas Djabata and Idadjo, which are much further from main roads, have greater richness. Alternatively, diversity may reflect either conservation due to respect for sacred pools – in the case of Djabata, where 14 sacred pools were actively maintained, compared with nine in Monka and five in Idadjo – or conservation that has been encouraged by a non-governmental organisation, PAMF (Projet d'aménagement des massifs forestiers), for the last decade, as in the case of Idadjo. Further analysis will quantify and compare riparian forest structure and diversity adjacent to sacred pools, agricultural land, and state-protected forest for each site.

The sacred pools occur where the river is particularly deep, the water gurgles, fishing is good (Figure 25.8.1), a historical event occurred, or where there is an interesting formation such as a suspended rock. Pools are home to spirits and upsetting them can have dire consequences, including floods, drought, disease and infertility. Most are surrounded by taboos ranging from the manner one must behave or dress near the fetish to specific rules regarding what one can or cannot do. In most cases, people can make requests to the spirit: for example, to improve business, conceive a child, or

Figure 25.8.1 Ya, a sacred pool near Djabata, is known for good fishing. The village
leader responsible for this pool makes an annual sacrifice of cheese or goat at this
point in the river. Anyone can make requests to the fetish that resides here.
Crocodiles swim in its serene waters (© N. Ceperley).

have a good harvest. There is usually an elder who is responsible for
organising the sacrifices and communicating with each particular
spirit.

However, will these cultural and spiritual motivations for conservation
stand up against the economic and demographic changes that are driving
land-use change? Major drivers of change of riparian vegetation include field
expansion adjacent to riparian forest, timber harvesting and cattle grazing.
Migrants who come from northern Benin to farm in the central Ouèmé Basin
are responsible for most of the field expansion. The village king designates

Figure 25.8.2 Exploitation of *Ceiba pentandra*. *Ceiba pentandra* planks from the riparian forest near the village of Idadjo. Migrant 'sciers' pay a nominal fee to the local king in order to be granted permission to transform these majestic tress that grow along the Oueme river into planks. Often the transportation is interrupted by the arrival of the rainy season (© N. Ceperley).

land far from the village for their use; often it is on the riskier, more fertile floodplain. *Ceiba pentandra*, *Diospyros mespilliformes* and the vulnerable *Albizia ferruginea* (IUCN, 2007) are harvested for timber to be sold in southern Benin by outsiders who pay a nominal fee to the local king (Figure 25.8.2). Cattle grazing has increased in the last decade as Peulh herders have been driven into the area due to regional droughts. They are perceived as the most severe threat to the landscape and water quality.

Conclusion

When combined with the social assessment of the importance of these pools, this study provides the argument for respecting and reinforcing *Íbú ódó*. Encouraging respect for sacred sites is particularly crucial among younger generations and migrants to the area.

Conclusions

A number of examples presented in this chapter suggest that many traditional societies are 'prudent' in their resource use by observing restraints for various reasons. Six different types of resource and habitat taboos are suggested to play a role in nature conservation and resource management in traditional societies. These societies undoubtedly have made a valuable contribution to conservation through their cultural practices. However, an important question is whether these cultural and spiritual motivations for conservation can withstand economic and demographic changes that are driving land use in a rapidly changing world. In Central Benin, for example, major driving forces of change in riparian vegetation include field expansion adjacent to riparian forest, timber harvesting and cattle grazing. Migrants who come from northern Benin to farm in the central Ouèmé Basin are responsible for most of the field expansion (Box 25.8). Can sacred water bodies in Benin withstand these changes? The example from Central Benin is representative of many other traditional practices that face similar challenges. The process of globalisation has added further to the complexity because many traditional societies have in fact become modernised in the recent past and undergone fundamental changes in their values. For example, the youth in these societies no longer subscribe to traditional practices or rituals. In many societies, migrants have changed the social fabric. The process of globalisation has also brought about 'cultural homogenisation' of a kind – similar to the 'biotic homogenisation' that many of the world's ecosystems have seen (Olden and LeRoy Poff, 2004). How can we then go about conservation of biocultural diversity in the face of cultural homogenisation?

There is no doubt that the challenges we face are unprecedented. The human species perhaps has not encountered such challenges for most of the last 10 000 years. However, there is evidence that landscapes and cultures have proved themselves to be remarkably resilient (Gunderson and Holling, 2002). There are examples where societies have been able to withstand natural catastrophes as well as social transformation and adapt to the new conditions. For example, despite the dramatic change in our natural surroundings, the Industrial Revolution, and the mind-boggling advancement in technology, faith still plays an important part in people's lives in many modern societies. Alliance of Religions and Conservation (ARC, 2008) estimates that 85% of the world's population still subscribes to a faith; and provides evidence that faith continues to play an important role in today's globalised world. It is estimated that over 15% of the Earth's land surface has a religious connotation (Palmer, 2007). To put this number into perspective, the global protected area network covers just over 12% of the Earth's land surface (WCPA, 2008). There is, therefore, hope for conservation of sacred species and associated biocultural diversity. Our own species has the capacity to respond to this unprecedented challenge and ensure the survival of many others.

References

ARC. (2008). Alliance of Religions and Conservation. Available from: www.arcworld.org (accessed January 2009).

Begg, C., Begg, K. and Muemedi, O. (2007). *Preliminary Data on Human–carnivore Conflict in Niassa National Reserve, Mozambique, particularly Fatalities due to Lion, Spotted Hyena and Crocodile*. Report to Sociedade para a Gestão e Desenvolvimento da Reserva do Niassa Moçambique.

Bhagwat, S. A. and Rutte, C. (2006) Sacred groves: potential for biodiversity management. *Frontiers in Ecology and the Environment*, **4**, 519–24.

Bowen-Jones, E. and Entwhistle, A. (2002). Identifying appropriate flagship species: the importance of culture and local contexts. *Oryx*, **36**, 189–95.

Brown, J. P. (1969). *The Lebanon and Phoenicia, Vol. 1*. Beirut: The American University of Beirut Press.

Catanoiu, S. and Deju, R. (2005). *Zimbrul-un simbol al Muntilor Carpati*. Piatra Neamt: Autograf, pp. 1–16.

Colding, J. and Folke, C. (2001). Social taboos: 'invisible' systems of local resource management and biological conservation. *Ecological Applications*, **11**, 584–600.

Dafni A., Levy, S. and Lev, E. (2005). The ethnobotany of Christ's Thorn Jujube (*Ziziphus spina-christi*). *Israel Journal of Ethnobiology and Ethnomedicine*, **1**(8); available from: http://www.pubmedcentral.nih.gov/articlerender.fcgi?artid=1277088 (accessed January 2009).

Dyikanova, C. K., Dykanov, T. K. and Samanchina, J. B. (2004). *Sacred Sites of Kyrgyzstan*. Bishkek: Turar.

Dymock, W., Warden, C. J. H. and Hooper, M. (1890). *Pharmacographia Indica*. London: Kegan Paul, Trench, Trubner & Co.

Efimenko, P. (1864). *Provincializmy Arkhangel'skoy gubernii*. Pamyatnaya knizhka Arkhangel'skoy gubernii na 1864 god.

Efimenko, P. (1877). *Materialy po etnografii russkogo naseleniya Arkhangel'skoy gubernii*. Chast' 1. Opisanie vnesdhnego I vnutrennego byta. Moscow.

Eliade, M. (1991). *Images and Symbols. Studies in Religious Symbolism*. Princeton, NJ: Princeton University Press.

EOL. (2008). *Encyclopedia of Life*. Available from: http://www.eol.org/index (accessed January 2009).

Gadgil, M. (1987). Social restraints on exploiting nature: the Indian experience. *Development: Seeds of Change*, **1**, 26–30.

Gorovei, A. (1995). *Credinti si superstitii ale poporului roman*, 2nd edn. Bucharest: Grai si suflet-Cultura Nationala.

Gunderson, L. H. and Holling, C.S. (2002). *Panarchy: Understanding Transformations in Human and Natural Systems*. Washington, DC: Island Press.

Hepper, N. (1992). *Illustrated Encyclopedia of Bible Plants*. Leicester: Three's Company.

INSAE (Institut National de la Statistique et de l'Analyse Economique). (2004). Cahier des villages et quartiers de ville: Département des Collines, Direction des Etudes Démographiques, Cotonou.

IUCN (International Union for the Conservation of Nature). (2007). Red List of Threatened Species. Available from: http://www.iucnredlist.org/ (accessed 20 October 2007).

Johannes, R. E. (1998). Government-supported, village-based management of marine resources in Vanuatu. *Ocean and Coastal Management*, **40**, 165–86.

Kyriakidou-Nestoros, A. (1989). *Laografika Meletimata, Vol. 1*. Athens: Etaireia Ellinikou Logotechnikou kai Istorikou Arxeiou. *Folk Studies, Vol. 1*. Athens: Society of Hellenic Literature and Historical archives. (In Greek.)

Makhzoumi, J. (2001). Learning from the vernacular. *Landscape and Art*, **22**, 20–1.

Marimuthu, G. (1988). The sacred flying fox of India. *Bats*, **6**, 10–1.

Mihailaris, P. D. (2004). *Aforismos: I prosarmogi mias poinis stis anagkaiotites tis Tourkokratias*, 2nd edn. Athens: Ethniko Idryma Erevnon – Kentro Neoellinikon Erevnon 60. Excommunication. Adaptation of a punishment to the needs of the Ottoman Occupation, 2nd edn. Athens: National Research Foundation – Center of Modern Greek Research 60. (In Greek).

MOE (Ministry of Environment). Available from: http://www.moe.gov.lb/ ProtectedAreas/categories.htm (accessed 8 April 2008).

Museum of Traditional Popular Civilisation ASTRA. The calendar of popular feasts, http://www.muzeulastra.ro/calendarul_manifestarilor.

Olden, J. D. and LeRoy Poff, N. (2004). Clarifying biotic homogenization. *Trends in Ecology and Evolution*, **19**, 282–3.

Palmer, M. (2007). Theology of land. Available from: http://www.arcworld.org/ projects.asp?projectID=369 (accessed September 2008).

Pamyatnaya knizhka Arkhangel' gubernii (1864).

Parikesit, D., Takeuchi, K., Tsunekawa, A., *et al.* (2005). Kebon tatangkalan: a disappearing agroforest in the Upper Citarum Watershed, West Java, Indonesia. *Agroforestry Systems*, **63**, 171–82.

Piegay, H. and Bravard, J. (1997). Reponse of a Mediterranean riparian forest to a 1 in 400 year flood, Ouveze River, Drome,Vaucluse, France. *Earth Surface Processes and Landforms*, **22**, 31–43.

Posey, D. A. (1985). Indigenous management of tropical forest ecosystems: the case of the Kayapo Indians of the Brazilian Amazon. *Agroforestry Systems*, **3**, 139–58.

Rackham, O. (2006). *Woodlands*. London: Collins.

Rossii, G. (1994). *Encyclopedia*, ed. G. M. Lappo. Moscow: Nauchnoe izdatel'stvo 'Bol'shaya Rossijskaya Encyclopedia'.

Sahay, K. N. (1965). Tree-cult in tribal culture. In S. S. Gupta, *Tree Symbol Worship in India*. Calcutta: Indian Publications.

Shangina, I. I. (2003). *Russkij traditsionny byt. Encyclopedichesky slovar*. St Petersburg: Azbuka-klassika.

Talhouk, S., Makhzoumi, J., Maunder, M., *et al.* (2001). You can't see the wood for the trees: the cedar of Lebanon as a symbol of a country and an ecosystem. *Archaeology and History in Lebanon*, **14**, 114–22.

WCPA. (2008). IUCN World Commission on Protected Areas. Available from: http://www.iucn.org/about/union/commissions/wcpa/index.cfm (accessed January 2009).

Zysk, K. G. (1985). *Medicine in the Veda*. Delhi: Motilal Banarsidass Publishers.

26

Sacred sites, sacred landscapes and biocultural diversity: applying the principles

GLORIA PUNGETTI and FEDERICO CINQUEPALMI

Introduction

This chapter aims to explore the sacred character of sites and landscapes, illustrating their link with biological and cultural diversity and indicating alternatives for the future with selected case studies. The European and global perspective has been tackled for the discussion, and six boxes by different authors are included to apply the general principles.

The value of protected areas in land and sea as venues of scientific inquiry, nature conservation and destinations for increasingly needed recreation is well known (Harmon and Putney, 2003). Similarly, settings of beautiful and scenic landscapes and their value for biological and cultural diversity are easily appreciated by people (Lucas, 1992). Landscape in particular embraces the ecological, natural, cultural and spiritual values of our environment (Makhzoumi and Pungetti, 1999) and, in turn, has been shaped by people and is a repository of their memories (Schama, 1995); it can be considered a pillar for local identity. The European perspective illustrated in this chapter is a representation of such identity.

The European approach to sacred landscapes

Although sacred landscapes contain important values for different faiths, the predominant link in Europe is with Christianity. However, in several cases, as discussed in Chapter 4, cultural landscapes connected with religions and traditions in Europe and in the Mediterranean basin are often more ancient and were associated with previous beliefs, such as Celts in the North, and Romans, Greeks and Etruscans in the South, rather than with the mainstream faith. Recent research has shown that these landscapes also retain high conservation values (Dudley *et al.*, 2005; Schaaf and Lee, 2006; Mallarach and Papayannis, 2007; McIvor and Pungetti, 2008) and are, therefore, important for studies of the relationship between the natural and the cultural heritage. The European Landscape Convention (ELC) by the Council of Europe (CoE) is a significant example.

One of the ELC theoretical foundations is to identify and assess landscape using research fields in particular conjunction with the local people. Each research field should consider both natural and artificial components, together with external factors that can induce changes to the general picture. Nevertheless, past landscape studies have focused largely on the physical and aesthetic character of landscape, taking into account, among other aspects, morphology, patterns, beauty, scenery, land use and, last but not least, nature and its wildlife habitats.

Another theoretical foundation of the ELC is to consider landscape as the basis of local identity. With the assumption that the well-being of the landscape is closely related to the level of public awareness and public involvement in decisions affecting living environments (Council of Europe, 2000), the ELC places people at the very heart of landscape conservation and management.

Sacred sites, landscapes and biocultural diversity

Elevated points or natural monuments have frequently been considered bridges towards the sky, namely places where people came in order to commune with the heavens and to escape from the terrestrial destiny of man. Such places were used, as in the Native American and Mediterranean traditions, as burial grounds (described in Boxes 26.1 and 26.5, respectively), whereas in other cultures these were favourite spots for building temples or sanctuaries. The list of these places is as long as the history of spiritual belief itself.

The mountain landscape had a special relevance in such a list. Volcanoes, in particular, with their distinctive conic outline and dangerous summits, have been considered sacred and emblematic of the mysterious forces that have governed natural phenomena since the dawning of history. Etna in Sicily and Mount Fuji in Japan are two ultimate examples.

In general, most elevated and unusual places have, at one time, represented some sort of religious reference point for the different communities who lived nearby, as clearly shown by the Holy San Francisco Peaks (Box 26.1) and the Mount Everest (Box 26.2) case studies presented here. On the other hand, lower altitudes have been enriched with the symbolic meaning of plants and cultural landscapes, as with the Mediterranean burial grounds mentioned above. They all reveal the co-existence of a variety of cultures living on different lands rich in biodiversity.

Moreover, the spiritual value associated with mountains across the world demonstrates how widespread this attitude has been since ancient times. Mount

Olympus, for example, was believed to be the home of the Greek gods and later came to be eponymous for the concept of divinity itself. Yet the concept can be easily extended to all 'acropolis' structures from Europe to Asia and throughout the Americas.

In the past, furthermore, mainstream faiths have sometimes misinterpreted their spiritual traditions, conquering and exploiting nature, its resources and indigenous peoples as well. One would expect that the challenges should be lesser in technologically developed countries (see Box 26.4), as they have the capacity and resources to manage their heritage more effectively. As proved by recent studies (Mallarach and Papayannis, 2007), however, this is not the always the case.

Yet sites sacred for indigenous peoples in some developed countries are threatened by the pressure of development and lack the protection and respect for spiritual beliefs. The ski resort planned on the Twin San Francisco Peaks in Arizona, sacred to 13 different Native American Nations, is an example. Similar cases throughout the USA are documented in literature and videos the Sacred Land Film Project.

Similarly, it is illustrated, i.e. in Box 26.3 how sacred groves in the Japanese landscape are threatened by contemporary society, and solutions for the conservation of their biocultural diversity are offered.

Initiatives have been launched to raise awareness of these threatened sites and landscapes connected to their sacred species, and to contribute to a better management of sacred natural sites, with the goal of maintaining their natural, cultural and spiritual values. Among these is the 3S Initiative on Sacred Species and Sites, which has been the origin of this book, and the Delos Initiative illustrated in this chapter.

Lastly, holy monuments hold a particular place in the history of some cultures and require special biocultural conservation. The last case study of this chapter (Box 26.6) reveals a relevant case from Sweden.

Holy landscapes and their peoples

Box 26.1 The Holy San Francisco Peaks, Arizona: cultural and spiritual survival of south-western indigenous nations

JENEDA BENALLY

Introduction

The Holy San Francisco Peaks are a distinct sight among the red rocks and dry sands of northern Arizona. Reaching 3851 m at the highest peak, this

Figure 26.1.1 Holy home to deities and rare species, the San Francisco Peaks are covered with snow (Photograph courtesy of Kelvin Long ©). See colour plate section.

volcanic massif serves as an oasis to the many forms of life that it sustains (Figure 26.1.1). Holy to 13 Native American Nations and culturally significant to 22 Native American Nations, this unique mountain has a distinct name and a distinct role in each of the indigenous native languages and customs. Although the Holy Mountain is not on Reservation land, it is situated on National Forest Service land. In the context of Native American history, such a land management situation is fairly recent. This has resulted in controversy and legal debate regarding Forest Service plans to manufacture snow utilising reclaimed wastewater on the Holy San Francisco Peaks.

Cultural significance

The San Francisco Peaks are known to the Dine' (Navajo) people as Dook'oo'sliid, the Abalone Shell Mountain. This prominence is a pillar of the Dine' universe. There are six sacred mountains and four are the pillars: Dooko'oo'sliid is the westernmost pillar and the traditionally given boundary. At the creation of time, the Creator gave these boundaries. It is within these Holy Mountains that the Dine' (Navajo) people were told to be caretakers. Through the soil bundles from the Sacred Mountain, used during ceremonies, Dook'oo'sliid controls the adulthood of the Dine' people's lives. Each individual has a spiritual, physical and mental bond that translates, for

Figure **26.1.2** View of the Holy San Francisco Peaks: an oasis in the high desert (Photograph courtesy of Klee Benally ©). See colour plate section.

tribal members, into their whole well-being. When prayers are made, they include every living being on this westernmost Holy Mountain, from the grasses and insects on the ground to the eagles in the sky. The prayers also include the Holy People that exist on Dook'oo'sliid. The Holy People have made their abode on this massif since the beginning of time. They aid and guide the traditionalists in everyday life, prayer and ceremony.

Sacred plants and minerals used for healing and restoring harmony are gathered from Dook'oo'sliid utilising specific sacred names and prayers. Offerings are made to establish gratitude to all life that nourishes these. It is recognised that the entire mountainous biosphere is a single living entity, identified as a female mountain that sustains and gives life just as a mother does to her children. It is with reverence and virtue that Dook'oo'sliid is acknowledged.

To the many bands of Apache, Dzil Cho, the San Francisco Peaks, are a portal into the next world. When a life has met its end, the spirit begins its voyage into the next world through Dzil Cho. It is said that all things attributed to Dzil Cho accompany the departed spirit into the next life. The Mountain Spirits make this mountain a home and come to the aid of their people when called upon.

The San Francisco Peaks are known to the Hopi as Nuvatukyaovi, 'Place of Snow on the Very Top' (Figure 26.1.2). The heart of the Hopi way of life is dependent upon their relationship with Katsinas. Also known as Kachinas, these Holy Ones make Nuvatukyaovi their dwelling place. These producers of holy precipitation are the lone source of water for the crops in this thirsty terrain. It is through prayer, ceremony and song that the Hopi people call to the Katsinas during particular times of the year. This relationship is the foundation for the Hopi people's existence in this dry desert landscape. For the Hopi, if man creates snow at the home of the Katsinas, the ones that are responsible for precipitation, then the Hopis fear that the Katsinas will leave the Hopi people.

Challenge

A small, privately operated ski resort presently exists on the Holy San Francisco Peaks, in opposition to the Native American Tribes that hold it Holy. The first ski lodge was allowed in the 1930s by the Forest Service, which continues to manage the land, and was then further developed in 1979 when the operation was officially introduced with a new ski lodge. Native Nations challenged the building of the ski resort in a legal battle. The tribes lost in the courts and the ski resort was permitted. The legal effort continues for Tribes supporting the protection and preservation of the natural land state as it presently occurs (Figure 26.1.3).

The ski resort and Forest Service want to expand the facility to include snowmaking with reclaimed wastewater. However, the Forest Service itself states that 'based on the belief systems of many of the tribes we must consider at least a portion of these impacts as a potentially irreversible impact to these tribes' religions' (Arizona Snowbowl Draft Environmental Impact Statement, pp. 3–28). The Forest Service later adds, 'Snowmaking and expansion of facilities, especially the use of reclaimed wastewater, would contaminate the natural resources needed to perform the required ceremonies that have been, and continue to be, the basis for the cultural identity for many of these tribes' (Arizona Snowbowl Facilities Improvements Environmental Impact Statement Vol. 1, Chapter 3, The affected environment and environmental consequences, pp. 3–18).

Conclusion

The tribal relationship with the Holy San Francisco Peaks is interconnected and it is of the utmost importance to maintain the spiritual sanctity of the mountain as well as the environmental integrity of this high

Figure 26.1.3 A prayerful ride through the high desert landscape to bring attention to the struggle to protect the Holy San Francisco Peaks.

desert oasis in order to support cultural survival. The existing ski resort is a wound for the Native American Tribes that hold it as a Holy Mountain; any expansion further altering the San Francisco Peaks' natural landscape adversely affects the spiritscape. When the spiritscape is altered it impacts the ancient living lifeways that are striving to maintain their cultural and spiritual existence.

Box 26.2 Buddhism, sacred places and Sherpa conservation in the Mount Everest region of Nepal

STAN STEVENS

Introduction

The Mount Everest area of Nepal, the high country on the border of Tibet that the Sherpa people call Khumbu, is one of the most sacred regions of the Himalaya (Figure 26.2.1). It is one of a small set of hidden, sacred valleys (*beyul*) consecrated by Guru Rinpoche (Padmasambhava) (Figure 26.2.2) and hidden by him more than 1200 years ago to be future

Figure 26.2.1 Khumbu. Central Khumbu looking east to Mt Everest (back, on left), Lhotse and Ama Dablam peaks. A protected temple grove can be seen in Khumjung, the largest Khumbu Sherpa village. (© Stan Stevens).

Buddhist sanctuaries. Sherpas believe that Guru Rinpoche visited Khumbu when it was an uninhabited wilderness, converted the mountain spirit Khumbu Yul Lha to Buddhism, and entrusted him with the care of the region, its wildlife and its future inhabitants as its guardian god. The ancestors of the Sherpas settled the sacred valley five centuries ago and have shared with Khumbu Yul Lha the stewardship of its scores of sacred mountains, nearly a dozen sacred forests (Figure 26.2.3), several hundred sacred trees, and many sacred springs, caves and other natural features. Today the region has a population of 6000, more than 90% Sherpa, and is a national park (Sagarmatha National Park and Buffer Zone) and World Heritage Site as well as a Sherpa homeland (Stevens, 1993, 2008).

Sacred places and Sherpa conservation

Sherpas care for and protect Khumbu's sacred natural sites today through household, clan and community rites (Figure 26.2.4) and by maintaining core values and conservation practices – including many local and regional Indigenous Peoples' and Community Conserved Areas (ICCAs). Indeed, Sherpa leaders consider that all of the Khumbu *beyul* is a Sherpa ICCA. Because of this, Khumbu remains an extraordinary wildlife sanctuary, with substantial populations of endangered and threatened species and

Figure 26.2.2 Padmasambhava (Guru Rinpoche), who declared Khumbu a sacred hidden valley (*beyul*) (© Stan Stevens). See colour plate section.

extensive forests, despite major regional economic, political, social and cultural changes associated with globalisation, international tourism development, and increased integration into the national, Hindu-dominated society and polity (Stevens, 2008).

Sherpas believe that it is a defining characteristic of Sherpa identity that as a Buddhist people they should not kill any form of life. They honour this belief by giving complete protection to all mammals, birds, reptiles, fish and insects. Sherpa religious leaders, moreover, have taught that protection of life is particularly important in Khumbu because it is a sacred valley and, as a result, Sherpas have attempted to prevent outsiders – including government officials, army, police and market hunters – from killing wildlife. Sherpa wildlife protection has made the region a celebrated

Figure 26.2.3 Pangboche temple and the lama's Forest at Yarin. This forest has been strictly protected for 400 years (© Stan Stevens).

wildlife sanctuary, home to Red List endangered species that include musk deer and snow leopard, threatened species such as Himalayan tahr (Figure 26.2.5), and vulnerable species that include the red panda and Himalayan black bear. Sherpas accept significant crop losses to Himalayan tahr, Himalayan monal pheasants, Nepal gray langur and rhesus macaque monkeys, Himalayan black bear and other wildlife without taking retaliation (Ale, 2007; Stevens, 1993, 2008).

In the past, however, Sherpas did kill predators in defence of their livestock and livelihoods. By the late twentieth century, the grey wolf, snow leopard and leopard had all been regionally extirpated. Since 2000, snow leopards and common leopards have re-colonised the region. Sherpa leaders have urged herders to co-exist with these predators and, thus far, herders have not taken any action against them. Sherpa leaders are now formulating a livestock insurance system that would compensate herders for their losses (Stevens, 1993, 2008).

The protection of sacred forests is an outstanding example of the Sherpa protection of sacred natural sites through local ICCAs. Sherpa communities strictly protect spirit (*lu*) trees, lama's forests (declared sacred by historical religious leaders) and temple/monastery forests from all tree felling (grazing, the collection of forest floor litter for composting material and the collection

Figure 26.2.4 Sherpas of Nauje village (internationally known as Namche Bazar) make offerings to the regional guardian god Khumbu Yul Lha at the Dumje festival (© Stan Stevens).

of wild foods and medicines are allowed). These forests vary in size from small temple groves scarcely a hectare in size to lama's forests and monastery forests of several hundred hectares. Several provide important habitats for endangered musk deer. Sacred forests have remained well protected despite new threats to them from outsiders, and still survive today (Stevens, 1993, 2008).

Since the 1970s, Khumbu has also been Sagarmatha (Mount Everest) National Park, and since 2002 the many Sherpa enclave settlements within and the park and the Sherpa lands adjacent to the park have been part of the Sagarmatha National Park Buffer Zone. Lack of government respect for

Figure 26.2.5 Himalayan tahr, a threatened species protected by Sherpas' Buddhist values and discouragement of outsiders' poaching (© Stan Stevens). See colour plate section.

Sherpa culture, sacred natural sites and conservation stewardship through ICCAs has led to continuing conflict (Stevens, 1993, 1997, 2008). Despite the lack of legal recognition of their conservation practices, however, Sherpas continue to take conservation stewardship responsibility for the region, protecting wildlife and sacred forests and managing livelihood commons through ICCAs that oversee community forests and rangelands (Figure 26.2.6). Sherpa leaders believe that Sherpas are responsible for 80% or more of the conservation responsibility and achievements of Sagarmatha National Park and Buffer Zone (Stevens, 2008).

Conclusion

It has been unfortunate that Sagarmatha National Park planning and policies have virtually ignored the sacred character of the region, the Sherpa's status as a legally recognised indigenous people, and customary Sherpa conservation values, institutions and practices. Sherpa leaders would welcome a change of spirit which would respect Sherpas' conservation stewardship through their values and ICCAs, and involve Sherpas in developing a new approach to Sagarmatha National Park management that

Figure 26.2.6 Sonam Hishi Shera (left), Urken Sherpa and Tenzing Tashi Sherpa examine a satellite photograph being used by a Sherpa mapping project to map Khumbu ICCAs as a proposed basis for future national park planning (© Stan Stevens).

is grounded in identity, Buddhist values and respect for natural sacred sites and all life.

Box 26.3 Sacred groves in Japanese *satoyama* landscapes: a case study and prospects for conservation

KATSUE FUKAMACHI and OLIVER RACKHAM

Introduction

Japan's *satoyama* cultural landscapes are dotted with a large number of sacred groves, small patches of forest which have traditionally been part of shrines and temples in almost every township. Many are at least a thousand years old. Their connection to ancient religions, legends and beliefs has been powerful enough to prevail over land development, urbanisation and land abandonment.

Sacred groves in Japan

Sacred groves occur in both principal religions of Japan, Shinto and Buddhism. In Shinto they are the focus of ceremonies and festivals which have their origin in ancient nature worship in which mountains, streams, rocks and trees are the abodes of deities or of the spirit ancestors and of legendary animals. Typically, they cover a few hectares, but can vary in size from a single tree to an entire mountain or island.

Rural Shinto shrines and the sacred groves around them have traditionally been maintained and managed by the *ujiko*, a committee of local shrine parishioners who play an important role in connecting the sacred sites to the life of the residents through regular festivals and ceremonies.

Taboos associated with the groves vary in each village, and often include a prohibition to fell trees or to use natural resources. Due to such taboos, vegetation in sacred groves has persisted over centuries and can be regarded in part as a relic of the natural regional vegetation of the past. The frequency of broadleaved evergreen trees such as *kusunoki* (*Cinnamomum camphora*), *tabu* (*Machilus thunbergii*), *shii* (*Castanopsis sieboldii*) and *shirakashi* (*Quercus myrsinifolia*) indicates that these species may have been part of the original natural vegetation.

The degree of management varies from one sacred grove to another. At one extreme, parts of the grounds of the larger temples and shrines are treated as formal gardens. At the other extreme, some areas look like undisturbed natural forest, with a great diversity of plants. Particularly conspicuous in such groves are *keyaki* (*Zelkova serrata*), *yamazakura* (*Prunus jamasakura*) and many shrubs and woody climbers. A particular feature of sacred groves is the presence of ancient trees, some of them marked as the homes of particular gods. Many species of tree can thus be designated: among the commonest are *keyaki*, *kusunoki* and *sugi* (*Cryptomeria japonica*). We are as yet unable to detect any difference between the tree species associated with Shinto and Buddhism. Even in formal gardens, ancient trees and dead trees are treated with veneration.

Sacred groves have varied down the centuries: they have a trajectory which is different from that of forests. This is shown not only in early maps (in which Japan is particularly rich), but in the groves themselves. The form of some trees displays a history of coppicing and pollarding. A general tendency is for sacred groves to be denser now than they have been in the past: young trees have grown up between the big spreading old trees which had plenty of room when they were young. This is associated with the increase of *sugi*, which was evidently a fashionable tree in the nineteenth century and was planted and encouraged in sacred groves as elsewhere.

Our case study is in a rice-farming area on the west side of Lake Biwa in Shiga Prefecture. The area is dotted with villages and covers a gentle east-facing slope up from the shore of the lake at 80 m altitude to 1000 m on

Figure 26.3.1 Sacred grove of Yama no kami between terraced rice fields (© Katsue Fukamachi).

Hora Mountain, which is covered by forests of *matsu* (*Pinus densiflora*), *nara* (*Quercus* spp.) and *buna* (*Fagus crenata*).

In this area, the *yama no kami*, one of the mountain goddesses, has been worshipped in shrines and sacred groves since ancient times. Worship of the mountain deity in this region is based on nature worship for the mountain that is the source of essential resources indispensable for rice farming, such as water. She therefore protects the farming environment and also the safety of woodcutters in the mountain forests. Taboos associated with the deity include not felling certain old trees and not entering the mountain on certain days. Non-observance is believed to result in misfortune or accidents.

The grove shown in Figure 26.3.1 is located in the midst of rice fields and lies close to a village located on the main road between the Hokuriku region and Kyoto; in the background, extended forests of *matsu* (pine), *nara* (Japanese oak) and *buna* (Japanese beech) can be seen. In this tiny *yama no kami* sacred grove, which covers only about 50 m², big old *dabunoki* camphor trees, *enoki* hackberry trees, *yabutsubaki* wild camellia, *egonoki* Japanese snowball and

Figure 26.3.2 Small shrine in a *yama no kami* grove that covers 50 m^2. A huge pair of *zori* straw sandals is dedicated to the mountain deity in a ceremony in January. The grove contains old *Machilus thunbergii*, *Celtis sinensis* var. *japonica*, *Camellia japonica*, *Styrax japonica* and many other rare native plant species (© Katsue Fukamachi).

many other rare native plant species can be found. Figure 26.3.2 shows a local shrine festival held each January during which a huge pair of *zori* straw sandals is dedicated to the mountain deity so that she can use them when patrolling the mountain for its protection. Figure 26.3.3 shows a *yama no kami* sacred grove in a neighbouring village. Every year in November and January, the *dondo* fire festival is held here. This festival, organised by the *ujiko* committee of local shrine parishioners, is dedicated to the *yama no kami* to express thanks and extend prayers for a good harvest and for the safety of the mountain workers.

Even though road-building and housing development have been spreading into this countryside since the end of World War II, many sacred groves were spared from destruction thanks to petitions by villagers who emphasised the cultural and spiritual value of the sites and insisted on the taboos (Fukamachi *et al.*, 2003).

In the study area, there has been a gradual influx of newcomers and tourists who are unfamiliar with ancient local customs and who have little interest in the preservation of sacred groves. Younger generations have little knowledge of ancient worship practices and often regard these as

Figure 26.3.3 *Yama no kami* sacred grove and site of the *dondo* Fire Festival, held each November and January. Organised by the *ujiko* committee of local shrine parishioners, it is dedicated to the mountain deity to express thanks and extend prayers for a good harvest and for the safety of the mountain workers (© Katsue Fukamachi).

superstition. Weakening spiritual connectivity of local people to sacred groves is a real threat to their survival.

Protective measures at the national level are lacking. Japan's nature conservation policy focuses on large-scale national parks or 'virgin forests', and there are hardly any regulations regarding small, sacred groves in the ordinary countryside. There is hope, however, as Japan has seen a recent rise in interest in sacred groves from the viewpoint of the preservation of rare species and biodiversity.

Conclusion

Sacred groves are of particular significance as a habitat because of their vast historical continuity, variety of tree species and presence of ancient trees. Given the loss of ancient beliefs and traditional knowledge among new generations, it is necessary to point out to the public the value of sacred groves in biodiversity and cultural significance. Support for their conservation must be gained by scientifically documenting their value as precious habitats for rare native flora and fauna, as well as treasures of culture.

Box 26.4 Sacred natural sites in technologically developed countries: from nature to spirituality

THYMIO PAPAYANNIS and JOSEP-MARIA MALLARACH

Introduction

Major spiritual facilities of mainstream faiths are subjected to intense tourism pressures, which undermine both their spirituality and functionality. A typical example is the Meteora site in Thessaly, Greece, with its monasteries on rocky pinnacles, subjected to heavy visitor flows and the uncontrolled urbanisation of the surrounding natural area (Lyratzaki, 2007). At other sites, incorporated in protected areas, the collaboration between their custodians and those responsible for the management of the areas (coming usually from the earth sciences sector) is defective or nonexistent, leading to conflicts and malfunctions. At times, spiritual events related to mainstream faiths may pose threats to protected natural areas, as in the case of the Virgin of El Rocío sanctuary in the Doñana National Park, Andalusia, Spain, which attracts over one million pilgrims by foot or by horse, at different times of the year, walking through the dunes and marshlands, praying, chanting and celebrating for several days (Falgarona *et al.*, 2007) (Figure 26.4.1). Another example is the arrival – usually by private car – of over two million visitors per year to the monastery of Montserrat in Catalonia (Mallarach, 2007).

Another recent phenomenon related to global immigration is the emergence of new sacred natural sites related to mainstream faiths coming from immigrants from distant countries, especially in parks around western metropolitan areas and, in somewhat different nuance, in a few of our case studies, such as the Holy Island of Arran, in Scotland, which was bought by a Tibetan Buddhist organisation (Soria, 2007) (Figure 26.4.2).

Figure 26.4.1 Doñana, Andalusia, Spain – *sin pecado* (© Josep-Maria Mallarach). See colour plate section.

Figure 26.4.2 Holy Island of Arran, Scotland – Tibetan Buddhist rite (© Isabel Soria). See colour plate section.

Figure 26.4.3 The island of Ukonsaari/Áddjá/Ärij (in Finnish and two Saami languages), Lapland, Finland, a sacred site for the Saami people (© Joseph-Maria Mallarach).

The approach of the Delos Initiative

To contribute towards the better management of sacred natural sites in developed countries, and thus to assist in maintaining both their natural and spiritual values, the Delos Initiative was launched in 2004 in the framework of the IUCN World Commission of Protected Areas Specialist Group on Cultural and Spiritual Values of Protected Areas. It was named after the Aegean island of Delos, a sacred site for both Greeks and Romans, dedicated to Apollo, the god of light. Delos was the centre of the Athenian Alliance, home to religious and peaceful political functions. The name of the Initiative was chosen because Delos has no links to any single living faith.

The approach of the Delos Initiative is twofold and complementary. A number of specific natural sites sacred to mainstream faiths or indigenous peoples were chosen in various parts of the world, attempting to reach a balance between regions and faiths (Figure 26.4.3). These sites were carefully analysed, usually by local experts, with the objective of assessing their biodiversity and spiritual values, understanding their specificities and identifying threats and opportunities. The studies produced were discussed with various local stakeholders, so that a deeper comprehension of the issues could be achieved. The results were presented to a peer group and debated among its members, and lessons were extracted from them.

In parallel, theoretical work was carried out by applying the basic metaphysical principles that all spiritual traditions share a belief in the symbolic character of nature and in the sacredness of some, if not all, natural theophanies. Thus, they profess awe and profound respect for the natural order as a terrestrial reflection of a divine order. Hence, at this level, the initiative attempts to identify the underlying principles and practices of different spiritual traditions, to assess their relevance and influence in various contexts, and to propose and validate analogies and potential relationships.

It is expected that the combination of these two approaches and the implementation of the lessons they provide can bring forward positive results for the conservation of sacred natural sites, in particular, as well as for nature in general.

Case studies

Current case studies of the Delos Initiative include protected areas from virtually all IUCN categories, found in Europe, North America, Asia and Oceania, related to the largest mainstream religions and several primal spiritual traditions and folk religions. Most of these cases combine outstanding natural, cultural and spiritual values. To mention just one of these cases: the Vanatori-Neamt Nature Park in Moldavia, north-eastern Romania, includes the largest concentration of living monasteries in Romania, many of them expanding and receiving a continuous flux of pilgrims (Figure 26.4.4). These are located in a beautiful mountain forested landscape which has a very diverse fauna, including healthy populations of all the top predators, such as wolf and brown bear, with a reintroduction programme for the European Bison, all of this in an area that is also considered one of the richest in Romania from a traditional cultural point of view (Catanoiu, 2007). It is also important to bear in mind that most of these sacred natural sites preceded the establishment of protected areas, often by several centuries, sometimes by thousands of years.

Conclusion

The work carried out up to now, both in the analysis of specific sites and in theoretical search for a better understanding, has led to a number of useful conclusions, which were encapsulated in the Montserrat Statement, the Ouranoupolis Statement and the Inari Statement. These are being further evaluated and refined, so that guidance can be provided, initially to

Figure 26.4.4 Romania – the new Skete of Poiana lui Ion under construction in the Vanatori-Neamt Nature Park (© Josep-Maria Mallarach).

the managers of protected natural areas that include sacred sites, but which can also be of use to the custodians of these sites and other concerned stakeholders. Specific guidelines for sacred natural sites related to mainstream religions is a need already recognised in the UNESCO–IUCN SNS Guidelines, which focus on indigenous and local communities' sacred natural sites.

Holy ancient monuments

Box 26.5 The study of prehistoric sacred sites and sacred plants: a case study of Son Ferrer funerary mound in Majorca, Balearic Islands

LLORENÇ PICORNELL GELABERT, GABRIEL SERVERA VIVES, SANTIAGO RIERA and ETHEL ALLUÉ

Introduction

Mediterranean landscapes constitute cultural environments, due to a long-term history of human–nature interaction (Roberts *et al.*, 2001). The understanding of current dynamics and structures of these landscapes requires studying this long historical process. The structure of the Mediterranean environments is not only the result of human land use, but also contains cultural footprints from the peoples who shaped it, such as identity and symbolic elements, cultural values, etc. In this context, the interaction between society and vegetation is also determined by different cultural patterns. Studies of vegetation history within a wide time frame can contribute towards an understanding of the shaping of current landscapes and, consequently, they can pave the way for new management tools and provide criteria for the conservation of nature and landscape.

The recent change of Majorcan landscapes as a consequence of the boom in tourism in the 1960s and 1970s has led to a new perception of land. This process jeopardises cultural landscapes and contributes to the disconnection of society from its own land. Furthermore, insularity aggravates the associated environmental problems. In this context, the study of past landscapes can contribute towards cultural development and social cohesion as well as by generating new sustainable strategies for local economies.

Son Ferrer funerary mound and the surrounding area

The region extending south from Calvià (south-west Majorca) provides us with a clear example of a prehistoric cultural landscape of the Bronze and Iron Ages (from 1800/1750 BC to 0 BC), when archaeological sites acquired a deep symbolic meaning. A research and management project on cultural heritage and landscapes has been carried out in this region.

The mound in Son Ferrer is, in itself, a summary of this process of space symbolisation during prehistory, since it has been used as a ritual–funerary place for 2000 years. Moreover, the presence of many ritual vessels provides abundant evidence of the symbolic practices of this site (Calvo *et al.*, 2005). The first ritual evidence dates back to 2000 BC, with the excavation of a hypogeous (Figure 26.5.1). At a later stage (1100–850 BC), new ritual areas were added (stratigraphical unit 17). In about 800 BC, a stepped tumulus was erected over the hypogeous, which in fact became a collective burial between 500 and 200 BC (stratigraphical unit 9). Finally, the external part of the mound was used for child burials between 200 and 0 BC (stratigraphical unit 64).

Methods

Symbolic and ritual uses of plants during prehistory have been discovered through an archaeobotanical approach. Plant remains preserved in archaeological sediments have been recovered and analysed. Both pollen

Figure 26.5.1 View and plan drawing of Son Ferrer funerary mound.

grains and charcoal particles have been identified and quantified in three stratigraphical units (SUs) corresponding to ritual and funerary contexts.

The presence of different plant remains in archaeological records could reflect a diversity of uses and practices. Thus, for example, pollen could have arrived at the sediments in a variety of ways, such as through flower offerings, vegetal layers or ritual drinks and meals. On the other hand, charcoal particles in sediments could be the aftermath of ceremonial fires, aromatic burnings or light torches.

Results

Pollen analyses have been carried out in SUs 17 and 9, corresponding to ritual and burial contexts. Both spectra record high percentages of *Lamium* pollen type, *Ephedra* sp. and Brassicaceae, as well as the presence of *Olea europaea* and *Pinus* sp. In addition, *Quercus ilex* type, *Salix* sp., *Junieprus* sp., Poaceae, Asteraceae, *Plantago* sp., Chenopodiaceae and *Lotus* pollen types are also found in the sediments (Figure 26.5.2).

Charcoal analyses were carried out at SUs 9 and 64. The first one reveals a high diversity of plants used as fuel. In this context, the high values of *Pistacia lentiscus* charcoal must be stressed, as well as the presence of *Rosmarinus officinalis* and other undifferentiated Lamiaceae. The presence of charcoal of *Pinus* cf. *halepensis*, *Cistus* sp. and *Olea europea* has been also reported (Figure 26.5.3). In the case of the SU 64, charcoal particles coming from a ceremonial fire related to child inhumation reveal that *Pistacia lentiscus* was the wood choice for this kind of event on almost every occasion (Figure 26.5.3).

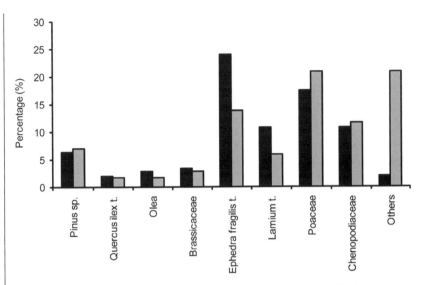

Figure 26.5.2 Histogram showing the percentage pollen data. The black columns correspond to SU 17 and the grey ones to SU 9.

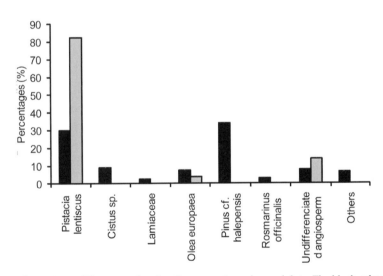

Figure 26.5.3 Histogram showing the percentage charcoal data. The black columns correspond to SU 9 and the grey ones to SU 64.

Pollen and charcoal spectra from these ritual archaeological sites differ from those reported in non-ritual/funerary contexts, supporting the interpretation that these palaeobotanical ensembles derived from rites based on the symbolic dimension of plants.

Figure 26.5.4 View of *Ephedra fragilis* (© Emili Garcia).

Discussion and conclusion

Both charcoal and pollen data suggest the use of Lamiaceae in ceremonial practices. In the Son Ferrer mound, the high values of *Lamium* type pollen grains and pollen clumps show the presence of flowers as offerings associated with burial and ritual practices. Moreover, charcoal remains indicate that the species *Rosmarinus officinalis* and other Lamiaceae were also burned during the funerary rites, probably for aromatic purposes. The cultural significance of this plant is supported by the fact that its charcoal has only been identified in funerary contexts in the Balearic Islands (Cova des Mussol, Cova des Pas, Son Ferrer).

The group of plants made up of *Ephedra* sp. and Brassicaceae reach higher pollen values in ritual contexts, strengthening their cultural/symbolic association. In this sense, high values of Brassicaceae pollen have also been reported in collective burials, such as Cova des Pas in Minorca, but their use and cultural significance remain unknown. The high pollen values of *Ephedra* in ritual contexts could reinforce the interpretation that this plant was used during the ceremonies carried out at Son Ferrer, probably related to the stimulant properties of this genus (Figure 26.5.4).

High percentages of *Pistacia lentiscus* charcoal particles have only been documented in ritual/funerary sites from Balearic prehistory, such as Cova des Càrritx (Lull *et al.*, 1999) or Cova des Pas, both caves located in

Figure 26.5.5 View of *Pistacia lentiscus* (© Marzia Boi).

Minorca. We could therefore suggest that mastic was also used in aromatic burnings in connection with these funerary practices. This is underlined by the fact that *Rosmarinus officinalis* and Lamiaceae charcoal always appears related to these high values of mastic (Figure 26.5.5).

The values of *Pinus* sp. and *Olea europaea* pollen in Son Ferrer mound are also higher in ritual samples than in constructive ones. This evidence could also suggest an intentional deposition related to rites.

In conclusion, the archaeological project in Son Ferrer reveals the need for an interdisciplinary approach, mainly based on the interrelation of different archaeobotanical and archaeological data, to study symbolic meanings of plants and cultural landscapes. In the future, the information generated through this approach will be able to contribute an additional value in cultural landscapes and nature conservation programmes.

Box 26.6 Registration and protection of sacred places in Sweden since 1666

LEIF GREN and MALIN BLOMQVIST

Introduction

The registration of information about sacred places in Sweden was first initiated by the government in 1630. The state antiquarians were requested to register not only all ancient monuments but also 'all chronicles, stories, poetries and fairy-tales'. In 1666 the government instituted the Ancient Monuments Act, which declared that all ancient monuments, remains and written stories from heathen times should be protected. It was absolutely prohibited to damage 'anything however small or unimportant it could seem'.

Legislation

The registration was mainly concerned with rune stones, but a large number of sacred places were also registered. The state had different motives: in the early seventeenth century it was important to 'prove' that Sweden had the historic right to conquer Danish provinces. In the late seventeenth century it was important for the state to show other countries in Europe, mainly France, that Sweden had a glorious history going back continuously to the times of the Old Testament – and was thus a reliable trade and war partner!

The Ancient Monuments Act of 1666 was declared by an absolute monarchy (see Figure 26.6.3). Thus the state actually confiscated the right to ancient monuments from private landowners without paying any financial compensation. The law remains valid today, although it has been revised several times, most recently in 1989. Concerning sacred places, the act protects places of assembly for the administration of justice, cult activities, commerce and other common purposes, and it also includes natural formations associated with ancient customs, legends or noteworthy historic events, as well as traces of ancient popular cults (Figure 26.6.1). One major motive for the state is the democratic right for every area in Sweden to preserve its own history, while at the same time the state wants to maintain central control against any misuse of history for political purposes or regional separatism.

Figure 26.6.1 Sacred stone, called the Stalo stone. Right against the stone many reindeer antlers were heaped by Sami people in past times. Jokkmokk parish, Lapland, Sweden (© Rikard Sohlenius, 7 May 2000, National Heritage Board).

Information system

The Swedish National Heritage Board has developed a geographic information system (called FMIS) which contains information about ancient sites and monuments in Sweden. FMIS includes information about historically/archaeologically interesting sites which are not protected by law. Today FMIS contains information on over 1.5 million individual monuments and sites in approximately 560 000 localities; more information is being added daily. This information is presented together with maps. Along with information about, for example, prehistoric graves, dwelling sites, rune stones, ruins of medieval monasteries, etc., FMIS also includes information about various 'sacred' or ritual sites, for instance sacrificial sites, church ruins, rock art sites and natural formations to which older traditions and legends are connected.

In FMIS around 160 different terms are used to classify different types of sites and monuments, but only some of those concern 'sacred' sites and/or sites connected with traditions and legends. A few of the relevant terms are listed below.

Figure 26.6.2 Sacred well-spring, called the Well of Svinnegarn. The well-spring is known in written sources since the fourteenth century and is connected with the Holy Trinity. The water is considered to give good health and it is still used for the same purpose today. Svinnegarn parish, Uppland, Sweden (© Bengt A. Lundberg, 3 May 2007, National Heritage Board).

- *Bear grave* – ritual burials of bones of bears. After killing a bear and cutting the meat up, the bones were buried in the belief that the bear could regenerate in another life. Total number in Sweden: 8.
- *Springs connected with older traditions* – includes springs connected with traditions about sacrifice, healing or obtaining luck, but also springs connected to legends about saints or other legends (Figure 26.6.2). Total number in Sweden: 2022.

Figure 26.6.3 Sacred places in Sweden have been protected by law since 1666. Frontispiece of the Act: 'His Majesty the King's edict and decree about ancient monuments and antiquities'.

- *Natural formations and objects to which older traditions, customs, legends and names are connected.* These include caves, erratic blocks, giant kettles, trees which are connected to ancient customs or traditions regarding, for example, healing, legends about saints, giants and trolls, and also trees from which bark or sap was collected in earlier times. Total number in Sweden: 5237.
- *'Sacrifice heap'* – sites connected with a specific event such as, for instance, a murder or an accident where people over time have heaped stones or wooden sticks in order to obtain luck or appease the ghost. Total number in Sweden: 535.
- *Sacrificial sites* – prehistoric and historic sacrificial sites not included in those described above. Total number in Sweden: 333.

- *Other sites to which old traditions, customs, legends and names are connected.* Total number in Sweden: 5633.

Conclusion

All ancient monuments and sacred places in Sweden have been protected by law since 1666, thus preserving the history of Swedish regions with their monuments, sites and the rights of their people (Figure 26.6.3).

Conclusions

Case studies around the world have confirmed the hypothesis that sacred natural sites and sacred landscapes serve to conserve both natural and cultural values (Bernbaum, 1997; Posey, 1999; Ramsar, 2001; Dudley *et al.*, 2005; Putney, 2006; Schaaf and Lee, 2006; Mallarach and Papayannis, 2007; McIvor and Pungetti, 2008). Nevertheless, these landscapes are also under increasing pressure and urgent measures to preserve them are necessary.

Yet the conservation of biological and cultural resources is often interrelated. Some indigenous people, like the Navajo with their Peaks, affirm that their culture can only survive if they are able to continue to live on the land and relate to nature as they have done for centuries (Lee and Schaaf, 2003; Hamilton and Benally, 2008). The importance of sacred landscapes, however, is not always acknowledged and currently its understanding is recognised more by international conservation programmes than national ones.

However, an exemption is the case of Sweden, where there was a need to prove its glorious history to other European countries in order to be preferred above other nations in matters of trade and war. Consequently, there was a need to register monuments and tales, some of which also included sacred sites. This situation allowed not only for the maintenance of an inventory of sacred sites and monuments, but also established the rights of the monarchy to own them and to preserve them in a certain way for their people. On the other hand, it empowered the state with the 'democratic right' to preserve Swedish regions with their history in order to prevent political crises and separatism.

In most of the case studies illustrated in this chapter, the natural, cultural and spiritual heritage of the site has developed continuously over time despite the cultural diversity of the peoples and the biological diversity of the natural areas. The Majorca funerary mound illustrated above is an example. This heritage is acknowledged today not only by spiritual communities but also by local citizens. However, present conflicts between the different needs of people, nature and spiritual realms are calling for democratic planning and improved management tools. These could help to develop an integrated strategy for the conservation of biocultural diversity through a participatory approach involving all the relevant communities of the area. Accordingly, the custodians of the sites should be consulted and involved in decision-making, and awareness should be raised on the prerequisite to pass on biological and cultural diversity to future generations.

A holistic approach should serve to foster a more sustainable development in tune with nature and sacred landscapes, which in turn should assist in preserving their biocultural diversity, as was done in the past with the use of traditional knowledge. This can also support awareness, understanding and respect for all landscapes, all necessary to help the efforts by the custodians of these sites in conserving both their natural and cultural heritage.

References

Ale, S. B. (2007). Ecology of the Snow Leopard and the Himalayan Tahr in Sagarmatha (Mt Everest) National Park, Nepal. PhD thesis. University of Illinois at Chicago.

Arizona Snowbowl Draft Environmental Impact Statement for Arizona Snowbowl Facilities Improvements. (2004) Coconino National Forest. Coconino County, Arizona. February 2004. United States Department of Agriculture.

Arizona Snowbowl Facilities Improvements Environmental Impact Statement, Vol. 1. (2005) Coconino National Forest. Coconino County, Arizona. February 2005. United States Department of Agriculture.

Bernbaum, E. (1997). *Sacred Mountains of the World*. Berkeley, CA: University of California Press.

Calvo, M., Fornés, J., Iglesias, M. A., *et al.* (2005). Condicionantes espaciales en la construcción del turriforme escalonado de Son Ferrer (Calvià, Mallorca). In *Mayurqa*, **30** (Vol. 1), 485–508. Palma de Mallorca: University of Balearic Islands.

Catanoiu, S. (2007). Vanatori-Neamt Natural Park. A Romanian Jerusalem. In *Nature and Spirituality in Protected Areas*, ed. J.-M. Mallarach and T. Papayannis. Spain: Abadia de Montserrat and IUCN, pp. 289–309.

Coconino National Forest Service. 17 December 2007. Available from: http://www.fs. fed.us/r3/coconino

Council of Europe. (2000). *European Landscape Convention*. Strasbourg: Council of Europe.

Dudley, N., Higgins-Zogib, L. and Mansourian, S. (2005). *Beyond Belief: Linking Faiths and Protected Areas to Support Biodiversity Conservation*. WWF, Equilibrium and Alliance of Religions and Conservation (ARC). Gland, Switzerland: WWF International and ARC.

Falgarona, J., García-Varela, J. and Estarellas, J. (2007). Doñana National and Natural Parks. Sanctuary of La Virgen del Rocío. In *Nature and Spirituality in Protected Areas*, ed. J.-M. Mallarach and T. Papayannis. Spain: Abadia de Montserrat and IUCN, pp. 175–99.

Fukamachi, K., Oku, H. and Rackham, O. (2003). A comparative study on trees and hedgerows in Japan and England. In *Landscape Interfaces. Cultural Heritage in Changing Landscapes*, ed. H. Palang and G. Fry. Dordrecht: Kluwer Academic Publishers, pp. 53–69.

Hamilton, L. and Benally, J. (2008). Holy San Francisco Peaks, California, USA. In *Proceedings of the 2nd Workshop of the Delos Initiative, Ouranoupolis 2007*, ed. T. Papayannis and J. M. Mallarach. Gland, Switzerland: IUCN, pp. 47–59.

Harmon, D. and Putney, A. D. (eds) (2003). *The Full Value of Parks: From Economic to the Intangible*. Lanham, MD: Rowman and Littlefield.

Lee, C. and Schaaf, T. (eds) (2003). *The Importance of Sacred Natural Sites for Biodiversity Conservation*. Proceedings of the international workshop held in Kunming and Xishuangbanna Biosphere Reserve, People's Republic of China, 17–20 February 2003. Paris: UNESCI-MAB.

Lucas, P. H. C. (1992). *Protected Landscapes: A Guide for Policy-makers and Planners*. London: Chapman & Hall.

Lull, V., Mico, R., Rihuete, C., *et al.* (1999). *Ideología y sociedad en la prehistoria de Menorca. La Cova des Càrritx y la Cova des Mussol*. Barcelona: Consell Insular de Menorca.

Lyratzaki, I. (2007). Meteora World Heritage Site. In *Nature and Spirituality in Protected Areas*, ed. J.-M. Mallarach and T. Papayannis. Spain: Abadia de Montserrat and IUCN, pp. 251–61.

Makhzoumi, J. and Pungetti, G. (1999). *Ecological Landscape Design and Planning: The Mediterranean Context*. London: Spon.

Mallarach, J.-M. (2007). Montserrat, Catalonia, Spain. In *Nature and Spirituality in Protected Areas*, ed. J.-M. Mallarach and T. Papayannis. Spain: Abadia de Montserrat and IUCN, pp. 151–62.

Mallarach, J.-M. and Papayannis, T. (eds) (2007). *Nature and Spirituality in Protected Areas: Proceedings of the 1st Workshop of the Delos Initiative*. Spain: Abadia de Montserrat and IUCN.

McIvor, A. and Pungetti, G. (2008). Can sacredness help protect species? *World Conservation*, **38**, 18.

Posey, D. A. (ed.) (1999). *Cultural and Spiritual Values of Biodiversity*. London: UNEP/ Intermediate Technology Publications.

Putney, A. (2006). *Sacred Dimensions: Understanding the Cultural and Spiritual Values of Protected Areas*. Gland, Switzerland: IUCN WCPA.

Ramsar. (2001). Wetlands and spiritual life. In: *Ramsar Briefing Pack: The Cultural Heritage of Wetlands*. Gland, Switzerland: The Ramsar Bureau.

Roberts, N., Meadows, M. E. and Dobson, J. R. (2001). The history of Mediterranean-type environments: climate, culture and landscape. *The Holocene*, **11**, 631–4.

Save the Peaks. 17 December 2007. http://www.savethepeaks.org/

Schaaf, T. and Lee, C. (2006). *Conserving Cultural and Biological Diversity: The Role of Sacred Natural Sites and Cultural Landscapes*. Paris: UNESCO.

Schama, S. (1995). *Landscape and Memory*. London: Harper Collins.

Soria, I. (2007). The Holy Island, Arran, Scotland. In *Nature and Spirituality in Protected Areas*, ed. J.-M. Mallarach and T. Papayannis. Spain: Abadia de Montserrat and IUCN, pp. 219–34.

Stevens, S. (1993). *Claiming the High Ground: Sherpas, Subsistence, and Environmental Change in the Highest Himalaya*. Berkeley, CA: University of California Press.

Stevens, S. (1997). Consultation, co-management, and conflict in Sagarmatha (Mount Everest) National Park, Nepal. In: *Conservation Through Cultural Survival: Indigenous Peoples and Protected Areas*, ed. S. Stevens. Washington, DC: Island Press, pp. 63–97.

Stevens, S. (2008). The Mount Everest Region as an ICCA: Sherpa conservation stewardship of the Khumbu sacred valley, Sagarmatha (Chomolungma/Mt Everest) National Park and Buffer Zone. Available from: www.iucn.org/about/union/commissions/ceesp/topics/governance/icca/grassroots/index.cfm

Swedish National Heritage Board, www.raa.se

27

Conclusions: the journey to biocultural conservation

GLORIA PUNGETTI, GONZALO OVIEDO and DELLA HOOKE

Introduction: natural and spiritual life

Early societies were small and close to nature. They were also intensely vulnerable and over the generations traditional ways of life evolved and enabled them to live in harmony within their customary habitat. Man also turned to religion to explain the features he could not understand and against which he sought protection, especially nature in its most dangerous and threatening forms such as storms, floods and earthquakes. Yet many societies also felt the need to thank nature for its bounties. Intervention with nature frequently involved a superior power and established rites which allowed communication with deities and the universe; shamanistic rituals suggested since millennia in prehistoric art may have been one of the earliest manifestations of such beliefs.

A sense of spirituality appears to have evolved within the human brain and soul, which renders it, as far as we are aware, different from that of all other creatures, and most early societies saw themselves as mere components of a richly endowed universe. There are also remarkable similarities across cultures: almost every society has its own creation story, for instance. As the raising of domestic animals and the cultivation of crops spread around the world, man had still to subjugate his needs to the requirements of nature and the resources available. Pests and diseases could be fatal to man and animal in growing societies; also, the over-exploitation of the land could result in soil erosion leading to the irrevocable destruction of local resources.

Today we live in a global society and over the last few hundred years immense changes have taken place with a vast increase in population numbers and with

Sacred Species and Sites: Advances in Biocultural Conservation, ed. Gloria Pungetti, Gonzalo Oviedo and Della Hooke. Published by Cambridge University Press. © Cambridge University Press 2012.

the spread of urbanisation and industrialisation across the world. 'Traditional' communities have often been swamped by so-called progress and many modern-day communities live far removed from 'natural' surroundings. Wildlife habitats have diminished to dangerously limited enclaves to such an extent that some have argued that we are on the brink of a further large-scale extinction of species.

In a world where many enjoy a life of plenty, albeit dependent upon other parts of the world for their lifestyle and food, it has been all too easy to forget that human vulnerability still remains, not only to the very occasional catastrophe of nature but to the results of human mismanagement of the resources of this planet. If we cannot live in harmony with nature, we cannot survive. We are but one of the species on this planet, but we are also the only one with the capacity to harm or heal on a grand scale, yet to have the intelligence and sense of spirituality that might conceivably ensure our future.

Traditional ecological knowledge

Traditional ecological knowledge is considered by scholars to be the basis for nature conservation by traditional societies, and it can become a powerful tool for conserving sacred species in cultural landscapes and traditional agricultural systems, both in developing and developed countries (see Chapter 1). Although sacred groves and sacred areas are recurrently spots of biodiversity, ecological networks and greenways can link them in the wider landscape (Jongman and Pungetti, 2004). In particular, cultural landscapes retaining sacred values frequently encompass both scopes and, when their dimension supports the carrying capacity of species, they form a means for biodiversity conservation. Therefore, these cultural sites become an important 'germplasm source' (Ramakrishnan, 2003, p. 39) for any rehabilitation activity in degraded ecosystems. Similarly, sacred species, with their keystone values, could assist in restoring degraded landscapes through community participation.

In this context, as suggested by several authors (Næss, 1989; Makhzoumi and Pungetti, 1999; Ramakrishnan, 2003; Oviedo and Jeanrenaud, 2006), it becomes imperative to link ecological and social dimensions, decoding the traditional intangible knowledge in order to integrate it into a modern scientific paradigm. A broader perspective in conservation biology is needed in these challenging times, reconciling scientific with cultural approaches, namely the ecological and economic perception of modern society with the ethics and spirituality of traditional communities. These in turn should work in conditions that enable them to understand the process required to preserve biocultural values, for their true participation in biocultural conservation and management.

The case studies in this volume confirm the hypothesis that sacred species and sites serve to conserve both natural and cultural values. However, the cases also underline the fact that sacred species and sites are increasingly threatened. Biological and cultural resources, likewise, are often highly interrelated in conservation. The indigenous peoples of Colombia and other parts of the world affirm that their culture can only survive if they are able to continue to live on the land and relate to nature as they have done in the past.

Lessons from the field

Most of the preceding 26 chapters illustrate fascinating examples of local relationships between spiritual beliefs and the natural world. Many demonstrate that sacred biocultural conservation is relevant, valuable and worthwhile.

Examples of sacred values of 'landscapes' have been presented first. The case study from Exmoor demonstrates how one landscape can bear different layers of significance simultaneously. The magical power of the spiritual imagination within a community means that while a landscape bears one type of precious significance for one individual or group, it can have another important meaning for others.

The same section of the book proposes the growing relevance of churchyards and their importance as guardians of the living, in the form of rare and diverse species, as well as protectors of species and their ecosystems.

Other examples given from around the world also confirm such multiple worth of sacred 'sites'. In the case studies from Italy, one becomes aware that what at first may seem to be ancient eco-spiritual knowledge and values of our forbears are alive and well in protected pockets of our current surroundings. As revealed in the Maori cases, the notion of metaphorically 'walking backwards' shows our past always ahead of us, guiding our actions with its tested wisdom.

The variety in examples of sacred 'species', both traditional and modern, provides much food for thought for the conservation arena. One dilemma is the fact that being sacred does not always guarantee protection of an animal or species, and sometimes results in quite the opposite. Further research in this area should help better understanding of such paradoxes and point to ways which allow us to deal with the negative effects of a species being held sacred and help us to take full advantage of protective worship. Continued investigation is also urgently required to catalogue as many sacred species as possible, in order to target potential candidates for improved protection from endangerment by appealing to their sacred value. However, in some cultures the 'sacred' is also 'secret', or at the very least, local people may be reluctant to identify their sacred sites for fear of desecration. In such cases, while the specific site, species or landscape may retain a certain anonymity, the related lessons they bring should be delineated and documented.

Of course, separate consideration of each of these elements – species, sites and landscapes – is artificial, since each of these levels is interdependent upon the others. Species occupy sites, and sites occupy landscapes. Humans occupy these spaces too, and viewing them from an outsider's perspective is erroneous. Playing on this interdependency will be vital in building upon the sacred value of any constituent part with a conservationist's agenda. This kind of 'biocultural ecosystem' approach could be one way of dealing with the example of a sacred species being threatened rather than protected by those who revere it.

Indeed, there are a number of new directions that can be pursued, taking the lead and carrying on from this publication. There is a need and an opportunity for creative innovations in bringing spiritual, traditional and conservation approaches closer together. The larger religions can be encouraged in further exploring their environmental values, in reinterpreting their beliefs to agree with a greener modernity and in aiding their faithful to act in ways more respectful of the planet, which many consider a divine creation. This is already beginning to happen, with initiatives such as the Forum for Religion and Environment (FORE) growing in stature. Environmentalists should be supported in becoming more aware of sacred sites and species, and urged to consider the potential benefit of certain natural entities being held sacred. The interdependency between cultural and ecological systems should also be made clearer and pursued at all levels. Finally, the power and role of cosmologies and belief systems to make sense of, and give meaning to, life should be harnessed by the biocultural movement.

Given some of these wider, broad-sweeping rallying cries, we can contemplate other details of the upcoming agenda for sacred species and sites within the context of biocultural conservation. First, we should consider what is needed. As stated in this publication, we need more research in this area. In addition to the points mentioned above, we need a better understanding of the global number of sacred sites. With the major religions already beginning this procedure, and in any case being easier to track in this sense, we especially need greater understanding of minor religions and beliefs, which are thus far unaccounted for in global counts. Similarly, the links between veneration of species, land and conservation need to be better explored, by looking at actual cases, for instance, and by quantifying their ecological impact. More research could also be done on how biocultural conservation can adapt to population change, and the effects of realities such as globalisation and tourism altering local demography and threatening cultural integrity. The Madagascan case studies, along this line, explain how very regional and local variations in beliefs are being eroded, and taboos disregarded, as the internal movement of people increases. These are but a few of the potential research directions to follow and, while several more have been identified by the authors, others could be added.

Pursuing this agenda and new directions will not be without challenges. The urgency of the actual need to address ecological and cultural threats is not the least of these. Another challenge will be the threats imposed by and between religions and cultures themselves. In Chapter 2 we learn of such clashes between colonial Catholicism and indigenous religions, with devastating consequences to the native sacred species and sites. A biocultural approach encourages an acceptance of other cultures and belief systems, and should bolster more recent improvements in relation to the larger religions and nature-based spiritualities, be they pantheistic, panentheistic, or otherwise, formerly considered as heretical, idolatrous 'paganism'.

Evolutionary approach

From Lamarck and Darwin to present times, the evolution of species has been a key for biological studies. The evolutionary synthesis at the beginning of the past century led to evolutionary biology, an interdisciplinary field which includes scientists from a wide range of disciplines.

Culture also evolves. Cultural evolution involves the study of cultural change over time and space, and frequently incorporates cultural transmission models. Cultural evolution, however, is not the same as biological evolution. Human culture involves the transmission of cultural information, which develops differently from human biology, although the study of cultural change is increasingly performed through genetic models.

Evolutionary anthropology is a link between the two. Concerning both the biological and cultural evolution of humans, and both the past and the present, it draws on many lines of evidence to understand the human experience during history through an interdisciplinary approach.

Neither nature nor culture remains static, but what we need to learn from past history is the danger of initiating or persevering with unsustainable practices. Some civilisations, for instance, have failed as a result of the effects of soil erosion following the removal of tree cover which has rendered further cultivation impossible. In addition, the removal of one dominant species by over-hunting for food or skins has sometimes led to the proliferation of other species that can themselves become destructive, a situation experienced in some parts of the world's oceans today. Moreover, the introduction of an alien species may irrevocably damage a native habitat.

Water, air, soil and species are major factors in maintaining the well-being of the Earth. Yet it has become obvious that the Earth's resources are not infinite. A sense of guardianship over these resources must be in place if we are to remain part of a successful biosphere, whether this arises from a particular religious belief, a wider sense of spirituality or a moral code.

Ethical approach

As Leopold (1987, p. 204) puts it, 'the land ethic simply enlarges the boundaries of the community to include soils, waters, plants, and animals, or collectively: the land'. It cannot prevent the alteration, management and use of natural resources, but it does affirm their right to their continued existence in a natural state.

Ecological consciousness in conservation biology has indeed increased since Leopold, and the biocultural journey has already started – in Barcelona in 2008. In order to implement such a journey, the conservation community should promote an ethical approach that respects the spiritual values of all human communities.

As indicated in previous chapters, further dialogue and development of such an approach is needed to achieve the effective integration of biological and cultural diversity in conservation.

Know-how, empowerment and participatory approach

'It is time to change' argued Taskha Yawanawa of Brazil at the IUCN WCC in Barcelona in 2008, urging all to care for Mother Earth before it is too late. We all have good intentions to save the planet for our future generations and the long-term health of the Earth. Sharing information and new discoveries between the many different countries, cultures and beliefs is imperative and needs to be followed by democratic cooperation, and to be guided by a clear mission.

Since the quality of life and species on Earth is strictly linked to the quality of their ecosystems, and therefore creates an ethical imperative to the conservation community, tackling this subject becomes imperative (Fisher *et al.*, 2005). Agricultural systems, for example, are often an important component of cultural landscapes and the stewardship of biological diversity. International initiatives such as the FAO GIAHS, the Globally Important Indigenous Agricultural Heritage Systems, can certainly support the identification and conservation of such systems.

That more research is needed on this topic is known. The establishment of appropriate mechanisms to apply both theoretical and practical principles on the understanding of biocultural diversity by scientists and local communities has been urged by the resolutions 4.038 'Recognition and conservation of sacred natural sites in protected areas' and 4.055 'Integrating culture and cultural diversity into IUCN's policy and programme' adopted by the 4th IUCN World Conservation Congress in Barcelona in 2008 (IUCN-WCC4, 2008). Besides this, it is necessary to develop policies which support the understanding of the relations between biological and cultural diversity consistent with these principles. This requires that the advocacy and participation of local stakeholders in the development of such policies, together with a sound understanding of the cultural and spiritual values, and of traditional practices, be brought into design and planning for biocultural conservation.

Resources, capacity, skills and power, moreover, should be made available for the conservation community. Empowering the poor and the local communities to be the main actors, furthermore, giving them voice and enhancing capacity, is the way forward. In order to take a full and effective part in the process, it is necessary to implement the participation of local people, who can be involved in the management of natural resources and be able to influence decision making.

A governmental approach which tackles knowledge, empowerment and participation in sacred species and sites should adopt laws and policies that:

- ensure that natural, cultural and spiritual values are considered in conserving sacred species and sites, and raise awareness and respect for them;
- foster multicultural values and acknowledge the importance of sacred species and sites as valuable for biodiversity conservation and ecosystem service and management;
- support effective participation and consent of peoples and communities concerned, and innovative governance models such as Community Conserved Areas of indigenous peoples;
- recognise the effectiveness of local communities to ensure protection over sacred species and sites, and assure support to those communities in doing so;
- respect customary use and management of sacred species and sites, and the rights of their custodians; and
- promote intercultural dialogue and conflict resolution with indigenous peoples, local communities and other actors interested in wider conservation.

Sustainable approach

A fundamental component of sustainability is the diversity of human cultures, with their knowledge, beliefs and social organisation. Indeed, sacred species and sites can play an important role in this as they go indistinctively to the minds of scientists and the hearts of people. They are custodians for the conservation of species, as well as of traditional cultures.

A new perspective on religions and the environment emerges from the research illustrated in this volume, addressing the compelling questions facing indigenous communities as they struggle with threats to their own sovereignty and the conservation of endangered species and sites. Traditional communities have different ways of maintaining a spiritual balance with larger cosmological forces while creatively accommodating current environmental, social, economic and political changes.

Most religions nowadays remind us that we are not owners but caretakers of the Earth, and have to act with consequential responsibility. They call for justice and equity for both people and nature. Preserving the integrity, stability and beauty of the biotic community is a duty for all people inhabiting the Earth, and in turn is a right of all species, including humans. Clearly, all communities need recognition of their rights.

However, rights-based policies and actions to maintain cultural and spiritual values are not enough. The commitment from all actors to preserve biocultural diversity, to reduce inequalities and to respect traditional cultures is a must. Moreover, more interaction between religion, science, education, policy and economy is advocated in order to address environmental challenges.

Undeniably, in recent years attempts to initiate such a dialogue have started. Bridges are being built with the custodians of the sacred lands of indigenous and traditional peoples, as well as with religious and monastic communities, and alliances between these communities and conservationists are sharing commitment to our planet. Furthermore, the increasing awareness of the need for partnership, and for the link between spirituality and conservation, directs actions for a sustainable future.

The biocultural approach to sacred species and sites

As discussed previously, the consideration of sacred species and sites in the context of environmental conservation can be seen as part of a wider, burgeoning movement striving to conserve biocultural diversity, 'the diversity of life in all of its manifestations – biological, cultural and linguistic – which are interrelated (and possibly co-evolved) within a complex socio-ecological adaptive system' (Maffi, 2007, p. 269).

Both ecological and cultural diversity hold inestimable values and, if managed carefully, could constitute inexhaustible goldmines for human well-being, whether physical, cultural or spiritual. However, both diversities are experiencing threats. Of known species, 21% of mammals, 30% of amphibians, 12% of birds,

28% of reptiles, 37% of freshwater fish, 70% of plants and 35% of invertebrates are threatened with extinction, according to IUCN's Red List of Threatened Species (IUCN, 2009). These alarming figures are mirrored in the plight of linguistic diversity. Of the approximately 6900 languages worldwide, 473 are considered nearly extinct, which means that only a handful of elders are speaking the language concerned. Hundreds more languages are at risk of a similar fate, as they fail to be passed down to younger generations (Lewis, 2009).

Indeed, if we take language as an indicator of culture, and, accordingly, linguistic diversity as an indicator of cultural diversity, the importance of safeguarding this becomes increasingly apparent, and all the more urgent. Using this representation, we begin to see more clearly some of the actual correlations between cultural and biological diversity and, by extension, between biocultural diversity and well-being. In appealing for language retention in the USA, the director of the Lakota Language Consortium argues the case for attempting to reverse language, and hence cultural, even spiritual, extinction:

> In the same way that a healthy planet requires biological diversity, a healthy cultural world requires linguistic diversity. Yet, language is also an elaborate phenomenon tied to real people and cultures. Language loss threatens a fundamental human right – that of the expression of the life and life ways of a people.

Each language relates ideas that can be expressed in that language and no other. Thus, when an indigenous community is no longer allowed to pray, sing or tell stories in its language, it is denied a fundamental human right. Unfortunately, linguistic rights have been seriously abused for hundreds of years by banning specific languages and indirectly by assaulting language-support structures such as land, economies and religions.

'Languages today are the next frontier in setting the country into moral and environmental symmetry' (Maffi, 2007, p. 274, quoting Meya, 2006).

This image of indigenous language, culture and spirituality is somehow rooted in, and evolving from, the same earth and landscape as the plants, the animals and the people. This is even more apparent when global mapping exercises show remarkable overlap between regions of biodiversity and regions of linguistic diversity. Similarly, the mapping of the world's threatened ecosystems surprisingly coincides with zones of threatened ethnolinguistic groups (see Maffi and Woodley, 2010). A further layer can be added to these: poverty–conservation mapping has shown that many areas considered biodiversity 'hot spots' correspond to areas of severe human poverty, as measured by the prevalence of stunting among children under five years of age.

While determining any causality and real links between these nature–culture–poverty correlations requires much further research, these associations between poor well-being, threatened ecosystems and species, and endangered languages cannot be ignored. They certainly contribute to the argument that combining landscapes and livelihoods in a biocultural approach can aid in improving the resilience of the world's most vulnerable species, ecosystems and people. The biocultural approach, it is argued, includes the growing recognition of the importance of traditional and indigenous sacred species and sites and their environmental conservation.

As aforementioned, the Biocultural Diversity Journey at the IUCN World Conservation Congress in Barcelona has been followed by a host of initiatives, such as the joint IUCN–UNESCO published guidelines on sacred natural sites in protected areas (Wild and McLeod, 2008), the Biocultural Diversity Conservation global sourcebook (Maffi and Woodley, 2010) and, most recently, this very publication on sacred species and sites.

The number of organisations, collaborations and institutions involved in this area is growing rapidly, from local associations and NGOs, to international organisations and academic and religious institutions. Moreover, as international and national development efforts aim towards the better harmonisation of projects and resources, the holistic and integrated biocultural approach is an innovative technical refocusing of perspective. These developments move in parallel with a reawakening of people and religious bodies to their environmental responsibilities and the connections between their spiritualities and beliefs, and the ecological plight. Studies on sacred species and sites are thus needed; this publication aims to provide a background.

Sacred species and sites for future generations

Many societies, especially indigenous and traditional peoples, recognise sacred species and sites as such, and engage in traditional practices for their protection as an expression of their worldview of the sacredness of nature and its link with culture. They also recognise sacred species and sites as a unique source of knowledge and understanding of their own culture, thus they are revered and cared for, and are a fundamental part of their territories, bringing significant benefits to local, national and global communities.

'Sacred' can mean for people 'hallowed, consecrated, set apart', but this can be extended to 'secured by religious sentiment, reverence, sense of justice, or the like, against violation, infringement, or encroachment' (OED), a sense that takes in the beliefs of all faiths as well as less religiously based conceptions. For many, sacred sites are those where divinity is concentrated, whether approachable by all members of a community or restricted to a priestly sect. Some places have developed such particular connotation as to become centres of pilgrimage. While some established religions may limit the places they hold most sacred to dedicated buildings, others are increasingly espousing sanctity in a wider sense to encompass other such foci of spirituality.

These can be pivotal in concentrating people's sense of values and outlook on the wider world. Paine has recently suggested categories of sacred sites, including places to which spiritual meaning is attributed: places of memory; places of innate energy; places created specifically to convey spiritual feelings; places formally set apart by an institution; and places consecrated by the presence of a holy object (Paine, 2004, pp. 14–26). A 'sacred site' is, therefore, distinct in a special way from others but within a spiritual context. A large variety of examples, together with the reasoning behind the selection of these fragile places in today's world, has been offered in the foregoing chapters.

Indeed, the majority of faiths now encompass within their spiritual outlook many facets of the natural world and man's role within it. Within such a view, aspects of sanctity may be conveyed to living creatures, which become regarded as 'sacred species', an integral part of the natural world. A respect for individual species, whether plant or animal, cannot only help to preserve those selected as having some sacred significance, but can also lead to respect for all living beings, helping to counteract the thoughtless exploitation of resources and to preserve the cultural and biological diversity of the planet. This wider outlook has never been as essential as in today's world. It is hoped that the themes covered in this book may go a small way towards focusing attention upon the contribution that sacred species and sites may make in maintaining the health of our planet for future generations.

However, as argued before, the path to a healthy planet presents numerous challenges. Overcoming them requires collaboration between numerous actors. Building on the research agenda, governments, religions, organisations and civil society should be engaged in encouraging and facilitating action and policy based on the evidence provided through biocultural findings, constituting a truly international response to an international crisis for all countries.

Biocultural conservation, in conclusion, is the key to collaboration, understanding and peaceful resolutions at every level, including global acceptance and the cohabitation of faiths and cultures. By placing nature at the centre, we put everyone on the same page, with the same goal. The interdependency of species, cultural landscapes and peoples is ever more apparent. Following the approach of biocultural diversity is crucial, we argue, to the resilience of the most vulnerable ecosystems, landscapes, cultures and peoples, including their spiritual values and beliefs.

References

Fisher, R., Maginnis, S., Jackson W., *et al.* (2005). *Poverty and Conservation: Landscapes, People and Power*. Gland, Switzerland: IUCN.

Jongman, R. H. G. and Pungetti, G. (eds) (2004). *Ecological Networks and Greenways: Concept, Design, Implementation*. Cambridge: Cambridge University Press.

IUCN. (2009). *Extinction crisis continues apace*. Available from: http://www.iucn.org/about/work/programmes/species/red_list/?4143/Extinction-crisis-continues-apace (accessed 3 November 2009).

IUCN-WCC4. (2008). *IUCN WCC4 Resolutions and Recommendations*. Available from: http://www.iucn.org/congress_08/assembly/policy/ (accessed 14 April 2009).

Leopold, A. (1987). *A Sand County Almanac: and Sketches Here and There* [1st edn, Oxford, 1949]. Oxford: Oxford University Press.

Lewis, M. P. (ed.) (2009). *Ethnologue: Languages of the World*, 16th edn. Dallas, TX: SIL International.

Maffi, L. (2007). Biocultural diversity and sustainability. In *Sage Handbook on Environmental Society*, ed. J. Pretty and A. Ball. Los Angeles, CA: Sage Publications, pp. 267–79.

Maffi, L. and Woodley, E. (2010). *Biocultural Diversity Conservation: A Global Sourcebook*. London: Earthscan.

Makhzoumi, J. and Pungetti, G. (1999). *Ecological Landscape Design and Planning: The Mediterranean Context*. London: Spon-Routledge.

Meya, W. (2006). Letter to The *Financial Times*, London, 11 March, 2006.

Næss, A. (1989). *Ecology, Community, Lifestyle*, trans. and ed. D. Rothenberg. Cambridge: Cambridge University Press.

OED. *Oxford English Dictionary*.

Oviedo, G. and Jeanrenaud, S. (2006). Protecting sacred natural sites of indigenous and traditional peoples. In *Conserving Cultural and Biological Diversity, The Role of Sacred Natural Sites and Cultural Landscapes*, ed. T. Schaaf and C. Lee. Paris, France: UNESCO, pp. 260–6.

Paine, C. (2004). *Sacred Places*. London: National Trust Enterprises Ltd.

Ramakrishnan, P. S. (2003). Conserving the sacred: the protective impulse and the origins of modern protected areas. In *The Full Value of Parks: From Economics to the Intangible*, ed. D. Harmon and A. D. Putney. Lanham, MD: Rowman and Littlefield, pp. 27–42.

Wild, R. and McLeod, C. (eds) (2008). *Sacred Natural Sites: Guidelines for Protected Area Managers*. Gland, Switzerland: IUCN.

28

Epilogue: a Spiritual Circle

Introduction

This publication is part of the 3S Initiative on Sacred Species and Sites, one of the activities of the IUCN–WCPA Specialist Group on Cultural and Spiritual Values of Protected Areas (CSVPA) coordinated by the Cambridge Centre for Landscape and People (CCLP).

The following selection of poetic contributions from some of the spiritual members of the 3S Community demonstrates an inherent caring for nature and the environment within spiritual traditions that embraces ecological ideals. While these contributions come from a variety of faiths and groups, the selection is not meant to be representative, nor does it cover the breadth and diversity of the community of researchers, scholars, practitioners and spiritual leaders who share the same goals.

The editors thank the contributors for blessing this publication with these words of wisdom and compassion.

Inspirational thoughts from Saint Francis of Assisi and the International Communities for the Renewal of Earth have also been included to close this circle of spirituality and nature. In particular, *The Earth Charter Guide to Religion and Climate Change*, published 11 November 2008, includes an appendix containing the reflection reported below, originally composed in 1991 by the International Communities for the Renewal of Earth (ICRE).

Sacred Species and Sites: Advances in Biocultural Conservation, ed. Gloria Pungetti, Gonzalo Oviedo and Della Hooke. Published by Cambridge University Press. © Cambridge University Press 2012.

Spirituality and religion: spiritualism and ancient wisdom from a Buddhist perspective

VENERABLE LAMA KARMA SAMTEN GYATSO

First of all it is very important to know the difference between spirituality and religion. Religion is belief and belief is taught by someone when you are young and through that you gain experience – then you believe. Belief is also faith and eagerness.

Some religions are taught through philosophy. Philosophy means you think, you examine, you investigate and you learn through your own experience – then you believe. This is also called faith and eagerness.

The first one relies on somebody. The circumstances may change and it is easy to lose faith and belief. The second one is more stable, because it does not rely on somebody but on one's own experience. Even if the circumstances change, your realisation does not change. This is religion.

Spirituality has many different meanings: culture, religion and language all play a part in it.

I can only refer here to the meaning of spirituality in accordance with Buddhism. Buddhist spirituality is a combination of two things: wisdom and compassion. If someone has wisdom and compassion then this is a spiritual person. Whether he or she is a religious person or not, whether he or she believes in something or not, this is a spiritual person.

In the world there are people at four different levels. The first is a spiritual as well as a religious person. The second is a spiritual but not necessarily a religious person. The third is a religious person but not necessarily a spiritual person. And the fourth is neither religious nor spiritual.

Therefore the world needs spiritual people with the combination of compassion and wisdom. Wisdom means having the understanding of one's own feelings and others' feelings. Compassion means tolerance and patience, with a capacity for forgiveness. That is why it is positive. A spiritual person fits in anywhere, because this person is understanding and tolerant. Religion is belief, and it depends on the person's belief whether it is used for good or bad and whether it creates conflict.

Other aspects of being spiritual are to do with ancient wisdom or indigenous belief. Indigenous people also have their own philosophy and belief. It is believed that the whole world is run by causes and conditions and the five elements. The outer world is run by the five elements of earth, water, fire, wind and space. The inner world, or being, is also run by these five elements. They operate together constantly and depend on each other.

The essence of the five elements has five different energies, sometimes called spirits or local deities. The first is Earth deity – *Yaksha* in Sanskrit, the second is Water deity – *Naga*, the third is Fire deity – *Raksha*, and the fourth is Wind deity – *Deva*. They have a sense of consciousness in the same way as a human being. Consciousness is related to the fifth element of Space. They are intrinsic to Nature; whether people believe it or not, they are naturally there.

In ancient times people respected the local deities. People would be aware of them and call their locations sacred sites, or sacred mountains, or sacred lakes. The word for sacred in Tibetan is *Ney*, which is an energy spot. Through the generations people would pay their respects to it. They would also express appreciation and respect to their own family elders and ancestors, their family 'lineage'.

But now in modern times people are not concerned about this. They deny and neglect it and the family lineage is broken. Then everything turns into chaos and the respect for the world is lost. We think we are very clever but actually we are destroying ourselves.

We depend on the outer world, so if we destroy it then what resources will future generations have? That is why we need ancient wisdom: to preserve and to conserve for the sake of all sentient beings now and in the future.

Man and Nature: environmental challenges versus inner wealth

PRASHANT KAKODAY

Since the human mind is the cause of much environmental harm, attention has to be given to the mind to rectify the problem. Only when we are sincere, can we address the problem. The problem is in the level of insecurity. An insecure human being cannot contribute to harmony.

Insecurities arise from material attachments and increased artificial needs. Surprisingly, increasing wealth doesn't necessarily address insecurities. That can only be a temporary solution.

The ultimate answer is spiritual. Human beings have to discover their inner true wealth and their immortality. That will entirely satisfy individuals. Only then can they be sincere in their attitudes and be truly caring and loving.

The human race operates like a herd. If a few bring about change, then the rest of the process will be automatic. The whole herd will change direction.

Maori Invocation for the 3S Community and for the world

JOSEF S. TE RITO

KARAKIA	INVOCATION
Mauri ora ki te rangi!	Blessings to the sky!
Mauri ora ki te whenua!	Blessings to the earth!
Mauri ora ki a tatau katoa!	Blessings to us all!
E nga atua	To the gods
E nga matua-tipuna	To the ancestors
E nga whakaruruhau wairua	To the spiritual mentors
O tena, o tena o matau	Of each and every one of us
I huihui ra ki Kemureti	Who gathered at Cambridge
I runga i te kotahitanga	In the unity of thought
Tena koutou katoa!	We greet and praise you all!
Tukua mai ra te aroha	We ask that you bless
Ki nga iwi o nga hau e wha	All peoples from the four winds
A, ka inoi atu ra matau	And we pray unto you all
Kia tiakina matau	To protect us
Me o matau whanau, hoa hoki	And our families and friends
A, kia hapaitia	And to ensure the success
Nga ahuatanga katoa	Of all aspects
O tenei pukapuka	Of this publication
E pa ana ki nga rakau tapu, kararehe tapu, wahi tapu hoki.	Pertaining to sacred plants, sacred animals and sacred sites.
Ko te tumanako hoki ia	Our ultimate desire is
Ka whai oranga	That well-being be accorded
Ka tu tangata	And human dignity be accorded
Nga iwi katoa, tae noa ki	To all peoples, inclusive of
Te hunga rawakore	The poverty-stricken
Te hunga e mamaetia ana	And the suffering peoples
O te ao katoa.	Of the world.
Tuturu whakamaua kia tina!	Let us affirm these words!
Tina!	*This we do!*
Hui e?	Each and every one of us?
Taiki e!	*Absolutely!*

Canticle of the Creatures: the unity of all things on this planet – both living and non-living

SAINT FRANCIS OF ASSISI

Cantico de le creature	Canticle of the Creatures
Altissimu, onnipotente bon Signore,	Most High, omnipotent, all good Lord!
Tue so le laude, la gloria e l'honore et onne benedictione.	All praise is Yours, all glory, all honour, and all blessing.
Ad Te solo, Altissimo, se konfano,	To You, alone, Most High, do they belong,
et nullu homo ène dignu te mentouare.	no mortal lips are worthy to pronounce Your name.
Laudato sie, mi Signore cum tucte le Tue creature,	Be praised, my Lord, with all Your creatures,
spetialmente messor lo frate Sole,	especially through my Lord Brother Sun,
lo qual è iorno, et allumini noi per lui.	who brings the day, and You give light through him.
Et ellu è bellu e radiante cum grande splendore:	And he is beautiful and radiant in all his splendour:
de Te, Altissimo, porta significatione.	of You, Most High, he bears the likeness.
Laudato si, mi Signore, per sora Luna e le stelle:	Be praised, my Lord, through Sister Moon and the stars:
in celu l'ài formate clarite et pretiose et belle.	in the heavens You have made them bright, precious and beautiful.
Laudato si, mi Signore, per frate Uento et per Aere et nubilo et sereno et onne tempo,	Be praised, my Lord, through Brothers Wind and Air, and clouds and storms, and all the weather,
per lo quale, a le Tue creature dài sustentamento.	through which You give Your creatures sustenance.
Laudato si, mi Signore, per sor'Acqua,	Be praised, my Lord, through Sister Water:
la quale è multo utile et humile et pretiosa et casta.	she is very useful, and humble, and precious, and pure.
Laudato si, mi Signore, per frate Focu,	Be praised, my Lord, through Brother Fire,
per lo quale ennallumini la nocte:	through whom You brighten the night:
ed ello è bello et iucundo et robustoso et forte.	and he is beautiful and cheerful, and powerful and strong.
Laudato si, mi Signore, per sora nostra matre Terra,	Be praised, my Lord, through our Mother Earth,
la quale ne sustenta et gouerna,	who feeds us and rules us,
et produce diuersi fructi con coloriti fior et herba.	and produces various fruits with coloured flowers and herbs.
Laudato si, mi Signore, per quelli ke perdonano per lo Tuo amore	Be praised, my Lord, through those who forgive for love of You
et sostengono infirmitate et tribulatione.	and those who endure sickness and trial.

Cantico de le creature	Canticle of the Creatures
Beati quelli ke 'l sosterranno in pace,	Happy those who endure in peace,
ka da Te, Altissimo, sirano incoronati.	for by You, Most High, they will be crowned.
Laudato si mi Signore, per sora nostra Morte corporale,	Be praised, my Lord, through our Bodily Death,
da la quale nullu homo uiuente pò skappare:	from whose embrace no living person can escape:
guai a quelli ke morrano ne le peccata mortali;	woe to those who die in mortal sin;
beati quelli ke trouarà ne le Tue sanctissime uoluntati,	happy those she finds doing Your most holy will,
ka la morte secunda no 'l farrà male.	the second death can do no harm to them.
Laudate et benedicete mi Signore et rengratiate	Praise and bless my Lord, and give thanks
e seruiteli cum grande humilitate.	and serve him with great humility.

Earth Charter: poetry from a spiritual perspective

INTERNATIONAL COMMUNITIES FOR THE RENEWAL OF EARTH

Preamble

I am because we are.
We have forgotten who we are;
We have lost our sense of wonder;
We have degraded the Earth;
We have exploited our fellow creatures;
And we have nowhere else to go.
In our ignorance we have disrupted the balance of life.
Now the air we breathe hurts us and the water we drink poisons us.
All things are bound together:
If we lose the sweetness of the waters,
we lose the life of the land;
If we lose the life of the land,
we lose the majesty of the forest;
If we lose the majesty of the forest,
we lose the purity of the air;
If we lose the purity of the air,
we lose the creatures of the Earth;
Not just for ourselves but for
our children – now and in the future.
But a new spirit is being born, a new awareness of

our place in this delicate balance. This spirit calls us to:
a transformation of our hearts and minds;
concrete changes in our way of life;
the renewal of our religions;
the creation of a global society;
Today,
We remember who we are;
We reclaim our sense of wonder;
We acknowledge our responsibility;
We commit ourselves to the Earth;
We turn toward each other in friendship;
We turn again together towards home.

Conclusions: a blessing for the 3S Initiative

VENERABLE LAMA KARMA SAMTEN GYATSO

I am very happy and appreciate all the effort made by so many people to compile this book. I rejoice and feel privileged to be a part of this contribution on behalf of the indigenous Tibetan people.

I wish in the future for all beings to have wisdom and compassion, so that they are able to see the whole world as our friend and not our enemy, and that our world is our precious resource.

Therefore everything and everyone is cherished and full of peace and harmony.

Index